Pricing Nature

In memory of David W. Pearce

Pricing Nature

Cost–Benefit Analysis and Environmental Policy

Nick Hanley

Professor of Environmental Economics, University of Stirling, UK

and

Edward B. Barbier

John S. Bugas Professor of Economics, University of Wyoming, USA

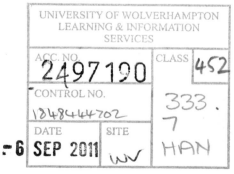
Edward Elgar
Cheltenham, UK • Northampton, MA, USA

Published by
Edward Elgar Publishing Limited
The Lypiatts
15 Lansdown Road
Cheltenham
Glos GL50 2JA
UK

Edward Elgar Publishing, Inc.
William Pratt House
9 Dewey Court
Northampton
Massachusetts 01060
USA

A catalogue record for this book
is available from the British Library

Library of Congress Control Number: 2009930428

Mixed Sources
Product group from well-managed
forests and other controlled sources
www.fsc.org Cert no. SA-COC-1565
© 1996 Forest Stewardship Council
FSC

ISBN 978 1 84542 789 4 (cased)
ISBN 978 1 84844 470 6 (paperback)

Printed and bound by MPG Books Group, UK

Contents

Acknowledgements

We would like to thank a number of people for making very helpful comments and suggestions on drafts of various parts of this book. These include Kerry Smith, Sue Chilton, Phoebe Koundouri, Robert Sugden, Iain Lange, Michael Harris, Bengt Kriström and Kerry Turner. Thanks also to Mikolaj Czajkowski for his help with the renewable energy chapter, and to Hanadi Musharrafiyeh for help with the water and hedonic pricing chapters.

Nick Hanley thanks the Commerce Division, Lincoln University, New Zealand for hosting his sabbatical during part of the writing of this book, and in particular Ross Cullen and Pip Lynch for their hospitality and all that nice wine.

1. Introduction

This chapter has four purposes:

- to explain the basic method of cost–benefit analysis (CBA);
- to reflect on why CBA might be a useful tool for environmental policy analysis and environmental management;
- to provide a very brief history of the use of CBA in policy and project appraisal;
- to explain what this book tries to achieve, and how it is organized.

1.1 COST–BENEFIT ANALYSIS: THE BASIC IDEA

In essence, the idea behind CBA is very simple. It is a technique for measuring whether the benefits of a particular action are bigger than the costs, judged from the viewpoint of society as a whole. By an 'action', we mean a deliberate decision to commit resources, which may involve two broad types:

- deciding on whether to introduce or reform a particular government *policy*, such as introducing a new energy tax; or
- deciding on whether to go ahead with a particular investment *project*, such as a new motorway or hydroelectric scheme.

To assess either type of decision using CBA, the analyst adds up the benefits of the project or policy and compares them with the costs. If the benefits are indeed bigger than the costs, then the project or policy makes society better off as a whole. If the costs are bigger than the benefits, then society is worse off as a whole if the project or policy goes ahead.

However, it quickly becomes clear that there are a lot of unresolved questions here. What do we mean by 'society'? What should we include as the 'benefits' and the 'costs' of a project or policy? How do we put a monetary value on these? What about projects where costs stretch far into the future? And how do we judge whether the benefits to society as a whole are bigger than the costs? This book will go some way to providing answers to these questions. To begin with, though, and to focus our discussion, we present an overview of how a cost–benefit analysis is conducted.

Let us take as an example a decision over whether to allow a new hydro-electric power scheme to be constructed in Scotland. The CBA method involves six stages of analysis:

i.   Project/policy Definition

This involves setting out exactly what is being analysed, whose welfare is being considered and over what time period. The CBA in this example is concerned with a new hydroelectric plant at a particular location, involving the building of access roads and a dam, the flooding of a valley, and the consequent generation of electricity, but a decision must be made about whether linked, ancillary investments (such as new transmission lines) should be considered as well. In terms of 'whose welfare', the usual answer is that it is national well-being that is considered, that is, all impacts are defined in terms of effects on people living within the UK. The analysis is to be carried out over the expected life time of the plant, say 30 years. Often, defining the 'relevant population' is a difficult issue. For instance, if the dam would threaten an internationally rare habitat, should the costs to non-UK conservationists also be counted? The relevant time period may also be problematic. If nuclear waste storage proposals are being analysed, then it is necessary to make allowance for the very long half life of some radioactive wastes.

ii.   Identification of Physical Impacts of the Policy/project

Any project/policy has implications for resource allocation: in this case, labour used to build access roads; additional electricity production due to the creation of a new power station; land used up in the creation of the reservoir; less pollution being generated from a coal fired power station which can now be closed early. The next stage of a CBA is to identify these outcomes in physical magnitudes: so many man-hours of labour, so many megawatt hours of electricity, so many hectares of land. For environmental impacts, Environmental Impact Analysis will often be used to produce predictions. Frequently, these changes in resource allocation will not be known with certainty – for example, how many tonnes of pollution will be displaced? How many hours of the year will the power station operate for? For environmental impacts, uncertainty in outcomes is to be expected to an even greater degree than with other impacts. The effects on inverte-brate fauna from a reduction in acid deposition, or the effects of enhanced global warming on species migration are examples.

Once physical impacts have been identified and quantified, it is then necessary to ask which of them are relevant to the CBA. Essentially, anything which impacts on the quantity or quality of resources, or on their price, may be said to be relevant if these impacts can be traced back to a link to the well-being of the relevant population. Since we specify relevant impacts in terms of utility impacts, it is not necessary to restrict attention to market-valued impacts, since non-market value changes (such as an improvement in air quality) are relevant if they affect people's utility.

iii. Valuing Impacts

One important feature of CBA is that all relevant effects are expressed in monetary values, so that they can then be aggregated. The general principle of monetary valuation in CBA is to value impacts in terms of their marginal social cost or marginal social benefit. 'Social' here means 'evaluated with regard to the economy as a whole'. Simple financial investment appraisal, in contrast, values costs and benefits in terms of their impact on firms and their shareholders only. But where are these marginal social benefits and costs derived from? Under certain conditions, this information is contained in market prices, as the next chapter explains. Market prices contain information on both the value to consumers of a particular product (say electricity) being supplied, and the costs to producers of supplying it. The market wage rate, similarly, shows both the value of labour to employers and the value of leisure to workers. Assuming that the impacts of the project are not large enough to actually change these prices, then market prices are a good first approximation to the values of benefits and costs (Sugden and Williams, 1978). Where markets work well, market prices and market supply and demand curves contain useful information about social costs and benefits of more electricity produced, or more land being used up. But markets often 'fail', for example when the actions of private firms and households impose costs on others, for example when pollution from a coal fired power station harms the health of those living nearby. Moreover, for some 'goods', like biodiversity and river water quality, no market exists at all from which a price can be observed. In such cases, market prices are no longer a good guide to social costs and benefits. Chapter 2 explains how in principle this valuation problem can be solved in CBA, while Chapters 3–6 contain detail on the methods which can be used to measure such 'non-market' values. Box 1.1 shows guidance from the US EPA (2000) on the different kinds of costs which can make up the social costs included in CBA.

BOX 1.1   DEFINING SOCIAL COSTS

The US EPA in its guidance on policy appraisal sets out four different kinds of costs which might make up the total social costs of implementing a new policy or project, or of changing existing government regulations. These are shown below:

Examples of social cost categories

Social cost category	Examples
Real-resource compliance costs	● Capital costs of new equipment ● Operation and maintenance of new equipment ● Waste capture and disposal, selling, or reuse ● Change in production processes or inputs ● Maintenance changes in other equipment
Government sector regulatory costs	● Training/administration ● Monitoring/reporting ● Enforcement/litigation ● Permitting
Social welfare losses	● Higher consumer and producer prices ● Legal/administrative costs
Transitional social costs	● Unemployment ● Firm closings ● Resource shifts to other markets ● Transaction costs ● Disrupted production

Source: US EPA (2000, p. 120).

Real resource costs are the value of scarce resources used up as a result of deciding to go ahead with a project/policy. For example, the costs of building a new nuclear power station, or the costs of installing better pollution treatment equipment to meet tougher pollution regulations. Government costs include those of monitoring compliance, and constitute the value of the scarce public resources (for example person hours) that are committed in this fashion. What the EPA calls 'social welfare costs' are changes in prices to consumers and producers as a result of the policy/project, for instance higher electricity prices resulting from a ban on new nuclear power stations being commissioned. Finally, 'transitional social costs' are defined by the EPA as being typically composed of (1) plant closings and resultant unemployment; (2) resources shifting to other markets; (3) transaction costs associated with setting up incentive-based programmes; and (4) disruptions in production. However, the EPA note that these transitional costs are often short-term in nature, yet hard to measure accurately.

iv. Discounting of Cost and Benefit Flows

Once all relevant cost and benefit flows that can be expressed in monetary amounts have been so expressed, it is necessary to convert them all into *present value* (PV) terms. This necessity arises out of the time value of money, or time preference. To take a simple example, suppose an individual is asked to choose between receiving £100 today and receiving that same £100 in one year's time. The more immediate sum might be preferred due to impatience (I want to spend the money right now). Alternatively, I may not want to spend the money for a year, but if I have it now I can invest it in a bank at an interest rate of, say, 10 per cent, and have £100 $\times$ (1 + i) = £110 in one year's time, where i is the rate of interest. The motives for time preference, and reasons for discounting, are discussed in Chapter 7: for now, all that need be recognized is that a sum of money, and indeed most kinds of benefit, are more highly valued the sooner they are received. Similarly, a sum of money to be paid out, or any kind of cost, seems less onerous the further away in time we have to bear it. A bill of £1 million to re-package hazardous wastes seems preferable if paid in 100 years' time rather than in 10 years' time. This is nothing to do with inflation, but more to do with the expectation that we might expect to be better off in the future, or to be able to pass the bill on to future generations.

So how is this time effect taken into account, and how are cost and benefit flows made comparable regardless of when they occur? The answer is that all cost and benefit flows are *discounted*, using a discount rate which, for now, is assumed to be the rate of interest, i. The present value of a cost or benefit (X) received in time t is typically calculated as follows:

$$PV(X_t) = X_t \left[(1 + i)^{-t} \right] \tag{1.1}$$

The expression in square brackets in equation (1.1) is known as a discount factor. Discount factors have the property that they always lie between 0 and +1. The further away in time a cost or benefit occurs (the higher the value of t), the lower the discount factor. The higher the discount rate i for a given t, the lower the discount factor, since a higher discount rate means a greater preference for things now rather than later.

Discounting may be done in CBA in one of two ways: either by finding the net value of benefits minus costs for each time period (usually each year), and discounting each of these annual net benefit flows throughout the life time of the project; or by calculating discounted values for each element of a project, then summing the discounted elements (for example, adding up total discounted labour costs, total discounted material costs and total discounted energy saving benefits). Both approaches should give identical answers.

v.   Applying the Net Present Value Test

The main purpose of CBA is to help select projects and policies which are efficient in terms of their use of resources. The criterion applied is the *Net Present Value* (NPV) test. This simply asks whether the sum of discounted gains ($\Sigma B_t(1 + i)^{-t}$ as it is written below) exceeds the sum of discounted losses (written as $\Sigma C_t(1 + i)^{-t}$). If so, the project can be said to represent an efficient shift in resource allocation, given the data used in the CBA. The NPV of a project is thus:

$$NPV = \Sigma B_t(1 + i)^{-t} - \Sigma C_t(1 + i)^{-t} \qquad (1.2)$$

where the summations Σ run from $t = 0$ (the first year of the project) to $t = T$ (the last year of the project). Note that no costs or benefits before year 0 are counted. The criterion for project acceptance is: accept if $NPV > 0$ (that is, is positive). Based on the criterion explained in the next chapter, any project passing the NPV test is deemed to be an improvement in social welfare.

There are a number of alternatives to the NPV criterion. The two most commonly employed are the Internal Rate of Return (IRR) and the Benefit–Cost Ratio. The IRR is a measure frequently employed in financial investment appraisal. It is the rate of interest which, if used as the discount rate for a project, would yield an NPV of zero, and is interpreted as the rate of return on the public funds used in the project. This can be compared with the opportunity cost of these funds, which might be the market rate of interest. However, the IRR is flawed as a measure of resource allocation for two principal reasons. First, many projects can generate multiple IRRs from the same data set, so the analyst does not know which to select as the decision-making criterion. Second, the IRR is unreliable when comparing performance across many projects in a portfolio. This is because the IRR only compares the return on one project relative to the opportunity cost of funds. The benefit–cost ratio is simply the ratio of discounted benefits to discounted costs. The decision rule becomes: proceed if and only if the benefit–cost ratio exceeds unity.

vi.   Sensitivity Analysis

The NPV test described above tells us about the relative efficiency of a given project, given the data input to the calculations. If this data changes, then clearly the results of the NPV test will change too. But why should data change? The main reason concerns uncertainty. In many cases where CBA is used, the analyst must make predictions concerning future physical flows (for example, the quantity of electricity produced per year) and future relative values (for example, the wholesale price of electricity). None of these predictions can be made with perfect foresight. When environmental impacts are involved, this uncertainty may be even more widespread; for example, if a policy to reduce global greenhouse gas emissions is planned, then the impacts of this in terms of avoided damage may be subject to a wide range of predictions. An essential final stage of any CBA therefore is to conduct sensitivity analysis. This means recalculating NPV when the values of certain key parameters are changed.

1.2   WHY IS CBA USEFUL?

In one very important sense, the practice of CBA addresses what might be called the fundamental economic problem: how to allocate scarce resources in the face of unlimited wants. Resources are scarce because the sum total of demands on them exceeds their availability, and using up scarce resources in one way imposes an opportunity cost on society in that we cannot use those same resources for some other purpose. For example, a proposal in 2007 to expand irrigated agriculture on the Canterbury Plains in New Zealand suggested diverting water from two rivers to a newly constructed reservoir which would then be used to supply irrigation schemes for dairy farmers. However, if land is used up to create a reservoir, that same land cannot also be used for sheep farming. If water is taken from a river to supply a reservoir and then to irrigate dairy farms, that same water is not available in the river to maintain in-stream ecological quality, or to support water-based recreation such as kayaking. Society might find it useful, in deciding whether to allow such schemes, to know whether the economic benefits of irrigated dairy farming are bigger or smaller than the costs of reservoir construction, lost sheep farming output, losses in river ecological quality and losses in kayaking opportunities.

CBA is a decision-aiding tool which conveys this manner of useful information to decision makers. Rowan describes the art of policy analysis as 'a set of procedures for exploring alternatives for achieving certain social ends . . . in a world limited in resources, in knowledge and in rationality'.[1] Not only does CBA allow a comparison of the benefits and costs of particular actions, reflecting therein the scarcity of resources, but it also allows for ordinary people's *preferences* to be included in government decision making. As Chapter 2 makes clear, economic values in a CBA

depend partly on what people like (their preferences), what they are prepared to give up to have more of what they like (their willingness to pay)
and what they can afford to pay (their budget constraint). In a sense, CBA
is an exercise in economic democracy, since every citizen gets an economic
vote in terms of their willingness to pay. However, the strength of votes is
constrained by resources – by people's incomes – which may seen unfair.
Nevertheless, CBA is a formal way of setting out the impacts of a project
or policy over time, of organizing debate over an issue, and of identifying
who enjoys the gains and who suffers the losses from such undertakings.
It is also, as Arrow et al. (1998) have noted, a good way of ensuring consistency and perhaps transparency in public-sector decision making. As
a procedure which must be gone through for policy decisions or project
funding to be approved, CBA has merits in that in this 'gatekeeper' role
it helps enforce an agreed set of principles in how decision making should
be undertaken over time. In the final chapter of the book, we return again
to the question of 'why CBA'?, and reconsider our case in the light of the
material which students will read in the intervening chapters.

1.3   A BRIEF HISTORY OF CBA

Other authors have presented a fuller account of the history of CBA in
policy and project analysis – see, for example, Turner (2007), and references therein. However, it is important to appreciate the context within
which CBA has developed, and its current position in decision support
within government. The first officially-sanctioned use of CBA as part of
national appraisal mechanisms was in the USA, for dam construction following the 1936 Flood Control Act (see Box 1.2). The US Army Corps of
Engineers was then required to take account of the benefits and costs 'to
whomsoever they may accrue' in appraising water management projects
(Pearce and Nash, 1981). This was followed in the US by the publication
in 1950 of the US Federal Inter-Agency River Basin 'Green Book', which
established guidance on how to carry out CBA of public projects. Later
in the US, the introduction by the Reagan presidency of Executive Order
12291 in 1981 required the benefit–cost appraisal of all new federal laws on
environment, health and safety (Arrow et al., 1998).

  In the UK, CBA began to be used in publicly-funded transport projects
in the 1960s, leading to the publication of the 'COBA' manual on how to
evaluate such projects in the 1970s. The Ministry of Agriculture, Fisheries
and Food also used CBA to appraise projects such as sea defences and
land drainage schemes. A major turning point in the UK occurred in
1991 with the publication of a short pamphlet by the Department of the

BOX 1.2 AN EXAMPLE OF COST–BENEFIT ANALYSIS OF HYDROPOWER REGULATION

The earliest official use of CBA was in the United States, in the context of the appraisal of new dam construction schemes from the 1930s. Kotchen et al. (2006) carry out a CBA of the relicensing of two hydroelectric dams in Michigan. The policy context involves a move to reduce the environmental impacts of hydropower operations by changing the way in which rivers are managed. The changes investigated by Kotchen et al. involve managing releases from dams and reservoirs in a way which more closely parallels natural fluctuations in water levels, rather than timing releases to coincide with maximum electricity demands. This change imposes costs in terms of lost electricity output on hydro operators at peak periods, which must be compensated for with more expensive output from other sources, here from fossil fuel-powered generation. The gain is an environmental one – in this case, an increase of about 270 000 salmon per year emigrating from the Manistee River to Lake Michigan. Due to the mix of fossil fuel power supplied to the grid, there is also an environmental gain from reduced net air pollution, since the peak-period demands are met from less polluting natural gas-powered generation rather than the more polluting coal sources.

The costs to producers of the change in operations is given by the differences in marginal costs per kWh between hydro and fossil fuel-derived electricity. This implies that annual costs for the two dams rise by about $310 000. For air pollution, the authors consider five pollutants, including NOx, CO_2 and SO_2. Changes in air pollution between the two water management regimes are then converted into dollars using estimates from the literature of marginal damage costs, reporting a range of possible values. Finally, changes in migrating salmon numbers are converted into changes in predicted catches for recreational anglers, and then valued using travel cost-derived estimates of the value of recreational fishing (see Chapter 4).

The conclusion of the study is that the benefits of changing the way in which the river system is managed for hydropower produces benefits that are bigger than costs. Annual losses in electricity output imply costs in the range of $219 132 to $402 094 with a best guess of $310 612. Annual benefits from emission reductions are in the range $67 756 to $246 680, whilst gains in recreational fishing are worth $301 900 to $1 068 600, with a most likely estimate of $738 400. The authors conclude that 'the benefits exceed the costs of the switch . . . . even ignoring the air quality benefits entirely, the best estimate of recreational fishing benefits exceeds the upper bound of producer costs'. In this case then, changing the way in which water resources are managed to reduce adverse environmental impacts seems to pass the cost–benefit test.

Environment called *Policy Appraisal and the Environment*, which called for the use of CBA thinking and the monetization of environmental impacts in policy (as distinct from project) appraisal throughout government, whilst central government guidance on how to carry out CBA continues to be issued in the form of HM Treasury's *Green Book*. The regulation of water pollution – and in particular, the setting of targets for private water companies for new investments in pollution treatment – is now very much driven by a CBA perspective under the Environment Agency's and Ofwat's Periodic Review process (see Chapter 10), whilst CBA-thinking has also influenced the design of agri-environmental measures, green belt land policy and transport policy.

At the level of policy making in the EU, Pearce (1998) argued that the Commission was guilty of not adopting a CBA approach in the appraisal of proposed Directives, but this now seems to be changing (Turner, 2007). As we note in Chapter 10, the implementation of water resource management policy in the EU under the Water Framework Directive explicitly occurs within a partial CBA framework.

1.4   THE REST OF THIS BOOK

The rest of this book is divided into two parts. Part I explains the 'tools' which CBA analysts need to possess. Chapter 2 gives an important theoretical background both to the measurement of changes in social welfare using the Net Present Value rule described above, and to the measurement of benefits and costs. Chapters 3–6 then present different approaches to putting monetary values on changes in environmental quality: stated preference methods, revealed preference approaches, and the valuation of ecosystem services. In Chapter 7, the awkward issue of discounting future benefits and costs is revisited, and we ask in particular whether one can identify a 'correct' discount rate or rates for use in public project and policy appraisal. Chapter 8 looks at the application of CBA in developing countries, and explains the differences that emerge in applying the technique here rather than in richer countries.

Part II of the book presents a series of case studies, where CBA techniques have been applied to actual environmental management problems. These are concerned with (1) valuing ecosystem services; (2) water quality issues; (3) habitat protection; and (4) renewable energy projects.

Finally, the concluding chapter, Chapter 13, returns to the question of what the benefits of undertaking CBA are in the context of environmental decision making, and what limits should be taken into account in using CBA as part of the policy appraisal process.

NOTE

1. This quote was taken from Turner (2007).

REFERENCES

Arrow, K., M. Cropper, G. Eads, R. Hahn, L. Lave, R. Noll, P. Portney, M. Russell, R. Schmalensee, V.K. Smith and R. Stavins (1998), 'Is there a role for benefit–cost analysis in environmental health and safety regulations?', *Environment and Development Economics*, **2**, 196–201.

Kotchen, M.J., M. Moore, F. Lupi and E. Rutherford (2006), 'Environmental constraints on hydropower: an ex post benefit–cost analysis of dam relicensing in Michigan', *Land Economics*, **82** (3), 384–403.

Pearce, D.W. (1998), 'Environmental appraisal and environmental policy in the European Union', *Environmental and Resource Economics*, **11**, 489–501.

Pearce, D.W. and C. Nash (1981), *The Social Appraisal of Projects*, London: Macmillan.

Rowan, H. (1976), 'Policy analysis as heuristic aid', in L. Tribe (ed.), *When Values Conflict*, Cambridge, MA: Ballinger.

Sugden, R. and A. Williams (1978), *The Principles of Practical Cost–Benefit Analysis*, Oxford: Oxford University Press.

Turner, R.K. (2007), 'Limits to CBA in UK and European environmental policy: retrospects and future prospects', *Environmental and Resource Economics*, **37**, 253–69.

US EPA (2000), *Guidelines for Preparing Economic Analyses*, Washington, DC: US Environmental Protection Agency.

PART I

The tools

2. The theoretical foundations of CBA

This chapter sets out some very important background on the economic theory which underlies the 'mechanics' of cost–benefit analysis. Whilst it may seem somewhat abstract at times, this material is essential to understanding the implicit assumptions that the analyst takes on board in undertaking a CBA; it also explains how we can interpret the outcomes of a CBA as being meaningful in terms of the likely impacts of a project on 'social welfare', and what the limitations of the approach are. We consider how risk and uncertainty can be included in CBA, and investigate the ways in which environmental values can enter a CBA. Much of the material presented below is a simple summary of an extensive body of work which dates back to the 1930s: for a more in-depth treatment of the issues, the reader is referred to Pearce and Nash (1981), Sugden and Williams (1979) and Zerbe and Dively (1994). We start by explaining a rather basic idea: how to measure benefits and costs for an individual.

2.1 INDIVIDUAL MEASURES OF VALUE

2.1.1 The Basics

As explained in Chapter 1, CBA is about comparing the gains and losses (benefits and costs) of undertaking a new project or policy. But how to measure these gains and losses? One fundamental requirement is that all gains and losses thought to be relevant are measured in the same units, otherwise they cannot be added together (aggregated), either across people or over time. The unit of measurement in CBA is money, but the conceptual basis is utility. Utility is a term used by economists to represent those factors that make people happy, or that explain people's choices. Ideally, CBA would evaluate gains and losses by adding up positive and negative changes in utility across individuals. However, for many years, economists have known that utility is difficult to translate into a cardinal measure (like kilometres per hour): we cannot measure how much extra utility Joe gets from listening to REM rather than Radiohead. Utility functions – a representation of those things that make a person happy, or help him to choose – are instead used to rank objects of choice, that is, to generate ordinal measures of preference: Joe prefers REM to Radiohead; he prefers two Radiohead CDs to one Radiohead CD in his collection.

To obtain a cardinal measure – a 'how much' measure – which approximates an underlying utility change (for example to Joe, how much happier he is following the release of a new REM collection), we instead use *money metrics* of underlying utility change, in particular either the most that someone is *willing to pay* to acquire more of something desirable, or less of something undesirable; and the least that someone is *willing to accept* in compensation for giving up something desirable, or tolerating something undesirable.

This means that we can use an individual's maximum Willingness to Pay (WTP from now on) as a measure of what an increase in the quantity of something good is worth to him. For example, suppose a project results in an improvement in water quality in a river in which Joe goes fishing: his maximum WTP for this change is a measure of the utility he gets from the improvement. As will be obvious, this means that WTP will represent both how much he cares about water quality and fishing – his preferences – and how much he is willing and able to give up of his income, or of expenditures on other items, to secure this change. It should also be apparent that WTP measures both the intensity of preferences (how much I like something) and the direction of preferences (do I prefer more or less of something). Similarly, if a project will increase the road noise Jill hears whilst sitting in her garden, then her minimum Willingness to Accept compensation (WTA) for this decrease in her utility tells us what peace and quiet is worth to her – or rather, what the proposed change in peace and quiet will 'cost' her in terms of lost utility.

These money metric measures, WTP and WTA, form the basic building blocks of individual valuations of gains and losses within CBA. A more precise definition of both can be provided in the context of 'exact' welfare measures.[1] These measures were first suggested by Hicks in 1943, in the context of changes in prices for consumer goods. Consider a policy that would increase the price of electricity to households. Hicks defined the *compensating variation* of this move as the minimum compensation an individual would have to be offered to make her as 'well off' without the price change, compared to the situation where prices were lower and no compensation was offered. This is her minimum WTA. By 'as well off', we mean that the level of utility in the two situations (lower prices, no compensation and higher prices, with compensation) is the same: this is the sense in which a minimum compensation sum is defined. The level of utility which is maintained or held constant here is the *initial* level of utility, that is at the original price of electricity.

An alternative measure of the effect of the price rise was defined by Hicks as the *equivalent variation*. This also looks at payments which hold utility constant, but now we fix utility at the level *after* the price change, not before it. In this case, the equivalent variation is the individual's maximum willingness to pay to avoid the price change.

Being more specific: imagine that the initial, pre-price rise level of utility for an individual is U_0. Initial prices for electricity and some other good the individual consumes are p_0^1 and p_0^2. The cost of obtaining level U_0 at these prices is $C(p_0^1, p_0^2, U_0)$. If the price of good 1 now rises to p_1^1, then to maintain the same level of utility U_0 the individual is going to have to be given more income, that is, compensated. This compensation sum – the Compensating Variation, CV – is defined as the difference between the expenditure needed to achieve utility level 0 at the old, lower price $C(p_0^1, p_0^2, U_0)$, and the expenditure needed to achieve utility level 0 at the new, higher price p_1^1, that is:

$$CV = C(p_0^1, p_0^2, U_0) - C(p_1^1, p_0^2, U_0).$$

Here, utility level U_0 is being used as the 'reference level' for welfare measurement.

Although these welfare measures are defined for price changes, most of the environmental applications we shall be considering in this book involve quality changes (for example, more or less forest conserved, a higher or lower level of pollution). However, the general principles of welfare change measurement remain, although as we will see below, some changes are needed.

The case examined above considered something which made electricity consumers feel worse off – a rise in prices. What about something which made them feel better off, such as a fall in prices? The relevant exact welfare measures are now simply reversed. Taking people's initial level of well-being as the reference level, the compensating variation measure of the benefit to an individual of this price cut would be their maximum WTP to have the price cut go ahead – since by taking away money from the individual, we can return them to their pre-price cut utility level, despite the fact that prices have in fact fallen and thus they feel better off. On the other hand, taking their post-change level of utility as the reference level, one could ask people what minimum compensation sum they would have to be offered to be as well off without the price cut as with it.

Summing up, it appears that there are four measures for the welfare change affecting an individual which can be quantified in monetary terms. These welfare changes can be in terms of changes in the price of something, or its quality. All assume that the individual can choose how much of the good to consume following the change. The measures are summarized in Table 2.1.

We stated above that an assumption was being made that 'the individual

Table 2.1   Welfare measures

For a change which:	Compensating Variation is:	Equivalent Variation is:
Increases someone's well-being	Your maximum WTP to have this change go ahead (Utility fixed at pre-change level)	Your minimum WTA to go without this change (Utility fixed at post-change level)
Decreases someone's well being	Your minimum WTA to accept this change (Utility fixed at pre-change level)	Your maximum WTP to stop this change from happening (Utility fixed at post-change level)

can choose how much of the good to consume following the change'. But when CBA is applied to environmental issues, this is often not the case. Suppose the government enacts a new law to restrict particulate emissions from buses and taxis in a city. Individuals living in the city either experience the pre-reform level of air quality or the post-reform level – they cannot exercise a perfectly free choice on the air quality they 'consume'.[2] If the government creates a new marine nature reserve which improves marine conservation, then people cannot choose what level of conservation to enjoy: they either face the pre-change level or the post-change level.

In such cases where individuals are *quantity-constrained*, which will often be the case in the instances of environmental applications of CBA considered in this book, then the concepts used for exact welfare measurement change somewhat. Instead of compensating variation we refer to *compensating surplus*; instead of equivalent variation we refer to *equivalent surplus*.[3] However, both will be measured using the same structure of WTP and WTA that is outlined in Table 2.1. So, for example, the value of an improvement in marine conservation to a sea-bird lover is their maximum WTP to have this improvement go ahead, which measures their compensating surplus. The cost of an increase in air quality to a person is their maximum WTP to avoid it, which equals their equivalent surplus.

2.1.2   Valuing Costs and Benefits when Prices do not Change

But where does this information on maximum WTP and minimum WTA come from? For the moment, let us focus on a project which has only a marginal (small) effect on the quantity of something provided, and/or on

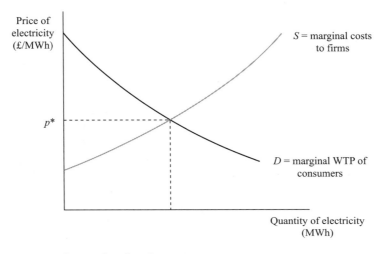

Figure 2.1 The market for electricity

the market for inputs. For example, imagine a proposal to construct a new wind farm in Scotland, the output of electricity from which would not be big enough to change the market price of electricity, and whose demand for inputs (say labour for construction) would not be big enough to change the market price of these inputs (in this case, the wage rate for construction workers in Scotland). Consider now the market for electricity. The new wind farm will generate, say, 10 megawatt hours of power per year. In Figure 2.1, we show the market for electricity in Scotland. The demand curve shows how much consumers are willing to buy at different prices; it also shows how much they value each extra unit of electricity supplied. This marginal willingness to pay declines as the quantity supplied increases (think of people bidding in an auction). The supply curve shows the marginal costs of producing electricity from the many competing power sources around the country, and reflects the opportunity costs of the scarce resources which are used up in electricity production. The electricity market is in equilibrium when demand equals supply, at price p^*. At this price, the marginal willingness to pay of customers just equals the marginal costs to producers of supplying electricity. If there are no external costs or benefits of electricity production (this is explained below), then the market price measures both what consumers are WTP at the margin for one more unit of electricity, and the costs of producers of supplying this unit – their minimum WTA (supply price) for producing this quantity. So marginal WTP can be measured, along with marginal WTA, by simply consulting the market price. Which is very handy!

Pricing nature

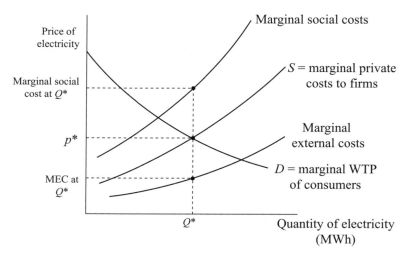

Figure 2.2   External costs and private costs

However, what we wish to measure in CBA is the *social* costs and benefits of an action, that is the costs and benefits to all members of society. In many cases, social and private costs, and social and private benefits, are the same thing, meaning that the market price tells us both marginal social and marginal private costs and benefits (recall that we have assumed no effects of the project on prices at the present). However, there are important instances where this does not hold. Economists refer to some of these instances as 'market failure' (Hanley et al., 2000). Take, for example, the production of electricity. If electricity is produced from coal, oil or gas, then burning these fuels will result in pollution from sulphur dioxide, nitrous oxides, particulates and CO_2. Take the example of particulates. These can have adverse effects on human health for people living close to the plant. Yet the costs of these pollution impacts do not fall on the private company generating the electricity – they are 'paid' by sufferers with chest complaints. Hydroelectric production can have adverse impacts on salmon fisheries, by hindering fish migration. These costs do not fall on the hydro company, but on fishermen who are deprived of the opportunity to fish. Carbon emissions from fossil fuel power stations contribute to global climate change, which may have adverse effects on people living in flood-prone areas of countries many thousands of miles away from the power station. Pollution is an example of the *external costs* referred to above: a cost which does not fall on (is not paid by) the agent responsible for causing it. In Figure 2.2, we show the same supply curve (= marginal *private* cost curve) for a competitive energy industry, and the demand curve for electricity. The market price is again at p^*. But now we also include a *marginal external cost* curve: this shows the marginal value of damages associated with emissions and other environmental impacts from electricity generation, which increase as a result of rising production. From society's point of view – and thus from the viewpoint of CBA – the relevant costs to consider are the social costs of production, that is the *sum* of marginal private costs and marginal external costs. As can be seen, the market price no longer provides a guide to this value. This means that using the market price of energy to value electricity output would overstate social benefits of increased electricity output, unless we also include in the analysis the external costs that result from this production. For a proposed expansion of electricity output above Q^*, then the social costs at the margin of this expansion include both the costs to the firm and the external costs. As can be seen, an expansion of electricity output above Q^* would actually fail a CBA test, since the marginal social benefits (shown by the demand curve) are less than the marginal social costs. Chapters 3–6 describe techniques for estimating such external costs.

A parallel concept to that of external costs is that of external benefits, and these constitute another reason why market prices can be a poor guide to marginal social costs or benefits. An external benefit arises when production activities result in benefits which are not valued by the market, or which are additional to those valued by the market. Consider, for example, a farmer who manages his land in a wildlife-friendly manner, creating many habitats for birds and butterflies. He also produces lamb for sale. The market rewards him for his lamb production, since he can sell his lamb to a buyer or buyers. But the market is unlikely to reward him for his 'production' of wildlife habitats, since these produce benefits known to economists as *public goods*. Such goods are undersupplied by the market system as they exhibit one or both of the following properties:

- They are 'non-excludable in consumption'. This means that if the good is provided at all, then the supplier cannot stop those people who pay him a zero price from consuming the good. Thus if a water company cleans up a lake by reducing sewage inputs, then all those who live around the lake benefit from this, and the water company would find it hard to charge them for this benefit. If a farmer plants a new native woodland which improves a local view, then it would be hard for the farmer to charge all those people who gain a benefit from the woodland when they pass by or view it from a distance.
- They are 'non-rival in consumption'. This means that the quantity or quality of the good is not diminished by more people enjoying

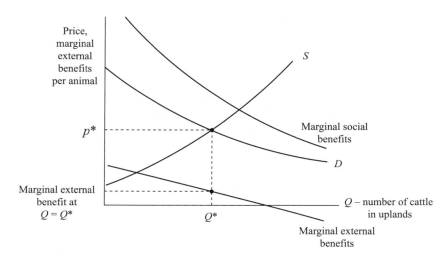

Figure 2.3   External benefits

it. Thus cleaning up the air in a city will provide a benefit which does not depend on how many people live there. Clearly some environmental 'goods' are not like this: if 1000 people turn up to my favourite fishing spot on a river, my enjoyment is probably going to be lower than when I am the only person there.

In Figure 2.3, we show the market demand and supply curve for cattle production in the Welsh uplands. The supply curve shows the marginal costs of cattle farmers, and the demand curve shows what customers are willing to pay for Welsh beef. There is an equilibrium at price p^*. Does p^* tell us about the social costs of a decline in cattle production in the hills? Not if the ecological quality of the uplands depends on them being managed for cattle (for example in terms of maintaining bird habitats). If people value birds, in the sense of deriving utility from watching them, and if birds depend on cattle farming in the uplands, then the marginal social benefits of cattle production will exceed the market price. This will also be so if people appreciate the kind of landscapes generated by upland cattle farming. In this case, the CBA analyst would have to include some measure of these external benefits in thinking about a policy which would result in a loss of cattle farming in the uplands.

The incorporation of both external benefits and external costs into a CBA is a reflection that the market price does not tell the analyst all of the costs and benefits of change in activity, when there are 'missing markets'. But another case which needs to be considered is where a market price exists, but this market price is in some sense wrong. CBA practioners have used the terminology of *shadow pricing* to refer to the case where market prices need to be adjusted to turn them into a better guide to marginal social benefits or costs. When does this need to be done? Sugden and Williams (1979) and Pearce and Nash (1981) provide a comprehensive guide. For our purposes, though, we can focus on just one example: where governments intervene in market prices.[4]

Government intervention in markets can be via the setting of price floors or price ceilings. For example, a government might set an upper limit on basic food prices in a developing country, or on consumer energy prices, for distributional reasons. Taxi prices in many cities are set by local councils. Housing rent controls have also been imposed by local authorities, again for reasons of equity. In Figure 2.4a, a government has set a maximum upper price of p_{max} on a basic food commodity (say maize in Mexico) which consumers can be charged. The demand for maize shows the marginal willingness to pay of consumers in Mexico, and the supply curve shows the marginal supply price of maize growers in Mexico (for simplicity, we ignore imports). At p_{max}, suppliers are only willing to offer Q_s to the market, even though Q_d is demanded by consumers – there is thus a government-induced shortage which much be 'solved' by some rationing device – such as queuing. Does this government-regulated price show the marginal social benefit of an increase in the supply of maize? No: this is shown by the marginal WTP of consumers, which, as can be seen, is much higher at p_{wtp}.

We can also use this diagram to show what happens if a government sets a price floor. Suppose a new government in Mexico decides instead to support poor farmers rather than poor consumers. It does this by taking away the price ceiling, and imposing a price floor of p_{min}, which shows (in Figure 2.4b) the minimum guaranteed price which maize farmers can expect to receive for their output. Now consumers only demand (can afford to buy) Q'_d units of maize, but producers supply Q'_s units. There is a surplus which the government must somehow deal with, for example by paying export subsidies to farmers. What is the value of an increase in maize production now? It is not the guaranteed price p_{min}, since this is the result of a political process, not an indication of social benefits and costs. Instead, the CBA analyst should note that to sell one more unit of maize to domestic customers would require a cut in prices, in fact to p'_{wtp}. This is the social value of one more unit of output being produced. Governments guaranteeing farmers a price above the market return is not uncommon as a phenomenon. During most of the lifetime of the Common Agricultural Policy, this was indeed the case, and a body of literature developed on how to value changes in farm output when agriculture was so subsidized. One

(a) A price ceiling

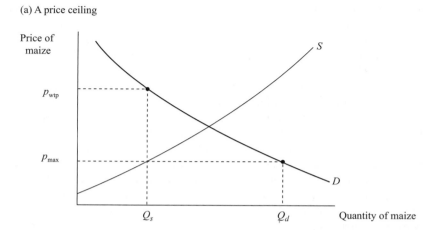

(b) A price floor

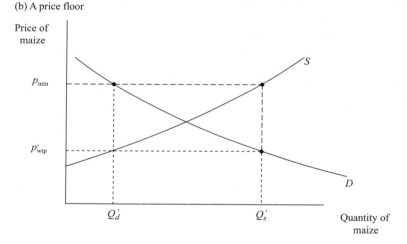

Figure 2.4   Effects of price intervention

important concept here is the 'producer subsidy equivalent' (PSE), which organizations such as the OECD calculated to convert private, farm-gate returns –which included subsidy payments and, for example, tariff protection (which we have not dealt with here) – into the social or economic benefits of increases in agricultural output. This need within the EU has changed since reform of the CAP in 2003 de-linked production from subsidy payments for most crops.

2.1.3 Valuing Costs and Benefits when Prices Change

Government intervention can have big effects on the prices paid by consumers and those received by producers. Two examples relate to climate
change policy. By imposing a tax on carbon dioxide emissions, governments increase the price that households pay for travelling by car, or
for heating their houses. By subsidizing renewable energy investments
through a higher 'feed-in' tariff for green electricity, governments can
change the price that renewable producers receive for their output. How
should we value those changes within a CBA? The answer is that we apply
the general principle laid out in section 2.1.1. For a price rise, we can ask:
'what is the most that consumers are willing to pay to avoid this?', or 'how
much compensation would we need to give consumers to maintain their
utility levels?'. We can also ask: 'what is the most that a firm would be
"willing to pay" to benefit from higher prices?' 'What is the compensation
they would need to make up for prices not rising?' Symmetrical questions
can be posed for price reductions.

Consider the case of consumers first. In Figure 2.5a, we show an ordinary demand curve for some good X for an individual. The usual way of
thinking about this demand curve is that it tells us about how much an
individual will want to buy of X as the price of X changes. But there is
another way of thinking about the demand curve which is more useful
here. It shows us how much an individual is willing to pay for successive
units of X being offered to her – in other words, the most she would bid
for X at an auction. For quantity q_1, the most this individual would bid for
one more unit is p_1, and at q_2, the most the individual would bid is p_2. This
maximum bid declines as the quantity of X offered rises due to the law of
diminishing marginal utility: as the amount of X consumed rises, the extra
utility we get falls. Now imagine collecting information on the maximum
this individual would bid for X for all possible levels of X up to q^*, and
then adding these amounts together. This sum would be their total willingness to pay for the quantity q^*, and is equal to the area under the demand
curve for X up to this point. *So the area under the demand curve shows the
total value of a good to an individual.*

Now in fact the market only charges the individual a price of p^* for consuming the quantity q^*. This means that the individual pays a total amount
($0p^*bq^*$) for the good (see Figure 2.5b). Yet we know that the value of q^*
to them is bigger than this, and in fact is equal to the area ($0abq^*$). This
means that the consumer has a 'surplus' of value over cost of the shaded
area (p^*ab). This area is known as *consumers' surplus,* and is a measure of
the welfare effect on consumers of being able to buy q^* at a price of p^*.
If prices were to rise, this area would shrink – the welfare measure would

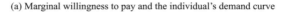

(a) Marginal willingness to pay and the individual's demand curve

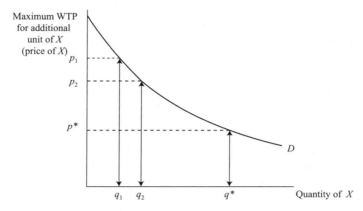

(b) From demand to consumers' surplus

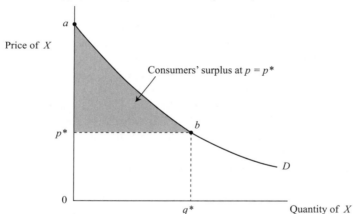

Figure 2.5   Consumers' surplus and the demand curve

fall as consumers now feel worse off. If prices were to fall, this area would increase, so the welfare measure again tracks the direction of how well off consumers are feeling. Consumers' surplus, as the area under a demand curve and above a price line, is thus a very useful measure of how the well-being of consumers changes when prices change. Since we can construct this measure for an individual – as in Figure 2.5 – so we can also construct it for many individuals if all consumers in a market are considered, and the change in aggregate consumers' surplus will be the area under the market demand curve above the price line. This is shown in Figure 2.5c.

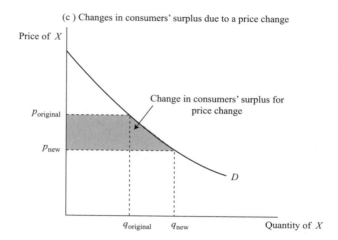

(c) Changes in consumers' surplus due to a price change

Figure *2.5* (continued)

One problem, however, exists if we try and relate this consumers' surplus measure to the 'exact' welfare measures discussed in Table 2.1. The Compensating Variation and Equivalent Variation measures constructed there held utility for an individual at some constant level, seeing what change in income was needed to maintain utility at this level following change in prices or environmental quality. For Compensating Variation (CV), utility was held constant at its pre-change level, and for Equivalent Variation (EV) at its post-change level. However, along an ordinary demand curve such as that shown in Figure 2.5, utility is not held constant. Income is held constant, but utility changes; for example a fall in prices (movement down the demand curve) will make consumers feel better off, even though their incomes have not changed. It is possible to draw 'compensated' demand curves which do hold utility constant at some level, and measure an exact consumers' surplus as the area under this and above a price (see Zerbe and Dively, 1994), but what we actually observe in market data is the ordinary demand curve in Figure 2.5. How wrong would we be if we used the consumers' surplus measure of a welfare change for consumers based on this? According to Robert Willig (1976), the answer is 'not very wrong at all'. Willig provided 'bounds' for the error resulting from using consumers' surplus, and showed that in most cases, this error would be small. The size of the error turns out to depend on how much of an individual's income is spent on a good, and on the relationship between increases in their income and increases in their demand (the income elasticity of demand). In general, it can be expected that, for a price fall, EV > CS > CV, and for a price rise, that CV > CS > EV.[5]

Pricing nature

(a) A firm's supply curve

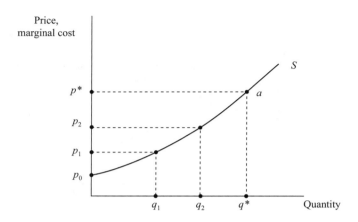

(b) From the supply curve to producers' surplus

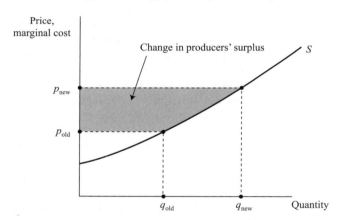

Figure 2.6   Producers' surplus

The material above discussed the measurement of the welfare impacts
on consumers of a price change. Is there an equivalent measure for producers? Yes: it is known as producers' surplus. However, precisely how it
is calculated has been debated in the literature. The majority view proceeds
as follows. In Figure 2.6, a supply curve for a competitive firm is shown: as
the price rises, the firm wishes to supply more to the market. This supply
curve shows the firm's marginal costs, since the firm will maximize profits
where price = marginal cost. The supply curve also shows, as noted above,

the least a firm would accept to supply a given level of output. So, to supply q_1, its minimum WTA (or 'supply price') is p_1, and for q_2 its minimum WTA is p_2. If the price falls below p_0, the firm will not produce anything. Now suppose that the market price is actually p^*, and that thus every firm receives this price (for example, think of this as the national milk price, for a dairy farmer). The firm chooses to produce q^*. But now it earns an excess over its minimum WTA for every unit of output between zero and q^*, equal to the area between the supply curve and the price line at p^*, area (p^*ap_0). This area is known as *producers' surplus*. It is equal to profits minus fixed costs, and shows the net benefits to firms from being able to sell at a price of p^* given their variable costs are consistent with marginal cost. If prices were to rise – as in Figure 2.6b – firms would feel better off, and the extent to which this is so would be measured by the change in their producers' surplus, shown by the shaded area. Since the measure applies to individual producers, it can be summed to apply to many producers: the area above the market supply curve and below the price will determine the aggregate (total) producers' surplus accruing to producers as a whole.

The issue with producers' surplus as a comparable measure of welfare to consumers' surplus is this: whose well-being are we trying to measure? As presented above, the changes in well-being accrue to firms. But what are firms? Are they entities, whose well-being matters in terms of CBA? Some authors have therefore preferred to trace changes in producers' surplus back to changes in the well-being of people who supply the factors of production which firms use. For simplicity, consider these are just labour, land and capital. In this case, one could examine the changes in returns to shareholders, landlords and workers in excess of the minimum supply price that these individuals have. This quantity of the excess of returns over minimum supply price (which is dictated by what the owner of the factors of production could get for employing them in their next best use) is known as *economic rent*. One can thus think of the change in producers' surplus as we have measured it being divided up into changes in economic rents to the owners of the factors of production. One could also trace out the effects on economic rent to owners of the factors of production if the prices of these inputs changes – for example, if land prices rise as a result of a new rural development policy.

2.2 MEASURING CHANGES IN SOCIAL WELL-BEING: THE KALDOR–HICKS COMPENSATION TEST

The Kaldor–Hicks compensation test, associated with John Hicks and Nicholas Kaldor, is the key principle underlying CBA.[6] It allows the analyst to infer changes in social well-being from the Net Present Value test set out in Chapter 1. The Kaldor–Hicks test examines whether a project or policy (project, from now on) brings about a 'Potential Pareto Improvement' (PPI). This means that those who would be better off as a result of the project are willing to pay more, in aggregate, to have the project go ahead, than those who would be worse off from the project would demand in compensation to allow it to occur. In other words, where the maximum aggregate WTP of the gainers (the social benefit) is greater than the aggregate minimum WTA of the losers (the social cost). Note that no compensation is actually paid to losers; we simply ask whether the gainers *could* compensate the losers, and still be better off. According to Sugden and Williams (1979), there are two ways to think about justifying the use of the Kaldor–Hicks test. The first is that it is a reasonable guess about how a decision maker with redistributive powers would choose to make decisions which impact on many people's well-being. Redistributive powers are important here since such a decision maker could, over time, correct any actual, undesirable redistributions of well-being using the tax system – for example, if energy policy which is justified on CBA grounds has bigger costs to poor households than rich households. The second justification revolves around what criteria for decision making we think *should be* applied. This idea recognizes that (i) projects that pass the CBA test increase economic efficiency and (ii) greater economic efficiency is, in and of itself, desirable as a social goal.

Some implications which need to be highlighted from adoption of the PPI criterion are as follows:

- social values are determined by the sum of individuals' values, and nothing else;
- individuals' valuations of the effects on them of a prospective project are the most appropriate measures of the costs or benefits to them;
- losses and gains are symmetrical, in the sense that a loss to one individual can be offset against a gain to another;
- all losses can be compensated for.

Clearly, these are controversial statements in some people's eyes.

Implementing the Kaldor–Hicks test consists of adding up the benefits of a project across all those who will gain, and then comparing this aggregate sum of benefits with the aggregate sum of costs. Notice that this means we are now effectively comparing changes in utility across people, the conceptual difficulties of which have not been discussed here so far. Costs might be measured in terms of people's WTA or WTP to tolerate or to avoid losses; costs might also consist of losses in consumers' surplus or producers' surplus; or of the value of resources used up in a project, valued in terms of market prices. We would also want to include in these benefits and costs any changes in external costs and benefits resulting from the project – such as an increase in air pollution, or a reduction in wildlife habitat. The analyst thus, on this view, adds up the real resource benefits of the project (the value of electricity generated by a new wind energy investment, the value of displaced carbon emissions) and compares it with the real resource costs of the project (the market price of steel and concrete used in construction, the opportunity cost of land, the environmental impacts on birds, the loss in utility to those who feel that landscape quality is diminished). In this sense, the 'adding up' is being done at the level of the project as a whole, broken down into benefits and costs. In this treatment, 'transfer payments' – such as taxes paid to the government on profits made, or subsidies offered by the government to the wind energy company – cancel out of the analysis, and so are ignored. So if the wind energy company receives a £1 million subsidy from the government, the CBA analysis would not include this as a benefit, since this equates to a £1 million cost to taxpayers. At the level of the economy as a whole, no net real cost or benefit occurs.

An alternative way of aggregating gains and losses is to divide the population into interest groups who are likely to be affected by the project: for example, taxpayers, electricity consumers, bird watchers, and the power company. Gains and losses can be added at the level of each group, and the net social benefit is then the sum of the changes across groups. In this treatment, transfer payments appear in the analysis, since they are gains to some groups, and losses to others. But when we add up gains and losses across groups, they cancel out transfers, so that this way of presenting the CBA should (!) give the same result as the 'real resource costs and benefits' approach outlined in the previous paragraph. An advantage of the 'by interest group' approach, in contrast, is that gains and losses are clearly set out according to whom they accrue: this may give more insight into the likely acceptability of the project, or of any compensation schemes that might need to be taken account of.[7]

We also need to think about the weighting of benefits and costs when aggregating gains and losses in a CBA. This is so since when costs and benefits are added up across people, and statements then made about the resultant change in social well-being, we are implicitly making a judgement about the relative importance of changes in well-being to each individual affected by the project – and, at the limit, to each individual in the economy. The concept that economists use to describe the function which reflects the relative importance of gains and losses across society is the *social welfare function* (SWF). This is not something we try and measure empirically, but rather a conceptual underpinning for how the evaluation of projects or policies proceeds. Imagine that there are only four people affected by a project: three gain (A, B and C), and one loses (D). The social welfare function in general terms could be written as:

$$W = f(b\text{A}, b\text{B}, b\text{C}, c\text{D}) \qquad (2.1)$$

where W is social well-being and b and c are the size of benefits and costs resulting from the project. Now the SWF is expressed in terms of aggregate utility, so that we need to make a judgement about the relative *weight* to put on the change in utility for each of these four people.[8] These weights are known as the marginal social utility for each individual i, (MSU_i). But benefits and costs are actually measured in monetary terms, so we also need to know how marginal changes in money income affect the utility of each person: their marginal utility of income (MUY_i). The overall weights on changes in money-valued benefits and costs in terms of utility-valued social welfare will depend on both of these terms, so that we could write:

$$W = \omega_1 b(\text{A}) + \omega_2 b(\text{B}) + \omega_3 b(\text{C}) - \omega_4 c(\text{D}) \qquad (2.2)$$

where the weights $\omega_1 \ldots \omega_4$ are the product of the MSU and the MUY for each individual (the combined weight is referred to as the marginal social utility of income). This kind of SWF is referred to as a Bergson–Samuleson SWF. Now the CBA analyst must make a judgement about the values of ω. Since the values of ω are not something we can observe,[9] this choice is a normative one – some would say, an ethical – choice. In the Kaldor–Hicks test, the default assumption is that all the ω values are equal. In other words, it is assumed that: (i) a marginal gain in the utility for any individual is as socially valuable as a gain in utility for anyone else and (ii) a gain in income for any individual generates as much utility as the same gain would for anyone else. In other words, the MSU and the MUY are assumed to be equal for everyone.[10] Now this has the merits of simplicity and clarity, but some might argue: surely gains in income are more highly valued by poor people than rich people? In this case, we could no longer assume that the MUY was equal for all people, and so even though the MSU was assumed to be the same for everyone, the weights ω_i will now vary across beneficiaries and losers as a function of their income. Pearce and Nash (1981) discuss how such weights could actually be computed: for example, if winners and losers could be divided into income groups $m_1 \ldots m_4$, we might compute the weights as:

$$\omega_m = \left(\frac{Y^*}{Y_m}\right) \qquad (2.3)$$

Where Y_m is the mean income of group m and Y^* is the mean income across all four income groups. This would ensure that benefits to poorer groups 'count' for more than benefits to richer groups. If we knew that the project would affect the output of certain goods in particular (for example electricity), then we could also reflect in these weights the income elasticity of demand for electricity. But then it would also be desirable to reflect how the social welfare function responds to changes in income (for example as more benefits flow to poorer groups). This effect is known as the elasticity of the marginal social utility of income, τ. This would change the weights in (2.3) to:

$$\omega_m^* = \left(\frac{Y^*}{Y_m}\right)^{-\tau} \qquad (2.4)$$

A discussion of the problems in actually calculating such weights can be found in HM Treasury (2003). But then an argument could be made that there are additional factors other than just income that society would wish to take into account in evaluating changes in social well-being across individuals: for instance, according to ethnic discrimination, or according to age, or rural versus urban location. . . Quickly we can see that there is no one obviously correct weighting system, and that all judgements over weights are just that – ethical judgements. They cannot thus be 'right' or 'wrong'. Moreover, the use of distributional weights implicitly assumes that utility is something we can measure on a cardinal scale (Adler and Posner, 1999). Perhaps because of these difficulties, CBA practice has largely avoided the unequal weighting of benefits and costs, other than in developing country applications where income inequalities are often extreme, and despite the observation that *not* employing distributional weights reduces our ability to say whether a project which passes the CBA test actually enhances social welfare (Adler and Posner, 1999 and Little and Mirrlees, 1994). In the UK, HM Treasury has in fact endorsed the use of distributional weights in CBA (HM Treasury, 2003), but this is not a position shared by most other central government guidelines (see Box 2.1).

In any case, an argument could be made that CBA is not the setting in which to solve income inequality issues, and that CBA should focus on economic efficiency only (maximizing the difference of benefits over costs). Using project appraisal as a way of redistributing income might in any case be much more expensive – in terms of potentially socially beneficial undertakings that get rejected – than redistributing income using the tax and benefits system (Harberger, 1978; Johansson-Stenman, 2005). CBA can in any case be used as a way of setting out the distributional impacts of a project, in terms of who gains and who loses. This suggestion, initially

---

BOX 2.1   DISTRIBUTIONAL WEIGHTS IN THE GREEN BOOK

HM Treasury present data for the UK showing how the population can be categorized according to income 'quintile'. The bottom quintile is the 20 per cent of households with the lowest gross or net household income; the 2nd quintile represents those households in the next-highest 20 per cent band of income. Using this categorization, and estimates of marginal utility of income taken from a utility function specified as $U = \ln(C)$, (where C is consumption), so that the marginal utility of income $= (1/C)$, gives the following weights:

Quintile	Weight
Bottom	1.9–2.0
2nd	1.3–1.4
3rd	0.9–1.0
4th	0.7–0.8
Top	0.4–0.5

Source: HM Treasury (2003, p. 92).

This shows that we would weight benefits accruing to households in the lowest income group by a factor of around 2, but benefits to households in the highest income group by a factor of around one half.

---

due to McKean (1958) is a very useful by-product of CBA. Indeed, the legislation background to the EU's Water Framework Directive *requires* this listing of benefits and costs by stakeholder as part of the appraisal of draft river basin management plans (see Chapter 10).

A few more comments on distributional issues are in order. The type of SWF shown in equation (2.2) is sometimes known as 'utilitarian', in the sense that the assumption underlying it is that social well-being is the sum of individual well-being across all people within a society, and that a desirable goal is to maximize this social well-being (W). However, alternatives exist. Most notably, a Rawlsian approach (named after the philosopher John Rawls) would have it that social welfare is determined only by the well-being of the worst-off individuals within society, since this is a more 'just' principle. In this case, the government's goal should be to maximize the well-being of the worst-off group (or individual), regardless of the implication for everyone else. Clearly this is a very different approach from the Kaldor–Hicks criterion. A related version is the suggestion by Willig and Bailey (1981) that a constraint should be imposed on CBA that at least the poorest group in society gets positive net benefits from a project for it to pass the CBA test. Yet it can be appreciated that even this might rule out projects that had big net benefits for everyone else, and that undertaking such projects and then redistributing via the tax and benefits system is probably a better bet. Other possibly desirable 'constraints' on the CBA process are discussed in Chapter 13. Finally, we note that accepting the Kaldor–Hicks principle as a way of thinking about CBA means we are also implicitly judging that the existing distribution of income is 'acceptable' as a part of the project appraisal process, since people's (unweighted) WTP and WTA values will depend partly on their income.

2.3 VALUING COSTS AND BENEFITS UNDER UNCERTAINTY

This short section addresses a fundamental problem in undertaking a CBA: that the analyst is not certain about the benefits and costs which will result from undertaking a project or policy. For example, planting a new forest, where timber production is the main expected benefit, will result in uncertain future benefits since we cannot be sure about the world timber price in 30 years' time. Creating a new wetland as a means of preventing storm surges and reducing flooding will have uncertain benefits, since future weather patterns are unknown. Investing in wave energy will result in uncertain benefits since the future demand for electricity is not known for sure, and since the cost evolution over time of alternative renewable sources is hard to predict. Costs can also be uncertain, for instance the cost of generating nuclear power will depend on what happens to uranium prices over the next 20 years, and how decommissioning and waste treatment technologies evolve.

A discussion of uncertainty is helped by distinguishing between *states of the world* and *probabilities of occurrence*. States of the world mean just that – future conditions for prices, costs, technologies, weather patterns and health impacts which are possible. For instance, a prediction for annual winter rainfall in Scotland in 2030 is that, relative to 2008, it could be (i) the same (ii) 5 per cent higher (ii) 20 per cent higher. These are alternative states of the world. A second type of useful information is the likelihood of these different states of the world occurring. For example, climate modellers might be able to say that state (i) has a 25 per cent chance of occurring, state (ii) a 55 per cent chance of occurring and state (iii) a 20 per cent chance. If these states-of-the-world are the only possible outcomes (unlikely!), then their probabilities must sum to 1, and we could compute an *expected* value for winter rainfall in 2030 which is equal to:

Expected winter rainfall in 2030 = (0.25* (state i) + 0.55* (state ii) + 0.20 (state iii))

More generally, if it is possible to identify all possible outcomes for a variable, X_i, and the chance with which they will occur at some point in the future, P_i, – or over some interval – then this means that the probability distraction of X is known, and the expected value of X is given by:

$$\sum_{i=1}^{n} X_i * P_i \qquad (2.5)$$

which shows that the expected value is a mean value computed over all possible outcomes, weighted by their probability of occurring.

Analysts typically identify two kinds of uncertainty in CBA. The first is where all possible states of the world are known along with their probability distribution. This means an expected value for the variable can be calculated. In practice, the analyst probably knows some of the more likely future outcomes (for example, for weather, for timber, for uranium prices. . .) and their likelihood of occurring. Where might this information on probability distributions come from? From statistical analysis of past trends in variables, and modelling of future possible outcomes. Such situations, where both states of the world and probability distributions are known, is referred to as *choice under risk*. Alternatively, the probability distributions may be unknown, and/or many possible states of the world unknown. This situation is referred to as *Knightian uncertainty*, named after the economist Frank Knight.

Where future states of the world can be identified along with their probability distributions – that is, for choice under risk – the expected costs and/or benefits can be calculated using the formula shown in equation (2.5). However, it should be noted that this implies that gainers and losers are equally concerned with outcomes which are higher than and lower than the expected outcome. Moreover, it assumes *risk neutrality*, that is, that people would be indifferent between a bet with an expected value of V and receiving V for sure. This does not describe many people! Individuals are typically assumed to be risk-averse, in that they would require a larger expected value, say ($V+v$), to be indifferent between receiving this and a sum V for sure. In this case, the idea of *certainty-equivalence* has been suggested, whereby the analyst would seek to identify those values for a future risky benefit or cost which gainers or losers would be indifferent between, in terms of receiving this risky outcome and a lower future benefit/cost for sure. More discussion is provided in Pearce and Nash (1981), and in Zerbe and Dively (1994), whilst Chapter 7 returns to the issue of risk in the context of choosing a discount rate.

Where outcomes are uncertain in the Knightian sense, expected values cannot be calculated, since the probability distributions and/or states of the world are unknown. In this case – and indeed, in the majority of cases in applied CBA – the main 'solution' to the problem is sensitivity analysis. This means recalculating the Net Present Value (NPV) when the values of certain key parameters are changed. These parameters will include:

I.   the discount rate;
II. physical quantities of inputs (for example days of labour input required for a construction project);
III. (shadow) prices of these inputs;
IV. the magnitude and value of external costs and benefits resulting from the project – for instance, the recreation benefits from a new forest;
V.   physical quantities of outputs (for example megawatt hours of electricity from a new wind farm);
VI. (shadow) prices of these outputs.

One intention is to discover to which parameters the NPV outcome is most sensitive, as each is varied independently, holding the other input variables constant. For example, in appraising a new coal mine where the NPV has been calculated as positive, by how much in percentage terms does the world coal price have to fall before the NPV becomes negative? By how much do labour costs need to rise before NPV goes negative? By how much does our forecast of the lifetime of the pit need to fall before NPV goes negative? What is the impact of changing the discount rate? Once the most sensitive parameters have been identified, (i) forecasting effort can be directed at these parameters to try to improve our best guess; and (ii) where possible, more effort can be made once the project is underway to manage these parameters carefully, although most will be outside the control of the decision maker. Monte Carlo analysis can be used to vary several of the decision parameters simultaneously (for example looking at the joint variability of future electricity prices and future coal prices). The NPV decision will often depend crucially on the choice of discount rate: this will certainly be so for projects with long-term effects, such as woodland planting, nuclear waste disposal, and research and development of alternative energy sources.

2.4 ECONOMIC VALUES AND THE ENVIRONMENT: A PREVIEW TO THE PROBLEM OF VALUING 'NON-MARKET' GOODS

2.4.1 In what Sense does the Environment have Economic Value?

The natural environment provides a multitude of vital goods and services to the economy and to the world's citizens. Environmental economics textbooks such as Hanley et al. (2000) characterize these links as being fourfold:

- The environment acts as a supplier of material and energy inputs such as iron ore, oil and timber to production.
- The environment acts as a 'waste sink' for the residuals of both production and consumption, such as emissions from fossil fuel burning.
- The environment acts as a direct source of amenity and quality of life for people, for example when people go mountaineering or bird watching.
- The environment provides vital basic life support services, such as global climate regulation, nutrient cycling and water cycling.

As noted above, market prices sometimes guide us to the value of these inputs; for instance, the world oil price contains a vast amount of information on global supply and demand. However, market failure – in particular, missing markets due to the absence of a complete and enforceable system of property rights for environmental resources – means that in many, many cases, environmental values are not revealed by the market. So, if a policy will threaten biodiversity in Brazil, there is no market price of 'biodiversity services' which we can consult to inform our CBA of such a policy. If a new policy on water resource management in New Zealand will result in pollution of groundwater increasing, then again there is no market price of pollution which can be consulted. Much of this book is taken up with explaining how to estimate such non-market environmental values.

In developing these environmental valuation methods, it is useful to think of a two-way classification for how environmental resources generate economic value. This involves a consideration of *direct* and *indirect* environmental values. Direct environmental values arise when an environmental resource impacts directly on people's well-being. For example, if we think about the value of improving water quality on a river, some benefits will come about in terms of people who directly use the river, say for kayaking or swimming. These benefits are then expressed through direct changes in utility; river water quality appears as a variable in people's utility functions:

$$U = U(\mathbf{X}, Z, W) \tag{2.6}$$

where $\mathbf{X}$ is a vector of market-valued goods and services, W is river water quality and Z are other environmental resources about which an individual cares. In this sense, an improvement in water quality has a *direct* benefit since it impacts directly on utility.

But imagine that water is also abstracted from the river as one input to the production of beer, and that beer is one item (good X_1) within the vector $\mathbf{X}$ in (2.6), as the production function in (2.7) shows:

$$Q_{x1} = Q(L, K, W) \tag{2.7}$$

Here, water quality W is an input to the production of beer (x_1), along with labour (L) and capital (K). If an improvement in water quality reduces the costs of producing beer since water treatment costs fall, then this reduction in the price of beer means that the environmental quality change has produced an *indirect* value for people, through its role as input to production. Many environmental services function in this way, for instance the role of wetlands in supporting coastal fisheries, or the role of rainfall and soils in crop production. The valuation methods in Chapters 3, 4, 5 and 6 can then be divided into whether they focus on the environment as a direct source of utility (for example contingent valuation), or whether they model the environment as an input to production (for example dose-response models), and as thus contributing indirect values.

A finer classification can also be made with regard to direct approaches to valuation. Impacts on the utility function from a change in environmental quality are measured conceptually using WTP and WTA, as we saw above. *Stated Preference Methods*, such as contingent valuation, use carefully constructed questionnaires to estimate these WTP and WTA amounts from individuals for a given environmental change. Chapter 3 discusses these methods. Alternatively, direct utility values can be estimated using *Revealed Preference Methods*, which examine people's behaviour in markets related to the environmental good in question, and infer WTP and WTA from this behaviour. The travel cost model (Chapter 4) and the hedonic price method (Chapter 5) are examples of revealed preference approaches. Indirect methods, on the other hand, study environmental values through the role of the environment as an input to production. Such methods are classified in this book as *Production Function Methods*.

2.4.2 'Total Economic Value' of an Environmental Resource

The concept 'Total Economic Value', or TEV, of environmental resources has recently become widespread in the environmental economics literature (Pearce and Turner, 1989). What does this mean, and how does it relate to the concepts of value discussed above? Take, as an example, the preservation of a wetland which is important to birds, but which also functions as a nursery for fish/shellfish and as a natural pollution control plant. How might the total economic benefits flowing from this wetland be described? Consider first what we have called direct benefits, that is, direct sources of utility. Some of those who benefit from the wetland in this way may participate in activities which make the wetland valuable to them, such as bird watching or duck hunting. Such benefits are often known as *use values*, since they require actual participation to enjoy them. Use values may be consumptive (hunting) or non-consumptive (bird watching). However, people other than those who actually visit the wetland may derive benefits, in terms of the utility they get from just knowing that the wetland is preserved. These types of benefit have become known as *non-use, passive use* or *existence values*. They may be motivated by selfish reasons, or by altruism, either for other members of the current generation, or for future generations. Existence values may be particularly high for unique, irreplaceable natural assets, such as the Grand Canyon in the USA, Stonehenge in England or Kakadu National Park in Australia. Both use and non-use values can be measured using WTP or WTA.

The sum of use and existence values gives the total direct benefits of preserving the wetland. The wetland's role as a nursery for fish and shellfish could be evaluated by estimating biological models of the contribution wetland makes to fish/shellfish populations, and then by looking at the economic (commercial) value of these species. Changes in these economic values, in terms of gains/losses in consumers' surplus and producers' profits from some change in the wetland could be calculated. Finally, the wetland's pollution control function could be valued either by using the value of avoided pollution damages (say, from sedimentation of coral reef fisheries, or from nutrient enrichment), or the pollution control costs that would have to be incurred to replace the role currently being undertaken by the wetland. The sum of avoided pollution/pollution control costs, and commercial fisheries value, would give the indirect benefits of preserving the wetland. Adding the wetland's direct and indirect benefits gives its Total Economic Value.

A further, separate element of TEV is known as 'option value'. This is claimed to be akin to an insurance premium, which potential or actual users of an environmental resource are willing to pay to secure that resource's availability at some time in the future. However, economists now know that option value does not exist as a separate element of total economic value, and moreover that both its sign and size are uncertain (Ready, 1995). Instead, the term 'option price' is used to describe willingness to pay under conditions of supply uncertainty (where an individual does not know for sure how much of a public good such as a designated wilderness area will be supplied), or demand uncertainty, where the individual is not sure of their future demand (for example how many trips to the wilderness area they will make in the next two years).

2.5 CONCLUSIONS

Cost–Benefit Analysis has a firm basis in the theory of welfare economics. The Kaldor–Hicks compensation test is used as the means of deciding whether a project or policy enhances social welfare by asking whether the gainers could compensate the losers and still be better off. This is implemented in practice by comparing the aggregate benefits and costs of a project/policy over time and across people. Welfare changes can be measured using market prices under certain conditions, or changes in consumers' and producers' surplus when prices change. However, in many cases the marginal social cost or marginal social benefit will not be equal to market prices, in which case shadow prices need to be calculated. Moreover, the lack of markets for many environmental goods and services means that non-market valuation methods must be used to produce estimates of changes in the Total Economic Value as a result of policy or project implementation.

NOTES

1. In fact, the word 'exact' is misleading here, since these measures will only be an exact measure of welfare change if people's behaviour corresponds completely with the underlying model of 'rational behaviour' which underlies standard welfare economics. In future, we will generally refer to such measures in terms of consumers' surplus, and compensating and equivalent surplus/variation, rather than talking about 'exact' measures.
2. Although the hedonic price analysis presented in Chapter 5 considers cases where people can choose their 'local' air quality to a degree, for example by moving house.
3. In fact, Hicks' 1943 article also outlined quantity-based measures of consumers' surplus, but these related to the case where the consumer could choose how much to consume at each price.
4. In fact, interest in shadow prices was much greater some years ago, for example in the 1970s. This decline in interest may reflect a general decline in government intervention

in markets, in foreign exchange controls, and in the power of trade unions since the 1980s.

5. Readers should note that this implies a particular relationship between WTP and WTA.
6. In fact, Hicks and Kaldor proposed somewhat different tests of whether a project improved social welfare, but these have been amalgamated, due to the work of Scitovsky (1941), and so now people refer to the 'Kaldor–Hicks' test. Hicks' compensation test takes the perspective of the losers from a change; Kaldor's takes the perspective of the gainers.
7. This 'by group' approach is used for the appraisal of transport and flood defence projects in the UK (Sugden, 1999).
8. See Pearce (2006) for a general discussion of the problem.
9. Although some authors have suggested we can infer weights from observing government decisions or tax schedules.
10. This is true so long as one sees the Kaldor–Hicks test as a test for increases in social welfare.

REFERENCES

Adler, M. and E. Posner (1999), 'Re-thinking cost–benefit analysis', *Yale Law Journal*, **109**(2), 164–247.

Hanley, N., J. Shogren and B. White (2000), *An Introduction to Environmental Economics*, Oxford: Oxford University Press.

Harberger, A.C. (1978), 'On the use of distributional weights in social cost–benefit analysis', *Journal of Political Economy*, **81**, S87–S120.

Hicks, J.R. (1943), 'The four consumer's surpluses', *Review of Economic Studies*, **11**(1), 31–41.

Hicks, J.R. (1945), 'The generalised theory of consumer's surplus', *Review of Economic Studies*, **13**(2), 68–74.

H.M. Treasury (2003), *The Green Book: Appraisal and Evaluation in Central Government*, London: The Stationery Office.

Johansson-Stenman, O. (2005), 'Distributional weights in Cost–Benefit Analysis – should we forget about them?', *Land Economics*, **81**(3), 335–52.

Little, I.M. and J. Mirrlees (1994), 'The costs and benefits of analysis: project appraisal and planning twenty years on', in R. Layard and S. Glaister (eds), *Cost–Benefit Analysis*, Cambridge: Cambridge University Press.

McKean, R.N. (1958), *Efficiency in Government Through Systems Analysis*, New York: Wiley.

Pearce, D.W. (2006), 'Framework for assessing the distribution of environmental quality', in Y. Serret and N. Johnstone (eds), *The Distributional Effects of Environmental Policy*, Cheltenham, UK and Northampton, MA, USA: Edward Elgar.

Pearce, D.W. and C. Nash (1981), *The Social Appraisal of Projects*, Basingstoke: Macmillan.

Pearce, D.W. and R.K. Turner (1989), *Economics of Natural Resources and the Environment*, New York: Harvester-Wheatsheaf.

Ready, R. (1995), 'Environmental valuation under uncertainty', in D.W. Bromley (ed.), *The Handbook of Environmental Economics*, Oxford: Blackwell.

Scitovsky, T. (1941), 'A note on welfare propositions in economics', *Review of Economic Studies*, **9**(1), 77–88.

Sugden, R. (1999), 'Developing a consistent cost–benefit framework for multimodal transport appraisal', report to the UK Department of the Environment, Transport and the Regions, University of East Anglia, Economics Research Centre.

Sugden, R. and A. Williams (1979), *The Principles of Practical Cost–Benefit Analysis*, Oxford: Oxford University Press.

Willig, R. (1976), 'Consumers' surplus without apology', *American Economic Review*, **66**(4), 589–97.

Willig, R. and E. Bailey (1981), 'Income distributional concerns in regulatory policy-making', in G. Fromm (ed.), *Studies in Public Regulation*, Cambridge, MA: MIT Press.

Zerbe, R.O. and D.D. Dively (1994), *Benefit–Cost Analysis in Theory and Practice*, New York: HarperCollins.

3. Stated preference approaches to environmental valuation

This chapter introduces two methods of environmental valuation which rely on the *stated preferences* approach: that is, they rely on the researcher directly asking people about their willingness to pay or willingness to accept compensation for changes in environmental quality. These two methods are contingent valuation, and choice experiments (which are sometimes referred to as choice modelling, or conjoint analysis). In this chapter, we will:

- Provide an overview of the contingent valuation and the choice experiment methods.
- Explain the main problems faced in applying these methods and interpreting their results.
- Present some recent examples of the use of contingent valuation and choice experiments in environmental policy analysis.
- Explain the process of 'benefits transfer'.
- Finally, we briefly review how stated preference methods can be used to value changes in risks in terms of mortality and illness, since such benefits can be important aspects of a CBA applied to environmental legislation.

3.1   THE CONTINGENT VALUATION METHOD

As stated in the previous chapter, the basis for the economic valuation of a change in prices or the availability of a good is to enquire what is the most an individual is willing to pay (WTP) for that change, if it is desirable, or the minimum compensation they are willing to accept (WTA) to forgo the change. Contingent valuation does just this – it asks people what they are WTP for an improvement in environmental quality, or what they are WTA to go without this improvement. Alternatively, people can be asked their maximum WTP to avoid a decrease in environmental quality, or their minimum WTA to put up with this decrease.

The contingent valuation method (CVM) for the valuation of

environmental goods was first used by Davis in a study of hunters in Maine in 1963. However, it was not until the mid-1970s that the method's development began in earnest (Hammack and Brown, 1974; Brookshire et al., 1976; Randall et al., 1974). Since then, the method has become the most widely used (and perhaps most controversial) of all environmental valuation techniques. Much argument surrounded the application of CVM to controversial environmental management and litigation issues such as the protection of the Kakadu National Park in Australia, and the use of the method to estimate damages from a major accident involving the oil tanker *Exxon Valdez* in Alaska in 1989. This latter incident gave rise to the commissioning of an eminent group of economists to apply CVM to measure lost non-use values which Exxon could be sued for in the US courts. As a response, Exxon commissioned another eminent group to publish a critique of the method. The consequence was a US federal government enquiry into the method (the 'NOAA Blue Ribbon Panel'), whose report was a qualified endorsement of the technique (Arrow et al., 1993; Bateman and Willis, 1999). This shows the importance which has become attached to the method (in Exxon's case, a prospective damage claim of $2.8 billion.) Since then, debate has continued over the best way in which to apply CVM, and into how reliable the values it produces can be judged to be. A comprehensive account of the CVM method may be found in Bateman et al. (2002), whilst an early overview of the method was (influentially) provided by Mitchell and Carson (1989). In what follows, we first run through the stages of a CVM, then review some problems in applying CVM and interpreting the results from a CVM survey. Since a very large amount of literature now exists on CVM, we focus on a selection of issues only.

3.1.1   Basics of a CVM Exercise

Most CVM exercises can be split into five stages: (1) setting up the hypothetical market; (2) obtaining bids; (3) estimating mean WTP and/or WTA; (4) aggregating the data; and (5) carrying out validity checks.

Stage 1: the hypothetical market
The first step is to set up a hypothetical market for the environmental good in question. For example, take a policy to improve air quality in a city centre by changing from diesel-powered buses to electric-powered trams, and by converting taxis to run on hydrogen-powered fuel cells. A decision would be made about the relevant population to sample for the CVM – akin to decisions over the relevant population in CBA generally – and a random sample drawn from this population. The description of the 'hypothetical market' needs to include:

- what change in environmental quality is envisaged, and over what time period;
- who would pay for this change, and why;
- how they would pay for this change;
- what would happen if the policy is not introduced (the 'status quo').

In our example, respondents might be told that the local government could engage in such a policy, describe what the policy would consist of, and explain that the policy could only go ahead if extra funds are generated. This sets up a *reason for payment* for the change in environmental quality. How funds will be raised also needs to be described; the *bid vehicle* must be decided upon; for example, through an increase in local property taxes, local income taxes, or a tax on car drivers. In this example, the bid vehicle could be higher local property taxes. The survey instrument (questionnaire) should also describe whether all consumers will pay if the change goes ahead, and how the decision on whether to proceed with the project would be taken.

Good questionnaire design is absolutely vital to a good CVM exercise. The questionnaire should be developed using focus groups drawn from the relevant population, and then pre-tested before the main survey occurs. The information given to respondents about all aspects of the hypothetical market, together with such information as is provided on the good being valued (in this case, an improvement in urban air quality), constitute the 'framing' of the good.

Stage 2: obtaining bids

Once the questionnaire has been designed, the survey is carried out. This can be done by face-to-face interviewing (in people's homes, or at a recreational site), telephone interviewing, via the Internet, or by mail. Telephone interviews are probably the least-preferred method since conveying information about the good may be difficult over the telephone. Internet surveys are growing in popularity. Mail surveys are frequently used, but suffer from potential non-response bias and often from low response rates. Personal, face-to-face interviews offer the most scope for detailed questions and answers, but are relatively costly. Typically, a CVM survey will ask some general questions about environmental attitudes; test for knowledge of the good in question and provide information on the hypothetical scenario; collect WTP/WTA information; ask for socio-economic data on the respondent; and pose some 'de-briefing' questions such as how hard the respondent found the exercise. Box 3.1 contains excerpts from a recent CVM questionnaire by way of illustration.

BOX 3.1   AN EXAMPLE FROM A CONTINGENT VALUATION QUESTIONNAIRE

This questionnaire was part of a study by the consultancy firm Jacobs for the Scottish Executive in 2003, which estimated the benefits of designating Natura 2000 sites in Scotland under the EU Habitats Directive (Jacobs et al., 2004). Most of the benefits were thought to involve non-use values. The survey was conducted in people's houses, using a random sample of Scottish households. After some warm-up questions on attitudes to nature conservation, interviewers asked the following question:

READ OUT and show map of Scotland with Natura 2000 sites shown

Natura 2000 is a new European network of conservation sites containing a representative sample of animals, plants and wildlife habitats of European importance. Most sites have had some form of protection for many years. So far around 300 Natura 2000 sites, excluding marine sites, have been established throughout Scotland.

They cover about 11% of the land in Scotland, and contain some of the most important and unique wildlife habitats in Europe. If the sites are not fully protected, many of the habitats, animals and plants will be damaged and, eventually, lost over time.

Public funds currently available may not be enough to pay for the conservation of the 300 Scottish Natura 2000 sites.

In principle, is your household willing to contribute additional money through your tax bill to ensure that all 300 sites remain fully protected for their wildlife and landscape?

Yes __ No ___ Not sure/don't know __

If the respondent said 'yes' the interviewer then asked:

You have said you would be willing, in principle, to contribute towards the conservation of the Natura 2000 sites throughout Scotland. We are very interested to know *how much* extra you would be willing to pay to ensure their complete protection for the next 25 years.

SHOW PAYMENT CARD

Using this card to help, what is the maximum total amount that your household would be willing to pay *in additional taxes each year* for the next 25 years towards the complete protection of all 300 Natura sites?

Before you answer this question, please bear in mind:
– You will no longer be able to spend this money on other things.
– Other sites in Scotland may still provide some similar wildlife habitats, although not as important.

Individuals can be asked to state their WTP/WTA in a number of ways (in what follows, we focus on WTP alone for simplicity, and since that is what most studies estimate in practice):

- As a *payment card*. A range of values is presented on a card, and the respondent is asked to pick that which most closely matches their WTP. Payment ladders can also be used. Data from such modes can either be treated as continuous information on WTP (that is, if someone ticks the $5 box, we interpret this as showing their maximum WTP is $5) or, more correctly, as interval-type data (so if they tick the $5 box but do not tick the next highest one – say $15 – we know their maximum WTP is at least as big as $5, but smaller than $15). People can also be asked how sure they are that they would pay each amount on the card.
- As an *open-ended question*. Individuals are asked for their maximum WTP with no value being suggested to them.
- As a *single bounded dichotomous choice*: a single payment is suggested, to which respondents either agree or disagree (yes/no). This is rather like voting on the provision of a public good at a fixed price.
- As a *double-bounded dichotomous choice*. Those respondents who say 'no' to the first amount are then asked if they would pay a lower amount, whilst those respondents who say 'yes' to the first amount are asked if they would pay a higher amount. Other variants exist.

Stage 3: estimating WTP
For open-ended responses, calculating mean or median WTP is simple, although researchers must take care to separate out *protest responses* first: these are zero values for WTP given for reasons other than a zero value being placed on the environmental good in question. These might occur because an individual objects on moral grounds to paying for the environmental good, or finds the hypothetical scenario hard to believe, or does not trust the government to actually deliver the environmental improvement on offer. Mean WTP is the relevant value for use in cost–benefit analysis, although authors often focus on median WTP since it is less impacted by extreme values, and since it is meaningful from a political consensus viewpoint (if median WTP for the air quality improvement is £70/household/year, then at least 50 per cent of the population would vote 'yes' to a policy costing £70). Confidence intervals for WTP should also be reported. For payment card designs, mean WTP could be calculated from the maximum value that people say they are WTP. *Bid functions* are usually estimated to investigate the determinants of variations in WTP for open-ended and

payment card data. A bid function is a regression equation which relates WTP to those variables thought likely to influence it. For example, we could take the individual WTP statements from our study and regress them on variables measuring household income, age, health status and whether the respondent has children of school age:

$$WTP = f(\text{Income, Age, Health Status, Kids}) \qquad (3.1)$$

The intention is to see how much of the variation in WTP can be statistically explained, and to see whether variables are related to WTP in a intuitively-consistent manner. In the air pollution example, other things being equal, we might expect WTP to be positively related to household income, and to whether people have children of school age, since children may be thought particularly vulnerable to air pollution. Old people or people of poorer health status might also care more about air quality improvements. Often, though, it is not possible to form a firm prediction about the relationship between WTP and variables we may collect as part of the survey. For payment card designs, estimating equation (3.1) is complicated by the fact that we only know that the respondent's maximum WTP is at least as big as the value they choose on the card, but less than the next highest value (see Haab and McConnell, 2002, for details).

For dichotomous choice (DC) designs (single and double-bounded), the researcher must estimate WTP, since all the respondent reveals is whether she is willing to pay a given amount, not her maximum. Several approaches are available to do this, the most popular being Hanemann's 'utility difference approach', which we now explain (Hanemann, 1984). Full treatments of these issues raised here can be found in Hanemann and Kanninen (1999), and in Bateman et al. (2002). Let us focus on a single-bounded DC design, and assume that Sue derives utility from an environmental good q. Let's assume that Sue has a utility function $U(q, y)$, where y is income. Let us also assume that the researcher cannot observe all of the aspects of this utility function: for example, we may not be able to measure Sue's preferences very well. This idea is known as the *random utility model*, which underlies the DC version of CVM, as well as choice modelling and multiple-site travel cost models. The random utility model can be represented like this:

$$U_j = v(y_j, q) + \varepsilon_j \qquad (3.2)$$

This says that utility is composed of two bits, a deterministic part v and a random part ε, which are 'additively separable'. It is assumptions about the distribution of this random term, and about the functional form of v which will give rise to different models of WTP.

Imagine that Sue, as part of a CVM questionnaire, is offered the option that environmental quality will rise from $q0$ to $q1$, where $q1$ is better than $q0$. Sue is asked whether she will pay £A for this change. She will answer yes with probability:

$$\Pr(yes) = Pr\{v(q1, y - A, e) \geq v(q0, y, e)\} \qquad (3.3)$$

and her maximum WTP for this change in q will be her compensating surplus C, defined as:

$$v(q1, y - C, e) = v(q0, y, e) \qquad (3.4)$$

which means that (3.3) can be re-written as:

$$\Pr(yes) = \Pr\{C(q0, q1, y, e) \geq A\} \qquad (3.3)'$$

To continue, the researcher must now estimate a statistical model which relates Sue's response, and those of everyone else in the valuation survey, to both the amount A and, typically, people's socio-economic character-istics. How exactly to proceed will depend on a range of factors, notably (as mentioned above), what we assume about the nature of people's utility functions, and what we assume about the distribution of the random part of utility. Haab and McConnell (2002) provide an excellent technical guide to these issues. The simplest case they consider is where the utility function is linear. This implies that the deterministic part of utility looks like this:

$$v_j = \alpha Z_j + \beta(y_j) \qquad (3.5)$$

where Z is a range of socio-economic characteristics and y is income for individual j. The deterministic part of the utility function for the hypotheti-cal CVM scenario is given by the difference between utility with the project and income less the offer amount A ($y - A$), and utility without the project and the original income y. We next need to choose a distribution for the random part of utility: the most common choices are that ε is distributed normally, which leads to a probit model, or logistically, which leads to the logit model. Using the latter assumption, the probability that someone will choose to say 'yes' in the CVM scenario to the offer amount A is:

$$\Pr(yes) = \frac{1}{(1 + \exp(-\alpha Z - \beta A))} \qquad (3.6)$$

To estimate this equation, simply create the dependent variable 'response', coded as $1 = $ yes and $0 = $ no, then regress this on the socio-economic variables Z and the offer amount A for each person, using the 'logit' command in a package such as STATA or LIMDEP.

We then want to calculate welfare measures, typically mean and median WTP. How this is done will again depend on what assumptions have been made about the functional form of v, and the distribution of ε. Again, Haab and McConnell (2002) give full details. For the simplest case of the linear utility function, then mean WTP is given by:

$$E(WTP) = \left(\frac{\alpha Z}{\beta}\right) \qquad (3.7)$$

Median WTP can be calculated as the value of A that there is a 50–50 chance a randomly selected person would agree to pay.

An alternative way of calculating mean WTP from dichotomous choice CVM data has also emerged, known as the 'non-parametric' or 'distribution-free' approach. This emerged because of a basic problem with the parametric approach set out above, namely that the mean WTP estimate obtained from a given data set depends on what assumptions the researcher makes about the forms of v and ε. Full details on how to use a non-parametric approach to analysing CVM data is given in Haab and McConnell (2002). But we can summarize the main details here of what is referred to as the 'Turnbull method'. First, we observe that if Joe says 'no' to a bid of t_j (we use t instead of A here to make comparison with Haab and McConnell easier), then his maximum WTP must be less than t_j. If he says 'yes', then his WTP must be equal to or greater than this amount. Define F_j as the (unknown) probability that Joe, and anyone like him, will say 'no' to price t_j. It turns out that if we knew F_j, we could calculate mean WTP for our sample. A good estimate of F_j is the proportion of all respondents asked whether they would pay amount t_j who answered 'no'. This can be calculated for each amount asked. We would end up with something like the data in Table 3.1. This CVM data is 'well-behaved', since the value of F_j rises every time the price increases. If the raw data do not have this property, then to apply this non-parametric procedure the analyst has to merge neighbouring price bands together until the merged data do have the property.

A 'lower bound' on WTP can now be calculated, using the formula:

$$E(WTP) = \sum_{j=0}^{M} t_j.(F_j + 1 - F_j) \qquad (3.8)$$

This means calculating the difference between the proportion of 'no' responses at a given price, and deducting from it the proportion of 'no' responses at the next lowest price; this gives the quantity $(F_{j+1} - F_j)$,

Table 3.1   Example data from a discrete choice contingent valuation study

Amount offered	Number of 'no' responses	Total number of people made this offer	F_j = (number of 'no' responses / number of people made the offer)
100	98	190	0.51
200	78	144	0.54
300	105	166	0.63
400	113	154	0.73

Table 3.2   Transformed discrete choice data for use of Turnbull Method

Amount offered, t	Number of 'no' responses	Total number of people made this offer	F_j = (number of 'no' responses / number of people made the offer)	$(F_{j+1} - F_j)$
100	98	190	0.51	0.51
200	78	144	0.54	0.03
300	105	166	0.63	0.09
400	113	154	0.73	0.1
400+			1	0.27

and then this is multiplied by the price. These amounts are then summed together. We assume that the probability of saying 'no' to a zero price is zero, and the probability of saying 'no' to some 'choke price' is one. This would give the data shown in Table 3.2.

The lower bound estimate on mean WTP, $E(WTP)$, would then be:

$$E(WTP) = (\$100 * 0.03) = (\$200 * 0.09) + (\$300 * 0.1) + (\$400 * 0.27)$$
$$= \$159$$

(notice that we ignore the first value for $(F_{j+1} - F_j)$ since this would be multiplied by zero). Haab and McConnell (2002) also give a formula for calculating the variance of WTP, so that a 95 per cent confidence interval for mean WTP can be worked out. For median WTP, we ask: 'at what value of t_j do just more than 50 per cent of people vote no?'. In the above data, this is at a price of $100. Median WTP will lie between this value and the next highest price.

Whilst the non-parametric approach outlined above has many advantages (it is simple to use, it does not involve making assumptions about the distribution of 'true' WTP), there are also some problems with the method. The main problem is that it is hard to take account of the variables that might be driving WTP. Suppose we think that how long people have lived in an area might well determine how much they are willing to pay to protect a local beauty spot from destruction. The main way of investigating this with the non-parametric approach is to divide the sample into, say, those that have lived in the area more than five years, and those who have lived in the area less than five years, and then to calculate separate means for each group. But you can imagine that this procedure gets rather limiting if one wants to investigate the impacts of many variables on WTP. Another problem is that splitting the sample in this way reduces the number of observations available to calculate each mean, which means that the standard error of our WTP estimate will increase, leading to less precise estimates.

Stage 4: aggregating the data
Aggregation refers to the process whereby the mean bid or bids are converted to a population total value figure. Decisions over aggregation revolve around three issues. First is the choice of the relevant population. This should have been decided when constructing the sampling frame from which the sample was drawn. The aim is to identify either (a) all those whose utility will be significantly affected by the action or (b) (which is the same or a smaller group) all those within a relevant political boundary who will be affected by the action. A decision must be made over the criteria to be used in deciding on who counts in (a) or (b). This group might be the local population, the regional population, the population of Scotland, or the population of the UK, or the whole of Europe. Clearly, where significant non-use values are involved, this population of beneficiaries could be very large. The second issue is moving from the sample mean to a mean for the total population. Several alternatives have been proposed. The sample mean could be multiplied by the number of households in the population, N. However, the sample might be a biased reflection of the relevant population; for instance, it might have higher income levels or show a lower level of educational achievement. If these variables have been included in a bid curve, an estimated population mean bid can be derived by inserting population values for the relevant variables in the bid curve. This number could then be multiplied by N. The third issue is the choice of the time period over which benefits should be aggregated. This will depend on the setting within which the CVM exercise is being performed.

Stage 5: carrying out validity checks
How good are the CVM estimates which the analyst produces? This is
clearly an important question from a policy perspective, and in terms of
the credibility of environmental valuation. Several 'validity checks' have
emerged. These are:

- scope tests;
- convergent validity;
- calibration factors;
- protest rates;
- construct validity.

Scope tests involve examining whether WTP varies significantly with
the quantity of q on offer. A simple scope test would be to test the null
hypothesis that WTP $(q2) >$ WTP $(q1)$, where we assume $q2 > q1$. For
example, this could mean that WTP to protect all wetlands in one region
of France was greater than WTP to protect a single wetland. Scope tests
arose as a validity criterion because of a worry that the failure of WTP to
show scope sensitivity would imply that a poor description of the environmental change/good in question had been provided, or that people's WTP
amounts were largely symbolic donations which could not be interpreted
as compensating surplus/equivalent surplus – although sometimes a CVM
survey may fail a scope test due to a small sample size. For more discussion, see Heberlein et al. (2005).

Convergent validity is a test for whether WTP for a given environmental
quality change estimated using CVM is significantly different from WTP for
the same change using some other technique; for instance, comparing CVM
and travel costs estimates for a day's fishing (see Chapter 4). This assumes
that CVM and, in this instance, travel costs measure the same underlying
value, which may not be true when non-use values are concerned.

Calibration factors address a fundamental weakness of CVM: that the
values stated are hypothetical commitments, not real ones. A calibration
factor is calculated by comparing a WTP value obtained from a CVM
survey with a comparable real commitment – obtained, typically, through
experimental economics methods (Fox et al., 1998), or occasionally by
means of a comparison with actual voting behaviour (Schlapfer et al.,
2004). If WTP (CVM) $\geqslant$ than WTP (real), then doubt is cast on the CVM
estimate. We come back to the problem of hypothetical versus real WTP
below in section 3.1.2. However, it is hard to calculate calibration factors
for many environmental goods since the reason why we undertake CVM is
precisely because some aspect of the good defies market valuation; this is
especially true for non-use values. Many experimental studies have shown

that stated WTP is bigger than actual WTP: could we therefore claim that CVM *always* produces numbers that are 'too big' by some fixed proportion? No: the current view is that the calibration factor varies according to the nature of the good and the nature of the valuation market, and does not lend itself to generalization.

Protest rates are another indicator of the quality of a CVM survey. The protest rate is defined as the percentage of responses which are protest bids (see above): too high a protest rate ('too high' is a subjective matter, but a protest rate of over 40 per cent would raise concerns) implies that there is something wrong with the design of the hypothetical market; for example, people did not find it believable, or found it morally objectionable. One useful exercise can be to try and statistically explain why some individuals protest and others do not. Finally, the worth of an individual CVM study can be assessed using the criterion of *construct validity*. This asks whether WTP varies in a manner which is consistent with theoretical expectations. Usually this question is addressed by estimating a bid function, and seeing whether parameter signs are in accord with a priori expectations (for example do people with more experience or knowledge of the good pay more? Does higher income boost WTP?), and also by considering what percentage of the variation in WTP can be explained statistically. However, for many variables it is hard to decide what the relationship with WTP should be (for example do we expect older people to value forest conservation more than young people? Do we expect locals to value it more than visitors?), whilst there are many different theoretically-consistent assumptions one could make about the nature of the underlying utility function. The construct validity notion is therefore not as useful as it first seems.

3.1.2   Some Problem Areas in Contingent Valuation

Hypothetical market bias
The most simple objection to CVM, as to any stated preference method, is that by asking a hypothetical question, one only receives a hypothetical answer. In other words, what people say they would pay in a CVM study for, say, a reduction in air pollution in their city, is more than they would actually pay if asked to do so. This tendency to overestimate true WTP – if we could observe it – has been called hypothetical market bias. The basic problem with addressing this issue is that we use CVM precisely because the market does not generate a price for many environmental goods – thus it is hard to know what 'true' WTP actually is for, say, an increase in biodiversity. Some authors have used experiments to compare stated with actual values for a range of goods. Harrison and Rustrom's

---

BOX 3.2   AN EXAMPLE OF A CVM STUDY: REDUCING
ECOLOGICAL DAMAGES DUE TO ACID RAIN

Banzhaf et al. (2006) report on a survey carried out to estimate the benefits of reducing acid rain damages in the Adirondacks National Park in
the US. Damages from acid rain in the Adirondacks have been important
historically in terms of the development of air pollution policy in the US,
as they are a well-known example of environmental damages from emissions of SO_2 and NOx. The health benefits of reducing SO_2 and NOx
emissions have been widely studied, but no previous study had looked
at the economic value of ecological benefits from avoided damages.
Non-use values were thought, a priori, to be an important component
of the Total Economic Value of reductions in acid rain emissions, thus
a stated preference method was chosen by the analysts – in this case,
contingent valuation. The sample population was composed of residents
of New York State, and most responses were collected through an
Internet panel. Considerable effort was made to translate current scientific understanding of how the ecology of the park would benefit from a
reduction in acidification into a format which was capable of conveying
this effectively to ordinary people: some 31 focus groups were used in
survey development.

Two versions of the survey were used, which varied according to the
extent of ecological damages under the 'policy off' or status quo scenario. The 'policy on' scenario referred to the use of liming (spreading
lime by helicopter) to reduce acidification, rather than the reduction of
emissions, since questionnaire pre-testing suggested that people would
protest against taxes being used to pay for pollution reductions directly
(since 'the polluter should pay'). Higher state taxes over a 10-year period
were used as the bid vehicle using a dichotomous choice format. For the
baseline case, mean WTP was between \$48–\$107 per annum, depending on how the data was analysed: this implied annual aggregate benefits
of between \$336 million and \$1.1 billion. Interestingly, these ecological
damage avoidance benefits were about one-third the size of the health
benefits estimated for the policy change.

This case study is a good example of a large CVM survey which has
been carefully analysed, and which relates to a specific policy question:
are the benefits of the damage restoration programme bigger than the
costs?

(2005) review of such work shows that 34 of 39 tests revealed hypothetical
bias, ranging from 2 to 2600 per cent. Another recent review is provided
by Murphy et al. (2005), who find a mean calibration factor of 1.35 (that
is, stated values exceed actual monetary values by 35 per cent on average),
although they note that for public goods, this hypothetical bias increases.
These results reinforce the argument that people tend to overstate their
actual WTP when confronted with hypothetical questions. Conversely, in

a study of 616 comparisons of contingent valuation results and estimates derived from actual markets via revealed preference methods, Carson et al. (1996) found that CVM estimates were on average *lower* than revealed preference estimates. List and Gallet (2001) review 174 sets of results from 29 papers, and find that the degree of hypothetical market bias seems to depend on certain characteristics of individual CVM studies, such as how the payment question is asked.

The extent of hypothetical market bias in any particular CVM study is thus hard to predict in any particular study, although a reasonable bet would be that true WTP is less than stated WTP. This is simply because the typical CVM study is 'non-consequential' for respondents: nobody is actually going to ask them to pay the amount they said they would be WTP, and environmental quality is unlikely to change directly as a consequence of their WTP statement. This brings us to a related issue, namely that of *incentive compatibility*. An incentive compatible CVM study would be one where for any respondent, their best bet is to truthfully reveal their exact maximum WTP. No actual CVM undertaken 'in the field' is likely to possess this characteristic. Instead, we can talk about how 'demand revealing' a particular CVM design is – how much of people's true WTP will be revealed by their WTP statement? In fact, this problem of incentive compatibility is not restricted to hypothetical markets, or to CVM. For example, when environmental charities ask for donations to meet a funding target for protecting a threatened habitat, an individual has an incentive to 'free ride' by offering to pay less than the true value. Why? Because if the benefits of the good – here, habitat conservation – are available to everyone regardless of whether they pay or not, then I can get a benefit even though I do not pay for it. This might be particularly true of non-use values for biodiversity or wilderness. For a recent overview of findings on hypothetical market bias (which includes a discussion of the importance of distinguishing between bias at the level of aggregate and individual responses), see Burton et al., 2007.

What can be done about hypothetical market bias? Besides testing for it, which is a rather hard thing to do in many contexts, one suggestion has been simply to tell respondents about the fact that, in a hypothetical survey, people tend to overstate their WTP, and then ask them not to! This is known as 'cheap talk' (Cummings and Taylor, 1999; Aadland and Caplan, 2003). A short version of this, used by Whitehead and Cherry (2007) reads: 'Now please think about the next question (the WTP question) just like it was a real decision. If you signed up for the program you would have A dollars less to spend on other things.' The evidence suggests that cheap talk can moderate hypothetical market bias, especially for those with higher WTP values.

Choice of response mode

One issue which has generated many articles in academic journals is which response mode should be used, and how data should be analysed. Open-ended CVM questions have been criticized for being too hard for respondents to complete, and for resulting in high-variance mean WTP distributions. However, the approach in principle tells us exactly what we want to know – the most someone is WTP for an environmental change, or the least they will accept in compensation. Open-ended designs thus continue to be used, although typically only for environmental goods that respondents are familiar with (for example fishing permits). Single-bounded DC formats became almost 'industry standard' following the 1993 National Oceanographic and Atmospheric Administration report into CVM produced by the US government, partly because it was alleged to be incentive-compatible – that is, that it would lead people to reveal their preferences truthfully, partly because it was argued to be more realistic (a fixed price for providing a public good), and because in the US respondents are familiar with voting on local public good issues.

However, single-bounded DC designs turned out to produce systematically-high mean WTP estimates ('yea-saying' being one explanation); required larger sample sizes because they are statistically inefficient; and produce mean WTP estimates which can be very sensitive to statistical assumptions about the functional form of WTP. Partly in response to these weaknesses, the double-bounded DC design was pioneered by Hanemann and Carson, and became widely used in the 1990s. But concerns arose over the effects of the size of the first bid on responses to the second bid (that is, whether both responses came from the same underlying distribution of WTP) (McLeod and Bergland, 1999). A further problem with the double-bounded DC design is that it typically fails to make the *decision* rule clear to respondents: will governments go ahead with a project if enough respondents vote 'yes' to the first amount, or to the second amount asked? Understanding what respondents believe about this would be important to understanding how much of their true WTP they will reveal. It has also been argued that single- and double-bounded DC formats do not encourage respondents to think carefully enough about the value they place on an environmental good, since 'yes' and 'no' are easy answers to give (Fror, 2008).

Alternative mechanisms are thus still widely used. Methods that have become popular include payment cards that allow respondents to say how sure they are they would pay the amount asked, over a series of amounts; and payment ladders which allow people to say the most they are sure they would pay, and the least they are sure they would *not* pay, thus typically identifying a range of uncertainty, given that people may be unsure

---

BOX 3.3   IS OUR ESTIMATE OF WILLINGNESS TO PAY
SENSITIVE TO HOW WE ASK THE QUESTION?
SOME EVIDENCE

As we noted above, there is a debate amongst CVM practioners about which format to use for WTP questions. Open-ended (OE), payment card (PC) and dichotomous choice (DC) formats all have advantages and disadvantages. But does it make a difference to our estimates of WTP, and if so, is this proof that hypothetical markets are somehow unreliable? Patricia Champ and Richard Bishop investigate this question using some rather unique data. As they show (2006, Table 1), many previous studies have compared mean WTP for DC, OE and PC formats. A typical finding is that WTP is sensitive to the choice of format, with DC designs usually giving higher WTP values. This sensitivity has been used to criticize contingent valuation, since the argument is that the underlying utility change should be invariant to how we try and measure it. However, Champ and Bishop show that this sensitivity also exists for actual payments for real goods. Their experiment involves customers of a Wisconsin power company being offered the chance to buy their electricity from renewable sources rather than from coal fired power stations. Respondents were told that renewable sources – in this case, wind power – had lower environmental costs than fossil fuel powered electricity, but that wind energy was more expensive. Consumers could thus opt, if they wanted, for more expensive, cleaner electricity. Two designs of the questionnaire were used, one with a DC format and one with a PC format.

Results showed that both the distribution of WTP and its mean value were different according to the format used, with the DC design giving higher WTP estimates. Since this was for real payments for an actual good, the authors concluded that the effect of format on WTP was nothing to do with hypothetical market problems! Rather, they suggest that different designs may convey different information about the good on offer to respondents, in that the payment format contains value 'clues' that cause people to respond differently. As the authors say, 'the bottom line is that, a priori, one elicitation format is not unequivocally better than the others'. All methods have advantages and disadvantages.

---

of their preferences for some environmental goods (Hanley et al., 2009). Non-parametric means of data analysis have also been introduced to try to get around sensitivities to distributional assumptions within the single- and double-bounded DC designs.

Information provision

An early concern in CVM was the sensitivity of WTP estimates to the amount and nature of information provided to respondents (see the survey in Munro and Hanley, 1999). For example, mean WTP for protecting

a not very well known species of wildlife could depend on what people
are told about this species as part of the CVM questionnaire process.
In a sense, we would want this to be so, since the value of market goods
depends on what people know about the characteristics of these goods (for
example my maximum WTP for a motorbike will depend on what I can
learn about its performance: if I am subsequently told that the reliability
of the brand is questionable, my willingness to pay will fall). Yet especially
where the analyst is dealing with unfamiliar environmental goods – such
as biodiversity – providing adequate information about the good to be
valued is crucial if we wish to elicit 'informed' preferences. But how best to
do this? And what constitutes 'adequate' information?

One new concept which addresses this question is the 'valuation workshop' technique, as explained in MacMillan et al. (2006), where respondents meet together with 'experts' over a number of occasions, discuss the
valuation problem with each other, and take time to think about their
preferences. Finally, an interesting new angle on the information story
is concerned with what people know about *why* environmental problems
occur: there is now some evidence to suggest that people are willing to pay
more to cure environmental problems that they believe to be caused by
human actions than they are for identical problems due to 'the forces of
nature' (Bulte et al., 2005).

Voluntary versus non-voluntary payments

In many cases, the use of a voluntary payment mechanism as the bid vehicle
is the most realistic choice in designing a CVM study. For example, if one
thinks about an increase in the protection of an endangered bird species in
the UK, then asking people their maximum WTP in terms of contributions
to an environmental charity which acts to buy up and safeguard this bird's
habitat is both realistic and in line with people's experience. However,
some researchers have recommended against using voluntary payment
mechanisms, since they encourage free-riding. With free-riding, respondents take advantage of the fundamental non-excludability of public goods
(see Chapter 2). They do this by stating a maximum WTP which is below
their true value, since they know that so long as the good is provided for
some, it will be available to them too. Stated WTP, obtained from a CVM
exercise, will thus be an underestimate of true value. One way of dealing
with this problem is the 'provision point mechanism', whereby respondents are told that a minimum level of aggregate contribution is required
for the public good to be supplied at all. This may be reinforced by either
a proportional rebate rule (all excess contributions are returned weighted
by your WTP), or an extending benefits rule, whereby additional amounts
of the public good are provided above the amount that has been set out,

should aggregate contributions exceed the minimum. Poe et al. (2002) show that this type of design can greatly improve the demand-revealing potential of voluntary contribution CV studies, by reducing free-riding. Stated WTP thus moves closer to true WTP.

3.2   THE CHOICE EXPERIMENT METHOD

3.2.1   Introduction

The choice experiment method is one method within a wider group of approaches known as choice modelling or conjoint analysis. The choice experiment method adopts a particular view on how the demand for the environment goods is best pictured, known as the *characteristics theory of value*. This states that the value of, say, a forest is best explained in terms of the characteristics or *attributes* of that forest. Different forests are actually different 'bundles' of attributes, and what people value is these bundles. Moreover, the value of any particular forest then can be broken down into the value of its different attributes. Using observations of people's choices between different bundles of attributes, the researcher can infer (i) which attributes significantly influence their choices; (ii) assuming price or cost is included as one attribute, what they are willing to pay for an increase in any other attribute; (iii) what they would be willing to pay for a policy that changed several attributes simultaneously.

The choice experiment (CE) method is becoming increasingly popular as a tool for estimating and indeed investigating environmental values. Policy makers have seen a powerful set of advantages for the CE method, in terms of being able to measure benefits for a wide range of policy changes. Bateman et al. (2002) give several examples of the use of the method in the policy process. For a very useful guide to the CE method, see Louviere et al. (2000) and Henscher et al. (2005).

3.2.2   How to Carry Out a Choice Experiment

In the choice experiment method, the researcher first of all identifies the main attributes that are relevant for describing the environmental good in question. This is done using focus groups, and by finding out from policy makers and administrators which aspects of the environmental good are likely to be affected by a policy action. For forests, the attributes might include species composition, age, type of felling regime, and the provision of recreational facilities. For a river, the attributes might be in-stream ecological quality, flow rates, and condition of the river banks. For a national park management problem, the attributes could be provision of guided walks, set-aside of conservation areas, traffic management, and management of agricultural areas. If the researcher wants to use the CE to measure economic values, then a price or cost attribute must also be included. For forest recreation, this could be the travel costs of a visit to the site; for river quality, it could be local water and sewerage rates; for a national park it could be a tourist tax. The researcher needs to be sure that the selected attributes are (i) likely to be relevant in terms of the preferences of the population to be surveyed; and (ii) likely to be amenable to change by environmental managers.

Different bundles of these attributes are then assembled, using experimental design principles. Software is available for this task (such as SAS), along with design catalogues. Bundles are then arranged in pairs, and respondents asked to choose between them and some status quo alternative; this is known as a 'choice set'. Typically, each individual might answer 4–8 choice sets. For example, a study by Morrison et al. (2002) looked at the benefits of protecting wetlands in Australia. Each respondent was asked to choose most preferred alternatives amongst pairs of different wetland management options, such as the choice set shown in Table 3.3 (this has been adapted a little from the original):

The questionnaire would be designed, piloted and implemented just like a contingent valuation study, as described in the previous section. Similar requirements exist for the description of the hypothetical market.

Table 3.3   Choice experiment for valuing Australian wetlands

Which option would you prefer that the government went ahead with? A, B or C?

	Management option A	Management option B	Management option C (status quo: no change on present)
Wetland area conserved	1000 ha	800 ha	700 ha
Bird species conserved (number)	40	30	25
Farm jobs protected	15	16	20
Cost to households in terms of increase in local taxes over next 5 years	$30/hsld	$15/hsld	$0/hsld

Source: Adapted from Morrison et al. (2002).

Once questionnaires have been completed, the researcher now has data on which options individuals chose (option A, option B, the status quo), and she can relate these choices to the levels that the attributes took in these options. In this way, choices can be statistically related to attribute levels, including price. The usual statistical model employed is known as the conditional logit model. This means we can write down the probability that an individual *i* chose a particular option like this:

$$P_i(choose\ A) = \frac{\exp(\mu V_{iA})}{\sum_j \exp(\mu V_{iJ})} \qquad (3.9)$$

where *V* is the 'observable' part of utility within a random utility model (as described briefly in section 3.1.1), μ is a 'scale parameter' which relates to the variance of the error component of the random utility model, and *J* are all the other options the individual could have chosen instead of *A*. A typical assumption is that *V* is a linear function of the choice attributes *X*:

$$V = \alpha + \beta_1 X_1 + \beta_2 X_2 + \ldots \beta_n X_n + \beta_c C \qquad (3.10)$$

We see that there are $(n + 1)$ attributes and that for each one, the model estimates a value β which shows the effect on utility of a change in the level of each attribute. Thus β_1 shows the effect of utility of a change in attribute X_1. The model also estimates a parameter β_c, which is the effect of a change (increase or decrease) in the price or cost of the option on the likelihood of choosing that option. Software packages such as *STATA* and *LIMDEP* can be used for this kind of estimation. Now knowing the β values is interesting, since now we know how much utility goes up or down when the attributes increase or decrease (albeit moderated by the scale parameter). These values tell us whether people prefer an increase or a decrease in each attribute; we can also see by looking at the *prob* or t-statistic values from the computer output whether these attributes are statistically significant or not. Box 3.4 shows the output from *LIMDEP* for one choice experiment, and how this is interpreted.

The final steps in a choice experiment are to calculate willingness-to-pay estimate, based on the β values already discussed. The β values show the effect on *utility* of changes in the attributes, but for cost–benefit analysis we need money-metric measures of willingness to pay. For a marginal change in an attribute, this WTP value is typically given by, for attribute X_1:

$$IP_{x_1} = \frac{\beta_{x_1}}{\beta_c} \qquad (3.11)$$

BOX 3.4   LIMDEP OUTPUT FROM A CHOICE EXPERIMENT

In this choice experiment of water quality improvements on a rather polluted river, there were four attributes being used: price (PRICE, below),
how much of the river was improved (RQ), the change in the number
of days when the river smelled bad (ODOUR), and the improvement in
ecological conditions (EC). We also collected data on a large number
of socio-economic characteristics of respondents, such as age and
highest level of education achieved: each socio-economic variable was
interacted with the constant (K) to let it enter the model. Data on how far
people lived from the river was also obtained (DIST).

```
+----------------------------------------------------------------------+
| Discrete choice (multinomial logit) model                            |
| Maximum Likelihood Estimates                                         |
| Model estimated: Mar 06, 2008 at 07:07:04PM.                        |
| Dependent variable                            Choice                |
| Weighting variable                              None                |
| Number of observations                          3059                |
| Iterations completed                               6                |
| Log likelihood function                    -2594.238                |
| Number of parameters                              16                |
| Info. Criterion: AIC =                       1.70660                |
| Finite Sample: AIC =                         1.70665                |
| Info. Criterion: BIC =                       1.73811                |
| Info. Criterion:HQIC =                       1.71792                |
| R2=1-LogL/LogL* Log-L fncn R-sqrd RsqAdj                             |
| Constants only     -3184.9785        .18548  .18334                |
| Response data are given as ind. choice.                             |
| Number of obs.= 3150, skipped 91 bad obs.                          |
+----------------------------------------------------------------------+
```

Variable	Coefficient	Standard Error	b/St.Er.	P[|Z|>z]
K	−5.46435700	.46862412	−11.660	.0000
RQ	−.00094221	.00513121	−.184	.8543
ODOUR	.00663149	.00665766	.996	.3192
EC	.60183041	.05772591	10.426	.0000
PRICE	−.09344849	.00473387	−19.740	.0000
RECREA	.74035732	.08679536	8.530	.0000
KNOW	.65302930	.14312736	4.563	.0000
DIST	1.17894781	.15266722	7.722	.0000
DIST2	−.09097955	.01760967	−5.166	.0000
AGE	−.13958176	.02960205	−4.715	.0000
EDU	.20341194	.07409420	2.745	.0060

If we look at the results, we can see that neither the RQ or ODOUR attributes had a significant effect on choices, since the prob value for these attributes is bigger than 0.05. But people did care about the improvements in ecological quality and the price of the option. We can also see that how far away people live from the river matters to their choices, but that this relationship is actually quadratic. Finally, we can see that age and education seem to affect people's choices, as did how many recreational visits they made to the river (RECREA) and how well informed they are about water quality in the river (KNOW).

This value for any attribute (other than price!) is called the *implicit price*, or *IP* in equation (3.11). For instance, in Table 3.3 one of the attributes was the number of bird species conserved. Dividing the β value for this attribute by the β value for the tax increase would show the (average) willingness to pay of people in the sample to increase the number of bird species conserved by one. However, often we wish to value multiple changes in attributes. For instance, a new policy on wetlands conservation could alter the area conserved (labelled A below), the numbers of bird species conserved (labelled B) and the provision of recreational trails, labelled R. The price for this would be an increase in local taxes, which are attribute c. The average willingness to pay for this suite of changes in attributes can be calculated using equations (3.12), (3.13) and (3.14) below:

$$CS = -\frac{1}{\beta_c}(V_1 - V_0) \qquad (3.12)$$

$$V_0 = \alpha + \beta_A A_0 + \beta_B B_0 + \beta_R R_0 \qquad (3.13)$$

$$V_1 = \alpha + \beta_A A_1 + \beta_B B_1 + \beta_R R_1 \qquad (3.14)$$

This might look a bit complicated but is actually very easy, and calculated with an Excel spreadsheet once you have got your estimates from the choice model in equation (3.9). Equation (3.12) says that the Compensating Surplus (*CS*) from an improvement in wetlands conservation – that is, the average person's willingness to pay for this package of changes – is given by the difference between their (measurable) utility before the improvement goes ahead, given by V_0, and their measurable utility after the change, V_1, converted into monetary units using the coefficient on the tax or price attribute, β_c. In turn, utility in the 'before' and 'after' cases is given by the levels of the attributes in each case (so A_0, B_0 and R_0 in the 'before' case, A_1, B_1 and R_1 in the 'after' case), multiplied by the attribute coefficients, and including the term α. This was the constant in equation (3.10), and is usually referred to as the *Alternative Specific*

Constant. It shows the utility people get simply from either staying in the status quo or leaving it (depending on whether it is positive or negative), independently of the values taken by the attributes. By fixing the status quo utility (as in equation 3.13), and varying the levels of the attributes, compensating surplus figures can be produced for as many combinations of attributes and levels as the design makes possible: that is, for a wide range of policy outcomes. We illustrate this in Box 3.5 for a soil conservation programme in Spain. It is this flexibility of choice experiments which makes the method so popular.

BOX 3.5   A SPANISH SOIL EROSION STUDY

Colombo et al. (2005) use the choice experiment to estimate the benefits of reducing soil erosion in Andalusia, Spain. The study considers the reduction of the off-site impacts of soil erosion in two watersheds, the Genil and the Guadajoz. Due to soil and climatic conditions and the nature of current farming practices, soil erosion levels in these catchments are well in excess of national average levels, and are known to result in widespread environmental problems. Among the most important of these are increased desertification, the siltation of water bodies, and reductions in biodiversity. To reduce these impacts it is necessary to provide subsidies to farmers to encourage them to adopt soil conservation measures in their land management. These measures include sowing a grass cover in olive orchards and reforesting degraded hill and mountain slopes. The choice experiment used the following attributes:

- desertification in semi-arid areas;
- quality of surface and groundwater;
- effects on flora and fauna;
- agricultural jobs safeguarded;
- area of countryside covered by the measures;
- cost to households in the area of the policy.

Attribute levels were defined in a number of ways. For example, for desertification, respondents were told what the current situation was, then it was explained that policy could change this to a small improvement or a moderate improvement. In both cases, respondents received an explanation of what this would actually mean 'on the ground', using words and pictures. The results showed that respondents had a positive willingness to pay for improvements in all of the policy attributes. Implicit prices were calculated and gave the following results (all values are in euros per household per year):

- For a change in desertification from continuing degradation (the status quo) to a 'small improvement': 17.78 (95% confidence interval: 12.02–25.21).

- For a change in desertification from continuing degradation (the status quo) to a 'moderate improvement': 26.51 (95% confidence interval: 20.05–35.76).
- For a change in water quality from 'low' to 'medium' quality: 18.39 (95% confidence interval 12.67–25.96).
- For a change in water quality from 'low' to 'high' quality: 26.27 (95% confidence interval 20.10–34.67).

Finally, the Compensating Surplus for a number of policy scenarios was measured, using the formulae given in this chapter. For instance, for a policy which produced a big improvement in desertification, high levels of water quality, good (versus declining) species numbers, 150 farm jobs and which covered 500 hectares, the mean WTP was €40.98, with a 95 per cent confidence interval from €34 to €47 per household per year.

3.2.3   Problems with the Choice Experiment Method

Accommodating variation in preferences across people
The standard approach to choice experiments which was described above has one important feature that needs a comment. This is that, if we use a Conditional Logit model to represent the choices that people make – as in equation (3.9) and the example in Box 3.4 – then we are effectively assuming that each person in the sample places the same value on each attribute used in the design. In other words, we effectively assume that the marginal utility for Joe if attribute X_1 is increased – β_1 – is the same as the marginal utility for Jane, and that the marginal utility for Joe of an increase in attribute X_2, β_2, is the same as that for Jane. This is because we only estimate one value for β_1 and one value for β_2 in equation (3.10). Now, as the example in Box 3.4 shows, we can allow that the value of a change away from the status quo can depend for an individual on their age or education, since we interact the constant with these terms. But this is a very limited way of handling *preference heterogeneity*, whereby we actually expect that people will care to different degrees about the same attribute.[1] We could also split the sample according to what we imagine might be a reasonable grouping according to preferences (for example between old and young, between rich and poor, rural and urban), but again this requires us to know how best to do this.

Choice experiment practitioners have thus looked for alternative ways of modelling preference heterogeneity. This literature is rather technical, so cannot be expanded on in detail here. But two approaches can be mentioned. One is known as the *random parameters logit model*. This represents variations in preferences by including two terms for each attribute in equation (3.7): a mean effect, which represents average preferences, and a standard deviation term, which represents how much preferences in the sample vary around this mean. The second approach is called the *latent class model*. This takes a rather different approach: respondents are divided by an algorithm into latent (that is, unobservable) classes according to how they have responded to the choice questions, or according to their observable characteristics. A set of preference parameters, that is the β values in equation (3.7) are then estimated for each class. For an example of how both approaches can be used, the reader can consult Birol et al. (2006).

Issues with experimental design
Designing a choice experiment is almost an art form! Decisions must be taken on a great number of issues:

i.   what attributes to include;
ii.   how to describe them to respondents;
iii. what levels are to be used for each attribute;
iv.   what price or cost term will be used;
v.   how the attributes and levels are combined in choice sets;
vi.   how many choice sets respondents can deal with;
vii. how many choice options are included in each choice set.

It is likely that the estimate we get for the willingness to pay of respondents for a change in any particular attribute, or how precise a measure we obtain of this, depends on what decisions are made above. The overall success of the choice experiment in terms of what it tells us about people's choices and values also depends on these steps. Many papers exist which investigate these issues, mostly in non-environmental applications of the method (for example in a transport, marketing and health context): lessons learnt can be found in the main choice experiment textbooks, such as Louviere et al. (2000) and Henscher et al. (2005). Suffice it to say that the best way of designing choice experiments is still an open question, partly because of the several ways in which 'best' can be interpreted. Moreover, choice experiments also depend, just as contingent valuation studies do, on the description of the hypothetical market and on sample selection.

Hypothetical market bias
Another parallel between choice experiments and contingent valuation is the possibility that responses in a hypothetical market setting will tell us little about how respondents would behave in a real market. This issue has been addressed in a couple of ways within the CE literature, comparing

real with hypothetical responses in terms of (i) how well hypothetical choices predict real choices, and (ii) how close predicted WTP from hypothetical choices is to real WTP in an actual market. Of course, the same problem faces the CE practitioner as faces the CVM analyst, that for most environmental goods we cannot observe 'real' market prices – that is the problem the method tries to address! However, some findings exist which compare real with hypothetical choices where this problem can be got around: these suggest that the extent of hypothetical market bias might not be too extreme in CE (Blamey et al., 2001; Carlsson and Martinsson, 2001). More recent evidence is presented by List et al. (2006), who compared actual with hypothetical scenarios for two choice experiments. They argue that two tests are of interest – whether a hypothetical choice experiment overstates the extent to which people would actually pay for, say, wetland conservation and the differences, if any, in the marginal values of the attributes used in the choice experiment between 'real' and 'hypothetical' choices. They found no statistically-significant differences between hypothetical and real WTP, or between the marginal values of attributes, when a 'cheap talk' script was used as part of the choice experiment – that is, when respondents were explicitly told about the problem of hypothetical market bias, and asked to consider their responses carefully.[2] Finally, choice experiment responses are also known to be liable to a 'status quo bias' – a tendency for respondents to choose the 'do nothing, zero additional cost' option for reasons other than utility differences between this and the other choice options. This can be diagnosed by testing whether the parameter estimate for the Alternative Specific Constant for the status quo choice is statistically significant or not.

Is the value of the whole equal to the sum of the parts?

One of the advantages of choice experiments is that they enable the researcher to do two things: (i) estimate the value for each of the attributes of an environmental good; and (ii) estimate the value for a policy which changes many of these attributes simultaneously. Now imagine that we wish to use CE to value the protection of a forest threatened with felling. A CE study is undertaken which estimates values for five forest attributes, which includes 'loss of the forest' as a level for each. Can these values be added up to show the economic loss from the forest being felled? Or imagine a landscape valuation study which identified five landscape attributes, and is then used to predict the economic value of changes in landscape quality. Can the value of a future landscape be inferred from the sum of the characteristic values? This is an issue revolving around whether people think about environmental goods as bundles of attributes (this is what the theory assumes), and around whether the CE designer has done a good job in selecting the attributes. But in cases where we are more concerned with the 'value of the whole' rather than the 'value of the parts', it might be wise to undertake a contingent valuation study rather than a choice experiment.

3.3   BENEFITS TRANSFER

Benefits Transfer (BT) is the practice of extrapolating existing information on the non-market value of goods or services (Brouwer, 2000). Typically, the practice involves predicting compensating or equivalent surplus values for an environmental quality or access change at one site, based on data collected using either stated or revealed preference methods at another, similar site. Adjustments are often made for differences between the environmental characteristics of the site to which values are to be transferred (known as the 'policy site') and those of the site at which the original data was collected, known as the 'study site' (Downing and Ozuna, 1996). Differences in socio-economic characteristics of the affected population between the study and policy sites can also be allowed for (Morrison et al., 2002).

The aim of BT techniques is to provide decision makers with a monetary valuation of environmental goods and service in a cost-effective and timely manner, since original valuation studies are both expensive and time-consuming. Demands for environmental valuation estimates are rising in the policy community in both Europe and the US. In Europe, this is partly being driven by the introduction of the Water Framework Directive, which requires benefit–cost analysis of water quality improvements throughout the European Union, and by the greater emphasis on the application of cost–benefit principles to environmental policy design in the EU (European Commission, 2002). In the UK, widespread use of benefits transfer has already occurred within policy making and regulatory bodies, for instance in the setting of water quality targets for private water companies.

Papers investigating the use and accuracy of BT have become increasingly frequent since an initial set of papers on the subject appeared in a special issue of *Water Resources Research* in 1992. Recent applications of BT include Rozan (2004) on improved air quality in France and Germany, Muthke and Holm-Müller (2004) on national and international transfers of water quality improvement benefits, Jiang et al. (2005) on coastal land management, and Colombo and Hanley (2008) on agricultural landscapes.

Many early BT studies used the contingent valuation method to undertake benefit transfers. However, Morrison et al. (2002) pointed out that, within the field of stated preference methods, Choice Experiments are arguably better suited to BT because it is possible to allow for differences in environmental improvements across sites as well as differences in socio-economics characteristics across impacted populations. Moreover, compensating surplus estimates for a wide range of potential policy scenarios can be calculated from the choice models estimated. Benefits transfer has also been investigated using the revealed preference methods of recreation demand modelling which we outline in the next chapter.

The accuracy of BT can be tested in a number of ways. Two main approaches have been followed in the literature. The first is the transfer of mean WTP values from the policy site to the study site. Transferring unadjusted mean values has been criticized since it does not take into account any possible differences between either the populations or the goods at the policy and study site. Because of that, an alternative adjusted mean value approach has developed, which adjusts mean WTP of the study site to account for differences in the environmental characteristics of the policy site and/or for differences in the socio-economic characteristics of the affected population between the two sites. In the case of unadjusted mean value transfer, the null hypothesis of benefits transferability is:

$$WTP_s = WTP_p \qquad (3.15)$$

where WTP_s and WTP_p are the mean WTP at the study and policy sites measured from two different original studies. In the case of the adjusted value transfer, the WTP_s is adjusted using data on socio-economic and environmental characteristics of the policy site, before the comparison takes place. Such adjustments are, to a varying degree, somewhat ad hoc.

The second approach to BT is benefit function transfer, where the entire demand function (or choice equation, in a CE setting) estimated at the study site is transferred to the policy site. Values at the policy site are predicted using independent variables (such as household income) collected from secondary data at the policy site and parameter values estimated from the study site. In the benefit function transfer the regression parameters of the study site and the environmental and population characteristics of the policy site are used to test:

$$\text{predicted } WTP \ (\beta^s, X^p) \ = \ WTP^p \qquad (3.16)$$

where predicted WTP (β^s, X^p) is the willingness to pay at the policy site estimated using the parameters of the benefit function of the study site (β^s) and the X values (site attributes, socio-economics characteristics and so on) of the policy site and WTP^p as defined above. An alternative test is the comparison of function parameters between the study and policy site:

$$\beta_s = \beta_p \qquad\qquad (3.17)$$

When several study site data sets are available, a further approach is to use a meta regression analysis. Here the analyst is concerned with understanding the influence of methodological and study-specific factors on WTP. Data can be pooled across study sites to produce a BT model for predicting policy site values. Here, the test is:

$$\beta_{s+p} = \beta_s \text{ and } \beta_{s+p} = \beta_p \qquad\qquad (3.18)$$

where β_s, β_p and β_{s+p} are the parameters of the study, policy and pooled regression models respectively. Which of these benefits transfer testing approaches is preferable is still open to debate.

Many of the case studies in part II of the book will involve instances where benefits transfer is an important part of applying CBA to the environment. Economists are still refining how benefits transfer is best carried out, and how to test its accuracy.

3.4 STATED PREFERENCE APPROACHES TO VALUING RISKS TO HUMAN HEALTH

There are many examples of government intervention which have implications for human health and indeed for lives saved. For instance, regulating dangerous chemicals, improving air pollution through tougher standards, and investing in public transport can all result in savings in lives and in illness – or, in the jargon, in reductions in mortality and morbidity. Arrow et al. (1997) note that many of the benefits which appear in CBAs of government intervention are for reductions in mortality and morbidity, but that there is evidence of inconsistency in how such benefits are valued. How then *can* such effects be expressed in monetary terms?

We begin by noting that both stated and revealed preference methods can be used. In Chapter 5 we explain briefly how the hedonic pricing method can be used to value changes in risks to human lives (see also Aldy and Viscusi, 2007). For now, though, the focus is on the use of stated preference methods such as contingent valuation.

Valuing Changes in Mortality

The idea of placing a monetary value on human life may seem morally repugnant. However, governments and individuals routinely make choices which impact on the risks of people dying. For example, public health agencies with limited budgets must decide how to prioritize spending in terms of which drugs to supply and which types of health campaigns to promote. Individuals make choices on a day-to-day basis which impact on their risks of dying sooner, such as choices over lifestyle (exercise, smoking and diet). The 'value of life', and how it varies across people, is implicit in these choices. Moreover, making public policy choices about whether to invest in a bypass around a town, or in safer trains, will involve benefits and costs which it would be useful to compare, given that many demands exist on scarce resources. Thinking about stated preference approaches, it would be unhelpful to ask people their maximum WTP or minimum WTA to avoid dying: this would be just their maximum income in the first case, and perhaps infinite in the second case. However, it can make sense to ask people what they are WTP to reduce the risk of them *or someone else* dying.

Two important concepts which we could try and measure in this context are the *value of a statistical life (VOSL)* and the *value of a life year (VOLY)*. The first is used to value changes in the expected number of lives saved by a decision, the latter to value the expected number of years of life saved. These are not the same, and depending on *who* stands to benefit from a policy, may give very different figures for benefits (Hammitt, 2007). For example, an air pollution regulation which predominantly benefits old people in terms of number of deaths avoided or number of life years saved might be viewed differently from an improvement in train safety which impacted more on risks to commuters. The VOSL is an abstract measure which takes expressions about WTP for a given risk reduction, and transforms this in the benefit of saving a statistical life (not the life of the respondent, or anyone in particular). If a CVM survey asked: 'If by paying higher train fares to generate money to invest in new signalling facilities, the risk of being killed in a train crash fell by one in one million, what is the most you would be willing to pay for this change?' and arrived at an average WTP of £3, then the VOSL would be £3/(1/1 000 000) or £3 million. Another way of thinking about this is that if one million people benefit from a project which reduces risk by one in a million, then the expected number of lives saved equals one. People are WTP £3 million in total (=£3 per person mean WTP multiplied by a population of 1 million) to have this one-death reduction in the population. As Hammitt (2007) explains, it is the slope of an indifference curve drawn between wealth and survival probability (= 1 – risk), evaluated at a particular risk level. Given a convex indifference curve, this means that an individual's maximum WTP for a risk reduction will depend on the current level of risk that they face, and the level of wealth from which they evaluate a change in this risk. VOSL estimates may also depend on whether the individual is asked to value a private or a public good: for instance, a car safety improvement might only benefit the driver and her family, whereas a reduction in air pollution could benefit many people in a city. Public good improvements may increase WTP if people are altruistic and care about the risks that others face too. Empirically, VOSL estimates seem to be sensitive to age of beneficiaries, as discussed below. For a discussion of whether society *ought* to differentiate according to which lives are saved in terms of the VOSL used, see Baker et al. (2008).

The Value of a Life Year measure of mortality takes a slightly different tack. The benefits of reducing the risk of death (of avoiding one statistical death) surely depend, the argument goes, on life expectancy. Given that we cannot postpone death indefinitely, this means that safety improvements targeted at children or young adults will result in more 'life-years saved' than improvements targeted at old people. The VOLY measure then estimates what people are WTP to save one life-year for a 'random' person of a particular age group. Overall, benefits will then depend on (i) how many life-years are saved (ii) what people in a particular age group are WTP to reduce risks per life-year saved.

Krupnick (2007) reviews the stated preference evidence on valuing mortality risks. He starts by noting the idea of the 'senior discount'. This is that the VOSL may be lower for older people than for younger people. This, in turn, relates to the net effects of how many life-years are saved by a policy, and who is being asked to state their maximum WTP for the risk reduction. Krupnick examines the results of 35 studies which relate WTP for mortality risk reductions to age group. Risk reductions used in the scenarios vary from five in one hundred to three in one million. These studies yield an average VOSL in 2006 US $ of 2.7 million, with a range of $150 000 –$12 million. Roughly half of them find a 'senior discount effect'.

Valuing Changes in Morbidity

Contingent valuation can also be used to value changes in non-fatal illness and ill-health episodes. For example, a policy to reduce air pollution could result in fewer instances of people with sore eyes, or fewer admissions to hospital for temporary breathing problems. A policy to reduce sewage pollution in coastal waters could result in fewer people experiencing stomach upsets after swimming. A typical approach is to value changes in 'health end-points' (avoiding one episode of sickness after swimming, for instance). These estimates can then be aggregated according to expected reductions in number of episodes and people so benefiting. Choice experiments could also be used in such cases, with the attributes being defined in terms of health end-points.

3.5 CONCLUSIONS

Contingent valuation and choice experiments are two stated preference methods that have been extensively used to estimate the value of non-market goods in the context of environmental policy and management. One advantage of the methods is their flexibility, in that a very wide range of environmental changes can be valued using these approaches. Another advantage is that they can be used to measure both use and non-use values. Contingent valuation focuses on the value of the 'whole', whilst choice experiments focus on the value of the 'parts'; which method is most appropriate to use thus depends on the policy context: what question are we trying to answer?

Both methods also suffer from a number of problems. For contingent valuation, much attention has been given to the extent to which it suffers from hypothetical market bias. For choice experiments, researchers have been more interested in how to model the choice data, and how to construct the choice sets. Environmental economists are now working with colleagues in other disciplines, such as behavioural psychology and statistics, to address some of these concerns. However, it seems likely that both methods will continue to be used as part of the policy process. For example, in the UK, the government has made extensive use of both methods in addressing policy and management questions over water quality improvements. In part II of this book, we will see such examples in a case study context.

NOTES

1. We could also interact socio-economic variables such as Age with any of the attributes.
2. The actual script read as follows 'In most questions of this kind, . . . folks act differently in a hypothetical situation where they don't have to pay real money. . . . (If I was choosing) I would ask myself: If this was a real situation, do I really want to spend my money in this way?'

REFERENCES

Aadland, D. and A.J. Caplan (2003), 'Willingness to pay for curbside recycling with detection and mitigation of hypothetical bias', *American Journal of Agricultural Economics*, **85**(2), 492–502.

Aldy, J. and W.K. Viscusi (2007), 'Age differences in the value of a statistical life: revealed preference evidence', *Review of Environmental Economics and Policy*, **1**(2), 241–60.

Arrow, K., R. Solow, P. Portney, E. Leamer, R. Radner and H. Schuman (1993),

'Report of the NOAA Panel on Contingent Valuation', *Federal Register*, **58**, 4601–14.

Arrow, K., M. Cropper, G. Eads, R. Hahn, L. Lave, R. Noll, P. Portney, M. Russell, R. Schmalensee, V.K. Smith and R. Stavins (1997), 'Is there a role for benefit–cost analysis in environmental, health and safety regulation?', *Environment and Development Economics*, **2**, 196–201.

Baker R., S. Chilton, M. Jones-Lee and H. Metcalf (2008), 'Valuing lives equally: defensible premise or unwarranted compromise?', *Journal of Risk and Uncertainty*, **36**, 125–38.

Banzhaf, H.S., D. Burtraw, D. Evans and A. Krupnick (2006), 'Valuation of natural resource improvements in the Adirondacks', *Land Economics*, **82**(3), 445–64.

Bateman, I. and K.J. Willis (1999), 'Introduction and overview', in I. Bateman and K.J. Willis (eds), *Valuing Environmental Preferences: Theory and Practice of the Contingent Valuation Method*, Oxford: Oxford University Press.

Bateman, I., R. Carson, B. Day, M. Hanemann, N. Hanley and others (2002), *Economic Valuation with Stated Preference Techniques*, Cheltenham, UK and Northampton, MA, USA: Edward Elgar.

Birol, E., K. Karousakis and P. Koundouri (2006), 'Using choice experiment to account for preference heterogeneity in wetland attributes: the case of Cheimaditita wetland in Greece', *Ecological Economics*, **60**, 145–56.

Blamey, R., J. Bennett, J. Louviere and M. Morrison (2001), 'Green product choice', in J. Bennett and R. Blamey (eds), *The Choice Modelling Approach to Environmental Valuation*, Cheltenham, UK and Northampton, MA, USA: Edward Elgar.

Brookshire D., B. Ives and W. Schulze (1976), 'The valuation of aesthetic preferences', *Journal of Environmental Economics and Management*, **3**(4), 325–46.

Brouwer, R. (2000), 'Environmental value transfer: state of the art and future prospects', *Ecological Economics*, **32**(1), 137–52.

Bulte, E., S. Gerking, J. List and A. de Zeeuw (2005), 'The effect of varying the causes of environmental problems on stated WTP values', *Journal of Environmental Economics and Management*, **49**, 330–42.

Burton, A., K. Carson, S. Chilton and W. Hutchinson (2007), 'Resolving questions about bias in real and hypothetical referenda', *Environmental and Resource Economics*, **38**(4), 513–25.

Carlsson, F. and P. Martinsson (2001), 'Do hypothetical and actual willingness to pay differ in choice experiments?', *Journal of Environmental Economics and Management*, **41**, 179–92.

Carson, R., N. Flores, K. Martin and J. Wright (1996), 'Contingent valuation and revealed preference methodologies: comparing the estimates for quasi-public goods', *Land Economics*, **72**(1), 80–99.

Champ, P. and R. Bishop (2006), 'Is willingness to pay for a public goods sensitive to elicitation format?', *Land Economics*, **82**(2), 162–73.

Colombo, S. and N. Hanley (2008), 'How can we reduce the errors from benefits transfer? An investigation using the Choice Experiment method', *Land Economics*, **84**(1), 128–47.

Colombo, S., N. Hanley and J. Calatrava-Requena (2005), 'Designing policy for reducing the off-farm effects of soil erosion using Choice Experiments', *Journal of Agricultural Economics*, **56**(1), 81–96.

Colombo, S., J. Calatrava-Requeno and N. Hanley (2006), 'Testing benefits transfer for choice experiments with preference heterogeneity', *American Journal of Agricultural Economics*, **89**(1), 136–51.

Cummings, R.G. and L.O. Taylor (1999), 'Unbiased value estimates for environmental goods: a cheap talk design for the contingent valuation method', *American Economic Review*, **89**, 649–65.

Downing, M. and T. Ozuna (1996), 'Testing the reliability of the benefit function transfer approach', *Journal of Environmental Economics and Management*, **30**, 316–22.

European Commission (2002), *Economics and the Environment: Guidance on Implementation of the Water Framework Directive*, Brussels: European Commission.

Fox, J.A., J.F. Shogren, D.J. Hayes and J.B. Kliebenstein (1998), 'CVM-X: calibrating contingent values with experimental auction markets', *American Journal of Agricultural Economics*, **80**, 455–65.

Fror, O. (2008), 'Bounded rationality in contingent valuation: empirical evidence using cognitive psychology', *Ecological Economics*, **68**(1–2), 570–81.

Haab, T. and K. McConnell (2002), *Valuing Environmental and Natural Resources*, Cheltenham, UK and Northampton, MA, USA: Edward Elgar.

Hammack, J. and G. Brown (1974), *Waterfowl and Wetlands: Towards Bioeconomic Analysis*, Baltimore: Johns Hopkins Press.

Hammitt, J.K. (2007), 'Valuing changes in mortality risk: lives saved versus life years saved', *Review of Environmental Economics and Policy*, **1**(2), 228–40.

Hanemann, M. (1984), 'Welfare evaluations in contingent valuation experiments with discrete responses', *American Journal of Agricultural Economics*, **66**, 332–41.

Hanemann, M. and B. Kanninen (1999), 'The statistical analysis of discrete response CV data', in I. Bateman and K. Willis (eds), *Valuing Environmental Preferences: Theory and Practice of the Contingent Valuation Method in the US, EU, and Developing Countries*, Oxford: Oxford University Press, pp. 302–441.

Hanley, N., B. Kristom and J. Shogren (2009), 'Coherent arbitrariness: on value uncertainty for environmental goods', *Land Economics*, **85**(1), 41–50.

Harrison, G. and E. Rustrom (2005), 'Experimental evidence on the existence of hypothetical bias in value elicitation methods', in C.R. Plott and V.L. Smith (eds), *Handbook of Experimental Economics*, Amsterdam: North Holland.

Heberlein, T.A., M.A. Wilson, R.C. Bishop and N.C. Schaeffer (2005), 'Rethinking the scope test as a criterion for validity in contingent valuation', *Journal of Environmental Economics and Management*, **50**(1), 1–22.

Hensher, D., J. Rose and W. Greene (2005), *Applied Choice Analysis: a Primer*, Cambridge: Cambridge University Press.

Jacobs, in association with NFO World Group, H. Gibson, N. Hanley, R. Wright, N. Coulthard and D. Oglethorpe (2004), 'An economic assessment of the costs and benefits of Natura 2000 sites in Scotland', Environment Group Research Report to Scottish Executive Environment and Rural Affairs Department, www.scotland.gov.uk/publications/2004/06/19426/38107.

Jiang, Y., S.K. Swallow and M.P. McGonagle (2005), 'Context-sensitive benefit transfer using stated choice models: specification and convergent validity for policy analysis', *Environmental and Resource Economics*, **31**, 477–99.

Krupnick, A. (2007), 'Mortality risk valuation and age: stated preference evidence', *Review of Environmental Economics and Policy*, **1**(2), 261–82.

List, J. and C. Gallet (2001), 'What experimental protocol influence disparities between actual and hypothetical stated values?' *Environmental and Resource Economics*, **20**(3), 241–54.

List, J., P. Sinha and M. Taylor (2006), 'Using choice experiments to value non-market goods and services: evidence from field experiments', *Advances in Economic Analysis and Policy*, **6**(2), 1–37.

Louviere, J., D. Hensher and J. Swait (2000), *Stated Choice Methods: Analysis and Applications*, Cambridge: Cambridge University Press.

MacMillan, D., N. Hanley and N. Lienhoop (2006), 'Contingent valuation: environmental polling or preference engine?', *Ecological Economics*, **60**(1), 299–307.

McLeod, D. and O. Bergland (1999), 'Willingness-to-pay estimates using the Double-Bounded Dichotomous-Choice Contingent Valuation format: a test for validity and precision in a Bayesian framework', *Land Economics*, **75**(1), 115–25.

Mitchell, R. and R. Carson (1989), *Using Surveys to Value Public Goods: the Contingent Valuation Method*, Washington, DC: Resources for the Future.

Morrison, M., J. Bennett, R. Blamey and R. Louviere (2002), 'Choice modelling and tests of benefits transfer', *American Journal of Agricultural Economics*, **84**(1), 161–70.

Munro, A. and N. Hanley (1999), 'Information, uncertainty and contingent valuation', in I.J. Bateman and K.G. Willis (eds), *Contingent Valuation of Environmental Preferences: Assessing Theory and Practice in the USA, Europe, and Developing Countries*, Oxford: Oxford University Press.

Murphy, J.T., G. Allen, T. Stevens and D. Weatherhead (2005), 'A meta-analysis of hypothetical bias in stated preference valuation', *Environmental and Resource Economics*, **30**, 313–25.

Muthke, T. and K. Holm-Müller (2004), 'National and international benefit transfer testing with a rigorous test procedure', *Environmental and Resource Economics*, **29**, 323–36.

Poe, G., J. Clark, D. Rondeau and W. Schulze (2002), 'Provision point mechanisms and field validity tests of contingent valuation', *Environmental and Resource Economics*, **23**, 105–31.

Randall, A., B. Ives and C. Eastman (1974), 'Bidding games for the valuation of aesthetic environmental improvements', *Journal of Environmental Economics and Management*, **1**, 132–49.

Rozan, A. (2004), 'Benefit transfer: a comparison of WTP for air quality between France and Germany', *Environmental and Resource Economics*, **29**, 295–306.

Schlapfer, F., A. Roschewitz and N. Hanley (2004), 'Validation of stated preferences for public goods: a comparison of contingent valuation survey response and voting behaviour', *Ecological Economics*, **51**, 1–16.

Whitehead, J. and T. Cherry (2007), 'Willingness to pay for a green energy program', *Resource and Energy Economics*, **29**, 247–61.

4. Revealed preference methods (1): the travel cost model

4.1 INTRODUCTION

The Travel Cost Method (TCM) can claim to be the oldest of the non-market valuation techniques. It originated in a letter from the economist Harold Hotelling to the director of the US Park Service in 1947, but was formally introduced to the literature by other economists, namely Wood and Trice (1958) and Clawson and Knetsch (1966). The TCM is predominantly used in outdoor recreation modelling, with fishing, hunting, boating and forest visits among the most popular applications.[1] Recreation activity can then be linked to environmental quality measures. The method is widely used by government agencies in the USA, and has been used extensively in the UK, both by the Forestry Commission for valuing forest recreation (Willis, 2003), and by the Environment Agency for valuing recreational fishing. In this chapter, we will look at how to apply the method, and at the problems that arise in doing so.

Travel costs are a measure of the price of recreation, and typically are thought of as being made up of both monetary expenses such as fuel costs (sometimes referred to as 'out-of-pocket' costs), along with the implicit time costs of travelling to a site. Two basic types of travel cost model exist. The first, which dates back to Clawson and Knetsch, is concerned with developing a relationship between how many visits individuals make to a particular site, and the travel costs they face in making such visits. The focus is on predicting how the number of trips to the forest, say, would change as the 'price' of visiting – the travel cost – varies. This version of the TCM is explained in section 4.2 under the heading 'Traditional travel cost models'. Such approaches are now often referred to as *visitation models*, since they focus on the 'how many trips?' question of recreation demand. An alternative approach, which has much in common with the choice experiment technique explained in the previous chapter, focuses instead on how recreationalists choose where to visit from amongst a group of options, or substitute sites. Site choice ('where to go') is represented as depending on the characteristics of recreation sites. These models make use of the random utility idea introduced in Chapter 3, and are explained under the heading 'The random utility site choice model' in section 4.3. Travel cost models of both types are examples of revealed preference methods, since they are based on people's actual behaviour in markets (in this case, markets for travel and for labour) which are somehow related to the environmental good of interest, such as a forest. As such, they are an alternative to stated preference approaches, but in section 4.4 we explain briefly how travel cost models can be combined with stated preference approaches. Finally, section 4.5 reviews some problem areas and limitations in using travel cost methods to measure environmental values.

4.2   TRADITIONAL TRAVEL COST MODELS

The TCM seeks to place a value on non-market environmental goods by using consumption behaviour in related markets. Specifically, the costs of accessing an environmental resource – such as forest recreation, or walking in a national park – are used as a proxy for a market price which does not exist. These consumption costs will include travel costs, entry fees, on-site expenditures, and the giving up of working time. The method assumes *weak complementarity* between the environmental asset and consumption expenditure (Freeman, 2003). This implies that when consumption expenditure is zero (people take no trips to the forest), the marginal utility of the public good is also zero. So if travelling to a forest becomes so expensive that no one goes any more, the marginal social cost of a decrease in the quality of that forest is also zero. The TCM therefore cannot estimate non-use values. Another implicit assumption made in most travel cost studies is that the representative visitor's utility function is 'separable' in the recreation activity being modelled. This means that, if the activity of interest is fishing, then the utility function is such that demand for fishing trips can be estimated independently of demand, say, for cinema trips (alternative.leisure activities) or for heating oil (alternative marketed non-leisure goods).

Simplifying, we can say that travel costs (*TC*) to a particular recreation site *j* depend on several variables:

$$TC_{ij} = f(DC_{ij}, WC_{ij}, F_j) \; i = 1 \ldots n, j = 1 \ldots m$$

Here, *DC* are distance costs for each individual *i*, dependent on how far he/she has to travel to visit the site and the cost per mile of travelling. *WC* are time costs: these depend on how long it takes to get to the site and the value of an individual's time, which on the whole is thought to depend on their labour market situation. *F* is the entry price, if any, which is charged for entrance to site j. Travel costs are then included in a regression equation such as equation (4.1), which predicts how many visits (V) will be undertaken by any individual i to site j.

$$V_{ij} = f(TC_{ij}) \qquad (4.1)$$

Visits are our measure of demand for the environmental good. Also included in the model could be individual socio-economic characteristics such as income, education and age level, as well as variables giving information on the type of trip. Examples of this case are dummy variables on whether a visit to the site is the sole purpose of that individual's journey from home, and whether the individual is on holiday or a local day-tripper. Data is obtained for estimating equation (4.1) through an on-site survey of recreationalists, or a mail/Internet survey of either recreationalists (for example registered fishermen, members of a national climbing association) or of the general public.

Historically, this approach was initially developed using a 'zonal' TCM. The zonal approach entails dividing the area surrounding a recreational site to be valued into 'zones of origin' from where site visitors are observed to travel. These zones may be concentric rings around the site, but are more likely to be local government administrative districts (such as counties or states). For example, we could categorize visitors to a marine national park in Malaysia according to which district of Malaysia they come from (for domestic tourists), or which country they come from (for overseas tourists). The zonal TCM typically also includes population levels for each zone of origin in order to predict trips per zone, and such population data are more readily available at the governmental level than for concentric rings around a site, although GIS (Geographic Information Systems) can be used to generate population data at any spatial scale. The regression equation for the zonal model is:

$$V_{zj} = V(TC_{zj}, Pop_z, S_z) \quad z = 1 \ldots Z \qquad (4.2)$$

where V are visits from zone z to site j, Pop is the population of zone z and S_z are socio-economic variables such as income averaged for each zone. The dependent variable is often expressed as (V_{zj}/Pop_z), or trips per capita. However, since equation (4.2) describes the average behaviour of groups of individuals (all those living within a particular zone), it does not fit at all well with the individual welfare measures developed in Chapter 2. For this reason, zonal travel cost models are now rarely used. In what follows, we focus just on models based on individual behaviour.

Once a travel cost model such as equation (4.1) has been estimated using

---

**BOX 4.1   AN EXAMPLE OF A SIMPLE TRAVEL COST
MODEL: NAVRUD AND MUNGATANA ON LAKE
NAKURU NATIONAL PARK IN KENYA**

Navrud and Mungatana (1994) estimated a zonal travel cost model for
visitors to Lake Nakuru in Kenya. They separated residents and overseas visitors into two groups, with a different travel cost model for each,
and used travel time plus financial costs of trips to define V, visits per
capita from different zones of origin. Travel time was valued at one third
of the wage rate. This gave, for overseas visitors, for example, the following travel cost model:

$$\ln V = -7.74 - 0.000658\ TC + 0.00004\ I - 0.00562\ A$$

where TC is travel costs, I is annual income, A is age. This gave a consumers' surplus of 75–79 US\$/day, and an implied annual aggregate
value of \$10 million for recreation trips to the lake. Another useful finding
was that demand by overseas visitors was price-inelastic, but for residents was price-elastic. This has big implications for the charging policy
adopted by the park authorities in future.

---

multiple regression, a demand relationship can be derived by simulating
what would happen to visits per annum as the 'fee' is increased. In this
way, a demand curve is traced out for each site. The fee is driven up until
visits either go to zero or to less than one (depending on the functional
form of the travel cost model). This is shown in Figure 4.1, where total
existing visits from all zones are v_T. This shows that visits will be made to
the site so long as the cost of the visit stays below p^*: p^* is referred to as
the 'choke price'. For example, at a fee of p_1, visits are predicted to fall
from v_T to v_1, and a further increase in the fee to p_2 reduces visits to v_2.
The reader should note that these fee/visit combinations (with the exception of the zero additional fee/v_T combination) are all predictions, based
on the observed relationship between travel costs and visits. The key
assumption behind the demand curve is that as the travel costs, defined
in equation (4.1), increase, the number of visits falls. Measuring the area
under this demand curve gives an estimate of consumers' surplus. This
value is most usually reported as consumers' surplus per visit. If the log of
visits is regressed on (un-logged) travel costs, then this has the convenient
property that the reciprocal of the travel cost coefficient gives consumers'
surplus per visit.

One important statistical feature of the travel cost model shown in equation (4.1) is that the dependent variable (V) can only take integer values:

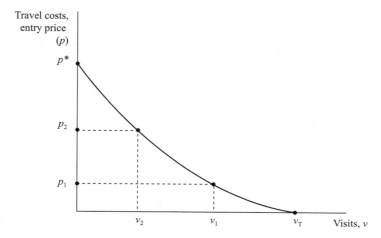

Figure 4.1   Relationship behind the travel cost method

1 visit per year, 2 visits per year and so on. This kind of data is known as count data, and using standard Ordinary Least Squares to estimate equation (4.1) is incorrect. Instead, a Poisson or negative binomial regression model should be used. The Poisson model has the property that the conditional mean (the expected value) of the dependent variable is equal to the variance; if this is not true for your data, a negative binomial model is used instead. Programmes such as LIMDEP and STATA will estimate both kinds of model. For more information on how to choose between Poisson and negative binomial regressions, see Haab and McConnell (2002). Another feature of travel cost data used in count models is that, if respondents have been interviewed on-site, no one can take less than one visit (otherwise we could not have interviewed them!). Samples obtained off-site cannot, or course, contain negative values for V. Finally, sampling on-site will tend to over-sample people who visit more often. This again can cause statistical problems: Haab and McConnell again offer some solutions to all of these problems.

Traditional travel cost models are often estimated for particular sites, such as Hanley's (1989) study of Achray Forest in Central Scotland. However, the approach can also be applied to groups of sites, for example, the study by Sellar et al. (1985) of lakes in East Texas, and the Smith and Desvouges (1986) study of water-based recreation sites in the USA. In either case, researchers may try to include the costs of visiting substitute sites. This is because, to take the example of a single site study, visits from an individual will also depend on the availability of substitute sites. Smith and Kaoru (1990) have shown that excluding the costs of visiting substitute sites biases the estimate of consumers' surplus per visit upwards on average. Indeed, it was dissatisfaction with the ability of the traditional travel cost model to deal with substitution in visits across sites, and with the role of site characteristics in determining choices, which led to the development of the random utility site choice model, which we now explain.

BOX 4.2   A MODEL OF RECREATION VISITS TO LOCH LOMOND, SCOTLAND

Loch Lomond is one of the most visited outdoor recreation sites in Scotland. Part of Scotland's first National Park since 2003, Loch Lomond draws people for fishing, boating, walking and picnicking. Recreational conflicts are present on the loch, for example between fishermen and jet ski users. In order to develop a management plan for the loch which helps resolve these conflicts, it is useful to develop an understanding of why people visit the loch, and the values they get from visiting.

Dalrymple and Hanley (2003) report on a simple travel cost analysis of informal recreation at the loch. Visitors were questioned at a number of locations around the loch, and data collected for a travel cost model, including how many trips people made to the loch in the last 12 months and the distance they travelled to get there. This was converted into a monetary travel cost using a figure of £0.10 per mile. Since the focus of the study was on recreational conflicts, visitors were also asked about their perceptions of how noisy (NOISE) or crowded (CROWD) the recreational sites they visited were, and their perceptions of environmental damages due to erosion (ENV DAMAGE). Results are shown below:

Variable name	Coefficient	T-statistic	Prob value
TRAVCOST	−.0487	−11.508	.0000
Length of visit	.1616	5.874	.0000
NOISE	−.1001	−1.656	.0978
ENV-DAMAGE	.0002807	.270	.7875
CROWD	−.000512	−.504	.6142
INCOME	.00783	.463	.6433
AGE	.14004	5.698	.0000
GENDER	.1770	3.621	.0003
CAR	.4725	3.913	.0001
HOME	−.000347	−.456	.6487
PASSIVE	.6697268924	6.501	.0000
Observations		443	
Log likelihood		−1154.427	
Restricted log likelihood		−1547.612	
Consumers' surplus/trip under current site conditions		£20.53	

Additional variables in the regression are people's income, their age, gender, whether they came by car, whether they travelled from home that day, and whether they were engaged in 'active' (such as mountain biking) or 'passive' (such as picnicking with family) recreation. Based on the coefficient on the travel cost variable, and given that this is a negative binomial model, the mean consumers' surplus accruing to visitors under current conditions is £20.53/trip (= 1/0.0487). As can be seen, visitors' rating of noise nuisance helped determine the number of trips they made in the previous 12 months, as did their age, gender and whether they were involved in 'active' or 'passive' recreation. Travel costs have a strongly negative influence on the frequency of visit.

4.3   THE RANDOM UTILITY SITE CHOICE MODEL

Most modern applications of the travel cost model have a rather different focus from that presented in the previous section. We can summarize the main purpose of traditional travel cost approaches as being to answer the question: 'What is the non-market value of recreation at a particular site under current site conditions?'. In other words, what would be the loss in welfare if a forest was to be felled, or a national park closed to public access? The Random Utility Site Choice model (RUSC), however, addresses a different question: 'What determines recreationalists' choice of site to visit from amongst a group of choice alternatives?'. The framework under which the method is implemented is also rather different, making use of the random utility model of Chapter 3.

We can summarize the RUSC approach as follows:

- We are interested in modelling *where* people choose to visit for outdoor recreation.
- People face a choice problem which requires them to select a destination site (for example for a mountain biking trip) from amongst a group of close substitutes (for example all mountain biking sites in Wales).
- The most useful way of explaining these choices is by considering the attributes or characteristics of each site.
- One of these attributes is the cost of visiting the site.

The method thus proceeds as follows. Imagine we are indeed trying to model the non-market recreation value of forests as destinations for mountain bikers in Wales. Using focus groups or some other means, the researcher compiles a list of characteristics for mountain biking sites which are thought likely to determine their attractiveness for bikers, and a list of sites which can be considered to comprise the 'choice set'. A sample of mountain bikers is put together, either through on-site surveys, Internet surveys or via club mailing lists. Each respondent in the sample is asked how many mountain bike trips they took in the previous 12 months, and how many visits they made to each of the sites in the choice set. Respondents may be asked to score each site in terms of the site attributes/ characteristics selected for the study, or else data could be obtained on characteristic values from other sources. Respondents are also asked how far they live from each site in the choice set, and how long it takes to travel to each site from their home. From this information, the researcher can work out the travel cost, or price, that each person faces in visiting each site in the choice set.

The researcher thus has, for each person in the sample, a count of how many times they have visited each site in the choice set (some sites will have zero visits for some people). They will also have a range of measures of site quality for each site, in terms of the scores for site characteristics, and a travel cost figure for each individual for each site. For simplicity, let us assume that there are only three sites in the choice set, and only two attributes besides travel cost. These are 'Difficulty' – how challenging the routes are, as rated individually by each person in the survey on a scale from 1 to 5; and 'Bike wash', whether the site has a bike wash facility or not. For the first two people in the sample, this data might look as in Table 4.1.

Joe lives further away from all sites than Gerry. He makes most visits to site 2, possibly because he likes difficult, challenging routes, even though it is further away than site 3. Gerry also takes the most trips to site 2, even though site 3 is also closer to him, since again he rates the routes as more

Table 4.1   Example data for a random utility site choice model

	Visits in last 12 months	Travel cost from home, £ per trip	Difficulty (1 = easy to 5 = hard)	Bike wash (1 = yes, 0 = no)
Joe				
Visits to site 1	2	40	3	1
Visits to site 2	5	25	4	0
Visits to site 3	4	20	1	0
Gerry				
Visits to site 1	0	18	3	1
Visits to site 2	3	10	4	0
Visits to site 3	2	7	2	0

challenging. Whether having a bike wash at a site is a significant determinant of site choice is hard to tell from just these two observations.

Imagine now that we had 400 observations from mountain bikers in and around Wales, and had organized the data as in Table 4.1. The random utility model states that utility can be decomposed into an observable, deterministic component V, which just as with the choice experiment method we assume to depend on site characteristics; and a random, unobservable element ε, which we must make assumptions about in order to undertake statistical analysis. Assume that recreationalists, in choosing which site to visit, select from the set of all possible sites in the choice set (C) according to the relative utility they obtain from each site, which in turn depends on the characteristics of that site. The deterministic part of utility is usually assumed to be a linear function of site characteristics:

$$V_{ij} = \beta_1 + \beta_2 X_2 + \beta_3 X_3 + \ldots + \beta_n X_n + \lambda(Y_i - p_{ij}) \qquad (4.3)$$

where X_j represent our mountain biking site attributes, Y is an individual's income and p_{ij} is travel costs of visiting site j for individual i. The probability that site j will be chosen over all other sites in C depends, for individual i, on:

$$\pi_i(j) = \text{Prob } [V_{ij} + \varepsilon_{ij} \geq V_{ik} + \varepsilon_{ik}; \forall k \in C]$$

If we assume that the error term is IID with an extreme value distribution, then this gives us the Conditional Logit model which we used in the choice experiment section:

$$\pi_i(j) = \frac{\exp(V_{ij})}{\Sigma_{k \in C}\exp(V_{ik})} \qquad (4.4)$$

Welfare measures such as compensating surplus (CS) for a site quality change can now be obtained, using the standard 'Hanemann' formula, where V_0 is (deterministic) utility in the initial situation, and V_1 is utility in some different situation: for example, when one measure of environmental quality has been improved at one site within the choice set. This equation can also be used to calculate the change in utility for a 'representative individual' if one of the sites in the choice set is shut down.

$$CS = -\frac{1}{\lambda}[\ln(\Sigma_{j \in C}\exp(V_{j0})) - \ln(\Sigma_{j \in C}\exp(V_{j1}))] \qquad (4.5)$$

Notice that this welfare expression asks us to sum up utility changes over all the different sites in the choice set, and also controls for the changing probabilities that we will visit any given site. Utility changes are converted into money-metric using the inverse of the marginal utility of income, which is here the parameter on the travel cost variable. This is basically the same expression for welfare changes we saw for choice experiment data.

Once data is in the format shown for Joe and Gerry in Table 4.1 for everyone in the sample, equation (4.4) can be estimated using a programme like *STATA* or *LIMDEP*. This will give us the β parameters from equation (4.3). The sign of these parameters will tell us the way in which site attributes influence site choice (for example whether an increase in perceived difficulty makes it more or less likely that people will choose a site), whilst the t-statistics on each parameter will tell us which attributes exert statistically significant influences on site choice (see Box 4.3 for an example). The parameter estimates can then be put into a spreadsheet for use in calculating the value of equation (4.5) for (i) changes in site quality and (ii) closure or opening of sites. For a range of applications of the method, see Hanley et al. (2003).

BOX 4.3   A RANDOM UTILITY SITE CHOICE MODEL OF WHITEWATER KAYAKING IN IRELAND

Stephen Hynes and co-authors (2007) describe the estimation of a site choice travel cost model for whitewater kayaking sites in Ireland. Data was collected from on-site and Internet samples of active kayakers in Ireland. Focus groups were used to arrive at a list of six site attributes and 11 rivers. Respondents rated each site they had visited in terms of these attributes, and told us how many trips they had made in the last 12 months to each site. This gave:

Mean visits to each whitewater site in the previous 12 months

Kayaking site	Mean visits per annum	Std. Deviation
The Liffey	16.59	42.32
Clifden Play Hole	2.63	5.54
Curragower Wave	3.34	6.46
The Boyne	5.65	14.73
The Roughty	0.82	2.00
The Clare Glens	1.00	2.14
The Annamoe	3.42	5.30
The Barrow	1.01	6.12
The Dargle	1.28	3.78
The Inny	1.07	1.82
The Boluisce	1.01	2.52
All Sites	37.83	47.16

The site attributes used were: quality of parking at the site, degree of expected crowding at the site, quality of the kayaking experience as measured by the star rating system used in The Irish Whitewater Guidebook, water quality, scenic quality, reliability of water information, travel distance to site, and travel time to site.

A conditional logit model was estimated and gave the following results for the site attributes (for fuller results, see Hynes et al., 2007):

	Parameter estimate	t-statistic
Quality of parking	−0.145	−2.04
Crowding	0.153	2.19
Star quality	0.351	2.82
Water quality	0.142	1.39
Scenic quality	0.285	2.99
Information	−0.08	−0.92
Travel cost	−0.07	−17.98

This shows that expected crowding, star quality, quality of parking and scenic quality all significantly affect which sites people choose to visit (t-statistic greater than 1.96 in absolute value), but the availability of information on water levels and water quality (a measure of perceived pollution) do not seem to matter on average (indeed the most popular site was the most polluted!). Travel costs are negatively related to visits, as is expected. Based on these figures, the authors calculate some illustrative welfare impacts for changes in site quality and availability. For example, closure of the Liffey site would reduce average consumers' surplus by €8.50 per kayaking trip (this closes off access to the most popular site), whilst a reduction of 50 per cent in the star rating of the Roughty (a very infrequently visited site) due to the creation of a new hydroelectricity scheme would only result in an average loss per trip of €0.56.

4.4   COMBINING STATED AND REVEALED PREFERENCE METHODS

An increasing use of combined stated preference (SP) and revealed preference (RP) models is now apparent in environmental economics. But what are the reasons for combining these two sources of data? Three reasons can be suggested:

- As a check on 'convergent validity': SP and RP data from the same sample can be compared to see whether they reveal the same underlying model of preferences.

- As a means of more efficient sampling. In most (but not all) combined approaches, each individual in the sample provides more than one observation.
- To combine the desirable features of the two approaches. We might want to ground SP estimates in actual behaviour, but extend the range of environmental variables of interest beyond that currently observed.

Two main approaches to using SP and RP data exist. These are Random Utility Models combining SP/RP data, and the Contingent Behaviour approach relating to either price or environmental quality changes. In the former approach, Adamowicz et al. (2003), for example, have used RP and SP data based on recreational choices, where choice alternatives are described in terms of site attributes. Data from the two sources is combined to produce an overall 'pooled' model. This approach is probably most suitable when the analyst wishes to focus on the value of different attributes of recreational goods and where changes in environmental quality produce site substitution effects across a group of sites (for example a group of fishing rivers when water quality alters).

Contingent Behaviour (CB) models are somewhat different. Here, the word 'contingent' implies that what is being measured is intended behaviour in some contingent market, rather than actual behaviour. For example, a respondent in a travel cost survey of beach recreation could be asked how their planned visits to the beach would change if water quality improved by a specific amount. Observations from contingent behaviour can be combined with observations of actual behaviour from the same individuals, using either pooled or panel data models. In Englin and Cameron (1996), anglers were asked how many fishing trips they had taken during the past year, and the starting point for these trips (the key pair of observations for a conventional travel cost model). They were then asked how their total trips would change if travel costs increased by 25 per cent, 50 per cent and 100 per cent. Four price-quantity estimates were thus made for each respondent, one real and three hypothetical. The main conclusions were that combining real and hypothetical behaviour improved the precision of consumer surplus estimates.

The principal feature of the Englin and Cameron paper is that the contingent behaviour relates to changes in trip frequency as *prices* change. A natural extension is then to look at contingent behaviour when *environmental quality* changes. Such an approach was followed by Hanley et al. (2003), who look at the benefits of improved water quality standards on Scottish beaches. Finally on this topic, it is of interest to note the paper by Grijalva et al. (2002), who test whether contingent (stated) behaviour is a good predictor of actual behaviour when environmental quality changes, or in their case, when access conditions to a rock climbing site change. The authors concluded that 'climbers do not appear to overstate (intended) changes in trip behaviour when presented with hypothetical questions about site access'. If this holds for changes in site quality also, then the implication is that combined revealed preference-contingent behaviour models do not suffer from the hypothetical market bias often associated with contingent valuation.

4.5 PROBLEMS WITH THE TRAVEL COST METHOD

Valuing Time

One methodological issue that affects both count models and site choice models is how to place a monetary value on leisure time. Travel to recreation sites is undertaken during leisure time, and time is scarce. This implies there is an opportunity cost of travel time which should be included into the calculation of travel costs. But at what rate? Most people will not be giving up an hour of work to drive to a forest for a picnic – so using the wage rate as the value of time is unlikely to be correct. Many analysts in the 1970s and 1980s made use of standard fractions of the wage rate as the price of leisure time (for example Smith and Desvouges, 1986), and this approach is still used in some studies (for instance, Train, 1998). Other authors have tried to estimate the value of time for individuals in the sample from data they provide as part of the questionnaire. In most situations, however, it will be better to include travel time in hours as a separate variable alongside travel cost, since the data requirements to estimate the value of leisure time at the individual-specific level are so great (Feather and Shaw, 1999). To complicate matters further, Chevas et al. (1989) argued that there was also a 'commodity value' to time spent in recreation, whereby the expenditure of time both on-site and travelling produced utility (if people enjoy the experience of driving to a site): the net cost of time was thus the difference between the commodity value and the scarcity value.

Combining Decisions over How Often to Go with Where to Go

Visitation models can be used to predict changes in participation: the total number of trips that people will make to a site as, for example, travel costs increase. Site choice models are used to predict how people will distribute a given total number of trips per season across sites. So an obvious question that arises is whether the two can be combined. The visitation rate portion of the combined model would then estimate changes in total trips, whilst the site choice part would predict where these will be taken. The answer is 'yes', but there is some debate over how best to do this (Parsons et al., 1999). Crucial features are that a feedback loop is needed between the change in site characteristics, the associated change in (the deterministic component of) utility, and the number of total trips taken: a second issue is that both components should be estimated simultaneously.

What is the Choice Set?

The random utility site choice model assumes that the researcher can accurately define the choice set that recreationalists face. This means knowing all the sites that they consider in choosing where to make a trip. But this raises the awkward issue of what to count as similar goods. If a rock climber is making a decision as to where to go climbing this weekend, will she just consider all those outdoor climbing areas within a day's journey, or will she also consider going to indoor climbing walls? Or perhaps she might instead decide to go windsurfing or mountain-biking instead? One approach to this issue is the idea of nested logit models, where a decision tree is constructed. For instance, the first level of the tree ('nest') might be a decision to go climbing indoors or outdoors. Perhaps this mainly depends on the weather! Then the second stage is where to go outdoors, given that one has decided on an outdoor trip, or which climbing wall to visit if one has decided on an inside experience. Given sufficient data, this decision process can be represented statistically. But more commonly the researcher falls back on the assumption of strong separability in the utility function: that is, we can consider the demand for outdoor climbing independently of the demand for other recreation activities.

How to Measure Site Characteristics

This issue revolves around a choice between two approaches: subjective and objective. Imagine we are constructing a travel cost model of recreational fishing, and we wish to measure the quality of different rivers in terms of their attributes. One approach is to use scientific, objective measures of site quality: for example, measurements of ecological quality, or species counts, or turbidity, taken from Environment Agency records. An alternative approach is to ask fishermen to rate rivers in terms of their attributes: for example, they could be asked to rate rivers as being 'very clean', 'quite clean' or 'rather polluted'. Adamowicz et al. (2003) comment on this issue. One can argue that, from a policy viewpoint, using objectively-measured attributes is more useful, since policy decisions are taken with respect to such objectively-measured values (for example maximum nitrate levels in a river). But from the point of view of explaining behaviour, one can argue that using subjective measures of site quality makes more sense, since it is the impressions of recreationalists about site qualities that determines where they decide to visit.

Preference Heterogeneity

The 'standard' version of the site choice travel cost model, estimated using conditional logit, makes an important assumption. This is that preferences can be adequately represented through their mean effect on choices. For example, in equation (4.3) and in Box 4.3, only one β value (marginal utility) is shown for each attribute. Yet people may have considerably varying preferences for site attributes, both in terms of how much they like them, and whether they like them or dislike them. This is known as *preference heterogeneity*. Hynes et al. (2008) review the different ways in which this can be accommodated within site choice travel cost models. Briefly, we can identify three main approaches:

- The researcher can decide that there are different types of people in her sample, segment the sample into these types, and then estimate separate site choice models for each type. For example, we could ask mountain bikers to rate their skill levels as 'beginner', 'moderate' and 'advanced', and then estimate separate conditional logit models for each.
- The researcher can let the data determine whether there are underlying 'latent' classes of people within the sample, and then estimate separate models for each. This approach is known as latent class modelling.
- The researcher can estimate a model where we allow for both a mean effect of an attribute on site choices, and the standard deviation of this effect. This approach is known as the random parameters model (Train, 1998).

Crowding

Congestion, or crowding, is a tricky issue to deal with in recreational demand modelling. Perceived congestion can be one factor which helps explain where people choose to go (as in Box 4.3). But actual decisions on site choice will then translate into different crowding pressures at alternative sites: crowding thus both determines and is determined by site choices. This raises some awkward issues.

BOX 4.4   FOREST RECREATION IN DENMARK: LINKING PARTICIPATION WITH SITE CHOICE

Zandersen et al. (2007) use travel cost modelling to explore two data sets of people visiting forests in the Northern Zealand region of Denmark in 1977 and 1997. Here we refer just to their 1997 data. A combined participation–site choice model was estimated. Trip data was recorded for people making day visits to 52 state-owned forests in this region, based on drop-off surveys at 321 parking locations. A response rate of around 50 per cent was achieved. This data set was supplemented with a national household survey of 2916 people in order to predict overall visit frequency or participation. This data set included information on income, age, how many trips people had made to forests in the last 12months, and distance to the nearest forest. Finally, data on forest characteristics was obtained from official records for each of the 52 sites. The character-istics included species diversity, age diversity, fraction of the forest taken up by rivers or lakes, and size of the forest.

Travel distance from people's homes to each forest were calculated, and converted into travel costs using a figure of €0.18/km (1997 prices). A linked site choice–participation model was then estimated. In the first stage of the model, people decide how many total forest trips to make in a year, depending on their income, age and other personal character-istics. In the second stage, they allocate this total across the 52 forests, depending on forest characteristics and travel costs from their home. The two stages are linked by an 'inclusive value', which captures the deterministic element of utility from the site choice model and which is then included in the count data model. This combined model is then used to predict the value of consumers' surplus per year for each of the 52 forests: this shows how much individuals are willing to pay for access to forests for recreation, and how this varies across forests.

BOX 4.5   AN ARCTIC TRAVEL COST MODEL

Berman and Kofinas (2004) present an interesting application of the multi-site travel cost model to hunting by native people in the Old Crow community in the Yukon. The model used allows the authors to explain both participation in hunting (how many trips) and where hunting trips are taken. The context of the study is the impact of climate change on well-being in a community that depends partly on caribou hunting.

Hunting caribou demands time and monetary resources on the part of hunters. The decision over how many trips to take for any hunter depends on expected hunting quality. Site choice across 10 hunting zones depended on time and resources needed to access each site, as rated by local hunters, and a range of other variables (for example whether the site was up- or down-river from Old Crow, and the likelihood of encountering caribou based on historic data). Statistical results for the site choice part of the model showed that remoteness and whether the site was down-river or not affected the probability that hunters would visit, as did the probability of caribou encounters. For the participation part of the model, which focuses on the decision of how many trips to make, household needs, whether the hunter had a full-time job or not, and the quality of hunting experience, all significantly affected the number of trips made in a season. Finally, the authors show what happens to the predicted number of trips and to consumers' surplus per trip (expressed, interestingly, in terms of 'lost family or leisure time') under a range of future climate change scenarios.

Aside from being one of the few travel cost applications to native subsistence hunting, this paper is also of interest in that a qualitative, focus group approach to understanding participation and success in hunting accompanied the travel cost analysis. The authors claim that combining these two approaches ('grounded' and 'rational' theory) led to a richer set of insights into the problem, for example by providing information on the set of hunting sites that were relevant to the community, and on the cost to hunters of accessing these sites.

4.6 CONCLUSIONS

Both the visitation rate and site choice versions of the travel cost model have proved very useful to economists interested in the economic benefits of outdoor recreation, and in the value of environmental quality changes which can be tied to outdoor recreation. However, it is worthwhile re-stating the two main limitations of the travel cost approach. First, it cannot be used to measure non-use values. Second, even for use values, it is restricted in terms of what problems it can be applied to.

NOTE

1. A fuller history of development of the method can be found in Hanley, Shaw and Wright (2003).

REFERENCES

Adamowicz, W., J. Swait, P. Boxall, J. Louviere and M. Williams (2003), 'Perceptions versus objective measures of environmental quality in combined revealed and stated preference models of environmental valuation', in N. Hanley, D. Shaw and R. Wright (eds), *The New Economics of Outdoor Recreation*, Cheltenham, UK and Northampton, MA, USA: Edward Elgar.
Berman, M. and G. Kofinas (2004), 'Hunting for models: grounded and rational

choice approaches to analyzing climate effects on subsistence hunting in an Arctic community', *Ecological Economics*, **49**, 31–46.

Chevas, J.P., J. Stoll and C. Sellar (1989), 'On the commodity value of travel time in recreational activities', *Applied Economics*, **21**, 711–22.

Clawson, M. and J. Knetsch (1966), *Economics of Outdoor Recreation*', Baltimore: Johns Hopkins University Press.

Dalrymple, G. and N. Hanley (2005), 'Using economic valuation to guide the management of outdoor recreational resources', *Tourism*, **53**(2), 105–14.

Englin, J. and T. Cameron (1996), 'Augmenting travel cost models with contingent behaviour data', *Environmental and Resource Economics*, **7**(2), 133–47.

Feather, P. and D. Shaw (1999), 'Estimating the cost of leisure time for recreation demand models', *Journal of Environmental Economics and Management*, **38**, 49–65.

Freeman, A.M. (2003), *The Measurement of Environmental and Resource Values*, Washington, DC: RFF Press.

Grijalva, T., R. Berrens, A. Bohara and W.D. Shaw (2002), 'Testing the validity of contingent behavior trip responses', *American Journal of Agricultural Economics*, **84**(2) May, 401–14.

Haab, T. and K. McConnell (2002), *Valuing Environmental and Natural Resources*, Cheltenham, UK and Northampton, MA, USA: Edward Elgar.

Hanley, N. (1989), 'Valuing rural recreation benefits: an empirical comparison of two approaches', *Journal of Agricultural Economics*, **40**(3), 361–74.

Hanley, N., D. Bell and B. Alvarez-Farizo (2003), 'Valuing the benefits of coastal water quality improvements using contingent and real behaviour', *Environmental and Resource Economics*, **24**(3), 273–85.

Hanley, N., W. Douglass Shaw and Robert E. Wright (eds) (2003), *The New Economics of Outdoor Recreation*, Cheltenham, UK and Northampton, MA, USA: Edward Elgar.

Hynes, S., N. Hanley and E. Garvey (2007), 'Up the proverbial creek without a paddle: accounting for variable participant skill levels in recreational demand modeling', *Environmental and Resource Economics*, **36**(4), 413–26.

Hynes, S., N. Hanley and R. Scarpa (2008), 'Effects on welfare measures of alternative means of accounting for preference heterogeneity in recreational demand models', *American Journal of Agricultural Economics*, forthcoming.

Navrud, S. and E.D. Mungatana (1994), 'Environmental valuation in developing countries. The recreational value of wildlife viewing', *Ecological Economics*, **11**, 135–51.

Parsons, G.J., P.M. Jakus and T. Tomasi (1999), 'A comparison of welfare estimates from four models for linking seasonal recreational trips to multinomial logit models of site choice', *Journal of Environmental Economics and Management*, **38**(2), 143–57.

Sellar, C., J. Stoll and J.P. Chevas (1985), 'Validation of empirical measures of welfare change', *Land Economics*, **61**(2), 156–75.

Smith, V.K. and W. Desvouges (1986), *Measuring Water Quality Benefits*, Boston: Kluwer Nijhoff.

Smith, V.K. and Y. Kaoru (1990), 'Signals or noise? Explaining the variation in recreation benefit estimates', *American Journal of Agricultural Economics*, **72**, 419–33.

Train, K. (1998), 'Recreation demand models with taste differences over people', *Land Economics*, **74**(2), 230–39.

Willis, K.J. (2003), *The Social and Economic Benefits of Forestry*, Edinburgh: The Forestry Commission.

Wood, S. and A. Trice (1958), 'Measurement of recreation benefits', *Land Economics*, **34**, 195–207.

Zandersen, M., Mette Termansen and Frank S. Jensen (2007), 'Evaluating approaches to predict recreation values of New Forest sites', *Journal of Forest Economics*, **13**(2–3), 103–28.

5. Revealed preference methods (2): hedonic pricing[1]

5.1 INTRODUCTION

Hedonic Pricing (HP) derives from the characteristics theory of value, developed by Lancaster (1966) and Rosen (1974), with the first HP studies being published in the late 1960s and early 1970s (see, for example, Anderson and Crocker, 1971). Since hedonic pricing focuses on the characteristics of goods, the method has something in common with the choice experiment method and the site choice travel cost model described in the previous two chapters.

The HP method identifies environmental service flows as characteristics which partly 'describe' a marketed good, typically housing. For example, the value of a particular house may depend on the number of bedrooms, whether it has a garden, and how close it is to a railway station, but also on the noise level in the neighbourhood and local air quality levels. HP seeks to find the relationships between the levels of environmental quality (such as noise levels or air pollution levels) and the prices of the marketed goods (houses), and then makes use of this relationship to measure the value of changes in environmental quality. HP has been used to value noise levels around airports and roads, earthquake risks, urban air quality changes and landscape values of woodland. The method is also applied to labour markets: the characteristics of a job (for example its degree of risk) are seen as determining the wage that is offered, and the analyst can infer something about the value of risk from observing the relationship between wages and risk in the labour market. HP can also be used to investigate the 'green premium' attached to products such as organic food.

In this chapter, the theoretical basis for HP is first considered, followed by an explanation of the method by which HP analyses are carried out. The chapter concludes by noting some of the problems associated with the technique. We can state the main problem with the technique at the outset: hedonic pricing as an environmental valuation method will always be limited to a small range of environmental goods and services – those that can be directly related to the price of specific marketed goods, such as environmental quality that affects housing prices and industrial pollution that affects wages.

5.2   THE CHARACTERISTICS THEORY OF VALUE

The characteristics theory of value, sometimes referred to as the Lancaster–Rosen approach, states that any given unit (for example your parents' house) within a commodity class (for example all houses in the town where they live) can be described by a vector of characteristics, **Z**. The price for which a given house (h_i) can be sold is a function of the characteristics of that house, $\mathbf{Z}_i$, that is:

$$p(h_i) = f(\mathbf{Z}_i) \tag{5.1}$$

Finding out the exact statistical relationship between a marginal change in any characteristic and the price of housing (that is differentiating the unit price with respect to the quantity of any characteristic) gives the *implicit price* of that characteristic (this terminology can be related to that used in the choice experiment method, where the 'implicit price' for an environmental characteristic was the average WTP of people in the sample for an incremental increase in the level of attribute). Individuals maximizing utility will rearrange their purchases of the commodity until the marginal rate of substitution[2] between a composite commodity (which represents everything else they buy), x, and each characteristic, z_j, is equal to the implicit price of that characteristic. Consumers will bid an amount $B_j[z,(.)]$ for an increase in the characteristic, depending on the value to them of that characteristic (for example greater peace and quiet, nicer views). If the market reaches equilibrium, then every consumer will be in a position where the marginal bid, $\delta B_j/\delta z_j$, is equal to the implicit price (that is, marginal cost) of the characteristic (Palmquist, 1991). This means that house prices should reflect the capitalized value of environmental quality to the home owner, and that we can use observations about the cost of 'buying' more peace and quiet – the implicit price – as an indicator of people's marginal WTP for that characteristic. Rosen (1974) showed how equilibrium in a hedonic market occurs when consumers maximize their utility and perfectly competitive firms maximize profits: the hedonic price function then describes this equilibrium, where sellers are supplying the quantities of (goods with) different attributes that they wish in terms of profit maximization, and buyers are purchasing the quantities of different attributes that they wish, in terms of utility maximization (see Taylor, 2003, pp. 337–8 for more detail).

In the HP approach, house buyers are assumed to have a utility function that is *weakly separable*. This means that the marginal rate of substitution between two goods *A* and *B* appearing in an individual's utility function is independent of the quantities of all other goods they consume. The implication in HP is that, if the representative individual's utility function is weakly separable in housing, then a demand curve for environmental quality can be estimated ignoring the prices of all other goods (see Freeman, 2003). *Weak complementarity* is also assumed to an extent. That is, if the level of purchases of the private good (here, housing) is zero, then the marginal willingness to pay for, or marginal demand price of, environmental quality is also zero.[3] Thus, HP is incapable of estimating non-user values and can only 'pick-up' those elements of environmental quality change reflected by house prices. However, we do not need to assume weak complementarity if we simply wish to investigate the effects of environmental amenities on house prices, without making inferences about the welfare values of changes in these amenities.

5.3   HOW THE METHOD WORKS

The first step in any HP study is to decide which environmental quality variables are of interest, and then to ascertain whether sufficiently disaggregated, spatial data are available for these environmental variables, along with data on house prices and housing characteristics. Once this has been verified, the method involves estimating a *hedonic price function* to show the relationship between the prices of a good, and the characteristics of that good. Some analysts then proceed to a second stage where a demand curve for individual attributes is constructed, although there are considerable problems with this second stage.

Estimation of the Hedonic Price Function

In this stage, the relationship between the environmental variable of interest and a related marketed good is estimated, including as explanatory variables all other characteristics thought to be relevant in determining the price of this marketed good. The choice of these explanatory variables is potentially crucial, for reasons that will become apparent. For example, house prices (p_h) within a city might depend on: site characteristics (S_i), such as the number of rooms, the size of garden and whether a garage is provided or not; neighbourhood characteristics (N_j), such as the crime rate and quality of schools in the area; and environmental quality variables (Q_k), such as air quality and noise levels. A *hedonic price equation* can be estimated to statistically test the relationships between these variables:

BOX 5.1   THE HEDONIC PRICE MODEL AND WATER
         QUALITY

Leggett and Bockstael (2000) look at the effects of varying faecal coliform
count levels in coastal waters on property prices in Anne Arundel county,
Maryland. The irregularity of this coastline means that water quality
levels vary substantially within the housing market. The analysis was
based on house sales data of waterfront properties from 1993–1997. The
authors argue that faecal coliform counts are a good measure of water
quality to use in HP studies, since it is something people are likely to care
about and know of, especially if they engage in water-based recreation
such as swimming and boating, because of health risks. High levels of
faecal matter also make the water smell and look bad. 'Emitter effects'
are incorporated in the analysis along with faecal coliform counts. These
emitter effects include the distance of the property from a sewage works,
distance from industrial pollution emitters, and surrounding land use (to
capture non-point run-off). Leggett and Bockstael explore different functional forms for the hedonic price equation, including linear, double-log,
semi-log and inverse semi-log. With the exception of the linear form, the
measure of faecal coliform concentration is highly significant and negative as an explanatory variable. Excluding the emitter effect variables
results in a higher value for the faecal coliform count parameter, and thus
an overestimate of the implicit price of this characteristic.

Welfare changes from reducing faecal coliform pollution are also estimated. Taking one particularly polluted stretch of coastline, where coliform levels currently range from 135–240 per 100ml water, the authors
find that property values would rise by $230 000 if levels were cut to 100
coliforms per 100ml, a 2 per cent gain in value (based on the inverse
semi-log hedonic price equation).

Another HP application to water quality is that by Poor et al. (2007).
They measure the effect of varying ambient water quality levels in the St.
Mary's River watershed in Maryland, US. The pollutants considered are
Total Suspended Solids (TSS) and Dissolved Inorganic Nitrogen (DIN).
The data set includes 1377 property sales for the period 1999–2003.
They find that a 1 mg/l increase in TSS reduces house prices on average
by $1086, whilst a 1 mg/l increase in DIN reduces prices on average by
$17 642 in 2003 US$.

$$p_h = p(S_i, N_j, Q_k) + \varepsilon \qquad (5.2)$$

where ε is an error term. The estimation of equation (5.2) will show
whether significant relationships exist between the market good (housing)
and the environmental variables of interest, and what the marginal value
is of an improvement in environmental quality. For example, Bjorner et
al. (2003) found a significant relationship between noise levels generated

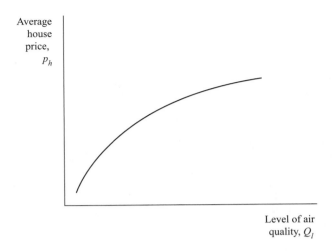

Figure 5.1   House prices and air quality

by traffic in Copenhagen and house prices in that city, with house prices declining by 0.49 per cent per decibel increase. Garrod and Willis (1992) found significant relationships between the area and type of nearby woodland cover and house prices in England.

The HP equation allows implicit prices for each characteristic to be calculated: that is, the marginal change in the house price associated with a marginal change in any characteristics – the partial derivative of equation (5.2) with respect to the characteristic of interest, or $\partial p_h/\partial Q_l$ for attribute Q_l. If (5.2) is linear, these implicit prices will be constants. However, as Rosen (1974) has observed, this is unlikely to be the case. But which non-linear form is most appropriate? In Figure 5.1, one possible partial relationship between house prices and some measure of environmental quality, Q_l (air quality), is shown. As may be seen, as the air quality level increases, the price of a house rises (higher levels of Q_l are thus desirable, *ceteris paribus*), but at a decreasing rate. The marginal cost of air quality (the implicit price) thus falls as the level of air quality rises. An alternative possibility is that house prices rise at an increasing rate as air quality rises; this means that the marginal costs of air quality are increasing.

The implicit price shows the marginal cost of *buying* an increase in the quality variable Q_l and, if the housing market is in equilibrium with respect to each attribute, the marginal benefit of a one-unit increase in the quality variable (Freeman, 2003). This implies that buyers in the housing market are fully aware of how characteristics vary across properties. Also, all individuals trading in the market are assumed to be able to adjust their buying

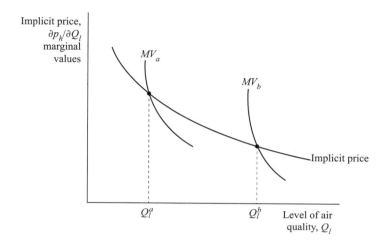

Figure 5.2   Equilibrium in the house market

behaviour, moving along the implicit price curve $\delta p_l/\delta Q_l$ until the marginal value to each buyer of an improvement in environmental quality is equal to the marginal cost of that improvement. In Figure 5.2, the function MV_a represents the marginal valuation of air quality by individual a, which declines due to diminishing marginal utility. Individual a will maximize his/her utility in this market by moving to point Q^a_l where marginal benefits and costs are equal. Similarly, individual b, with different preferences shown by MV_b, will choose the air quality level Q^b_l. Thus, the implicit price (which is observed) can be used as a measure of the (unobservable) benefits of a marginal increase in air quality, at the equilibrium.

Two 'value' measures can be obtained for any attribute from the hedonic price function. The first is the implicit price, as already discussed – the marginal change in average house prices for a one-unit change in the attribute. The second is the increase or decrease in house prices from a non-marginal change in an attribute, or in several attributes together. This is given by the difference in the predicted average house price between an 'original' level for noise, say, and at the 'new' level of noise. For example, suppose we had estimated a linear hedonic price equation on houses in Glasgow using particulates concentrations as one of the environmental attributes, and found that the coefficient on this attribute was -800, with a standard error of 100. This shows that, on average, a one-unit increase in particulates (from the current mean level of 20 microgrammes per cubic metre) would reduce house prices by £800. A 10 per cent reduction in particulates to 18 µg/m³ would *increase* house prices by (800 * 2) or £1600 on average, recalling that a linear hedonic price function has constant implicit prices for each attribute. The 95 per cent confidence interval for this value of an improvement based on the estimated implicit price is (£1600 +/− (2 * 1.96 *100)). To find the aggregate value of this change in particulates, we would compute the predicted price differ- ence between the with- and without-improvement scenarios for all houses affected by the change, and add these together. If there are costs of moving house, then these can be subtracted from the aggregate price difference to give an approximation of the change in utility for home owners.

However, if environmental improvements or declines are sufficiently great to shift the hedonic price function for a city, such changes would imply a shift in the supply of houses with given quality levels. In such cases, 'welfare' measures based on implicit prices are not reliable. Instead, we need to try and actually measure demand for housing attributes. This is discussed in the following paragraph.

Estimating a Demand Curve

Stage 2 of the HP process involves estimating a demand curve for environ- mental quality using the information gained from stage 1. In other words, we try and recover measures of preferences from observations about the implicit price, using variations in attribute levels and prices across proper- ties, along with information on the socio-economic characteristics of buyers in the market. This was originally suggested by Rosen (1974) as a logical second stage after the hedonic price function itself had been estimated. The (inverse) demand function for attribute Z_1 would in principle look like:

$$Q(Z_1) = f(p(Z_1), p(Z_2), p(Z_3), \mathbf{S}) \qquad (5.3)$$

Where $Q(Z_1)$ is the quantity of Z_1 demanded, $p(Z_1)$ is the observed implicit price for Z_1, $p(Z_2)$ and $p(Z_3)$ are the implicit prices for other characteristics, and $\mathbf{S}$ is a vector of socio-economic characteristics describing the buyers. Haab and McConnell (2002) note that estimating such a demand curve involves some awkward 'identification' problems statistically. Equilibrium in the housing market in the hedonic model occurs when marginal willing- ness to pay for each attribute is equal to the implicit price of each attribute, and the same attributes enter into both the marginal cost and benefit expressions. Palmquist (1991) observed that the problem revolved around the lack of information available to the researcher to trace out the price that a given individual would have been willing to pay for a different level of the attribute than the one she is observed to purchase. This means that, in Figure 5.2, we observe the point (Q^a_1, p_1) for individual a: this is one point on their marginal value curve, given by the interaction of MV with

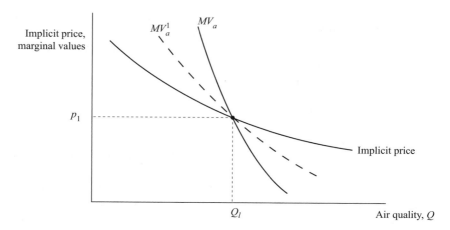

Figure 5.3a   Problems with measuring demand

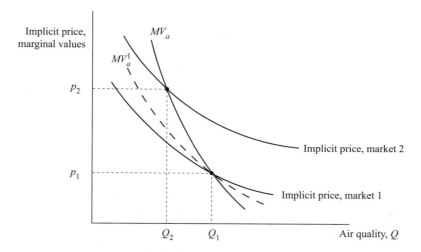

Figure 5.3b   Solving the problem via segmented markets

the implicit price function. But we do not know what their MV curve looks like above and below this point – in Figure 5.3a, whether it is the dashed line or the solid line. Freeman (2003) suggests one way of getting around this problem through the separation of a housing market into several sub-markets, and estimating implicit prices faced by an individual in each sub-market. This would mean having a second implicit price schedule in Figure 5.3b. By assuming that buyers with the same observable, socio-economic characteristics in separate sub-markets have the same preferences, we can look at the intersection of the MV curve with this second implicit price curve, $Ip2$. This defines another point of equilibrium for 'type a' buyers, and now we can identify the MV curve as being the solid line rather than the dashed line. This is the approach taken by Boyle et al. (1999). A second statistical problem relates to the fact that in choosing the quantities of each attribute to purchase when buying a house, people are also effectively determining the implicit price we observe. This gives rise to a problem of endogeneity of the regressors in the second stage demand equation, so that the researcher must try and implement an instrumental variables approach (Taylor, 2003).

Haab and McConnell (2002) conclude that 'with a few exceptions, researchers have abandoned attempts to (measure) preferences, and work instead with the hedonic price function'. Indeed, as McConnell and Walls (2005) note in their review of HP studies of the value of open space 'almost none of the studies attempt to carry out a second stage estimation of the demand function . . . most focus on the marginal price of an additional acre of open space'. This focus on implicit prices is common in the HP literature, and is due to the statistical problems of second stage demand estimation noted above. For examples of a study which does manage to estimate a second-stage demand curve, see the work by Day et al. (2007)

BOX 5.2   THE VALUE OF GREEN SPACE IN GUANGZHOU,
           CHINA

A study by Jim and Chen (2006) explores the amenity value provided by environmental and landscape attributes such as urban green spaces, water bodies and noise that influence residential housing prices in the city of Guangzhou, China. The environmental features included in the model specification were: window orientation, view of green spaces, traffic noise, nearby water bodies and presence of nearby wooded areas. Linear and semi-logarithmic functions were applied to test the relationship between the housing units' sale prices and their characteristics, including these environmental features. In both models, the number of bedrooms, exposure to traffic noise and proximity to wooded areas were statistically insignificant. The possession of southward and northward-facing windows had a positive effective on apartment selling price, as did proximity to water bodies and a 'green view', while increasing distance from the town centre lowered the selling price. Using the implicit prices obtained from the semi-log model, the authors conclude that 7.1 per cent of the selling price is due to a 'green space' view, whilst 13.2 per cent is contributed by proximity to water bodies.

BOX 5.3   ECO-LABELS AND THE CLOTHING INDUSTRY

Most of the discussion of the HP method in the main text is concerned with the relationship between environmental quality and house prices. But as hinted, the approach can be used to search for relationships between any marketed product and the characteristics of that product, which can include different indicators of environmental quality. Nimon and Beghin (1999) use HP to investigate whether consumers are willing to pay a price premium for 'environmentally-friendly' clothing. As the authors note, some manufacturers seek to differentiate their products on the basis that they are 'organic', or 'natural', based on the expectation that some consumers will be willing to pay extra for a shirt, say, which has been made from a production process (organic cotton growing) which, it is claimed, has lower environmental impacts than conventional cotton farming. Indeed, a glance at the Greenpeace clothing catalogue will show many examples of such differentiated goods on offer. People may also be willing to pay more for a product which is differentiated in terms of possible health impacts of its production: this was claimed to be the case for cotton clothing in terms of the nature of dyes used to colour material. The environmental and health attributes the authors consider are thus 'organic cotton', 'environmentally-friendly dyes' and 'no dyes'.

A semi-log functional form was used for the hedonic price equation, based on 750 products on sale. Results show that a large and statistically significant relationship exists between the organic cotton label and prices, with an average mark-up of 34 per cent being found for organic clothes. Interestingly, only 37 per cent of this mark-up is accounted for by the higher cost of producing organic cotton. No significant effects were found, however, for environmentally-friendly dye labels (interestingly, no-dye clothes sold for a discount). The authors note that a stronger relationship might be expected for health-related characteristics in the case of children's clothing, since parents might care more about their children's health than their own, but they find no evidence for this in the data.

on the value of peace and quiet in the housing market in Birmingham, UK; and the study by Boyle et al. (1999) on water quality in Maine, USA.

5.4   PROBLEMS WITH THE HP METHOD

Omitted Variable Bias

If a variable that significantly affects house prices is omitted from the HP equation, which is in addition correlated with one of the included variables, then the coefficient on this included variable will be biased.

This might be a particular problem when 'emitters' cause more than one impact. For instance, paper mills will affect water quality, which impacts on house prices, but may also impose disutility due to odours. Traffic can cause disutility due to noise, but also due to dust and safety concerns. Including only either noise or water quality in the HP equation will result in biased estimates for the marginal values of noise/water quality (Leggett and Bockstael, 2000); this was suspected to be the case in the Copenhagen noise study referred to above. Leggett and Bockstael (2000) solve the problem by including separate variables for water quality levels and for the distance of houses from pollution sources; fortunately, due to the nature of the natural processes relating emissions to water quality levels, these two variables are not too correlated with each other.

Multi-collinearity

Some attributes in the hedonic price function may be highly correlated with each other. For example, houses close to a river may score highly in terms of both 'peace and quiet' and 'scenic quality of views'. Houses in deprived neighbourhoods may score badly both in terms of 'local crime rates' and 'quality of local amenities'. This means that the parameter estimates for implicit prices will be imprecise, and that the effects of attributes that are highly correlated with each other (for example two measures of air pollution in a city) will be difficult to disentangle from each other. The researcher might decide in such cases either to leave out some explanatory variables from the hedonic price equation, or to seek for alternative ways of representing their influence on house prices.

Choice of Functional Form for the Hedonic Price (HP) Function

Economic theory does not specify which functional form should be used for the HP equation, yet the choice of functional form will influence the value that implicit prices take. We can reasonably suggest that the functional form used should allow house prices to rise as more of a desirable attribute is supplied, and that linear models may be rather unrealistic, since they imply that the cost of buying cleaner air quality or more bedrooms does not vary with the quantity of these attributes purchased. Choice of which form to use will thus depend on econometric considerations, and flexible forms such as the Box–Cox have been suggested and used (Cropper et al., 1988). Semi-log forms where the natural log of house prices is used as the dependent variable are also popular, since they also allow for non-linear implicit prices, which can be calculated using a simple formula (for example Geoghegan et al., 2003). In Leggett and Bockstael (2000), results

BOX 5.4   THE VALUE OF OPEN SPACE

McConnell and Walls (2005) undertook a review of non-market valuation methods and the value of 'open space'. They review 40 studies published between 1967 and 2003, organized according to whether they were concerned with 'general open space, parks and natural areas', green-belts, wetlands and forests, and agricultural lands. Some of the implicit prices for open space were found to be negative, and some statistically insignificant, but in most cases proximity to open space is correlated with an increase in house prices. Some of the results surveyed are shown below:

Study	Type of open space	Marginal value in $ for living 200 metres closer
Anderson and West, 2003	State/regional parks, wildlife refuges	600
Schultz and King, 2001	Wildlife habitat	429
Doss and Taff, 1996	Open-water wetland	1980
Mahan et al, 2000	Wetland of any type	286
Smith et al, 2002	Public open space	−553
		Marginal value from conversion of 1 acre
Irwin, 2002	Conservation land	3307

They conclude that open space values seem to depend on location, type of open space and research methods.

for four different functional forms are presented. For a comprehensive guide to how implicit prices will vary according to the functional form of the HP function, see Taylor (2003, p. 354).

Market Segmentation

The hedonic price function relates, in theory, to the equilibrium implicit prices for housing attributes in a single market. How big this market is in spatial terms can be difficult to assess. If we study the relationship between traffic noise and house prices in Glasgow, should we consider the whole of the city to be one housing market, or are there separate markets North and South of the river, with separate hedonic price functions for each? It can be hard to test for this market segmentation econometrically, since we are unsure about both functional form and market size (Palmquist, 2003). Michaels and Smith (1990) use definitions of separate markets from realtors (estate agents) to solve this problem. Geoghegan et al. (2003) estimate separate HP models for three neighbouring counties in Maryland to look at the effects of protecting open space (agricultural, forest, and parkland and golf courses) on property values. They found that the implicit price of open space varied a lot across these three counties: for one county (Carroll), open space had no significant effect on house prices, whilst for the other two, the effects on house values of increasing open land conservation by 1 per cent was much higher in Calvert County than in Howard County.

Expected or Perceived Versus Actual Characteristic Levels

House sales may be a function of expected future environmental conditions in addition to current observed conditions. For example, the implicit price for noise may also show what people expect to happen to noise levels in that part of town in the next 10 years, not just what noise levels are when the study is undertaken. Also, implicit prices for open space may depend on what people think will happen to this open space in the future (Smith et al., 2002). McCluskey and Rausser (2003) look at the effects over time of the discovery and eventual remediation of toxic wastes from an old lead smelter, which affected house values in Dallas County, Texas. The authors allow for the effects of distance from the smelter on housing values to vary with time. One can argue that one factor which varies with time is people's beliefs about the extent of the risk from wastes left behind by the smelter (which were used as part of landfill for construction), and the likelihood and extent of eventual remediation of the risks. Thus, people's beliefs about how risk levels were changing over time, as well as actions which actually reduced risks (such as the various stages of clean-up which occurred at the site), may be what drives house prices.

Another problem arises in that individuals' subjective values of such risks are likely to be either less than or greater than the scientific probability of health damages occurring. People often tend to overestimate the likelihood of low probability, high cost events (such as a plane crash) occurring, and underestimate the likelihood of high probability events happening. The implication is that hedonic prices may either overestimate or underestimate welfare changes according to whether a low or high objective probability event is being considered, and to the amount and quality of information available to individuals (Kask and Maani, 1992). Recent work on this issue has looked at how people learn about risks, and how this relates to behaviour in housing markets. For example, Hallstrom and Smith (2005) study the effects of a 'near miss' hurricane, Hurricane

Andrew, on housing markets in Lee County, Florida. The argument is that this near-miss caused local residents to re-evaluate the risks of living in a hurricane-prone part of the US, and that this re-appraisal of risks should be reflected in house prices. The authors indeed find that the near miss caused a fall in house prices due to a re-evaluation of risks, this fall being equivalent to about 3 per cent of average annual income in Lee County.

Spatial Auto-Correlation

Spatial auto-correlation refers to the phenomenon whereby certain factors influence house prices for all properties in a neighbourhood, but are not observable to the researcher. This means that the error term in equation (5.2) is correlated across neighbouring properties. The effects are to make the estimates of the hedonic price equation parameters inefficient, and to bias standard errors (making the associated t-statistics 'too big'). This means we might incorrectly infer that an attribute has a significant effect on house prices, when in fact it does not. Spatial auto-correlation can be tested for, and steps taken to remove its effects – see Geoghegan et al. (2003) for details.

Restrictive Assumptions

The HP gives an accurate estimate of the value of environmental quality only if (i) all buyers and sellers in the housing market are well informed of attribute levels at every possible housing location; (ii) all buyers in the market are able to move to utility-maximizing positions (otherwise, marginal cost is not equivalent to marginal WTP); (iii) the housing market is in equilibrium; the vector of implicit prices is such that the market clears at all times. Clearly, these assumptions will never fully describe reality. For example, buyers could be more poorly informed about the characteristics of certain houses than sellers. Pope (2008) notes that information disclosure laws in the US over house sales implies that the government indeed thinks that buyers do not 'know enough'. He looks at the effects of airport noise disclosures on house prices around Raleigh-Durham Airport in North Carolina. He found that disclosure laws increased the implicit price of aircraft noise by 37 per cent, leading him to conclude that the 'information environment' should be carefully considered when using HP to value amenities and disamenities. In the case of aircraft noise he looks at, one might say that a HP study carried out on the disamenity of aircraft noise prior to the implementation of information disclosure laws would have undervalued the costs of noise nuisance.

BOX 5.5   VALUING THE DISAMENITIES OF LANDFILL SITES

Landfill sites, whether for municipal solid waste or industrial wastes, have long been associated with impacts on house prices, since the assumption is that no one wants to live next to a landfill. Other things being equal, then, house prices will have to be lower, the closer one gets to a landfill site, to compensate buyers for the negative externalities of such facilities – noise, smell and seagulls! Several HP studies of landfill impacts on house prices can be found in the literature, including an interesting article by Hite et al. (2001). Hite et al. explain that both distance to a landfill site and the expected lifetime of that site can be expected to have an effect on house prices; whilst how well-informed house buyers are about landfill sites in an area could also matter to the implicit prices the analyst can uncover. They also allow for the fact that property taxes matter to the house buyer, and these depend both on public goods supplied in a neighbourhood (for example spending on schools) and on house prices.

The study is based on 2913 house sales in Franklin County in Ohio in 1990. House sales information was supplemented with data on household socio-economic characteristics for buyers. Environmental and neighbourhood characteristics data was also collected. Four landfill sites exist within the study area, and the distance of each house in the data base to each site was measured. Information was also included on how long these sites had left to operate (two had already closed in 1990). The authors find a significant effect of distance from all of the four landfill sites on property values, and that this effect persists even after a landfill has closed. The longer the lifespan a landfill site has at the time of sale, however, the lower the house price. They conclude that 'welfare losses from decreased property values near landfills can be of a significant magnitude'.

A similar study is that by Eshet et al. (2007) for waste transfer facilities in Israel. The authors use data from four cities to study the relationship between distance from the waste site and house prices. The data set consists of 9505 house sales located within 4 km of a waste site. Regression results using the quadratic model showed that the maximum distance affected by disamenities varied between the four cities from 2.29 to 3.29 km. Housing prices increase at a decreasing rate away from the transfer station: moving from the second to the third kilometre adds US$4460 to the price of an average house, whereas moving from the third to the fourth kilometre away adds only US$3150 to the price of an average house.

5.5   CONCLUSIONS

As has been pointed out in the preceding section, there are many problems associated with the HP technique. Perhaps the most important of these are the assumptions made about the related market (the housing market, in this chapter). Moreover, the method cannot be used to measure non-use values, and is restricted in terms of the kinds of environmental goods to which it can be applied (some tie has to be found to marketed goods). However, the method does make use of data on actual behaviour, unlike the stated preference methods described in Chapter 3. Although this chapter on HP has concentrated on house prices and environmental quality levels, the technique is applicable to other goods. HP can be used to estimate the implicit price of any observable characteristic of any good, so long as adequate data is available. HP can therefore be used to estimate the value of the 'green premium' on environmentally-friendly consumer goods (see Box 5.3), or the value of environmental risks on human health through wage differentials.

How reliable are hedonic price estimates of environmental benefits? Smith and Huang (1993) conducted a meta-analysis of 37 HP studies, to see how well they could detect the influence of air pollution on house prices. The authors report that 74 per cent of the studies found a negative and significant relationship between measures of air quality and house prices. They find that, overall, 'there is a systematic relationship between the modelling decisions, the descriptions used to characterise air pollution, the condition of local housing markets, and the conclusions reached about the relationship between air quality and house prices' – see also their 1995 meta-analysis (Smith and Huang, 1995). Palmquist cautions in his review of the HP literature that 'there is still substantial room for improvement' (Palmquist, 2003, p. 64), but this comment could equally be applied to all valuation methods!

As a means of measuring marginal values for certain environmental goods, the hedonic price method has much to recommend it.

NOTES

1. We thank V. Kerry Smith for his extensive and very helpful comments on this chapter.
2. That is, the rate at which an individual is willing to exchange one good for another: the slope of an indifference curve.
3. As with the travel cost model.

REFERENCES

Anderson, R.J. and T.D. Crocker (1971), 'Air pollution and residential property values', *Urban Studies*, **8**, 171–80.
Bjorner, T., J. Kronbak and T. Lundhede (2003), *Valuation of Noise Reduction: Comparing Results from Hedonic Pricing and Contingent Valuation*, Copenhagen: AKF Forlaget.

Boyle, K., J. Poor and L. Taylor (1999), 'Estimating the demand for protecting freshwater lakes from eutrophication', *American Journal of Agricultural Economics*, **81**(5), 118–22.

Cropper, M., L. Deck and K. McConnell (1988), 'On the choice of functional form for hedonic price functions', *Review of Economics and Statistics*, **70**, 668–75.

Day, B., I. Bateman and I. Lake (2007), 'Beyond implicit prices: recovering theoretically consistent and transferable values for noise avoidance from a hedonic price model', *Environmental and Resource Economics*, **37**, 211–32.

Eshet, T., M.G. Baron, M. Shechter and O. Ayalon (2007), 'Measuring externalities of waste transfer stations in Israel using hedonic pricing', *Waste Management*, **27**, 614–25.

Freeman, A.M. (2003), *The Measurement of Environmental and Resource Values*, Washington, DC: RFF Press.

Garrod, G. and K.G. Willis (1992), 'The amenity value of woodland in Great Britain', *Environmental and Resource Economics*, **2**(4), 415–34.

Geoghegan J., L. Lynch and S. Bucholtz (2003), 'Capitalization of open spaces into housing values and the residential property tax revenue impacts of agricultural easement programs', *Agricultural and Resource Economics Review*, **32**(1), 33–45.

Haab, T. and K. McConnell (2002), *Valuing Environmental and Natural Resources: The Econometrics of Non-market Valuation*, Cheltenham, UK and Northampton, MA, USA: Edward Elgar.

Hallstrom, D.G. and V.K. Smith (2005), 'Market responses to hurricanes', *Journal of Environmental Economics and Management*, **50**(3), 541–61.

Hite, D., W. Chern, F. Hitzhusen and A. Randall (2001), 'Property value impacts of an environmental disamenity: the case of landfills', *Journal of Real Estate Finance and Economics*, **22**, 185–202.

Jim, C.Y. and W.Y. Chen (2006), 'Impacts of urban environmental elements on residential housing prices in Guangzhou (China)', *Landscape and Urban Planning*, **78**, 422–34.

Kask, S. and S. Maani (1992), 'Uncertainty, information and hedonic pricing', *Land Economics*, **68**(2), 170–84.

Lancaster, K.J. (1966), 'A new approach to consumer theory', *Journal of Political Economy*, **74**, 132–57.

Leggett, C.G. and N. Bockstael (2000), 'Evidence on the effects of water quality on residential land prices', *Journal of Environmental Economics and Management*, **39**, 121–44.

McConnell, V. and M. Walls (2005), 'The value of open space: evidence from studies of non-market benefits', Discussion Paper, Resources For the Future, Washington, DC, available from www.rff.org.

McClusky, J. and G. Rausser (2003), 'Hazardous waste sites and housing appreciation rates', *Journal of Environmental Economics and Management*, **45**(2), 166–76.

Michaels, R. and V. Smith (1990), 'Market segmentation and valuing amenities with hedonic models: the case of hazardous waste sites', *Journal of Urban Economics*, **28**, 232–42.

Nimon, W. and J. Beghin (1999), 'Are eco-labels valuable? Evidence from the apparel industry', *American Journal of Agricultural Economics*, **81**(4), 801–12.

O'Byrne, P., J. Nelson and J. Seneca (1985), 'Housing values, census estimates, disequilibrium and the environmental cost of airport noise', *Journal of Environmental Economics and Management*, **12**, 169–78.

Palmquist, R. (1991), 'Hedonic methods', in J. Braden and C. Kolstad (eds), *Measuring the Demand for Environmental Improvement*, Amsterdam: North Holland.

Palmquist, R. (2003), 'Property value models', in K.-G. Maler and J. Vincent (eds), *Handbook of Environmental Economics, Volume 2*, Amsterdam: North Holland.

Poor, P.J., K.L. Pessagno and R.W. Paul (2007), 'Exploring the hedonic value of ambient water quality: a local watershed-based study', *Ecological Economics*, **60**, 797–806.

Pope, J.C. (2008), 'Buyer information and the hedonic: the impact of seller disclosure on the implicit price of aircraft noise', *Journal of Urban Economics*, **63**(2), 498–516.

Rosen, S. (1974), 'Hedonic prices and implicit markets: product differentiation in pure competition', *Journal of Political Economy*, **82**, 34–55.

Smith, V.K. and Ji Chin Huang (1993), 'Hedonic models and air quality: 25 years and counting', *Environmental and Natural Resource Economics*, **3**(4), 381–94.

Smith, V.K. and Ji Chin Huang (1995), 'Can markets value air quality? A meta-analysis of hedonic property value models', *Journal of Political Economy*, **103**, 209–27.

Smith, V.K., C. Poulos and H. Kim (2002), 'Treating open space as an urban amenity', *Resource and Energy Economics*, **24**, 107–29.

Taylor, L. (2003), 'The hedonic method', in P. Champ, K. Boyle and T. Brown (eds), *A Primer on Non-Market Valuation*, Dordrecht, NL: Kluwer.

6. Valuing the environment: production function approaches

6.1 INTRODUCTION

In addition to providing services directly to individuals as consumers, environmental and resource systems can affect the costs and output levels of producers in an economy. The effects of these changes will be transmitted to individuals through the price system in the form of changes in costs and prices of final goods and services, and through changes in factor prices and incomes. By properly modelling the way in which environmental quality affects production and costs, it is possible to determine the changes in producers' and consumers' surpluses associated with environmental changes, and thus the welfare impacts of these changes.

This method of valuing the environment is what characterizes *production function (PF) approaches*, which is also called 'valuing the environment as input' (Barbier, 1994, 2000 and 2007; Ellis and Fisher, 1987; Freeman, 2003, ch.9; Heal et al., 2005). Such approaches assume that an environmental good or service essentially serves as a factor input in the production of a marketed good that yields utility. Thus, changes in the availability of the environmental good or service can affect the costs and supply of the marketed good, or the returns to other factor inputs, or both. Applying PF approaches therefore requires modelling the behaviour of producers and their response to changes in environmental quality that influence production. As the various PF modelling methods develop, they are increasingly being applied to valuing a diverse range of environmental benefits, including the effects of flood control, coastal habitat-marine fishery linkages, groundwater recharge, pollution abatement by firms, maintenance of biodiversity and carbon sequestration, storm protection, pollution mitigation and water purification.

In this chapter we explore production function modelling approaches for valuing the environment. We explain the general methodology and discuss some key measurement issues, including the key differences between production function modelling and related but older methods of estimating dose-response functions. We illustrate the basic methodology using some examples from the literature, although some applications of PF approaches are also shown in the later case study chapters of this book. Here, our main purpose is to show how various production function models and methods can be used to value 'the environment as input'.

6.2   THE DEVELOPMENT OF PRODUCTION FUNCTION METHODS

The concept of 'valuing' the environment as an input is not new. Older methods of valuation, such as dose-response, change-in-productivity and damage function models, can be considered special cases of the PF approach in which the production responses to environmental quality changes are greatly simplified (Freeman, 1982). These older methods focused on measuring the physical changes in output due to environmental changes, such as crop yield losses due to soil erosion and damages due to pollution or floods, and then using market prices or costs to value these impacts.

For example, a typical early study of the impact of soil erosion on crop losses or the cost of fertilizer run-off would start with estimating a physical damage function relating the decline in agricultural yield or applied fertilizers to the loss in topsoil depth due to erosion. The resulting damage function would then simply be multiplied by the unit price or cost estimate, such as the market price of the affected crop or the cost of purchasing additional fertilizer. The problem with such a simplified approach, however, is that it ignores any possible modification in the economic behaviour of the individuals affected by the environmental change. A farmer faced with soil erosion, for example, might switch to other types of crops more tolerant of soil erosion, or alter the application of other inputs, such as labour, fertilizers, farm machinery, irrigation water or so forth. Without modelling carefully the role of the environment as one of many possible inputs in the production activity affected by an environmental change, a simple damage function or change-in-productivity approach to estimating the value of that change may be misleading.

Figure 6.1 uses a soil erosion example to illustrate this problem with the change-in-productivity approach (see Barbier, 1998). Assume for simplicity that soil erosion does not affect the costs of production but only revenues, through impacts on crop yields. Let R_0 be the gross revenues per hectare of the farm initially before erosion. As soil erosion occurs over time, actual yields for any time $T > T_0$ will be less than R_0. As shown in the figure, the change-in-productivity approach assumes that for any particular time period T the (undiscounted) revenue impacts of yield losses from soil erosion in that period will be the distance AB. However, this method

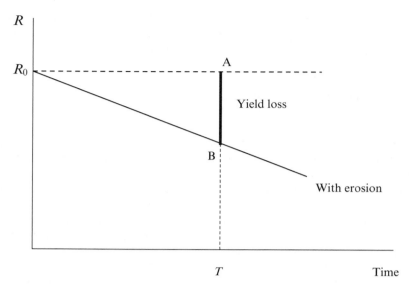

Note: R = gross revenue per hectare.

Source: Barbier (1998, Fig. 13.2).

Figure 6.1 Change in productivity approach for valuing the impact of erosion on crops

is likely to overestimate the on-site costs of soil erosion. The assumption that gross revenues R_0 could be maintained indefinitely from T_0 onwards is unrealistic. Even if it is technically feasible to reduce soil erosion, the costs of investing in soil conservation on some plots of land may not be economically worthwhile. For other plots of land, it may be worthwhile reducing erosion and thus improving yields, but it may be too costly to restore crop yields and gross revenues from production to the initial levels at time T_0 before erosion sets in. Thus measuring on-site costs in terms of all the yield and income losses associated with productivity changes before and after erosion occurs on all cropland may be misleading.

Modern production function methods of 'valuing the environment as input' attempt to correct these limitations arising from ignoring economic behaviour in response to environmental change. The basic modelling approach underlying PF methods is similar to determining the additional value of a change in the supply of any factor input. For example, if an environmental change affects a marketed production activity, such as growing crops, commercial fishing or electricity generation by utilities, then the effects of these changes will be transmitted to individuals through the price system via changes in the costs and prices of the final marketed good. This means that any resulting 'improvements in the resource base or environmental quality' as a result of enhanced environmental quality, 'lower costs and prices and increase the quantities of marketed goods, leading to increases in consumers' and perhaps producers' surpluses' (Freeman, 2003, p. 259). The sum of changes in consumer and producer surpluses in turn provides a measure of the willingness to pay for the improvement in environmental quality.

An adaptation of the PF methodology is required in the case where the benefit provided by the environment has a protective value, such as the storm protection and flood mitigation provided by coastal wetlands or the reduction of soil run-off downstream provided by forested upper watersheds. In such cases, the environment may be thought of as producing a non-marketed service, such as 'protection' of economic activity, property and even human lives, which benefits individuals through limiting damages. Applying PF approaches requires modelling the 'production' of this protection service and estimating its value as an environmental input in terms of the expected damages avoided (Barbier, 2007).

For now, we will focus on the general production function modelling approach applied to the case of the environment as an input supporting or enhancing a marketed production activity. Later in the chapter, we will address the special case of applying the production function method to value the environment when it protects an economic activity from damage.

6.3   GENERAL METHODOLOGY

A two-step procedure is generally invoked in implementing production function methods (Barbier, 1994). First, the physical effects of an environmental change on an economic activity are determined. Second, the impact of this environmental change is valued in terms of the corresponding change in the marketed output of the relevant activity. These steps can be analysed together if the physical impact on production due to the environment is treated as an 'input' into the economic activity, and like any other input, its value can be equated with its impact on the productivity of any marketed output.

More formally, if Q is the marketed output of an economic activity, then Q can be considered to be a function of a range of inputs:

$$Q = Q(E_i, \ldots, E_k, S), \tag{6.1}$$

where $E = E_i, \ldots E_k$ represents the conventional economic inputs used in production, such as labour, machinery, tools, land, and so forth, and S is the support provided to the economic activity by the environment. For example, the latter support could be coastal wetland or coral reef habitat enhancing the productivity of a marine fishery, groundwater recharge supporting irrigated agriculture, pollination of tree crops by wildlife, improved air quality enhancing the total productivity of firms, water filtering affecting the hydroelectric output of dams, and so forth.

Although the presence of the environmental input supports or enhances the productivity of the economic activity, this input is not paid for, and thus from an economic standpoint is a 'non-marketed' input, or positive externality, used in production. However, if the other conventional inputs are marketed and have corresponding prices $w = w_i, \ldots w_k$, then any profit-maximizing owner of the economic activity would seek to minimize the costs of production, C

$$\min C = wE \qquad\qquad (6.2)$$

$$\text{s.t. } Q = Q(X, S).$$

For a given output Q, it follows that the cost-minimizing function is $C^* = C(Q, w, S)$. If all production activities are affected identically by the environment and employ the same production technology with respect to conventional inputs, then C^* would also represent the optimal cost function of all suppliers of Q to a market. Suppose that this market is competitive, and that its inverse demand function has the normal properties, $p = p(Q)$, $\partial p_h/\partial Q < 0$, where p is the market price for the output Q. Equilibrium in the market place for given input and output prices, and for some initial level of environmental quality $S = S_0$, would be determined by the standard competitive market conditions that the marginal cost of supplying Q by all producers is equal to the price determined by demand, $\partial C^*(Q, w, S_0)/\partial Q = p(Q)$. The latter expression can be rearranged to yield the equilibrium level of output in the market

$$Q_0 = Q(w, p, S_0), \partial Q_0/\partial S_0 > 0. \qquad\qquad (6.3)$$

Equation (6.3) indicates that a change in environmental quality will lead to an increase in the initial equilibrium output, Q_0. This comes about because an environmental improvement essentially represents an increase in a fixed factor, and thus increases the productivity of the conventional inputs employed in production. The result is a reduction in the marginal

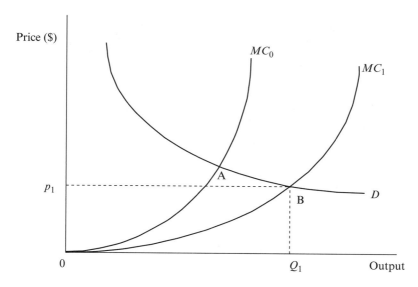

Notes:
MC = marginal cost of market supply.
D = demand curve for output.
p_1 = market price after environmental change.
Q_1 = market output after change.
$0AB$ = change in consumer and producer surplus.

Figure 6.2   Valuing a change in the environment as input

costs, $\partial^2 C^*/\partial Q \partial S_0 < 0$, and thus a new and higher equilibrium output is attained in the market.

This outcome is shown in Figure 6.2. An environmental improvement lowers the marginal cost of supplying any level of marketed output, from MC_0 to MC_1. The result is that market price falls and output increases. Both consumer and producer surplus increase, and the total welfare gain is measured by area $0AB$. The latter represents the value of the additional environmental improvement – the 'value of the environment as input'.

Of course measuring this welfare gain from an environmental improvement will vary from case to case. Box 6.1 draws on the example of groundwater recharge of cropland irrigation to illustrate how the general production function methodology can be estimated in practice to estimate the change in consumer and producer surplus as shown in Figure 6.2. As illustrated in Box 6.1, using this method, Acharya and Barbier (2000) value the welfare impacts from groundwater recharge changes due to floodplain wetland loss affecting 6600 ha of irrigated dryland farming

BOX 6.1   PRODUCTION FUNCTION APPROACH APPLIED
           TO GROUNDWATER RECHARGE OF DRYLAND
           FARMING

Acharya and Barbier (2000) apply a production function approach to
value the groundwater recharge function of the Hadejia-Nguru wetlands
in northern Nigeria. The groundwater recharge function supports dry
season agricultural production, which is dependent on groundwater
abstraction for irrigation. The recharge function is valued as an environmental input into the dry season agricultural production, allowing the
welfare changes associated with a change in recharge to be calculated.
The basic methodology is as follows.

Let Y_i be the aggregate output of the ith crop (vegetables, wheat,
and so on) produced by farmers in a semi-arid region. Production of Y_i
requires a water input W_i abstracted through wells and $j = 1, \ldots, J$ other
inputs (for example fertilizers, seed, labour), which can be denoted as
$x_{i1}, \ldots, x_{iJ}$ or X_J in vector notation. Assume that the water input in the wells
is dependent on the level of naturally recharged groundwater, R. The
aggregate production function of crop i is

$$Y_i = Y_i(x_{i1}, \ldots, x_{iJ}, W_i(R)) \qquad \text{for all } i$$

The associated costs of production are

$$C_i = C_x X_J + c_w W_i \qquad \text{for all } i$$

where C_i is the minimum costs associated with producing Y_i during a
given period of time, c_w is the cost of pumping water and C_x is the vector
of $c_{x1}, \ldots, c_{xJ}$ strictly positive input prices. Assume that there exists an
inverse demand curve for the aggregate crop output Y_i

$$p_{Yi} = p_i(Y_i) \qquad \text{for all } i$$

Denoting Ω_i as social welfare arising from producing Y_i, it is measured as
the area under the demand curve less the costs of production. Thus

$$\Omega_i = \Omega(x_{i1}, \ldots, x_{iJ}, W_i(R)) = \int_0^{Y_i} p_i(u) \, du - C_i \quad \text{for all } i, j$$

The first-order conditions for choosing input x_{ij} and water use W_i to maximize social welfare are

$$\frac{\partial \Omega_i}{\partial x_{ij}} = p_i(Y_i) \frac{\partial Y_i}{\partial x_{ij}} - c_{xj} = 0 \quad \text{for all } i, j$$

$$\frac{\partial \Omega_i}{\partial W_i} = p_i(Y_i) \frac{\partial Y_i}{\partial W_i} - c_w = 0 \quad \text{for all } i$$

The socially efficient level of input use occurs where the value marginal product of each input equals its price. The first-order conditions can be used to derive optimal input demands $x_{ij}^* = x_{ij}^*(c_{xj}, c_W, R)$ and $W_i^* = W_i^*(c_{xj}, c_W, R)$. Substituting the optimal inputs back into the production and welfare functions yields the optimal Y_i^* and Ω_i^*.

A change in R will clearly affect production through an impact on water use $W_i(R)$. However, if we assume that all other inputs are held at their optimal levels, $x_{ij} = x_{ij}^*$, then it follows from the envelope theorem applied to the (optimal) welfare function

$$\frac{d\Omega_i}{dR} = \frac{\partial \Omega_i \partial x_{ij}}{\partial x_{ij} \partial R} + \frac{\partial \Omega_i \partial W_i}{\partial W_i \partial R} = \frac{\partial \Omega_i \partial W_i}{\partial W_i \partial R}\bigg|_{x_{ij}=x_{ij}^*}$$

Substituting the first-order condition for optimal water use yields

$$\frac{d\Omega_i}{dR} = \left[p_i(Y_i)\frac{\partial Y_i}{\partial W_i} - c_W \right]\frac{\partial W_i}{\partial R} \quad \text{for all } i$$

Thus the net welfare change is the effect of a change in recharge levels on the value marginal product of water less the per-unit cost effects of a change in water input.

For a non-marginal change, that is from R_0 to R_1, the welfare change can be found by integrating over this change in groundwater levels

$$\frac{d\Omega_i}{dR} = \int_{R_0}^{R_1} \left[p_i(Y_i)\frac{\partial Y_i}{\partial W_i} - c_W \right]\frac{\partial W_i}{\partial R}dR \quad \text{for all } i$$

Thus the welfare impact associated with a change in R is the resulting change in the value of production less the impacts on pumping costs. As long as per-unit pumping costs were not too high, one would expect an increase in groundwater levels to lead to a welfare benefit, whereas a decrease would result in a welfare loss. An alternative calculation of the welfare impact can be made if the initial and final output levels, Y_i^0 and Y_i^1, and the cost function, C_i are known

$$\frac{d\Omega_i}{dR} = \int_0^{Y_i^1} p_i(Y_i)dY_i - C_i(Y_i^1, R_1) - \int_0^{Y_i^0} p_i(Y_i)dY_i - C_i(Y_i^0, R_0) \quad \text{for all } i$$

This is none other than the change in consumer and producer surplus, that is the change in area under the demand curve less the change in area under the supply (marginal cost) curve. In Figure 6.2, this is equivalent to area 0AB.

in northern Nigeria. A fall in groundwater levels from 6 to 7 metre depth results in losses of US$32.5 per vegetable farmer, approximately 7.65 per cent of yearly income, and US$331 for vegetable and wheat farmers, or around 77 per cent of annual income. The total loss associated with the 1 m change in naturally charged groundwater levels was estimated to be US$62 249 for all 6600 ha of dryland farming.

As PF approaches continue to develop, they are being increasingly employed for a diverse range of environmental quality impacts. Some examples include maintenance of biodiversity and carbon sequestration in tropical forests (Boscolo and Vincent, 2003); nutrient impacts in the Baltic Sea (Gren et al., 1997) and the Gulf of Mexico (Smith, 2007); pollination by tropical forests supporting coffee production in Costa Rica (Ricketts et al., 2004); modelling joint production of timber and wildlife from forests (Nalle et al., 2004); substitution possibilities between pollution emissions, fuels, labour, and capital in electric power generation (Considine and Larson, 2006); mangrove deforestation affecting mangrove habitat–fishery linkages in Thailand (Barbier, 2003 and 2007); soil conservation improving reservoir services (Hansen and Hellerstein, 2007); tropical watershed protection services (Kaiser and Roumasset, 2002); coral reef habitat support of marine fisheries in Kenya (Rodwell et al., 2002); marine reserves acting to enhance the 'insurance value' of protecting commercial fish species in Sicily (Mardle et al., 2004) and in the Northeast cod fishery (Sumaila, 2002); and nutrient enrichment in the Black Sea affecting the balance between invasive and beneficial species (Knowler et al., 2001; Knowler and Barbier, 2005).

6.4   MEASUREMENT ISSUES IN IMPLEMENTING PRODUCTION FUNCTION APPROACHES TO VALUATION

However, successful implementation of PF modelling approaches requires overcoming a number of important measurement issues.

First, application of the PF approach requires properly specifying the production function model that links the physical effects of the environmental quality change to changes in market prices and quantities and ultimately to consumer and producer surpluses. Such modelling has its own demands in terms of ecological and economic data, and there must be sufficient scientific knowledge of how environmental goods and services support or protect economic activities. For example, the case study in Box 6.1 of modelling how changes in groundwater recharge affect irrigated dryland agriculture was based on hydrological evidence linking the extent of floodplain wetlands with mean water depth of the shallow aquifers used for crop irrigation by farmers (Thompson and Hollis, 1995). Thus, as shown in Box 6.1, changes in the groundwater level impact the water available in wells for irrigation and thus raise the cost of pumping.

For other environmental effects on production, it has proven difficult to provide a direct measure of the environmental quality change, and 'proxy' methods have been employed. For example, it has been recognized for some time that coastal wetlands provide valuable support for commercial and recreational marine fisheries by serving as breeding grounds and nursery habitat for fish fry. However, directly measuring this nursery and breeding habitat support is complicated. Instead, since the early coastal habitat–fishery model developed by Lynne et al. (1981), the standard approach adopted is to allow the wetland area to serve as a proxy for the productivity contribution of the nursery and habitat function (see Barbier, 2000 for further discussion). It is then relatively straightforward to estimate the impacts of the change in the coastal wetland area input on fishery catch, in terms of the marginal costs of fishery harvests and thus changes in consumer and producer surpluses.

In addition, market conditions and regulatory policies for the marketed output will influence the values imputed to the environmental input (Freeman, 1991 and 2003, ch. 9). Market distortions, imperfect competition, and of course, the complete absence of markets will mean that the well-behaved market conditions for measuring the impact of environmental quality on changes in consumer and producer surplus, as illustrated in Figure 6.2, will not apply. Freeman (2003, ch. 9), for example, illustrates how the basic method illustrated so far in this chapter can be adapted for cases such as multi-product firms with joint production technologies, vertically linked markets in which the output of one set of firms is purchased as an input by another set of firms, monopoly markets and price supports in agriculture. Another common problem occurs if environmental quality affects harvesting of a renewable resource that is subject to open access (Freeman, 1991). Under these conditions, profits from harvesting would be dissipated, and equilibrium prices would be equated to average and not marginal costs. As a consequence, there is no producer surplus, and the welfare impact of a change in wetland habitat is measured by the resulting change in consumer surplus only.

In cases where environmental quality does support a harvested natural resource system, such as a fishery, forestry or a wildlife population, then it may be necessary to model how changes in the stock or biological population affects the future flow of benefits. If the natural resource stock effects are not considered significant, then the environmental changes can be modelled as impacting only current harvest, prices and consumer and producer surpluses, exactly as shown in Figure 6.2. If the stock effects are significant, then a change in an ecological service will impact not only current but also future harvest and market outcomes. In the production function valuation literature, the first approach is referred to as a 'static model' of environmental change on a natural resource production system, whereas the second approach is referred to as a 'dynamic model' because it takes into account the inter-temporal stock effects of the environmental change (Barbier, 2000 and 2007; Freeman, 2003, ch. 9).

Finally, a single environment, habitat or ecosystem may support various economic activities in more than one way, and it may be important to model any tradeoffs among these various ecological–economic linkages as environmental change occurs. Integrated economic–ecological modelling may be necessary to capture more fully the ecosystem functioning and dynamics underlying the provision of these linkages, and can be used to value multiple impacts on activities arising from environmental change. Such modelling is essentially an extension of the production function approach, but from a single environment–economic production relationship to encompassing multiple, possibly interrelated, relationships. Examples of such multi-relationship PF modelling include analysis of salmon habitat restoration (Wu et al., 2003); eutrophication of small shallow lakes (Carpenter et al., 1999); changes in species diversity in a marine ecosystem (Finnoff and Tschirhart, 2003); introduction of exotic trout species (Settle and Shogren, 2002); rangeland management with dynamic interactions between livestock, grass, shrubs and fire (Janssen et al., 2004); and cattle stocking on rangeland threatened by invasive plants and nitrogen deposition (Finnoff et al., 2008).

We can illustrate the first three of these measurement issues by using the example of coastal habitat–fishery modelling. We will return to the issue of integrated ecological–economic modeling of multiple PF relationships in Chapter 9.

6.5 CASE STUDY: MODELLING COASTAL HABITAT–FISHERY LINKAGES

The development of PF models to value how a change in coastal wetland habitat area affects the market for commercially harvested fish not only illustrates some important measurement issues that need to be considered in implementing these models but also shows how PF modelling approaches have evolved.

Many initial PF methods to value habitat–fishery linkages, for instance, were based on a 'static model' of these linkages; that is, the environmental changes were modelled as impacting only current harvest, prices and consumer and producer surpluses, similar to the outcome shown in Figure 6.2. For example, using data from Lynne et al. (1981), Ellis and Fisher (1987) constructed such a static PF model to value the support by Florida marshlands for Gulf Coast crab fisheries in terms of the resulting changes in consumer and producer surpluses from the marketed catch. Freeman (1991) then extended Ellis and Fisher's approach to show how the values imputed to the wetlands in the static model are influenced by whether or not the fishery is open access or optimally managed. Sathirathai and Barbier (2001) also used a static model of habitat–fishery linkages to value the role of mangroves in Thailand in supporting near-shore fisheries under both open access and optimally managed conditions.

However, most near-shore fisheries are not optimally managed but *open access*, which assumes that fishermen are free to enter or leave the fishery, and no one controls how much each fisherman harvests. As a consequence, any profits in the fishery will attract new entrants until all the profits disappear. However, the general PF approach outlined above that treats environmental quality, such as coastal wetland habitat, as an 'input' into the economic activity, can still be used. Although in the open access equilibrium any producer surplus disappears, a change in coastal habitat will still affect welfare through its impact on consumer surplus. More formally, if h is the marketed harvest of the fishery, then a standard assumption in most static habitat–fishery models is that the general production function (6.1) takes the Cobb–Douglas form, $h = AE^aS^b$, where E is some aggregate measure of total 'effort' in the off-shore fishery (number of boats, hours spent fishing, and so on) and S is coastal wetland habitat area. It follows that the optimal cost function of a cost-minimizing fishery is

$$C^* = C(h, w, S) = wA^{-1/a}h^{1/a}S^{-b/a}, \qquad (6.4)$$

where w is the unit cost of effort. Assuming an iso-elastic market demand function, $p = p(h) = kh^\eta$, $\eta = 1/\varepsilon < 0$, then the market equilibrium for catch of the open access fishery occurs where the total revenues of the fishery just equals cost, or price equals average cost, that is $p = C^*/h$, which in this model becomes

$$kh^\eta = wA^{-1/a}h^{1-a/a}S^{-b/a}. \qquad (6.5)$$

One can see immediately from equation (6.5) that a change in wetland area is equivalent to 'shifting' the average cost of the fishery. The actual change in harvest as a result of this shift can be seen by rearranging equation (6.5) to yield the equilibrium level of fish harvest

$$h = \left[\frac{w}{k}\right]^{a/\beta} A^{-1/\beta} S^{-b/\beta}, \beta = (1 + \eta)a - 1. \tag{6.6}$$

It follows from (6.6) that the marginal impact of a change in wetland habitat is

$$\frac{dh}{dS} = -\frac{b}{\beta}\left[\frac{w}{k}\right]^{a/\beta} A^{-1/\beta} S^{-(b+\beta)/\beta}. \tag{6.7}$$

The change in consumer surplus, CS, resulting from a change in equilibrium harvest levels (from h^0 to h^1) is

$$\begin{aligned}
\Delta CS &= \int_{h^0}^{h^1} p(h)\,dh - [p^1 h^1 - p^0 h^0] = \frac{k[(h^1)^{\eta+1} - (h^0)^{\eta+1}]}{\eta + 1} \\
&\quad - k[(h^1)^{\eta+1} - (h^0)^{\eta+1}] \\
&= -\frac{\eta[p^1 h^1 - p^0 h^0]}{\eta + 1}.
\end{aligned} \tag{6.8}$$

By utilizing (6.7) and (6.8) it is possible to estimate the new equilibrium harvest and price levels and thus the corresponding changes in consumer surplus associated with a change in coastal wetland area, for a given demand elasticity, γ. Later, we will provide an example of this calculation. For now, we present in Figure 6.3 a diagrammatic representation of the welfare measure of a change in wetland area on an open access fishery corresponding to equation (6.6). As shown in the figure, a change in wetland area that serves as a breeding ground and nursery for an open access fishery results in a shift in the average cost curve, AC, of the fishery (see equation (6.5) above). The welfare impact is the change in consumer surplus (area p^*ABC).

However, as we argued previously, if the stock effects of a change in coastal wetlands are significant, then valuing such changes in terms of the impacts on current harvest and market outcomes is a flawed approach. To overcome this shortcoming, a dynamic model of coastal habitat–fishery linkage incorporates the change in wetland area within a multi-period harvesting model of the fishery. The standard approach is to model the change in coastal wetland habitat as affecting the biological growth function of the fishery (Barbier, 2003). As a result, any value impacts of a change in this habitat-support function can be determined in terms of changes in the long-run equilibrium conditions of the fishery. Alternatively, the welfare analysis could be conducted in terms of the harvesting path that

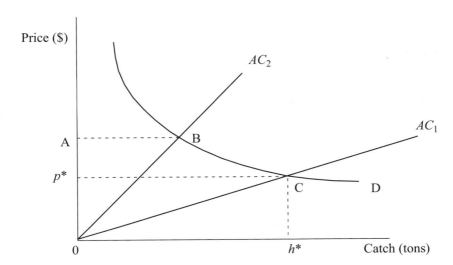

Notes:
AC = average cost.
D = demand curve.
p^* = price per ton.
h^* = fish catch in tonnes after change.
p^*ABC = change in consumer surplus.

Source: Adapted from Freeman (1991).

Figure 6.3   *Valuing the effects of a change in coastal habitat on an open access fishery*

approaches this equilibrium or the path that is moving away from initial conditions in the fishery.

Most attempts to value habitat–fishery linkages via a dynamic model that incorporates stock effects have assumed that the fishery affected by the habitat change is in a long-run equilibrium. Such a model has been applied, for example, in case studies of valuing habitat fishery linkages in Mexico (Barbier and Strand, 1998), Thailand (Barbier et al., 2002; Barbier, 2003) and the United States (Swallow, 1994). Similar 'equilibrium' dynamic approaches have been used to model other coastal environmental changes, including the impacts of water quality on fisheries in the Chesapeake Bay (Kahn and Kemp, 1985; McConnell and Strand, 1989), nutrient enrichment and jellyfish invasion impacting the Black Sea anchovy fishery (Knowler et al., 2001), and the effects of mangrove deforestation and shrimp larvae availability on aquaculture in Ecuador (Parks and Bonifaz, 1997).

However, valuing the change in coastal wetland habitat in terms of its impact on the long-run equilibrium of the fishery raises additional methodological issues (Barbier, 2007; Smith, 2007). First, the assumption of prevailing steady state conditions is strong, and may not be a realistic representation of harvesting and biological growth conditions in the near-shore fisheries. Second, such an approach ignores both the convergence of stock and harvest to the steady state and the short-run dynamics associated with the impacts of the change in coastal habitat on the long-run equilibrium. The usual assumption is that this change will lead to an instantaneous adjustment of the system to a new steady state, but this in turn requires local stability conditions that may not be supported by the parameters of the model.

There are examples of pure fisheries models that assume that the dynamic system is not in equilibrium but is either on the approach to a steady state or is moving away from initial fixed conditions. The latter approach has proven particularly useful in the case of open access or regulated access fisheries (Bjørndal and Conrad, 1987; Homans and Wilen, 1997), and both Barbier (2007) and Smith (2007) show how this approach can be adapted for PF models of environmental quality affecting fisheries. Here, we follow Barbier (2007) to show how this approach can be used to value a change in wetland habitat in terms of the dynamic path of an open access fishery.

Defining X_t as the stock of fish measured in biomass units, any net change in growth of this stock over time can be represented as

$$X_t - X_{t-1} = F(X_{t-1}, S_{t-1}) - h(X_{t-1}, E_{t-1}), \ \frac{\partial^2 F}{\partial X_{t-1}^2} < 0, \ \frac{\partial F}{\partial S_{t-1}} > 0. \tag{6.9}$$

Thus, net expansion in the fish stock occurs as a result of biological growth in the current period, $F(X_{t-1}, S_{t-1})$, net of any harvesting, $h(X_{t-1}, E_{t-1})$, which is a function of the stock as well as fishing effort, E_{t-1}. The influence of wetland habitat area, S_{t-1}, as a breeding ground and nursery habitat on growth of the fish stock is assumed to be positive, $\partial F/\partial S_{t-1} > 0$, as an increase in wetland area will mean more carrying capacity for the fishery and thus greater biological growth.

As before, it is assumed that the near-shore fishery is open access. The standard assumption for an open access fishery is that effort next period will adjust in response to the real profits made in the past period (Clark, 1976; Bjørndal and Conrad 1987). Letting $p(h)$ represent landed fish price per unit harvested, w the unit cost of effort and $\phi > 0$ is a parameter indicating the degree to which fishing effort adjusts to profit, then the fishing effort adjustment equation is

$$E_t - E_{t-1} = \phi[p(h_{t-1})h(X_{t-1}, E_{t-1}) - wE_{t-1}], \quad \frac{\partial p(h_{t-1})}{\partial h_{t-1}} < 0. \quad (6.10)$$

Assume a conventional bioeconomic fishery model with biological growth characterized by a logistic function, $F(X_{t-1}, S_{t-1}) = rX_{t-1}[1 - X_{t-1}/K(S_{t-1})]$, and harvesting by a Schaefer production process, $h_t = qX_tE_t$, where q is a 'catchability' coefficient, r is the intrinsic growth rate and $K(S_t) = \alpha \ln S_t$, is the impact of coastal wetland area on carrying capacity, K, of the fishery. The market demand function for harvested fish is again assumed to be iso-elastic, that is $p(h) = kh^\eta$, $\eta = 1/\varepsilon < 0$. Substituting these expressions into (6.9) and (6.10) yields

$$X_t = rX_{t-1}\left[1 - \frac{X_{t-1}}{\alpha \ln S_{t-1}}\right] - h_{t-1} + X_{t-1} \quad (6.11)$$

$$E_t = \phi R_{t-1} + (1 - \phi w)E_{t-1}, \quad R_{t-1} = kh_{t-1}^{1+\eta}. \quad (6.12)$$

Both X_t and E_t are predetermined, and so (6.11) and (6.12) can be estimated independently (see Homans and Wilen, 1997). Following Schnute (1977), define the catch per unit effort as $c_t = h_t/E_t = qX_t$. If X_t is predetermined, so is c_t. Substituting the expression for catch per unit effort in (6.11) produces

$$\frac{c_t - c_{t-1}}{c_{t-1}} = r - \frac{r}{q\alpha \ln S_{t-1}}c_{t-1} - qE_{t-1}. \quad (6.13)$$

Thus equations (6.12) and (6.13) can also be estimated independently to determine the biological and economic parameters of the model. For given initial effort, harvest and wetland data, both the effort and stock paths of the fishery can be determined for subsequent periods, and the consumer plus producer surplus can be estimated for each period. Alternative effort and stock paths can then be determined as wetland area changes in each period, and thus the resulting changes in consumer plus producer surplus in each period are the corresponding estimates of the welfare impacts of the coastal habitat change. As along its dynamic path the open access fishery is not in equilibrium, producer surpluses, or losses, are relevant for the welfare estimate of a change in coastal wetland habitat.

This approach to modelling and estimating a dynamic coastal habitat–fishery linkage is undertaken by Barbier (2007) to value the effect of mangrove loss on the artisanal shellfish and demersal fisheries of Thailand over 1996 to 2004. Moreover, Barbier compares the dynamic PF approach to a static valuation following the methodology outlined in the above model equations (6.4) to (6.8). The results of the two contrasting valuations are

Table 6.1   *Valuation of mangrove–fishery linkage in Thailand, 1996–2004*
              (US$)

Production function approach	Average annual mangrove loss	
	FAO (18.0 km²)[a]	Thailand (3.44 km²)[b]
Static analysis:		
Annual welfare loss	99,004	18,884
Net present value (10% discount rate)	570,167	108,756
Net present value (12% discount rate)	527,519	100,621
Net present value (15% discount rate)	472,407	90,108
Dynamic analysis:		
Net present value (10% discount rate)	1,980,128	373,404
Net present value (12% discount rate)	1,760,374	331,995
Net present value (15% discount rate)	1,484,461	279,999

Notes:
a FAO estimates from FAO (2003). 2000 and 2004 data are estimated from 1990–2000 annual average mangrove loss of 18.0 km².
b Thailand estimates from various Royal Thailand Forestry Department sources reported in Aksornkoae and Tokrisna (2004). 2000 and 2004 data are estimated from 1993–1996 annual average mangrove loss of 3.44 km².
All valuations are based on mangrove–fishery linkage impacts on artisanal shellfish and demersal fisheries in Thailand at 1996 prices. The demand elasticity for fish is assumed to be –0.5.

Source: Barbier (2007).

shown in Table 6.1. As the table indicates, there are two different estimates of the 1996–2004 annual mangrove deforestation rates in Thailand, namely the FAO estimate of 18.0 km² and the Royal Thai Forestry Department estimate of 3.44 km².

For the welfare impacts arising from the FAO estimates of annual average mangrove deforestation rates in Thailand over 1996–2004, the static analysis suggests that the annual loss in the habitat–fishery support service is around US$99 000. The net present value of these losses over the entire period is between US$0.47 and 0.57 million. For the much lower Thailand deforestation estimates, the annual welfare loss is just under US$19 000, and the net present value of these losses from 1996 to 2004 is US$90 000 to 108 000. The results for the dynamic mangrove–fishery linkage analysis are also depicted in Table 6.1, which indicates annual welfare losses of over US$1.98 million and US$373 404 associated with the FAO and Thailand deforestation estimates over 1996–2004, respectively. If the FAO estimate of mangrove deforestation over 1996–2004 is used, then the net present value of the welfare loss ranges from around US$1.5

to 2.0 million. In contrast, the lower Thailand deforestation estimation for 1996–2004 suggests that the net present value welfare loss from reduced mangrove support for fisheries is around US$0.28 to 0.37 million.

The welfare estimates in Table 6.1 indicate that the losses in the habitat–fishery support service caused by mangrove deforestation in Thailand over 1996–2004 are around three times greater for the dynamic production function approach compared to the static analysis. This large disparity in estimates between the two approaches suggests that the static analysis, which by definition ignores stock effects and focuses exclusively on the impact of changes in mangrove area on fishing effort and costs in the same period in which the habitat service changes, may seriously underestimate the value of changes in habitat–fishery linkages due to mangrove deforestation. In other words, the comparison of the dynamic and static analysis in the Thailand case study of mangrove–fishery linkages confirms that the multi-period stock effects resulting from mangrove loss are clearly an important component of the impacts of mangrove deforestation on the habitat–fishery service in Thailand. Thus, the Thailand case study reviewed here suggests caution in using the static analysis in preference to the dynamic production function approach in valuing the ecological service of coastal wetlands as breeding and nursery habitat for offshore fisheries. The static PF approach may prove misleading for policy analysis, particularly when considering options to preserve as opposed to convert coastal wetlands. Certainly, the perception among coastal fishing communities throughout Thailand is that the habitat–fishery service of mangroves is vital, and local fishers in these communities have reported substantial losses in coastal fish stocks and yields, which they attribute to recent deforestation (Aksornkoae et al., 2004; Sathirathai and Barbier, 2001).

6.6   VALUING THE ENVIRONMENT WHEN IT PROVIDES PROTECTION FROM DAMAGE

An adaptation of the PF methodology is required in the case where natural environments have a protective value, such as the storm protection and flood mitigation services provided by coastal wetlands. In such cases, the environment may be thought of as producing a non-marketed service, such as 'protection' of economic activity, property and even human lives, which benefits individuals through limiting damages. Applying PF approaches requires modelling the 'production' of this protection service and estimating its value as an environmental input in terms of the expected damages avoided.

This expected damage function (EDF) approach, which is a special category of 'valuing' the environment as 'input', is nominally straightforward;

it assumes that the value of an asset that yields a benefit in terms of reducing the probability and severity of some economic damage is measured by the reduction in the expected damage. The essential step to implementing this approach, which is to estimate how changes in the asset affect the probability of the damaging event occurring, has been used routinely in risk analysis and health economics, for example as in the case of airline safety performance (Rose, 1990); highway fatalities (Michener and Tighe, 1992); drug safety (Olson, 2004); and studies of the incidence of diseases and accident rates (Cameron and Trivedi, 1998; Winkelmann, 2003). In fact, the expected damage function approach predates many of the PF methods discussed so far, and has been used extensively in environmental economics to estimate the risk of health impacts from pollution (Freeman, 1982, ch. 5 and 9). Here we show that the EDF approach can also be applied, under certain circumstances, to value any environmental change that also reduces the probability and severity of economic damages, which could include storm protection, flood mitigation, prevention of erosion and siltation, pollution control and maintenance of beneficial species.

The following example illustrates how the expected damage function (EDF) methodology can be applied to value the storm protection service provided by a coastal wetland, such as a marshland or mangrove ecosystem. The starting point is the standard 'compensating surplus' approach to valuing a quantity or quality change in a non-market environmental good or service, which we introduced in Chapter 2.

Assume that in a coastal region the local community owns all economic activity and property, which may be threatened by damage from periodic natural storm events. Assume also that the preferences of all households in the community are sufficiently identical so that it can be represented by a single household. Let $m(p^x, z, u^0)$ be the expenditure function of the representative household, that is the minimum expenditure required by the household to reach utility level, u^0, given the vector of prices, p^x, for all market-purchased commodities consumed by the household, the expected number or incidence of storm events, z^0.

Suppose the expected incidence of storms rises from z^0 to z^1. The resulting expected damages to the property and economic livelihood of the household, $E[D(z)]$, translates into an exact measure of welfare loss through changes in the minimum expenditure function

$$E[D(z)] = m(p^x, z^1, u^0) - m(p^x, z^0, u^0) = c(z), \qquad (6.14)$$

where $c(z)$ is the *compensating surplus*, which we defined in Chapter 2. In this example, compensating surplus is the minimum income compensation that the household requires to maintain it at the utility level u^0, despite the expected increase in damaging storm events. Alternatively, $c(z)$ can be viewed as the minimum income that the household needs to avoid the increase in expected storm damages.

However, the presence of coastal wetlands could mitigate the expected incidence of damaging storm events. Because of this storm protection service, the area of coastal wetlands, S, may have a direct effect on reducing the 'production' of natural disasters, in terms of their ability to inflict damages locally. Thus the 'production function' for the incidence of potentially damaging natural disasters can be represented as

$$z = z(S), z' < 0, z'' > 0. \tag{6.15}$$

It follows from (6.14) and (6.15) that $\partial c(z)/\partial S = \partial E[D(z)]/\partial S < 0$. An increase in wetland area reduces expected storm damages and therefore also reduces the minimum income compensation needed to maintain the household at its original utility level. Alternatively, a loss in wetland area would increase expected storm damages and raises the minimum compensation required by the household to maintain its welfare. Thus, we can define the marginal willingness to pay, $W(S)$, for the protection services of the wetland in terms of the marginal impact of a change in wetland area on expected storm damages

$$W(S) = -\frac{\partial E[D(z(S))]}{\partial S} = -E\left[\frac{\partial D}{\partial z}z'\right], W' < 0. \tag{6.16}$$

The 'marginal valuation function', $W(S)$, is analogous to the Hicksian compensated demand function for marketed goods. The minus sign on the right-hand sign of equation (6.16) allows this 'demand' function to be represented in the usual quadrant, and it has the normal downward-sloping property (see Figure 6.4). Although an increase in S reduces z and thus enables the household to avoid expected damages from storms, the additional value of this storm protection service to the household will fall as wetland area increases in size. This relationship should hold across all households in the coastal community. Consequently, as indicated in Figure 6.4, the marginal willingness to pay by the community for more storm protection declines with S.

The value of a non-marginal change in wetland area, from S_0 to S_1, can be measured as

$$-\int_{S_0}^{S_1} W(S)\,dS = E[D(z(S))] = c(S). \tag{6.17}$$

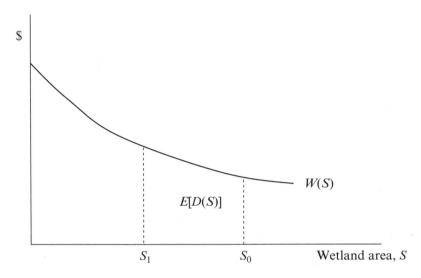

Source: Barbier (2007).

Figure 6.4   Expected damage costs from a loss of wetland area

If there is an increase in wetland area, then the value of this change is the total amount of expected damage costs avoided. If there is a reduction in wetland area, as shown in Figure 6.4, then the welfare loss is the total expected damages resulting from the increased incidence of storm events. As indicated in (6.17), in both instances the valuation would be a compensation surplus measure of a change in the area of wetlands and the storm protection service that they provide.

Box 6.2 provides an example of the EDF approach applied to valuing how the loss of mangrove area in 21 coastal provinces in Thailand over 1979–1996 increases the expected number of economically damaging natural disasters affecting these provinces.

6.7   CONCLUSION

As we learn more about the environment, we also find out that it assists and protects economic activity in many ways. In addition to providing benefits directly to individuals as consumers, the environment supports production of goods and services as well as protecting economic activity, property and even human lives. The 'production function' methods introduced in this chapter illustrate how environmental change that supports

BOX 6.2   VALUING THE COASTAL STORM PROTECTION
            SERVICE OF MANGROVES IN THAILAND

Barbier (2007) has shown that the EDF approach can also be applied, under certain circumstances, to value the protection service of coastal wetlands that reduce the probability and severity of economic damages from natural storm disasters. Two components are critical to implementing the EDF approach to estimating the changes in expected storm damages:

- the influence of wetland area on the expected incidence of economically damaging natural disaster events;
- some measure of the additional economic damage incurred per event.

The most important step is the first, and provided that there is sufficient data on the incidence of past natural disasters and changes in wetland area in coastal regions, this step can be done through employing a *count data model*, which we first introduced in Chapter 4. Count data models explain the number of times a particular event occurs over a given period. In economics, count data models have been used to explain a variety of phenomena, such as explaining successful patents derived from firm R&D expenditures, accident rates, disease incidence, crime rates and recreational visits (Cameron and Trivedi, 1998; Winkelmann, 2003; see also Chapter 4). Count data models could be used to estimate whether a change in the area of coastal wetlands, S, reduces the expected incidence of economically damaging storm events.

   For example, suppose that for a number of coastal regions, $i = 1,\ldots,N$, and over a given period of time, $t = 1,\ldots,T$, the *i*th coastal region could experience in any period *t* any number of $z_{it} = 0, 1, 2, 3 \ldots$ economically damaging storm event incidents. The expected number of incidences per period occurring in each region, $E[z_{it}|S_{it}, x_{it}]$, can therefore be explained by the area of wetlands, S_{it}, plus other factors, x_{it}. The most common formulation for the Poisson variable is loglinear, that is $\ln \lambda_{it} = \alpha_i + \beta_S S_{it} + \beta' x_{it}$, in which case the expected number of storm events per period is given by

$$E[z_{it}|S_{it}, x_{it}] = \lambda_{it} = e^{\alpha_i + \beta_S S_{it} + \beta' x_{it}}, \quad \frac{\partial E[z_{it}|S_{it}, x_{it}]}{\partial S_{it}} = \lambda_{it}\beta_S.$$

Estimation of β_S, along with an estimate of the conditional mean λ_{it}, provides the 'marginal effect' estimate of how a change in mangrove area influences the expected incidence of economically damaging natural disaster events, $\lambda_{it}\beta_S$.

   The count data analysis for 21 coastal provinces in Thailand over 1979–1996 by Barbier (2007) shows that loss of mangrove area in Thailand increases the expected number of economically damaging natural disasters affecting coastal provinces. The point estimate for β_S indicates that a 1-km² decline in mangrove area increases the expected number of disasters by 0.36 per cent. Using the corresponding 'marginal effect' (−0.0031), it is possible to estimate the resulting impact on expected damages of natural coastal disasters. Over 1996–2004, the estimated real economic damages per coastal event per year in Thailand averaged around US$61.0 million (1996 prices). This suggests that the marginal effect of a 1-km^2 loss of mangrove area is an increase in expected storm damages of about US$187 898 per km^2. Using two different mangrove deforestation estimates for Thailand over 1996–2004, a low rate of 3.44 km^2 per year and a high rate of 18 km^2 per year, the paper estimates that the net present value of the welfare loss from reduced coastal protection ranges from US$16.1 to 19.5 million (low deforestation estimate) and around US$3.1 to 3.7 million (high deforestation estimate).

or protects human economic activity and livelihoods can be valued. Such methods have undergone considerable change in recent years. Earlier approaches, such as dose-response, change-in-productivity and damage function models, focused on measuring the physical changes in output due to environmental changes, such as crop yield losses due to soil erosion and damages due to pollution or floods, and then using market prices or costs to value these impacts. In contrast, the newer production function methods introduced in this chapter start by modelling economic behaviour in response to environmental change. In the case where the environmental change affects production, environmental quality is treated as an additional 'input' into the production function of a good or service. Thus, if an environmental change affects a marketed production activity, such as growing crops, commercial fishing or electricity generation by utilities, then the effects of these changes will be transmitted to individuals through the price system via changes in the costs and prices of the final marketed good. Any resulting impacts on the consumer and producer surpluses of the marketed good serve as a measure of the welfare effects of the environmental change. In the special case where the natural environment has a protective value, such as protection against storm or flood damages, the environment may be thought of as producing a non-marketed service, such as 'protection' of economic activity, property and even human lives. The correct approach is to model the 'production' of this protection service and the economic benefits it provides, and then possibly to estimate its value as an environmental input in terms of the expected damages avoided.

As we apply production function approaches to an increasing array of environmental valuation problems, we are learning more about both the limits of these approaches and some important measurement issues. First, application of these methods requires properly specifying the production function model that links the physical effects of the environmental quality change to changes in market prices and quantities and ultimately to consumer and producer surpluses. Second, market distortions, imperfect competition, regulatory policies, and of course, the complete absence of markets will influence the values imputed to the environmental input. Third, when environmental quality supports a harvested natural resource system, such as a fishery, forestry or a wildlife population, or causes other 'inter-temporal' changes over time, then it may be necessary to model the 'dynamic' changes in environmental quality on both the present and future flows of benefits. Finally, because a natural environment, habitat or ecosystem may support various economic activities in more than one way, it may be important to model any tradeoffs among these various ecological–economic linkages as environmental change occurs.

REFERENCES

Acharya, G. and E.B. Barbier (2000), 'Valuing groundwater recharge through agricultural production in the Hadejia-Jama'are wetlands in Northern Nigeria', *Agricultural Economics*, **22**, 247–59.

Aksornkoae, S. and R. Tokrisna (2004), 'Overview of shrimp farming and mangrove loss in Thailand', in E.B. Barbier and S. Sathirathai (eds), *Shrimp Farming and Mangrove Loss in Thailand*, Cheltenham, UK and Northampton, MA, USA: Edward Elgar.

Aksornkoae, S., R. Tokrisna, W. Sugunnasil and S. Sathirathai (2004), 'The importance of mangroves: ecological perspectives and socio-economic values', in E.B. Barbier and S. Sathirathai (eds), *Shrimp Farming and Mangrove Loss in Thailand*, Cheltenham, UK and Northampton, MA, USA: Edward Elgar.

Barbier, E.B. (1994), 'Valuing environmental functions: tropical wetlands', *Land Economics*, **70**(2), 155–73.

Barbier, E.B. (1998), 'The economics of soil erosion: theory, methodology and examples', Chapter 13 in E.B. Barbier (ed.), *The Economics of Environment and Development: Selected Essays*, Cheltenham, UK and Northampton, MA, USA: Edward Elgar, pp. 281–307.

Barbier, E.B. (2000), 'Valuing the environment as input: applications to mangrove–fishery linkages', *Ecological Economics*, **35**, 47–61.

Barbier, E.B. (2003), 'Habitat–fishery linkages and mangrove loss in Thailand', *Contemporary Economic Policy*, **21**(1), 59–77.

Barbier, E.B. (2007), 'Valuing ecosystem services as productive inputs', *Economic Policy*, **22**(49), 177–229.

Barbier, E.B. and I. Strand (1998), 'Valuing mangrove–fishery linkages: a case study of Campeche, Mexico', *Environmental and Resource Economics*, **12**, 151–66.

Barbier, E.B., I. Strand and S. Sathirathai (2002), 'Do open access conditions affect the valuation of an externality? Estimating the welfare effects of mangrove–fishery linkages', *Environmental and Resource Economics*, **21**(4), 343–67.

Bjørndal, T. and J.M. Conrad (1987), 'The dynamics of an open access fishery', *Canadian Journal of Economics*, **20**, 74–85.

Boscolo, M. and J.R. Vincent (2003), 'Nonconvexities in the production of timber, biodiversity, and carbon sequestration', *Journal of Environmental Economics and Management*, **46**, 251–68.

Cameron, C.A. and P. Trivedi (1998), *Regression Analysis of Count Data*, Cambridge: Cambridge University Press.

Carpenter, S.R., D. Ludwig and W.A. Brock (1999), 'Management of eutrophication for lakes subject to potentially irreversible change', *Ecological Applications*, **9**(3), 751–71.

Clark, C. (1976), *Mathematical Bioeconomics*, New York: John Wiley and Sons.

Considine, T.J. and D.F. Larson (2006), 'The environment as a factor of production', *Journal of Environmental Economics and Management*, **52**, 645–62.

Ellis, G.M. and A.C. Fisher (1987), 'Valuing the environment as input', *Journal of Environmental Management*, **25**, 149–56.

FAO (2003), 'Status and trends in mangrove area extent worldwide', by M.L. Wilkie and S. Fortuna, *Forest Resources Assessment Working Paper*, No. 63, Forest Resources Division, Food and Agricultural Organization of the United Nations, Rome.

Finnoff, D. and J. Tschirhart (2003), 'Harvesting in an eight-species ecosystem', *Journal of Environmental Economics and Management*, **45**, 589–611.

Finnoff, D., A. Strong and J. Tschirhart (2008), 'A bioeconomic model of cattle stocking on rangeland threatened by invasive plants and nitrogen deposition', *American Journal of Agricultural Economics*, **90**(4), 1074–84.

Freeman, A.M. III (1982), *Air and Water Pollution Control: A Benefit–Cost Assessment*, New York: John Wiley.

Freeman, A.M. III (1991), 'Valuing environmental resources under alternative management regimes', *Ecological Economics*, **3**, 247–56.

Freeman, A.M. III (2003), *The Measurement of Environmental and Resource Values: Theory and Methods*, 2nd edn, Washington, DC: Resources for the Future.

Gren, I.-M., K. Elofsson and P. Jannke (1997), 'Cost-effective nutrient reductions to the Baltic Sea', *Environmental and Resource Economics*, **10**, 341–62.

Hansen, L. and D. Hellerstein (2007), 'The value of the reservoir services gained with soil conservation', *Land Economics*, **83**(3), 285–301.

Heal, G.M., E.B. Barbier, K.J. Boyle, A.P. Covich, S.P. Gloss, C.H. Hershner, J.P. Hoehn, C.M. Pringle, S. Polasky, K. Segerson and K. Shrader-Frechette (2005), *Valuing Ecosystem Services: Toward Better Environmental Decision Making*, Washington, DC: The National Academies Press.

Homans, F.R. and J.E. Wilen (1997), 'A model of regulated open access resource use', *Journal of Environmental Economics and Management*, **32**, 1–21.

Janssen, M.A., J.M. Anderies and B.H. Walker (2004), 'Robust strategies for managing rangelands with multiple stable attractors', *Journal of Environmental Economics and Management*, **47**, 140–62.

Kahn, J.R. and W.M. Kemp (1985), 'Economic losses associated with the degradation of an ecosystem: the case of submerged aquatic vegetation in Chesapeake Bay', *Journal of Environmental Economics and Management*, **12**, 246–63.

Kaiser, B. and J. Roumasset (2002), 'Valuing indirect ecosystem services: the case of tropical watersheds', *Environment and Development Economics*, **7**, 701–14.

Knowler, D. and E.B. Barbier (2005), 'Managing the Black Sea anchovy fishery with nutrient enrichment and a biological invader', *Marine Resource Economics*, **20**, 263–85.

Knowler, D., E.B. Barbier and I. Strand (2001), 'An open-access model of fisheries and nutrient enrichment in the Black Sea', *Marine Resource Economics*, **16**, 195–217.

Lynne, G.D., P. Conroy and F.J. Prochaska (1981), 'Economic value of marsh areas for marine production processes', *Journal of Environmental Economics and Management*, **8**, 175–86.

Mardle, S., C. James, C. Pipitone and M. Kienzle (2004), 'Bioeconomic interactions in an established fishing exclusion zone: the Gulf of Castellammare, NW Sicily', *Natural Resource Modeling*, **17**(4), 393–447.

McConnell, K.E. and I.E. Strand (1989), 'Benefits from commercial fisheries when demand and supply depend on water quality', *Journal of Environmental Economics and Management*, **17**, 284–92.

Michener, R. and C. Tighe (1992), 'A Poisson regression model of highway fatalities', *American Economic Review*, **82**(2), 452–6.

Nalle, D.J., C.A. Montgomery, J.L. Arthur, S. Polasky and N.H. Schumaker (2004), 'Modeling joint production of wildlife and timber', *Journal of Environmental Economics and Management*, **48**(3), 997–1017.

Olson, M.K. (2004), 'Are novel drugs more risky for patients than less novel drugs?', *Journal of Health Economics*, **23**, 1135–58.

Parks, P. and M. Bonifaz (1997), 'Nonsustainable use of renewable resources: mangrove deforestation and mariculture in Ecuador', *Marine Resource Economics*, **9**, 1–18.

Ricketts, T.H., G.C. Daily, P.R. Ehrlich and C.D. Michener (2004). 'Economic value of tropical forest to coffee production', *Proceedings of the National Academy of Science*, **101**(304), 12579–82.

Rodwell, L.D., E.B.Barbier, C.M. Roberts and T.R. McClanahan (2002), 'A model of tropical marine reserve–fishery linkages', *Natural Resource Modeling*, **15**(4), 453–86.

Rose, N.L. (1990), 'Profitability and product quality: economic determinants of airline safety performance', *Journal of Political Economy*, **98**(5), 944–64.

Sathirathai, S. and E.B. Barbier (2001), 'Valuing mangrove conservation in Southern Thailand', *Contemporary Economic Policy*, **19**, 109–22.

Schnute, J. (1977), 'Improved estimates of the Schaefer production model: theoretical considerations', *Journal of the Fisheries Research Board of Canada*, **34**, 583–603.

Settle, C. and J.F. Shogren (2002), 'Modeling native-exotic species within Yellowstone Lake', *American Journal of Agricultural Economics*, **84**(5), 1323–8.

Smith, M.D. (2007), 'Generating value in habitat-dependent fisheries: the importance of fishery management institutions', *Land Economics*, **83**, 59–73.

Sumaila, U.R. (2002), 'Marine protected area performance in a model of a fishery', *Natural Resource Modeling*, **15**(4), 439–51.

Swallow, S.K. (1994), 'Renewable and nonrenewable resource theory applied to coastal agriculture, forest, wetland and fishery linkages', *Marine Resource Economics*, **9**, 291–310.

Thompson, J.R. and G. Hollis (1995), 'Hydrological modeling and the sustainable development of the Hadejia-Nguru Wetlands, Nigeria', *Hydrological Sciences Journal*, **40**, 97–116.

Winkelmann, R. (2003), *Econometric Analysis of Count Data*, 4th edn, Berlin: Springer-Verlag.

Wu, J., K. Skelton-Groth, W.G. Boggess and R.M. Adams (2003), 'Pacific salmon restoration: trade-offs between economic efficiency and political acceptance', *Contemporary Economic Policy*, **21**(1), 78–89.

7. Discounting and the discount rate

7.1 INTRODUCTION

As will be recalled from Chapter 1, the key statement in a CBA is the Net Present Value (NPV) test. This asks whether the *discounted* value of future benefits is greater or less than the *discounted* value of future costs, added up over a defined time period. Chapter 1 also briefly explained how discounting is carried out. To repeat: cost and benefit flows are discounted using a discount rate which, for now, is assumed to be the rate of interest, *i*. The present value of a cost or benefit (X) received in time t is typically calculated as follows:

$$PV\,(X_t) = X_t[(1 + i)^{-t}] \qquad \text{(7.1, as shown initially as (1.1))}$$

The expression in square brackets is known as a *discount factor*. Discount factors have the property that they always lie between 0 and +1. When a benefit or cost happens in the period in which the analysis is being undertaken ('year 0'), no discounting occurs, and the discount factor equals 1. As we consider benefits and costs further and further into the future, the effect of discounting increases and the discount factor falls towards zero. The further away in time a cost or benefit occurs (the higher the value of *t*), the lower the discount factor (the greater the effect of discounting). Since the discount factor is less than 1, this reduces the present value of future benefits or costs. The higher the discount rate *i* for a given *t*, the lower the discount factor, since a higher discount rate means a greater preference for things now rather than later.

Discounting may be done in CBA in one of two ways: either by finding the net value of benefits minus costs for each time period (usually each year), and discounting each of these annual net benefit flows throughout the lifetime of the project; or by calculating discounted values for each element of a project, then summing the discounted elements. For example, adding up total discounted labour costs, total discounted material costs and total discounted energy saving benefits. Both approaches should give identical answers.

So, for example, suppose that a project to improve river quality undertaken in 2008 will generate £400 000 a year in revenues to the owner of

Table 7.1 *Benefits over time from a river improvement scheme with a 5 per cent discount rate*

Year (t)	Benefits in year t, £k	Discount factor at 5%	Discounted value
2009	400	0.9523	380.92
2010	400	0.907	362.8
2011	400	0.8638	345.52
2012	400	0.8227	329.08
2013	400	0.7835	313.4
		Sum PV	1731.72

Table 7.2 *Benefits over time from a river improvement scheme with a 3 per cent discount rate*

Year (t)	Benefits in year t, £k	Discount factor at 3%	Discounted value
2009	400	0.9708	388.32
2010	400	0.9426	377.04
2011	400	0.9151	366.04
2012	400	0.88884	355.536
2013	400	0.8626	345.04
		Sum PV	1831.976

fishing rights on a river, through greater licence sales. If the discount rate is 5 per cent, then for the first five years after the improvement, the discounted value of these benefits is calculated as shown in Table 7.1. Here, 'Sum PV' is the sum of the discounted values over years 1–5 of the project, and the discount factor is $(1 + i)^{-t}$, which is $(1 + 0.05)^{-t}$ in this case. Notice that the discount factor declines as we have to wait longer for the benefits. By convention, the year in which the first spending of resources on a project occurs is referred to as year zero, and we do not discount year zero costs and benefits, so that the present value and the current-period value are the same. The example in Table 7.1 assumes that initial investments in water quality happen in 2008 (year zero), and that benefits start to appear in year 1 (2009). What can be seen is that the same current-value amount (£400 000) gets smaller in present value terms as it gets further away in the future – compare the discounted values in 2012 (year 4) and 2013 (year 5). If a lower discount rate had been used, say 3 per cent, all present values would be increased, as shown in Table 7.2. As can be seen, with the same current value revenue stream, the total present value is higher with a 3 per cent discount rate than with a 5 per cent rate. This effect of discount rates on the PV of costs and benefits gets more pronounced the further into the future benefits and costs occur. For example, planting a forest today might generate an expected current value of £50 000 in 50 years' time. At a 5 per cent discount rate, this is worth £4360. At a 3 per cent discount rate, it is worth £11 405 in present value terms. Avoiding damage costs of £500 000 due to a severe flood in 100 years' time is worth £3802 today at 5 per cent and £26 016 at 3 per cent. Box 7.1 shows the effects of choosing a higher or lower discount rate in terms of appropriate policy choices over climate change.

BOX 7.1   DISCOUNT RATES AND CLIMATE CHANGE POLICY (1)

The Stern Review (2007) was a UK government-sponsored enquiry into the economics of climate change, which focused on the question of 'what action is justified now in terms of avoiding future damages?'. The report attained a very high degree of prominence in the popular press, and was cited by the then UK Prime Minister, Tony Blair, as providing evidence that urgent action to cut greenhouse gas (GHG) emissions by a substantial amount was justified. The report states that 'If we don't act (now), the overall costs and risks of climate change will be equivalent to losing at least 5% of global GDP each year, now and forever. If a wider range of risks and impacts is taken into account [this] could rise to 20% of GDP' (Summary, p. xv). These are clearly worrying statements that prompt urgent action by all countries to reduce future climate change by cutting emissions.

The Review has, however, attracted a lot of critical comment from economists. Here we focus on issues around the choice of discount rate. This matters enormously in the context of climate change, since the 'optimal' economic response is to cut emissions to the point where the marginal cost of pollution abatement is equal to the *present value* of avoided future damages. It is in calculating this present value that the discount rate matters, especially given that damages are likely to extend far into the future, and to be potentially increasing over time as the stock of GHGs rises and as environmental systems get more sensitive to increased temperatures. Nordhaus (2007) notes that the main conclusion of the Review – cut emissions by a substantial amount now – is at odds with most economic analysis of the problem, which suggests that emission reductions should begin at a low rate, but then 'ramp up' over time. Put another way, the sacrifice in current-period consumption or GDP per capita should begin low, but then rise. Nordhaus notes that the Stern Review uses a very low discount rate of 1.4 per cent per annum, which leads it to recommend steep reductions in the short term since, at this low rate, damage costs far into the future (for example from 2200 on) count for relatively more. The 1.4 per cent rate comes from the use of equation (7.3) with values of ρ = 0.01 and η = 1 and g = 1.03. The value of 0.01 for the pure time preference rate is defended on the grounds of being consistent with an ethical position that the only aspect for pure time preference which should be allowed for is 'ultimate extinction'. The value of 1 for the elasticity of consumption implies a rather unusual shape for the utility function.

Nordhaus notes that using a 1.4 per cent discount rate would lead us to accept a big reduction in the incomes of poor people living today (in his example, from $10 000 to $4400) to reduce future annual damages from $130 000 to $129 870 some 200 years from now and continuing thereafter. Clearly what seems 'fair' or 'ethical' depends on whether you are a poor person living today or a rich person living 200 years from now. Nordhaus also runs the DICE climate change model comparing the effects of using a discount rate of 1.4 per cent with his 'more realistic', higher discount rate. He finds that, using the 'more realistic' values, the model comes up with an optimal emission reduction of 14 per cent on 1990 levels by 2015 and an associated carbon price of $35/ton, rising to $85/ton C in 2050 and $206 in 2100. In contrast, using the Stern Review's discount rate of 1.4 per cent gives an optimal reduction in 2015 of 53 per cent, and an associated carbon price of $360/ton C.

The judgement that the discount rate used in the Stern Review is 'too low' is also shared by Weitzman (2007), in his commentary on the review. Weitzman uses the example of a policy to sacrifice 1 per cent of GDP today to avoid damages of 5 per cent of GDP in 100 years' time. Using the Stern Review discount rate of 1.4 per cent, this has a benefit–cost ratio of 4.5, so the advice would be that the policy improves net social welfare over time. However, using what Weitzman refers to as more realistic values for pure time preference and the consumption elasticity (ρ and η respectively in equation (7.3)) of 2 per cent per annum and 0.02, and a growth rate of the economy of 2 per cent gives a social discount rate of 6 per cent. At this rate, the benefit/cost ratio for the same 1 per cent sacrifice in today's GDP to avoid expected future damages of 5 per cent of GDP in 100 years is 0.1; in other words, the present value of costs is *ten times* the expected value of benefits, which would cause us to advise against the project.

Finally, Gollier et al. (2008) have noted that declining discount rates should be applied to calculations of optimal climate policy, since costs and benefits stretch over such a long period. Applying such rates to costs and benefits as used in the Stern Review they reach a similar conclusion to that reached by Nordhaus and Weitzman: namely, that Stern's recommendations will lead to welfare losses over time.

One extra 'trick' concerns the PV of a cost or a benefit which goes on forever. This seems a strange notion, but consider a proposal to allow a development which will result in a species becoming extinct (for example because its last habitat is destroyed. One cost of the project would be the forgone benefits of conserving this species, which would be lost forever.

Such perpetual costs result from *irreversible* actions (Krutilla and Fisher, 1985). The PV of a perpetual stream of lost benefits, B_t, is given by:

$$\text{PV } (B_t) = \sum_{t=0}^{\infty} B_t (1 + i)^{-t}$$

$$= \left(\frac{B_t}{i} \right) \qquad (7.2)$$

where B_t is the forgone annual benefits from protecting the species – for example, people's WTP to protect it – and i is the discount rate. Krutilla and Fisher (1985) noted that for many protection/development decisions, one might expect the benefits of protection to grow over time, because (i) as economic growth occurs, natural environments become more developed, and thus for example wilderness areas become more scarce; and (ii) because there is a general presumption that as people get richer, their WTP for environmental protection rises faster than their WTP for other goods (Kriström and Riera, 1996; Jacobsen and Hanley, 2008). This growth over time in the benefits of protecting natural assets acts to offset the effects of discounting: if benefits are growing in real terms at rate g, then the present value of lost protection benefits (assuming an infinite period time horizon) becomes $(B_t/i - g)$. Allowing for the differential growth rates of development and protection benefits and costs in this way in calculating Net Present Values is known as the *Krutilla–Fisher model* – see Chapter 12 for more details on this. A comprehensive treatment is given in Krutilla and Fisher (1985), whilst the approach is also discussed in Hanley and Spash (1993).

7.2   WHY DISCOUNT AT ALL?

Discounting means placing a lower value on benefits and costs, the further away in time they occur. Why might this make sense? First, we should make clear that this is nothing to do with inflation. Inflation causes the prices of all goods and services to rise at some average rate (for example 3 per cent per year). But even if we removed the effects of inflation from the projected future benefits of, say, a new wind farm, converting them from 'nominal, current values' into 'real, current values', we would still want to discount these real, current values. But again, why?

Two main reasons have been given for discounting. These revolve around:

- the productivity of capital, and
- preferences.

7.2.1 The Social Opportunity Cost of Capital

Economies grow over time for many reasons, but an important one is that by building up the stock of capital, an economy increases its potential output. Investing in a new factory is expected to generate a flow of returns over time to the owner of that capital, in terms of annual sales of goods produced. Across the entire economy, invested capital generates a positive rate of return, meaning that the value of consumption goods in year $t + 1$ that could be produced should all of the resources of an economy be invested in year t, will be greater than the maximum value of consumption goods that could be produced in year t. However, capital is scarce: investing £1 million in a new factory means we cannot invest the same £1 million in another scheme. Choosing to invest in a particular scheme thus involves an opportunity cost, which is the return on capital forgone from some other use (in particular, from its most profitable alternative). Across the economy as a whole, we could rank investment projects in terms of their rates of return.

These rates of return show the net benefits from investing resources rather than consuming. At the margin, this is known as the *opportunity cost of capital*;[1] and, if transfer payments are excluded, and externalities internalized, it can be used to measure the *social opportunity cost of capital*, r. As Pearce (1983, p. 43) explains: 'To use the [social opportunity cost of capital] for discounting purposes is very appealing [and] is equivalent to saying that our project in the public sector must do at least as well as the projects it displaces'.

Indeed, we could say that using up any resources in a particular activity has an opportunity cost which can be incorporated in a forgone rate of return measure. As Nordhaus (2007) notes, for risk-free US Treasury securities, the rate of return on capital was 2.7 per cent in 2007, whilst the average rate of return to capital in the US economy was around 6 per cent per annum. Thus, we could choose to discount future benefits and costs at 6 per cent, since this represents the return that could have been earned elsewhere in the economy had we not undertaken a project.

Pearce et al. (1989) reviewed 'environmental critiques' of such opportunity cost-based discounting. The first of these is that the rationale behind discounting only works if one assumes that all returns from a project are re-invested. But if they are partly consumed, then this merely suggests that the discount rate should be reduced, rather than that the way in which discounting occurs be changed. The second relates to the idea that a future environmental damage of £x can be compensated for by investing £y ($y < x$) now, so that it accumulates sufficiently to pay for an offsetting of the environmental damage of £x in the future. What if such re-investment does not occur, or what if future damages cannot actually be compensated for? The former objection misinterprets the Kaldor–Hicks compensation test set out in Chapter 2 – recall that this only talks about the potential for compensation of losses, not that compensation is actually put in place. However, the second is more serious, and speaks to the need to believe that we could potentially offset a future damage. Pearce et al. (1989) also point out that lowering the discount rate on environmental criteria might well result in increases in environmental damage.

BOX 7.2   DISCOUNT RATES AND CLIMATE POLICY (2)

As explained in the main text, rates of return on capital vary across the economy, a useful distinction being between a risk-free rate, r_f, and a risky rate r_m, the latter being positively correlated with economy-wide fluctuations in returns. We expect the risk-free rate to be substantially lower than the risky rate, the difference representing the average pay-off for risk-taking which an efficient capital market should reward. But which should be used to discount the costs and benefits of climate change policy, the risk-free or the risk-adjusted discount rate? Weitzman (2007) explains that the answer depends on whether the pay-off from investing in emission reductions is independent from returns to investment across the economy as a whole,[2] since the 'climate policy discount rate' should be a weighted average of the risky and risk-free rates, the weights being the correlation between returns from climate investments and returns across the economy as a whole, and should decline over time (so that the climate policy discount rate should be lower in 100 years than now: see Weitzman, 2007, equation 7). Weitzman argues that the implicit value for this correlation coefficient in the kinds of models of climate change damages that the Stern Review uses is equal to 1, implying that returns from the climate change project and the economy-wide returns are perfectly correlated with each other. This implies that it is the average of returns on capital across the economy as a whole – rather than the risk-free rate – which should be used to discount costs and benefits. Yet this implies a discount rate much bigger than the Stern value of 1.4 per cent. As we saw in Box 7.1, this will make a big difference to conclusions on the optimal time profile of actions to reduce emissions. Concluding that a risky rate of return should be used to discount public policy choices also chimes with Lind's earlier statement that in general, there is no reason to suppose that the returns from public investments are uncorrelated with returns across the economy as a whole (Lind, 1982). But, in closing, Weitzman observes that there are actually some good reasons to think that this correlation is not a strong as one might suppose, implying that some weighted average of the risky and risk-free discount rates should be used.

7.2.2 Time Preferences

The other motivation for discounting is that 'pure time preference' – the desire for benefits to come sooner rather than later – is a fundamental feature of human desires. We are all impatient! Various motivations have been suggested for time preference: impatience, the fact that we might not be around in the future to collect on benefits, that future benefits are less certain than present-day benefits, and that we might expect to be richer in the future and thus will value each extra pound of income as less valuable than we do today.

An important distinction is between a discount rate that applies to individual well-being, and that which might be applied to collective well-being. We could refer to the former as being a reflection of individual time preference, and the latter as a reflection of social time preference. It is also important to distinguish between the discounting of future utility, and the discounting of future consumption – more on this below. Finally, we can distinguish between time preference rates which are inferred from people's behaviour (such as in Box 7.3: see also Warner and Pleeter, 2001), and time preference rates which reflect some judgement by the analyst on what they ought to be. This latter might reflect notions of inter-generational fairness (section 7.4). Future interest rates can also be econometrically estimated through the use of a time series model where the future properties of the interest rate are determined by its own past behaviour (see Hepburn et al., 2009).

We begin with the notion of individual time preferences. People, as argued above, have a number of motives for preferring benefits the sooner they occur. Rob would rather have a free test ride around Brands Hatch on the new Honda Fireblade this month than wait 12 months. Why? Because Rob is impatient, or because he thinks there is a risk that the deal will fall through in 12 months' time, or because he might be physically unable to ride such a mean machine around Brands in 12 months' time if he puts his R1 through a hedge before then. More generally, assume that from people's behaviour or stated choices a 'pure' time preference rate could be inferred for a random sample of individuals in the UK. This rate, ρ, would show the rate at which people discount future benefits in terms of the utility they provide; it would be given by the slope of their indifference curve between utility now and utility at some point in the future. The question then becomes: should governments base their policy and project decisions on the basis of a discount rate founded on individual pure time preferences? Marglin (1963) argued that they should not, since saving and therefore investment generates public good-type benefits which would be under-supplied if decisions were based on individual time preference rates. Moreover, following Sagoff (1988), we

BOX 7.3   DISCOUNTING LIVES SAVED

Anne Alberini and colleagues looked at the rate at which people in Italy discount future lives saved (Alberini et al., 2007). The idea is quite simple: society sometimes faces choices between investing in programmes which can save a few lives in the present, or more lives in the future – for example, in terms of the clean-up of toxic waste sites. At what rate do people discount future life saving? In other words, how many more lives need to be saved at some future point in time for people to prefer this to a project which, say, saves 100 lives right now? 150? 200? Alberini et al. devised an experiment where people were asked to choose between two alternative programmes for cleaning up contaminated land in Italy:

1.   Programme A saved 100 years as soon as it was complete;
2.   Programme B saved a greater number of lives (call this number X) but would take longer to complete (call the waiting time T).

People were told that the costs of the two programmes were the same, and then asked to choose between them. By varying the rates of X and T across people in the sample, the authors found that (i) on average, the rate at which people discount future lives saved is 12 per cent; but that (ii) this rate declined as the value of T increased. For example, if the delay in saving lives was 10 years, the discount rate was 16 per cent, but if the delay was 40 years, the discount rate fell to 4 per cent: the graph below shows the results. This is evidence of 'non-constant' discounting happening in people's minds, which can be contrasted to the usual assumption of constant, exponential discounting of benefits and costs.

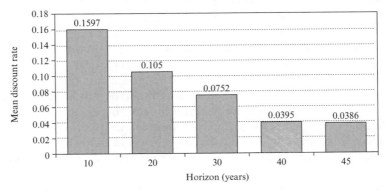

Discount rates for saving lives by horizon

Evidence that people's behaviour is consistent with declining discount rates can be found now in many studies (see Hepburn and Koundouri, 2007, for references).

might think that individuals have different time preferences in their role as citizens rather than in their role as consumers. This suggests that the rate of *social time preference* should not necessarily be the same as individual time preference rates (see Sugden and Williams, 1978, p. 220).

An additional complication is that the benefits and costs of a given policy or project will be measured in terms of monetary values, rather than in terms of utility. This means that a preference-based discount rate defined in terms of consumption is needed, rather than one defined in terms of utility. Consider a simple utility function $U = U(C)$, so that utility depends only on consumption. What might affect preferences for consumption over time (for example C_t, C_{t+1}, C_{t+2}...)? The answer clearly lies in the functional form of $U(C)$. As people get richer, the extra utility from each extra pound's worth of consumption might be expected to fall: that is, the marginal utility of consumption falls with rising income. This suggests that to identify a discount rate based on preferences but defined in terms of consumption, we need to know about the growth rate of (per-capita) consumption or income over time, and how marginal utility responds to this increase. Refer to the former as g and the latter as η. The term η is known as the elasticity of the marginal utility of consumption, or more concisely as the consumption elasticity, and describes the curvature of $U(.)$.[3] We can now define a *consumption rate of interest*,[4] i, as:

$$i = \rho + \eta g \qquad (7.3)$$

As Weitzman (2007) points out, ρ and η are measures of preferences, and g depends on technological progress and resource accumulation in the economy. The value of η measures both the rate at which utility rises with consumption, and the average rate of risk aversion. Imagine that we had calculated from observations that the average rate of pure time preference for Germans was 2 per cent (0.02), that their economy has a long-run growth rate of 3 per cent, and that the consumption elasticity was 1.5. Then the consumption rate of interest for use by the German government in undertaking CBA analysis of policy decisions would be equal to (0.02 + (1.5*0.03)) or 0.065, that is $i = 6.5$ per cent. Arrow et al. (2004) review the components of equation (7.3), and arrive at an estimate of i for the US economy of between 3 per cent and 6 per cent.

There are thus two candidates for use as 'the' social discount rate in public policy and project appraisal – the social rate of time preference, measured as the consumption rate of interest, i; and the social opportunity cost of capital, r. In an optimal economy, these will actually be equal, that is we would find that consumption patterns and investment spending had been arranged by market forces such that:

$$r = i = \rho + \eta g \qquad (7.4)$$

This is known as the Ramsey condition, named after the economist Frank Ramsey, who was the first to formalize the optimal inter-temporal behaviour of an economy. In reality, we might expect that the two measures will be different, so that the government needs to choose the discount rate. Indeed, the choice of discount rate is as much a political decision as an economic one. Arguing for a zero discount rate, or a very low discount rate, is a value judgement which needs to be justified as much as arguing for a higher rate, as Pearce et al. (1989) pointed out. However, we might be

---

BOX 7.4   DISCOUNTING FORESTS

Forests generate benefits which can stretch many hundreds of years into the future, for example in terms of acting as a habitat for wildlife, or as a carbon store. Planting forests for their timber can also have long-term benefits depending on the 'rotation period', the length of time it takes trees to reach their economic optimum size. This will depend on species, climate and location, and can range from as short as 20 years for fast-growing species in New Zealand or Africa, to over 100 years for hardwoods planted in the UK. Hepburn and Koundouri (2007) show the effects of discount rate choice for a number of forest investments. Here we make use of their results for two forest types:

- Type A: a forest where trees take 60 years to reach economic maturity; and
- Type B: a forest where trees take 120 years to reach economic maturity.

The main costs and benefits for each type are shown below:

Year(s)	Activity	Real cost/benefit (£/ha)	
		Type A forest	Type B forest
0	Site preparation	−50	−100
0	Planting	−200	−800
1	Weed control	−50	−100
15 (A), 5, 20 (B)	Initial thinning/ pruning	−50	−200
40 (A), 60 (B)	Thinning 1	1,000	4,000
50 (A), 80 (B)	Thinning 2	2,000	8,000
100 (B)	Thinning 3	–	10,000
60 (A), 120 (B)	Final felling	4,000	12,000

Three different discount rate regimes were considered: a constant 6 per cent, a constant 3.5 per cent, and a declining 3.5 per cent rate as per HM Treasury (2003). Results were as follows:

	Net Present Value*, Forest A (60 years to felling), £/hectare	Net Present Value*, Forest B (120 years to felling), £/hectare
Using a constant 6% rate	−200	− 1250
Using a constant 3.5% rate	+400	− 300
Using a declining rate, starting at 3.5%	+550	+ 250

Note: * numbers are rounded.

Looking first at Forest A, we see that it fails the NPV test at a constant discount rate of 6 per cent, but passes at a constant rate of 3.5 per cent; this shows the effects of cutting the discount rate on the present value of the bulk of benefits received when the forest is felled in 60 years' time. The declining rate schedule increases the NPV again, since by year 60 we are only discounting at 3 per cent rather than 3.5 per cent. For Forest B, the effects of discounting are more pronounced, since the bulk of benefits are not forthcoming until 80–120 years from now. The NPV is now negative using either constant rate, but the declining schedule means that the present value of benefits is increased so that the NPV becomes positive. Note that the authors did not include any non-market benefits or costs of forests in these calculations.

able to develop a positivist argument which addresses the question of *how* we discount for environmental benefits and costs, rather than a normative argument about the value which society should decide for the social rate of time preference in CBA. In this light, we now consider some alternatives to 'conventional' discounting.

7.3 ALTERNATIVES TO 'CONVENTIONAL' DISCOUNTING

7.3.1 Declining Discount Rates over Time

The conventional approach to discounting assumes that there is one value for the discount rate which is 'correct' for discounting costs and benefits, irrespective of how far into the future they occur. Thus, if a benefit in 10 years' time is discounted at 5 per cent, so will a benefit received in 100 years' time. For far-in-the-future benefits and costs, small changes in the discount rate have very big impacts on present values. Recently, economists have questioned this practice of using a constant discount rate, and have recommended instead that the discount rate should *decline* as costs and benefits further into the future are appraised. The main reasons for this are summarized by Hepburn and Koundouri (2007), and Groom et al. (2005).[5] First, there appears to be experimental evidence that people discount near-in-time benefits and costs at a higher rate than further-away-in-time benefits and costs (see Box 7.3). If this is so, then the time profile of the social discount rate used in CBA should reflect this phenomenon. A second argument is that there is uncertainty over the future value of the social rate of discount. As we saw in equation (7.3), this rate depends partly on growth in per capita consumption. Yet this is hard to predict, even if we are only looking forward a few years from the present. The effect of such uncertainty is to produce an uncertainty-adjusted discount rate which declines over time, on one view because of the desire for precautionary saving in the face of a risky future. This would modify equation (7.3) in the following way:

$$i = \rho + \eta g - \frac{1}{2}\eta P \operatorname{var}(g) \tag{7.5}$$

In (7.5), P is a measure of precautionary saving, and var(g) is the variance of the growth rate of per capita consumption. The effect is to reduce the value of i over time, according to people's attitudes to risk and what they believe about future growth prospects (for more details, see Groom et al., 2005). Hepburn and Koundouri (2007) show how the 'certainty-equivalent' discount rate – the rate they recommend for use in CBA – declines with time, in a situation where there are two equally likely possible future outcomes for the growth in per capita consumption with implied social discount rates of 2 per cent and 6 per cent. This sees the certainty-equivalent discount rate falling from 4 per cent in year 1 to 2.4 per cent for benefits or costs accruing in 200 years' time (see Table 7.3).

Theory suggests that in an uncertain economic environment it is the persistency of the shocks on the growth rate of consumption (in the consumption-based approach) and of the shocks on short-term interest rates (in the production-based approach) which determines the time path of the socially efficient discount rate. These two explanations are coherent with each other: persistent shocks on growth expectations translate into persistent shocks on interest rates, both yielding Declining Discount Rates (DDRs) (see Gollier et al., 2008).

The official guidance for CBA for public policy and projects in the UK – the Treasury's *Green Book* – now recommends a declining discount rate

Table 7.3 Numerical example of a declining certainty-equivalent discount rate

Time (years from present)	1	10	50	100	200
Discount factor for 2% rate	0.98	0.82	0.37	0.14	0.02
Discount factor for 6% rate	0.94	0.56	0.05	0.00	0.00
Certainty-equivalent discount factor	0.96	0.69	0.21	0.07	0.01
Certainty-equivalent (average) discount rate	4.0	3.8	3.1	2.7	2.4

Source: Hepburn and Koundouri (2007).

Table 7.4 HM Treasury (2003) Green Book discount rates

Period of years	0–30	31–75	76–125	126–200	201–300	301+
Discount rate (%)	3.5	3.0	2.5	2.0	1.5	1.0

Source: HM Treasury (2003, p. 99).

is used, falling from 3.5 per cent for benefits and costs up to 30 years in the future, to 3 per cent for years 31–75, to 2.5% in years 76–125 (see Table 7.4). The effects of this scheme, relative to conventional constant-rate discounting, is to increase the present value of long-term benefits and costs.

7.3.2 Generational Models

In fact, a number of alternatives to the conventional approach to discounting have been put forward. One idea has been suggested by Sumaila and Walters (2005), to address the ethical problems of using the time preferences of the current generation to discount benefits and costs occurring to those born into future generations. Sumaila and Walters' method involves breaking down the practice of discounting into two components: applying conventional discounting to benefits and costs of those living at the time resources are committed; but then including an additional present value calculation for those 'entering the stakeholder population' in later years. These latter individuals are assumed to only start discounting benefits and costs from the point in time at which they 'enter the population'. Thus, for example, if a nuclear waste storage programme, begun in 2010, imposes costs of £1 billion in 2060, this is discounted using a factor of $(1 + i)^{-50}$ for those who were living in 2010, but is only discounted using a factor of

$(1 + i)^{-5}$ for those born in 2055. Note that the same ethical parameter (i) is used in both cases, since it is hard to calculate what the time preference rate of those born in the future will be, but that this procedure reduces the effects of discounting on costs to future generations. An extension would allow for inclusion of a separate rate of i, say i^{fg}, which represents the willingness of the present generation to give up consumption today in favour of those born in the future – an altruistic endowment again based on the preferences of those living now.

Schelling (1995) has also cautioned that we need to think carefully about discounting benefits and costs which stretch over several generations. He notes that the key point about climate change policy is that, by engaging in emission reductions today, we are incurring costs so that others in the future can enjoy benefits (reduced climate change impacts). In such long-term schemes, the arguments for a positive discount rate based on pure time preference (impatience) are less appealing, but we may still prefer to benefit those future people closer in time to us than further away in time. He also notes that the other justification for discounting – that people get richer over time, and that the marginal utility of income falls as part of this progress – may not hold for climate change policy, since those who pay for abatement are, on the whole, the rich West, and those who benefit in the future are, on the whole, the still poorer and thus *higher* marginal utility people in developing countries. However, the logical implication is consequently that the rich West should sacrifice current consumption to benefit people in poor countries *now*, rather than investing in greenhouse gas abatement to benefit them in the future. Why? Because if the incomes of poor countries are expected to rise over time, then the highest marginal utility of 'aid' (broadly defined), is now, not in 50 years' time. This means that abatement policies in the West should be compared with development projects, so that we can find out where the biggest return on sacrificing

---

BOX 7.5   DISCOUNTING AND NUCLEAR POWER

For many governments worldwide, deciding on whether to invest in nuclear power is a vital aspect of energy policy. In the UK, the government has recently confirmed that new nuclear power stations – probably sited at the same locations as existing nuclear plants – will form a key part of energy supply over the next 50 years. Applying CBA to potential nuclear power investments shows up some of the implications of discount rate choice, since major costs are associated with decommissioning at the end of the reactor's life, whilst wastes must be stored far into the future. Investing in nuclear power thus implies a large capital cost at the beginning of the project, a series of operating costs and revenues from electricity sales stretching over the lifetime of the plant, a stream of decommissioning costs at closure, and then a stream of storage costs far into the future. We might also include the value of displaced CO_2 emissions over the operating period of the plant, if nuclear energy displaces fossil fuel-powered energy in terms of national electricity supply.

Groom et al. (2005) use nuclear power as a case study to show the effects of declining discount rates on NPV. The main working assumptions they adopt are:

- construction costs of £2250 per kW, and a construction time of 6 years;
- an 85 per cent load factor;
- operating and fuel costs of 0.6p and 0.4p per kWh respectively;
- reactor lifetime of 40 years;
- decommissioning from year 40 to year 110, at a cost of £40 per kW per year;
- waste costs are included in decommissioning costs.

They then compare the NPV of the investment using three scenarios: a constant discount rate of 6 per cent, a constant rate of 3.5 per cent and a declining rate according to the work of Newell and Pizer (2003). This yields the following results:

Costs and benefits of a new nuclear power station, per kW

Revenues and costs (present values)	Constant 6% discount rate	Constant 3.5% discount rate	Declining discount rate over time
Sale of electricity	2527	4062	4210
Carbon credits	90	228	255
Capital costs	−2054	−2173	−2181
Operating costs	−1453	−2336	−2421
Decommissioning costs	−90	−427	−497
NPV	−980	−646	−634

Source: Adapted from Groom et al. (2005).

This shows that the effects of moving from a constant 6 per cent rate to a constant 3.5 per cent rate are actually more pronounced than moving to a declining rate (unlike the forestry example in Box 7.4). Observe that moving from 6 per cent to 3.5 per cent increases the PV of both benefits and costs, but that overall the NPV is still negative. Groom et al. (2005) also show the effects of using alternative approaches to calculating which declining discount rates to use: this turns out to have a noticeable effect on the size of NPV, although NPV remains negative in all their calculations.

current consumption in the West lies: benefiting the poor now, or the future poor?

With specific reference to discounting and climate change policy, we can note another modification to conventional discounting which has been suggested by Nordhaus (1991). Nordhaus was one of the first authors to apply quantitative economic analysis to investigate what reduction in greenhouse gas emissions might be optimal, under different assumptions about damage costs. He shows that the answer to this question depends on the present value of marginal damage costs, and that the discount rate for calculating this present value depends not just on economic parameters such as the growth rate of consumption over time, but also on 'natural' parameters, namely the rate at which increases in the stock of greenhouse gases feed into changes in global mean temperatures, and the rate at which greenhouse gases decay in the upper atmosphere.

7.4   DISCOUNTING AND RISK

All policies have uncertain outcomes. We do not know how much car drivers will reduce their annual mileage if we introduce a carbon tax; we do not know for how long a nuclear power station will last, nor how reliable it will be over a 30-year period. We do not know for sure the value of climate change damages due to storm events in the UK in 2020. Analysts are used to working with *estimates* of these future benefits and costs, and to categorizing possible *states of the world* which will influence the magnitude of these benefits and costs. For example, we could imagine a 'gloomy' prediction and an 'optimistic' prediction for the incidence of storms in 2020, and various alternative scenarios for how people will have adapted to flooding. These constitute the states of the world relevant to the problem of applying CBA in the face of uncertain events. As noted in Chapter 2, economists have differentiated between situations of *risk* and situations of *uncertainty*. In the former case, sufficient information exists to allow us to (i) predict all possible, relevant states of the world *and* (ii) assign a probability to their occurrence. In the latter case, we may not know all possible states of the world, or the likelihood of their occurrence. In what follows, the focus will be on risk: the assumption is that it is feasible to write down all possible outcomes relevant to a policy, and to assign a probability to each outcome. We refer back to Chapter 2, section 2.3, for recommendations on how to tackle the rather more difficult problem of uncertainty in CBA.

Financial analysts have developed a standard approach to incorporating risk in investment appraisal. 'Risk' here relates to the future variability in costs and benefits from investing in a new product, or building a factory, or buying a portfolio of shares (stocks). Risk can be measured using the standard deviation or variance of expected (predicted, possible) returns on an investment. One can think of two different kinds of return on an investment:

- the return that investors would demand if there is no risk attached to the investment;
- the *higher* return that risk-averse investors would demand for investing in a project with a particular level of risk.

The difference between the risk-free and the risky return can be called a 'risk premium'. For a particular investor, the risk premium he would demand for undertaking a particular project will depend on (i) the level of risk (the variability of costs and benefits) and (ii) his attitude to risk, which as we have already seen is referred to as his risk preferences. Many individuals are risk-averse, meaning that (a) their marginal utility of income is declining as their income (or wealth) increases and (b) they would require some payment for taking on a gamble where the expected value is zero (see Zerbe and Dively, 1994, chapter 15, for more details on the theoretical background to this).

However, the risk from undertaking a particular investment does not just depend on the variability of returns from this action, but on how this affects the variability of all sources of income to the investor – the returns from their portfolio. This will in turn depend on whether returns from a new investment are correlated with returns from the current portfolio, and if so, whether positively correlated (as returns from project X go up, returns from all projects I have invested in are also rising – perhaps because all are linked to overall economic activity), or negatively correlated so that returns from project X tend to go up when my other returns are actually declining. The extent to which returns from different investments move with each other is given by their covariance.[6] The risk attached to a portfolio of investments depends on how much is invested in each investment, their individual risk levels as measured by the standard deviation of returns, and the covariance between the investments in the portfolio. This portfolio risk will be lower than a simple average of risks across the elements of the portfolio, unless returns are perfectly correlated with each other. By diversifying (adding more investments to the portfolio), individuals can thus reduce the overall risks that they face. This focus on how actions affect returns from the whole portfolio of investments is relevant to the public sector as well as to individuals or firms. In considering how to undertake a particular project or policy, the government should thus

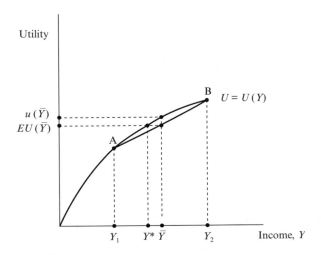

Source: Adapted from Pearce and Nash (1981, p. 68).

Figure 7.1 Utility income and risk

evaluate the extent to which risks from this project/policy are correlated with the costs and benefits of other projects/policies.

We are now in a position to figure out how to deal with risk in CBA. In fact, there are two approaches, which turn out to be two sides of the same coin. The first involves using a risk-free discount rate (say, the return on long-term government securities), and to 'adjust' costs and benefits to reflect their risk. This is done by transforming future flows into *certainty equivalents* – a concept we introduced above. To be more precise, consider Figure 7.1. This shows utility as a function of income for a representative voter. As income rises, utility rises, but at a decreasing rate: the utility function thus displays diminishing marginal utility and the individual is classified as risk-averse. Now consider a project which can impact on the individual's income depending on which state of the world occurs:

- State 1: individual gets income of Y_1, with a probability of 50 per cent.
- State 2: individual gets income of Y_2, with a probability of 50 per cent.

The utility from outcomes Y_1 and Y_2 *if they happened for certain* can be read off the utility function as $U(Y_1)$ and $U(Y_2)$. The expected outcome is $(\overline{Y}) = 0.5(Y_1) + 0.5(Y_2)$. If this level of income was received with certainty, then it would generate utility equal to $U(\overline{Y})$. However, this outcome is not certain. The expected utility of the project to the individual is:

$$EU(\overline{Y}) = 0.5\ U(Y_1) + 0.5\ U(Y_2)$$

This can be read off the straight line AB joining points Y_1 and Y_2 on the utility function, as $EU(\overline{Y})$. We can see that, because the utility function is shaped the way it is, the expected utility of the risky project is less than the utility which would arise should its expected value occur for sure: $EU(\overline{Y}) < U(\overline{Y})$. Moreover, we can define the certainty equivalent of the project with possible outcomes (Y_1, Y_2) and probabilities of $(0.5, 0.5)$ as Y^* in Figure 7.1. This gives the same level of utility $(EU(\overline{Y}))$ as the risky project.

So, one approach that the analyst could take to risk is to (i) express all uncertain benefits and costs in terms of their certainty equivalents and then (ii) discount these using the risk-free rate of discount. We use the risk-free rate since risk has been allowed for in the process of calculating certainty equivalents. All the discount factor has to then do is control for the effects of time passing.

However, actually calculating certainty equivalents for costs and benefits is difficult: we need information on all possible states of the world, on outcomes in each state, on the probability of each state, and on the degree of risk aversion on the part of everyone impacted by the project, along with their initial wealth levels. Is there an alternative? The main alternative is to incorporate risk into the discount rate itself. To do this, we draw on the finance literature concerned with evaluating the required return from risky investments. This makes use of the 'Capital Assets Pricing Model'. Investors demand an extra return from taking on more risk. But in an efficient capital market, where risks at the portfolio level can be reduced to a degree by diversifying (that is, spreading one's wealth across different investments), only a certain element of risk-taking will be rewarded: this is risk that relates to the economy as a whole, which cannot be 'removed' by diversifying. The capital assets pricing model states that the required return on a particular investment, r_i, is given by:

$$r_i = r_f + \beta_i[r_m - r_f] \tag{7.6}$$

Here, r_f is the rate of interest or return on risk-free assets, r_m is the rate of return on the market portfolio, and β_i is the 'beta' value for investment i. This shows the extent to which the benefits from investing in project i co-vary with returns from the portfolio held by the investor, or with average market returns. It is defined as:

$$\beta_i = \frac{\text{cov}(r_i, r_m)}{Var(r_m)} \tag{7.7}$$

that is, as the extent to which returns between investing in i and investing in the market portfolio are correlated with each other, relative to the variance of returns at the level of the market. If $\beta = 0$, this implies that the project's risk is uncorrelated with market returns (an unlikely outcome). If β is negative, it means that investing in the project actually reduces overall risk (provides insurance), with the implication that the risk-adjusted discount rate is actually less than the risk-free rate. More commonly, we find that β values are positive, so that the risk-adjusted discount rate is greater than the risk-free rate.

Equation (7.6) above defines the risk-adjusted discount rate, since it incorporates a measure of how investing in a particular project changes the overall level of risk attached to a portfolio held by an individual, a firm or even a government (see Zerbe and Dively, 1994 for a worked example of this idea applied to local government). It assumes that individuals, firms and governments will diversify their investments such that they reduce overall risk to the greatest amount possible, given overall fluctuations in economic and environmental conditions.

The second option for dealing with risk in CBA is thus now clear: use a risk-adjusted discount rate to discount future benefits and costs, without converting them into certainty equivalents. Now the discount rate is doing two jobs: controlling for the effects of risk and controlling for time passing. Should the government use the risk-adjusted discount rates it observes being used in the market? One reason not to take this approach is the presence of taxes on firms. Such taxes mean that firms will have to earn a higher return to pay their taxes such that they earn sufficient post-tax to reward their shareholders. Since taxes are a transfer payment (in the language of Chapter 2), this implies the government should use the after-tax rate of return on the market portfolio as the risk-adjusted discount rate: Lind (1982) estimated this at 4.6 per cent for the US in the early 1980s.

However, there is also an argument that the investment risks the government faces, or that each individual voter implicitly faces, is lower than that faced by private firms. This idea, known as the Arrow–Lind Theorem, is due to the fact that the government can spread risk across a very large number of taxpayers. As the number of taxpayers gets bigger, the risk faced by each gets less. At the limit, this suggests that governments should use a risk-free rate of discount. However, as Pearce and Nash (1981) point out, there are problems applying this idea to environmental policy, since the number of people suffering from a negative externality such as pollution does not affect how much each suffers. Finally, we note that current UK government guidance is to avoid trying to deal with risk by adjusting the discount rate (HM Treasury, 2003). For an exemplary overview of all the issues discussed in this section, see Lind (1982).

7.5 CONCLUSIONS

No matter what finesses are placed around it, the practice of discounting the future still raises considerable unease. Yet, as we have argued in this chapter, it appears to be based on both market behaviour and people's choices. One could argue that, even though individuals may discount, governments do not need to when deciding on future actions. However, if governments did ignore evidence of positive discounting in their decision making through CBA by using a zero discount rate, they would be acting contrary to the preferences of their voters, which is inconsistent with the underlying assumption of CBA, as noted in Chapter 2, that preferences should count in making judgements over social welfare and the resource allocation decisions that affect it.

Whilst it is possible to find many ethical critiques of the practice of discounting in the literature, Goulder and Stavins (2002) have cautioned against 'mixing up' ethical and efficiency criteria in the choice of discount rate. If they are correct, then this might mean discounting on pure dynamic (social) efficiency grounds, but then imposing constraints on decision making which reflect ethical concerns in some situations. This is in line with Randall's general suggestion, discussed in Chapter 13, that CBA might be constrained by ethical trump cards in some situations (Randall, 2002). Issues of fairness can cause us to question the nature of the social welfare function which the CBA analyst has in mind, as noted in Chapter 2, but adjusting the discount rate to take account of fairness concerns is wrong. Even if concern for future well-being were to lead us to revise the social welfare function that CBA aims to maximize, such a revision on the grounds of being 'fair to the future' is difficult. For example, Padilla (2002) has commented that it is hard to know what future generations will 'want' or 'need', and to conceptualize the rights of imagined individuals who are not around today.

In conclusion, the choice of discount rate matters a great deal to the outcomes of CBA, especially where long-term benefits and costs are involved. People discount future gains and losses, and so should governments in applying CBA. However, deciding on a single, *correct* rate of social discount is difficult, since many factors influence this, including time preferences, the social opportunity cost of capital, time itself, risk and uncertainty. What is important is then that any CBA should include a sensitivity analysis which shows how the NPV of a policy or project changes as we vary the discount rate (Arrow et al., 1996).

NOTES

1. Also known as the marginal efficiency of capital.
2. In finance, this means asking what the *investment Beta* is for climate policy, as per section 7.5.
3. Formally, η is given by the ratio of the second derivative of the utility function with respect to consumption over the first derivative – see Dasgupta (1982).
4. This is the term used by Dasgupta (1982). Arrow et al. (2004) refer instead to the 'social rate of interest of consumption'.
5. Another motivation for declining discount rates over time, which is driven by uncertainty over what the rate should be, is provided by Weitzman (2001).
6. For two investments X and Y, the covariance COV $x, y = \text{corr}_{x,y} \cdot \sigma(X) \sigma(Y)$, where $\sigma(X)$ and $\sigma(Y)$ are the standard deviation of returns for X and Y, and $\text{corr}_{x,y}$ is the correlation coefficient between these returns.

REFERENCES

Alberini, A., S. Tonin and S. Turvani (2007), 'Rates of time preference for saving lives in the hazardous waste site context', paper submitted to the 2007 EAERE conference, College Park, MD, USA.

Arrow, K., M. Cropper, G. Eads, R. Hahn, L. Lave, R. Noll, P. Portney, M. Russell, R. Schmalensee, V.K. Smith and R. Stavins (1996), 'Is there a role for benefit–cost analysis in environmental, health and safety regulation?', *Science*, **272** (April 12), 221–2.

Arrow, K.J., P. Dasgupta, L. Goulder, G. Daily, P. Ehrlich, G. Heal, S. Levin, K.-G. Maler, S. Schneider, S. Starrett and B. Walker (2004), 'Are we consuming too much?', *Journal of Economic Perspectives*, **18**(3), 147–72.

Dasgupta, P. (1982), 'Resource depletion, research and development and the social rate of discount' in R.C. Lind (ed.), *Discounting for Time and Risk in Energy Policy*, Baltimore, MD: Johns Hopkins Press.

Gollier, C., P. Koundouri and T. Pantelides (2008), 'Decreasing discount rates: economic justifications and implications for long-run policy', *Economic Policy*, **23**(56), 757–95.

Goulder, L. and R. Stavins (2002), 'Discounting: an eye on the future', *Nature*, **419**, 673–74.

Groom, B., C. Hepburn, C. Koundouri and D.W. Pearce (2005), 'Discounting the future: the long and short of it', *Environment and Resource Economics*, **31**(4), 445–93.

Hanley, N. and C. Spash (1993), *Cost–Benefit Analysis and the Environment*, Cheltenham, UK and Northampton, MA, USA: Edward Elgar.

Hepburn, C. and P. Koundouri (2007), 'Recent advances in discounting: implications for forest economics', *Journal of Forest Economics*, **13**(2–3), 169–89.

Hepburn, C., P. Koundouri, E. Panopoulou and T. Pantelidis (2009), 'Social discounting under uncertainty: a cross country comparison', *Journal of Environmental Economics and Management*, **57**(2), March, 140–50.

HM Treasury (2003), *The Green Book: Appraisal and Evaluation in Central Government*, London: The Stationary Office.

Jacobsen, J. and N. Hanley (2008), 'Are there income effects on global willingness to pay for biodiversity conservation?', *Environmental and Resource Economics*, forthcoming. Published online 8 August 2008

Kriström, B. and P. Riera (1996), 'Is the income elasticity of environmental improvements less than one?', *Environmental and Resource Economics*, **7**, 45–55.

Krutilla, J.V. and A.C. Fisher (1985), *The Economics of Natural Environments*, Baltimore, MD: Johns Hopkins Press.

Lind, R.C. (1982), 'A primer on the major issues relating to the discount rate for evaluating national energy options', in R.C. Lind (ed.), *Discounting for Time and Risk in Energy Policy*, Washington, DC: Resources for the Future.

Marglin, S. (1963), 'The social rate of discount and the optimal rate of investment', *Quarterly Journal of Economics*, **77**, 95–111.

Newell, R. and W. Pizer (2003), 'Discounting the benefits of climate change mitigation: how much do uncertain rates increase valuations?', *Journal of Environmental Economics and Management*, **46**(1), 52–71.

Nordhaus, W.D. (1991), 'A sketch of the economics of the greenhouse effect', *American Economic Review*, **81**(2), 146–50.

Nordhaus, W.D. (2007), 'A review of the Stern review of the economics of climate change', *Journal of Economic Literature*, **45**(3), 686–702.

Padilla, E. (2002), 'Intergenerational equity and sustainability', *Ecological Economics*, **41**, 69–83.

Pearce, D.W. (1983), *Cost–Benefit Analysis* (2nd edn), Basingstoke: Macmillan.

Pearce, D.W. and C.A. Nash (1981), *The Social Appraisal of Projects*, London: Macmillan.

Pearce, D.W., A. Markandya and E. Barbier (1989), *Blueprint for a Green Economy*, London: Earthscan.

Randall, A. (2002), 'B–C considerations should be decisive when there is nothing more important at stake', in D. Bromley and J. Paavola (eds), *Economies, Ethics and Environmental Policy*, Oxford: Blackwell.

Sagoff, M. (1988), *The Economy of the Earth*, Cambridge, MA: Cambridge University Press.

Schelling, T. (1995), 'Intergenerational discounting', *Energy Policy*, **23**(4/5), 395–401.

Sen, A. (1982), 'Approaches to the choice of discount rates for social cost–benefit analysis', in R.C. Lind (ed.), *Discounting for Time and Risk in Energy Policy*, Washington, DC: Resources for the Future.

Stern, N. (2007), *The Economics of Climate Change: The Stern Review*, Cambridge: Cambridge University Press.

Sugden, R. and A. Williams (1978), *The Principles of Practical Cost–Benefit Analysis*, Oxford: Oxford University Press.

Sumaila, U. and C. Walters (2005), 'Intergenerational discounting: a new intuitive approach', *Ecological Economics*, **52**, 135–42.

Warner, J.T. and S. Pleeter (2001), 'The personal discount rate: evidence from military downsizing programs', *American Economic Review*, **91**(1), 33–53.

Weitzman, M. (2001), 'Gamma discounting', *American Economic Review*, **91**(1), 261–71.
Weitzman, M. (2007), 'A review of the Stern review of the economics of climate change', *Journal of Economic Literature*, **45**(3), 703–24.
Zerbe, R.O. and D.D. Dively (1994), *Benefit–Cost Analysis in Theory and Practice*, New York: HarperCollins.

8. CBA in developing countries: what's different?

8.1 INTRODUCTION

The application of cost–benefit analysis to environmental problems in developing countries must take into account that these problems are often very different from those occurring in industrialized economies.

Most developing economies, and certainly the majority of the populations living within them, are directly dependent on exploiting natural resources. For many of these economies, primary product exports account for the vast majority of their export earnings, and one or two primary commodities make up the bulk of exports (Barbier, 2005, ch. 1). On average across these countries, agricultural value-added accounts for 40 per cent of GDP, and nearly 80 per cent of the labour force is engaged in agricultural or resource-based activities (World Bank, 2006). By 2025, the rural population of the developing world will have increased to almost 3.2 billion (Population Division of the United Nations, 2008).

Much of this rural population in developing countries depends directly on the exploitation of natural resources and the environment for agriculture, livestock raising, fishing, basic materials and fuel – to meet their own subsistence requirements and to sell in markets for cash income. The lack of basic water supply, sanitation and other infrastructure services suggests that increased public provision of such basic services is highly valued by many households. Rapid land-use change has meant that many natural environments and habitats are disappearing quickly, with the result that critical ecological services are being disrupted or lost (see Chapter 9). The demise of key ecosystems of the developing world includes mangroves (35 per cent either lost or degraded), coral reefs (30 per cent) and tropical forests (30 per cent) (Houghton, 1995; Millennium Ecosystem Assessment, 2005; UNEP, 2006; Valiela et al., 2001).

Poor people in developing countries are particularly vulnerable to the resulting loss in critical ecological services. Currently one quarter of the people in developing countries – almost 1.3 billion – survive on 'fragile lands', which are defined as 'areas that present significant constraints for intensive agriculture and where the people's links to the land are critical for the sustainability of communities, pastures, forests, and other natural resources' (World Bank, 2003, p. 59; see also Box 8.1 below). These populations living on fragile land in developing countries account for many of the people in extreme poverty, living on less than $1 per day, and include 518 million living in arid regions with no access to irrigation systems, 430 million on soils unsuitable for agriculture, 216 million on land with steep slopes and more than 130 million in fragile forest systems.

However, the rapid growth of rural populations in the developing world will be outpaced by the even faster growth of urban populations. In 2007, 2.38 billion people, approximately 44 per cent of the population, lived in the urban areas of developing countries (Population Division of the United Nations, 2008). By 2019, half of the developing world will live in cities, and by 2050 5.33 billion people, or 67 per cent of the population in developed countries, will inhabit urban areas. This brisk pace of urbanization means that the growing populations in the cities will continue to face increased environmental problems associated with congestion, pollution and rising energy, water and raw material demands. In addition, the rising numbers of middle to high-income households in urban areas will mean higher demands for recreation and amenity services. Although such environmental problems are similar to those faced by industrialized countries, the pace and scale of population growth in the urban areas of developing countries are likely to lead to more severe and acute problems, especially in terms of health effects.

The environment in developing countries is therefore very much related to health and welfare of rural and urban households, and in turn, the basic production and consumption decisions of these households have a considerable impact on natural resources and the environment. As a result, the environmental impacts of rapid urbanization and of rural resource degradation, and the implications for the economic livelihoods of the urban and rural poor, are now an important policy concern in developing countries. Thus, many of the valuation methods that we have discussed so far in this book (see Chapters 3–6) are increasingly being applied in developing countries to assess these environmental impacts. In this chapter, we will discuss recent progress in such applications of economic valuation of environmental problems in developing countries.

However, in assessing such progress, we must always remember the 'bigger picture' of how environment and development are mutually intertwined in low and middle-income economies. As the problem of widespread and endemic poverty is a major concern in these economies, we will begin by examining the role of economic valuation in assessing the importance of environment benefits to the livelihoods of the poor in developing countries. In addition, as the livelihoods of the rural poor are often dependent on major ecosystems and habitats, we will discuss the current trends in the loss of these key environments and the role of valuation in helping to assess these trends. We will also examine the major trends in urban environmental problems, such as pollution and congestion, and explore how valuation studies have helped to assess the resulting health and welfare impacts, especially for improvements to urban environments and reductions in key environmental risk factors responsible for high mortality in many developing countries.

8.2 ECONOMIC VALUES AND THE ENVIRONMENT IN DEVELOPING COUNTRIES

One pertinent feature of many ecosystems and habitats, particularly those found in developing regions such as coastal and marine systems, rainforests, watersheds, rangelands and floodplain wetlands, is that they provide multiple benefits, or values, to neighbouring communities. As Table 8.1 indicates for the case of tropical coastal and marine systems, these benefits cover a wide variety of 'use' and 'non-use' values, as well as a range of 'goods', 'services' and other 'intangible benefits'.

For example, typical direct use values, which refer to both consumptive and non-consumptive uses that involve some direct physical interaction with the ecosystem and its services, include harvesting of fish and wild resources, transportation by waterways, recreation and tourism. Some unique coastal and marine habitats are also important stores of genetic

Table 8.1 Various values provided by tropical coastal and marine ecosystems

Use values		Non-use values
Direct values	Indirect values	Existence and bequest values
Fishing	Nutrient retention and cycling	Cultural heritage
Aquaculture	Flood control	Resources for future generations
Transport	Storm protection	Existence of charismatic species
Wild resources	Habitat for species	Existence of wild places
Water supply	Shoreline stabilization	
Recreation		
Genetic material		
Scientific and educational opportunities		

Source: Adapted from Barbier (2001, Table 1.1) and Heal et al. (2005, Table 2-1).

material and have educational and scientific research value as well. But in developing regions, some of the more important uses of coastal and marine systems tend to involve both small-scale commercial and 'informal' economic activity to support the livelihoods of local populations, for example through fishing, hunting, fuelwood extraction, and so forth.

Some important regulatory and habitat functions of ecosystems underlie the key economic benefits provided by tropical coastal and marine systems. As indicated in Table 8.1, these include nutrient retention and cycling, flood control, storm protection, providing species habitat, and stabilization of shorelines. The values derived from these services are considered to be 'indirect', as they are derived mainly from the support and protection of economic activities and livelihoods that have directly measurable values (Barbier, 1994). For example, in the case of tropical coastal wetlands such as mangrove systems, the mangrove swamps may serve as a nursery and breeding habitat for many important fish species, some of which may migrate as adults to offshore fisheries. In addition, mangroves can provide 'storm protection' by reducing the economic damages inflicted by tropical storms on coastal property and communities. Finally, mangrove systems are thought to prevent coastal erosion, thus preserving valuable agricultural land and coastal properties.

Many unique natural environments are considered to have substantial 'non-use values', even in developing regions. These include existence and bequest values, which may be high among indigenous communities in rural areas, as they see their culture, heritage and traditional knowledge closely intertwined with the surrounding environment. Even some of the poorest rural communities have expressed interest in seeing their 'way of life' passed on to their heirs and future generations (Berkes, 1999).

Another way of looking at the way in which the environment impacts human livelihoods is through the risks that various environmental hazards pose to human health. These can be significantly different for developing countries as opposed to more developed countries. Table 8.2 shows the contribution to mortality of five important environmental risk factors: unsafe water, sanitation and hygiene; indoor smoke from solid fuels; urban air pollution; lead exposure; and climate change. All of these risk factors impact mortality in various ways. For example, unsafe water, sanitation and hygiene are responsible for widespread outbreaks of diarrhoea. Indoor smoke from burning solid fuels causes acute respiratory infections in children, chronic obstructive pulmonary disease and lung cancer. Urban air pollution is linked to cardiovascular mortality, respiratory mortality, lung cancer, and mortality in children from acute respiratory infections. Lead exposure is known to cause mild mental retardation and is associated with cardiovascular disease. Climate change may be responsible for

Table 8.2   Attributable mortality by environmental and other major risk factors, 2000

	High mortality developing countries		Low mortality developing countries		Developed Countries	
	Males	Females	Males	Females	Males	Females
Total deaths ('000)	13,758	12,654	8,584	7,373	6,890	6,601
Share (%) to environmental risks						
Unsafe water, sanitation and hygiene	5.8	5.9	1.1	1.1	0.2	0.2
Indoor smoke from solid fuels	3.6	4.3	1.9	5.4	0.1	0.2
Urban air pollution	0.9	0.8	2.5	2.9	1.1	1.2
Lead exposure	0.4	0.3	0.5	0.3	0.7	0.4
Climate change	0.5	0.6	<0.1	<0.1	<0.1	<0.1
Share (%) to other major risks						
Underweight child and mother	12.6	13.4	1.8	1.9	0.1	0.1
Unsafe sex	9.3	10.9	0.8	1.3	0.2	0.6
Tobacco	7.5	1.5	12.2	2.9	26.3	9.3
Blood pressure	7.4	7.5	12.7	15.1	20.1	23.9
Cholesterol	5.0	5.7	5.1	5.6	14.5	17.6

Notes: High mortality developing countries include Sub-Saharan Africa; the Latin American and Caribbean countries of Bolivia, Ecuador, Guatemala, Haiti, Nicaragua and Peru; the North African, Middle Eastern and West Asian countries of Afghanistan, Djibouti, Egypt, Iraq, Morocco, Pakistan, Somalia, Sudan and Yemen; and the Asian countries of Bangladesh, Bhutan, Democratic People's Republic of Korea, India, Maldives, Myanmar, Nepal and Timor-Leste. The low mortality developing countries include the remaining countries of Latin America and the Caribbean; North African, Middle Eastern and West Asian countries; Asia and the Western Pacific. Developed countries include Europe and the former Soviet Union; Canada, Cuba and the United States; and Australia, Brunei, Japan, New Zealand and Singapore.

Source: Adapted from (WHO, 2002, Table 4.9).

deaths for a variety of means, including diarrhoea outbreaks, flood injury and mortality, malaria and even malnutrition.

Table 8.2 indicates the contribution of these environmental risk factors to mortality in three groups of countries: high mortality developing countries, low mortality developing countries and developed countries. Table 8.2 also compares the five environmental risk factors with other major risk factors responsible for mortality, especially in developing countries. The table shows that environmental risk factors, especially unsafe water, hygiene and sanitation as well as indoor smoke pollution, are particularly important sources of mortality in high mortality developing countries, which include most of the poorest countries of the world. In contrast, urban air pollution tends to be particularly significant for low mortality developing countries, which include many rapidly industrializing and urbanizing economies. Although other major risk factors, such as childhood and maternal undernutrition, unsafe sex, tobacco use and diet-related risks, may be slightly more important sources of mortality, the table shows that environmental risk factors are significant causes of death in developing countries. With the exception of lead exposure, these risk factors are generally much lower in the richer, developed economies of the world.

8.3 COST–BENEFIT ANALYSIS, THE ENVIRONMENT AND THE ECONOMIC LIVELIHOODS OF THE POOR

Several CBA studies have indicated the importance of the various coastal and marine ecosystem values outlined in Table 8.2 to the economic livelihoods of the poor in developing countries. Other natural environments, such as coral reefs, forested watershed and floodplains, also yield significant benefits to poor communities.

For example, in Chapter 9 we discuss in detail a case study from Thailand (Barbier, 2007b), which through employing various production function methods outlined in Chapter 6, estimates three benefits to local coastal communities arising from mangroves. The study estimates that the net present value (in 1996 $) over 1996–2004 arising from the net income to local communities from collected forest products from coastal mangroves ranges from $484 to $584 per hectare (ha). The net present value of mangroves as breeding and nursery habitat in support of offshore artisanal fisheries ranged from $708 to $987 per ha, and the storm protection service was $8966 to $10 821 per ha. Such benefits are considerable when compared to the average incomes of coastal households; a survey conducted in July 2000 of four mangrove-dependent communities in two different coastal provinces of Thailand indicates that the average household income per village ranged from $2606 to $6623 per annum, and the overall incidence of poverty (corresponding to an annual income of $180 or lower) in all but three villages exceeded the average incidence poverty rate of 8 per cent found across all rural areas of Thailand (Sarntisart and Sathirathai,

2004). The authors also found that excluding the income from collecting mangrove forest products would have raised the incidence of poverty to 55.3 per cent and 48.1 per cent in two of the villages, and to 20.7 per cent and 13.64 per cent in the other two communities.

The Thailand example is not unusual; poor households across the developing world typically display considerable direct and indirect use values for mangroves (Badola and Hussain, 2005; Bandaranayake, 1998; Barbier and Strand, 1998; Brander et al., 2006; Chong, 2005; Hammitt et al., 2001; Janssen and Padilla, 1999; Naylor and Drew, 1998; Othman et al., 2004; Rönnbäck, 1999; Rönnbäck et al., 2007; Ruitenbeek, 1994; Walton et al., 2006). However, there is also evidence that coastal people hold important non-use values associated with mangroves. A contingent valuation study of mangrove-dependent coastal communities in Micronesia demonstrated that the communities 'place some value on the existence and ecosystem functions of mangroves over and above the value of mangroves' marketable products' (Naylor and Drew, 1998, p. 488).

Coral reefs are another critical habitat throughout the developing world that both support near-shore fisheries harvested by poor coastal communities and provide valuable shoreline protection (Cesar, 2000; Chong, 2005; Moberg and Folke, 1999; Moberg and Rönnbäck, 2003; Jackson et al., 2001; Worm et al., 2006). For example, Cesar (2000) estimates the losses, in net present value per square kilometer (km^2), in terms of support for near-shore artisanal fisheries and coastal protection from the destruction of coral reefs in Indonesia. The main threats to coral reefs are from poison fishing, blast fishing, mining coral, sediment pollution from logging onshore, and over-fishing. Together, these threats account for present value losses in coastal fisheries of around $0.41 million per km^2 of coral reef destroyed, and present value losses in coastal protection $0.011 to $0.453 million per km^2 of coral reef destroyed. Evidence from Kenya indicates that coral reefs may also be critical to larval dispersal to fishing areas, which could influence the effectiveness of marine reserves and closed fishing grounds in inducing stock recovery and thus eventual re-opening to fishing (Rodwell et al., 2003). Coral reefs also have important cultural and non-use value to neighbouring coastal communities; many cultural and religious traditions have evolved in tropical coastal zones that honour the dependence of local communities on adjacent reefs and reflect the 'bequest value' of preserving this way of life into the future (Moberg and Folke, 1999).

Cesar (2000) also uses CBA to determine who 'gains' or 'loses' from the major human-induced threats to coral reef systems in developing regions in terms of destructive and non-sustainable fishery practices. Some of these activities may be engaged in by poor coastal communities, such as the unsustainable fishing practices and coral mining, but most of the gains from coral reef destruction accrue to large-scale commercial interests. For example, Cesar (2000) calculates that in Indonesia, the harmful activities most likely undertaken by poor coastal households are overfishing and coral mining, but these activities generate low returns, a net present value of $1400 per family for mining and $200 per fisher through over-fishing. In contrast, the net present value per investor from poison fishing and logging-induced sedimentation is significantly larger, ranging from $2 million per company in the case of logging to over US$0.4 million per boat in the case of poison fishing.

Forested watersheds in developing regions also provide a number of hydrological benefits that can impact the livelihoods of the poor, such as water filtration/purification; seasonal flow regulation; erosion and sediment control; and habitat preservation (Alix-Garcia et al., 2005; Chomitz and Kumari, 1998; Diwakara and Chandrakanth, 2007; Guo et al., 2001; Kaiser and Roumasset, 2002; Kremen et al., 2000; Landel-Mills and Porras, 2002; Pattanayak and Kramer, 2001; Postel and Thompson, 2005; Richards, 1997; Silvano et al., 2005). These benefits will become increasingly important as more and more river basins in developing areas experience rising water use relative to freshwater supplies (Rosegrant et al., 2002). In addition, the forests of upper watersheds provide a number of direct uses to poor communities living there, including timber, collected non-timber products and community forestry (Guo et al., 2001; Kremen et al., 2000; Pagiola et al., 2005).

Some of the most important benefits of maintaining and improving land uses in upper watersheds accrue to poor communities living downstream. In the central highlands of Bolivia, for example, Richards (1997) finds that a project to improve watershed protection and reduce soil erosion on farmers' fields in the uplands yields a net present value of nearly $34.9 million, with the majority of the benefits due to flood prevention and the increased water availability resulting from aquifer recharge in the lower watershed. Similarly, improvements to the upper watersheds in Karnataka, India through afforestation and construction of tanks, artificial ponds, check dams and other reclamation structures lead to significant benefits to downstream farmers through improving groundwater recharge and availability, thus reducing the cost of irrigation and the need for developing new wells or extending existing wells (Diwakara and Chandrakanth, 2007). Pattanayak and Kramer (2001) estimate that increased water flows associated with afforestation of watersheds in Eastern Indonesia yield economic values for downstream farmers reported equivalent to 1 to 10 per cent ($3.5–$35) of annual agricultural profits. However, land uses other than forests in some tropical watersheds may also yield beneficial hydrological flows; for example, Aylward and Echeverría (2001) show that conversion of forests to pasture for livestock in the upper watersheds of Río Chiquito, Costa Rica actually increases water flow downstream, generating net present values in the range of $250 to $1000 per hectare of pasture.

In many poor countries, an economically important natural environment downstream is the seasonally inundated savanna or forested flood-plains located in the lower river basins. During seasonal flood events, water often leaves the main river channel and inundates these floodplains. As the floods abate and recede, crops are planted in the naturally irrigated soils, fish are caught more easily in the retreating waters, and the increased alluvial deposits increase the biological productivity of forests, wildlife and other harvested resources. Around half of Africa's total wetland area consists of floodplains, including huge large-scale ecosystems of several thousand square kilometres such as the Inner Niger Delta in Mali, the Okavango Delta in Botswana, the Sudd of the Upper Nile in Sudan and the Kafue Flats in Zambia (Lemley et al., 2000). Millions of people across the continent depend directly on the floodplains for their economic liveli-hoods through production activities such as flood-recession agriculture, fishing, grazing and wood and non-wood harvesting of riparian forest resources, and millions more in surrounding arid land depend on the groundwater recharge service of floodplains for drinking water and irriga-tion (Barbier, 2003). Similar benefits are found in other extremely poor countries, such as Bangladesh, where 80 per cent of the country consists of floodplains created by the confluence of the Ganges, Brahmaputra, Meghna and other rivers (Islam and Braden, 2006).

For example, upstream dam developments are threatening the economic livelihoods of millions of poor agricultural households dependent on the Hadejia-Jama'are floodplain in North-east Nigeria. Full implementation of all the upstream dams and large-scale irrigation schemes is estimated to produce overall net losses in terms of agricultural, fuelwood and fish production to these households of around US$20.2–20.9 million in net present value terms (Barbier, 2003). In addition, the reduction in mean peak flood extent is predicted to cause a one-metre fall in groundwater levels in the shallow aquifers that are recharged by the standing water in the floodplain wetlands, leading to additional annual losses of around $1.2 million in tubewell irrigated dry season agriculture and $4.76 million in domestic water consumption for rural households. Islam and Braden (2006) show that, in Bangladesh, fishing and flood-recession agriculture are important joint products to poor rural households utilizing natural floodplains, although it is largely the landless who benefit from floodplain fish production rather than agricultural landowners. As a consequence, a natural floodplain means more land devoted to fishing rather than agriculture but actually yields higher overall net economic returns, especially compared to traditional management scenarios of upstream dam developments to limit flooding, increase agricultural area and expand crop production downstream. Such studies are important, because across the developing world downstream floodplains and rivers are being threatened by major upstream water diversion projects for agriculture and urban development (Nilsson et al., 2005; Tockner and Stanford, 2002).

In the case of tropical forests, the implications of deforestation for the livelihoods of the poor are more complex. Across the tropics, the principal activity responsible for deforestation appears to be the direct conversion of forests to permanent agriculture (Chomitz et al., 2007; FAO, 2001 and 2003). Stratified random sampling of 10 per cent of the world's tropical forests reveals that direct conversion by large-scale agriculture may be the main source of deforestation, accounting for around 32 per cent of total forest cover change, followed by conversion to small-scale agriculture, which accounts for 26 per cent. Intensification of agriculture in shifting cultivation areas comprises only 10 per cent of tropical deforestation, and expansion of shifting cultivation into undisturbed forests only 5 per cent (FAO, 2001). However, there are important regional differences. In Africa, the major process of deforestation (around 60 per cent) is due to the conversion of forest for the establishment of small-scale permanent agriculture, whereas direct conversion of forest cover to large-scale agriculture, including raising livestock, predominates in Latin America and Asia (48 per cent and 30 per cent, respectively). Although agricultural conversion is the principal cause of tropical deforestation, in many forested regions uncontrolled timber harvesting is responsible for initially opening up previously inaccessible forested frontiers to permanent agricultural conversion and for causing widespread timber-related forest degradation and loss (Ascher, 1999; Barbier, 2005; Chomitz et al., 2007; Matthews et al., 2000). In some regions, large-scale plantation development is initiating the 'opening' of forested areas to subsequent smaller scale cropland expansion. Wassenaar et al. (2007, p. 101) note that 'Amazonian cropland expansion hot spots in Brazil and Bolivia for example are adjacent to current large soybean production zones, the creation of which, largely driven by increasing animal feed needs, has caused large scale deforestation in the recent past'.

CBA of different tropical forest land management regimes highlight the economic tradeoffs for developing countries of these various land-use change scenarios (see Table 8.3). In Cameroon, small-scale farmers would gain from conversion of the forest to agriculture; however, oil palm plantations are only profitable because of the existence of extensive subsidies and

Table 8.3 Private, social and global benefits of competing tropical forest land uses ($/ha)

Benefits	Cameroon[a]			Sri Lanka[b]		Malaysia[c]	
	Sustainable logging	Conversion to oil palm	Conversion to small-scale agriculture	Sustainable logging	Conversion to tea	Sustainable logging	Unsustainable logging
Private	309	−1,695	1,472	1,212	4,596	2,361	1,401 to 1,922
Social	206	10	34	158		610	1,230 to 1,547
Global	2,055	601	608			8,270	10,048 to 10,076

Notes:

a Net present value at 10 per cent discount rate for 32 years; private benefits for oil palm are negative due to removal of market distortions (taxes, subsidies); social benefits include non-timber forest products, flood prevention and sediment control; global benefits include carbon storage and undiscovered plant drugs.

b Net present value at 8 per cent discount rate for 20 years; social benefits include non-timber forest products; external costs of soil erosion and sedimentation damages from tea cultivation were not estimated.

c Net present value at 8 per cent discount rate for 100 years; social benefits include non-timber forest products, domestic water, fish, recreation, hydrological benefits; global benefits include carbon storage and endangered species preservation.

Source: Adapted from Turner et al. (2003, Table 4).

tax breaks. Sustainable logging generates much lower private returns per hectare but yields much higher social benefits in terms of non-timber forest products, flood prevention and sedimentation control. In Sri Lanka, tea cultivation is highly profitable to farmers converting forest land, although it generates substantial external damages from soil erosion and sedimentation downstream. In comparison, sustainable logging yields lower private returns per hectare but yields positive wider benefits in terms of non-timber forest products. In Malaysia, unsustainable logging yields immediate and large financial gains but more sustainable timber practices can still generate significant private returns in addition to non-timber social and global benefits. Thus, the examples in Table 8.3 indicate that CBA can generate important information on the various benefits accruing from competing tropical forest land uses, as well as the extent to which poorer communities are likely to gain or lose from the various management options.

In sum, the dependence of the poor on the benefits provided by surrounding natural ecosystems and habitats should not be surprising, given the location of many of the poorest people of the world. As discussed in Box 8.1, nearly 1.3 billion people – almost a fifth of the world's population – live in fragile environments found in developing economies. The rural poor comprise almost half of the people living in these fragile environments, and they outnumber the poor living on favoured lands by two to one (see Box 8.1).

8.4 VALUING CRITICAL ENVIRONMENTAL GOODS AND SERVICES

Because of the economic dependence of many poor rural households on exploiting the surrounding natural environment for key commodities,

---

BOX 8.1   THE POOR AND FRAGILE ENVIRONMENTS

The table below indicates that nearly 1.3 billion people – almost a fifth of the world's population – live in fragile environments found in developing economies. Almost half of the people (613 million) consist of the rural poor, who throughout the developing world outnumber the poor living on favoured lands by two to one. These fragile environments are prone to land degradation, and consist of upland areas, forest systems and drylands, yet are areas 'where the people's links to the land are critical for the sustainability of communities, pastures, forests and other natural resources' (World Bank, 2003, p. 59). In other words, the economic livelihoods of the people living on fragile lands are directly and indirectly affected by the services provided by surrounding ecosystems.

Distribution of world's population and rural poor on fragile land

(a) Distribution of world's population[a]

Region	Population in 2000 (millions)	Population in fragile lands	
		Number (millions)	Share of total (%)
Latin America and the Caribbean	515.3	68	13.1
Middle East and North Africa	293.0	110	37.6
Sub-Saharan Africa	658.4	258	39.3
South Asia	1,354.5	330	24.4
East Asia and Pacific	1,856.5	469	25.3
Eastern Europe and Central Asia	474.7	58	12.1
OECD Group[b]	850.4	94	11.1
Other	27.3	2	6.9
Total	**6,030.1**	**1,389**	**23.0**
Total Developing Economies[c]	**5,179.7**	**1,295**	**25.0**
Total Latin America, Africa and Asian Developing Economies[d]	**4,677.7**	**1,235**	**26.4**

(b) Distribution of rural poor in developing regions[e]

Region	Rural poor on favoured lands (millions)	Rural poor on fragile lands	
		Number (millions)	Share of total (percent)
Central and South America	24	47	66
West Asia and North Africa	11	35	76
Sub-Saharan Africa	65	175	73
Asia	219	374	63
Total	**319**	**613**	**66**

Notes:

a   This table is from Barbier (2005, Table 1.7) and adapted from World Bank (2003, Table 4.2). Fragile lands are defined as areas that present significant constraints for intensive agriculture and where the people's links to the land are critical for the sustainability of communities, pastures, forests and other natural resources; they include arid regions with no access to irrigation, areas with soils unsuitable for agriculture, land with steep slopes and fragile forest systems (see World Bank, 2003).

b   OECD stands for Organization for Economic Cooperation and Development, and the OECD Group of countries include Australia, Austria, Belgium, Canada, Denmark, Finland, France, Germany, Greece, Iceland, Ireland, Italy, Japan, Luxembourg, Netherlands, New Zealand, Norway, Portugal, Spain, Sweden, Switzerland, United Kingdom and United States.

c   World Total less OECD Group.
d   World Total less OECD Group, East Europe and Central Asia and Other.
e   This table is adapted from the Comprehensive Assessment of Water Management in
     Agriculture (Molden, 2007, Table 15.1) and Scherr (1999). Fragile lands are equated with
     marginal lands, which are defined as areas with the greatest potential for land and water
     degradation; i.e., land with highly weathered soils, steep slopes, inadequate or excess
     rainfall, and high temperatures (see Comprehensive Assessment of Water Management
     in Agriculture, 2007).

The figure below further illustrates that rural poverty is correlated with the fraction of the population in developing countries found on fragile lands. As the figure indicates, the sample of 60 countries which have substantial numbers of people living in fragile environments – ranging from 20 to 30 per cent of the population to over 70 per cent – also have a high percentage of the rural population living in extreme poverty (45.3 per cent on average). What is more, the incidence of rural poverty rises as developing countries have more of their populations concentrated on fragile lands.

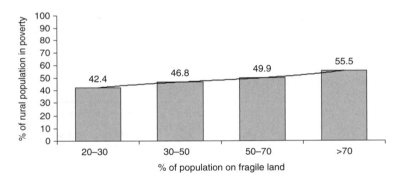

Notes:
Developing regions are defined as low and middle-income countries in Africa, Latin America, Asia and Oceania, based on World Bank definitions (countries with 2003 Gross National Income per capita of $9385 or less), from World Bank (2006).
Percentage of rural population in poverty is from World Bank (2006).
Percentage of population on fragile land is from World Bank (2003, Table 4.3). Number of observations = 60 countries, of which 24 (20–30 per cent of population on fragile land), 29 (30–50 per cent), 5 (50–70 per cent) and 2 (> 70 per cent). The average rural poery rate across all countries is 45.3 per cent, and the median is 43.1 per cent.

The tendency for the rural poor to be clustered in the most marginal environments is also supported by studies at the regional and country level, although there can be important differences within and between countries. For example, researchers from the World Bank have examined the 'poverty–environment nexus' in three of the poorest countries in Southeast Asia – Cambodia, Laos and Vietnam (Dasgupta et al., 2005; Minot and Baulch, 2002). In Cambodia, the core poor in rural areas appear to be located in areas that are already heavily deforested; on the other hand, poor populations tend to be more concentrated in the lowlands rather than steeply sloped lands. In Laos, the poorest provinces in the north and northeast also have the highest incidence of poor rural populations, who appear to be concentrated in forested areas and the highlands. In Vietnam, large poor populations confined to steep slopes exist in the provinces comprising the Northern and Central Highlands, but extensive rural poverty is also found along the North Central Coast and the Red River Delta.

many valuation studies focus on estimating these non-market benefits. The behaviour of poor households and communities with respect to the environment is complex, and must be modelled carefully to determine how the range of choices and tradeoffs available to the poor is affected by their access to key markets (for example, for land, labour, credit as well as goods and services) as opposed to the quality and state of the surrounding environment on which their livelihoods depend (for reviews, see Barbier, 2005, ch. 6, 2007a and 2008; Barrett, 2004; Caviglia-Harris, 2004; Dasgupta, 1993; Fisher, 2004; Gray and Mosley, 2005; Narain et al., 2008; Pascual and Barbier, 2006 and 2007; Reardon and Vosti, 1995; Scherr, 2000; Vedeld et al., 2004; World Bank, 2008). As summarized by Dasgupta (1993, p. 475) 'in rural communities of poor countries a great many markets of significance (e.g. credit, capital, and insurance) are missing, and a number of commodities of vital importance for household production (potable water, sources of fuel and fodder, and so forth) are available only at considerable time and labour cost.' In the absence of local labour markets capable of absorbing all the poor and landless households looking for work, or well-functioning rural credit markets to lend needed capital, the landless and near landless in rural communities depend critically on exploitation of common-property resources for their income and nutritional needs. Thus, it may be the 'assetless' poor who end up most dependent on exploiting the surrounding environment for survival.

The application of CBA methods to value important benefits to poor rural households, such as potable water, fuelwood and fodder, has to take into account the complex behaviour of the households involved in allocating time and labour to obtain these commodities from the environment. As noted by Barbier (2001), developing travel cost models and other household production function approaches to value non-market environmental resource use by rural households in developing countries often shares many similarities with standard agricultural household models, which have been used extensively to model labour, land and other resource decisions of rural households. Such modelling of rural household behaviour, for example, is now routinely used to examine the economic value of time spent by rural households in various non-market, resource-based activities, such as water and fuelwood collection. The traditional approach has focused on household labour time allocation, which is a similar approach to the travel cost and allocation of time models we discussed in Chapter 4.

Three studies from rural Nepal are illustrative of how this approach has developed. Amacher et al. (1993) examined household production and consumption of fuelwood in two hill districts of Nepal. Households in the district characterized by lower prices for purchased wood, briefer travel time to the surrounding forests, and a larger forest inventory relied on fuelwood from the forested commons. Households in the district where fuelwood was scarcer produced more supplies from their own lands, and tended to substitute combustible agricultural residues for fuelwood and to adopt improved cook stoves. Bluffstone (1998) develops a more complete model to examine the allocation of rural household labour to four activities: cutting fodder and grazing cattle in forests, agricultural production, fuelwood collection and off-farm work. Kerosene purchases are assumed to be a substitute source of fuel. Model simulations are run on the effects of different fuel policy options on household behaviour as well as changes in the available fuelwood biomass stock. The results suggest that both improved cooking stove promotion and a kerosene price subsidy reduce fuelwood collection and deforestation while increasing fodder and grazing demands; however, the subsidy is the less preferred option due to its higher cost and income effects on households. Cooke (1998) also developed a time allocation model to examine the effects of natural resource scarcity on agricultural households' collection of fuelwood, leaf fodder, grass and water. The gender component of labour allocation was an important focus of the study, as over 80 per cent of the collection of environmental goods in Nepali households is usually done by women. However, the results of the study do not support the claim that households, and women in particular, spend less time farming when the costs of collecting natural resource products rise. Seasonal factors, landholding size, household composition and traditional gender roles in agriculture exert more influence on household agricultural labour allocation than an increase in the costs of collecting environmental products.

Applications of time allocation models to estimating the benefits of fuelwood, fodder and other commodities collected from the surrounding environment must frequently take into account other important factors, such as the effects of 'open access' collection and increasing resource scarcity on the time allocation decisions of poor households. Cooke et al. (2008) review household time allocation studies of fuelwood use, and find that most studies show that households alter their behaviour in the presence of sufficient fuelwood scarcity to reduce labour and time costs of collection. The presence of formal or informal institutional arrangements to control 'open access' collection also had a bearing on household costs and behaviour. Increasingly, household time allocation studies must take into account such factors affecting the collection decisions of rural households in order to estimate accurately the benefits accruing from natural resource products gathered from the surrounding environment. For example, as Bluffstone et al. (2008) show in rural Bolivia, changes in common forestry management practices have a significant impact on the behaviour of individual households, including their collection of forest products and on-farm planting of trees. Similarly, Barbier (2007a) finds that coastal households in Southern Thailand that depend on the surrounding mangroves for collected products and fishing alter the allocation of male and female labour, including their employment in activities outside the household, in response to mangrove deforestation as well as to the extent to which community controls on such deforestation exist.

Applications of time allocation models in developing countries have also employed discrete choice, or random utility, models to model the household's choice of collecting its own resource supplies as opposed to other options available to it. The advantage of this approach is that, assuming each option is mutually exclusive, it is possible to determine how changes in the key characteristics of a resource-collection activity, including the time spent collecting, will affect the decision of the individual to select that activity over other available options. This in turn allows an implicit price to be imputed to the time spent in resource collection activities.

One early application of the random utility approach involved examining choices between collecting water from an open well, purchasing water from door-to-door vendors or purchasing water from a kiosk by households in Ukundu, a large village near Mombassa, Kenya (Whittington et al. 1990). Although only the last two choices involve cash purchases of water, all three sources of supply require time spent hauling water by households, and particularly its female members. This time clearly involves an opportunity cost, or 'value', in that it may be put to other productive household uses such as child care, wage employment, agricultural labour or food preparation. The results of the random utility estimation reveal that the households in the village place a very high value on the time they spent collecting water, approximately US$0.31 per hour. This is almost 25 per cent more than the prevailing market wage rate for unskilled labour in Ukundu, which was US$0.25 per hour. This finding has important implications for public water supply decisions, as it suggests that piped distribution systems are an economically attractive technology in villages such as Ukundu.

Random utility models have also been employed to analyse household decisions over fuel choice in both urban and rural areas of developing countries. Such analysis is important for understanding the costs and benefits of different fuel choices on reducing indoor air pollution, which, as we have seen, is a major source of mortality risk in developing countries, especially among females (see Table 8.2). For example, Farsi et al. (2007) find that lack of income and the price of liquid petroleum gas are the main factors in constraining urban households in India from using cleaner fuels and reducing indoor air pollution. Heltberg (2005) finds that income is also a constraint on the choice of fuels by rural and urban households in Guatemala, but the opportunity costs of fuelwood play an additional role. However, because there is a tendency for all Guatemalan households to use a 'mix' of solid fuels, households may continue to pay high prices for fuelwood bought in local markets. In contrast, An et al. (2002) find that providing a cheaper and better quality electricity service in rural China could lead households to switch from fuelwood collection to electricity for cooking and heating, as they are already using electricity mainly for lighting and some electronic appliances. As emphasized by Larson and Rosen (2002), further analysis of the household demand for control of indoor pollution needs to develop household-based random utility models to address four critical areas: (1) improving information on dose-response relationships between indoor air pollution and various health effects (for example increased mortality and morbidity risks); (2) improving information on impacts from interventions in terms of air pollution reductions and also cooking times, fuel use and heat intensities; (3) improving information on household shadow values for improved health, with separate information for adult and child health; and (4) considering more directly household information, and its adequacy, for their ability to evaluate the relationships between fuel use and health.

As we saw in Chapter 3, choice experiments are also based on the random utility model framework, and allow assessment and valuation of tradeoffs in choices between various environmental goods and services, especially where differences in the attributes of the various choices matter. In recent years, choice modelling and experiments have also been increasingly used in developing countries. For the most part, however, the studies are limited to choices concerning preferences of national and international tourists in relation to the development or preservation of unique natural environments and national parks, such as rainforest conservation in Vanuatu (Rolfe et al., 2000), ecotourism development in

Costa Rica (Hearne and Salinas, 2002) and improved mangrove management in Malaysia (Othman et al., 2004). Choice modelling has also been used in Costa Rica to assess how sensitive urban households' choice of travel mode is to changes in travel time, changes in costs for each mode of travel and other key attributes (Alpizar and Carlsson, 2003). These various applications have shown that choice modelling can be applied in developing countries and can yield implicit values for key environmental attributes. For example, Othman et al., (2004) find that non-user households were, on average, willing to pay US$0.21 for an additional 1 per cent of preserved forest area and US$0.36 for an additional 1 per cent of migratory bird species to be present in the Matang mangroves of Malaysia. Such results hold promise that the approach can be extended to value the key attributes determining the choices that rural user households make over management of critical environmental goods and services.

In the meantime, both contingent valuation and contingent behaviour methods are being used more extensively in developing countries. Contingent Valuation (CV) has been used for a diverse range of applications and settings, including the value to local residents of preserving a variety of important environmental services including flood control, wildlife habitat, waste treatment, and recreational opportunities in the Kuantu wetland in Taiwan (Hammitt et al., 2001); the use and value of mangroves to villagers in Kosrae, Micronesia for fuelwood and other ecosystem services, such as erosion control, storm protection and nutrient flows to shoreline fisheries (Naylor and Drew, 1998); determination of national park entry fees in Costa Rica (Shultz et al., 1998); assessing the welfare losses to local villagers of reduced access to tropical forest as a result of the creation of the Mantadia National Park in Madagascar (Shyamsundar and Kramer, 1996); willingness to pay for a malaria vaccine in Ethiopia (Cropper et al., 2004); the valuation of community forestry in Ethiopia (Mekonnen, 2000); and the willingness to pay for improved water services in Manaus, Brazil (Casey et al., 2006).

Despite the recent proliferation of such studies, conducting CV methods in developing countries needs to address a number of important issues that arise to ensure high quality results (Whittington, 1998 and 2002). First, non-economists in developing countries are often confused about the distinction between willingness and ability to pay for an improvement in environmental quality. As many interviewers may lack economics training, it is important that they understand that the objective of the CV study is to determine how much respondents are willing and able to pay. In addition, cultural and language differences may make it difficult to understand and interpret respondents' answers to the hypothetical questions and scenarios posed. Even 'yes' and 'no' responses to a contingent referendum questionnaire can be easily misinterpreted. Another common problem in implementing referendum-style surveys is that the range of prices utilized is too low, which can undermine the credibility of the CV results. Correctly modelling the household's behaviour with respect to provision of an environmental commodity and accurately presenting this scenario may also be critical to the CV outcome. This is particularly important in the case of water supply, sanitation and other infrastructure services, where the service may be provided publicly to a community but may involve individual households deciding to connect to the service once it is provided. Also, few CV studies conducted in developing countries are designed to test whether some of the key assumptions that the researcher made were the right ones, and whether the results are robust with respect to simple variations in research design and survey method. Finally, conducting CV surveys in developing countries raises some unique ethical issues, such as ensuring that public agencies that have access to survey responses respect their confidentiality, which researchers need to be aware of in conducting such surveys.

Some of these problems can be overcome through combining revealed preference and stated preference techniques to value environmental goods and services. As discussed in Chapter 3, contingent behaviour methods that combine information on actual market transactions and direct household surveys have been used extensively to value environmental amenities. Such approaches are beginning to be applied in developing countries as well. For example, Rosado et al. (2006) demonstrate how combining averting behaviour with CV data can be employed to estimate the willingness to pay for improved drinking water in Espírito Santo, Brazil. Box 8.2 summarizes the case study by Acharya and Barbier (2002), who combine contingent behaviour and household production function modelling to determine the loss in household welfare to villagers in Northern Nigeria whose village well water supply is affected by a decline in the recharge of local aquifers caused by the loss of inundation area in the surrounding floodplain.

8.5   VALUING IMPROVED ENVIRONMENTAL QUALITY AND REDUCTION IN ENVIRONMENTAL RISK FACTORS

As we have discussed previously, a growing concern in developing economies is the high mortality caused by certain environmental risk factors. Valuation methods are increasingly being employed to assess the willingness to pay for reducing these risk factors as well as for improving environmental quality in general, particularly pollution and congestion problems in urban areas.

BOX 8.2   VALUING VILLAGE WATER DEMAND AND
GROUNDWATER RECHARGE IN NORTHERN
NIGERIA

Upstream dam developments are threatening the economic livelihoods of millions of poor agricultural households dependent on the Hadejia-Jama'are floodplain in Northeast Nigeria (Barbier, 2003). One of the concerns is that disruptions to the flood extent will affect the annual recharge of the underlying aquifer, which will in turn impact the welfare of local populations dependent on this groundwater for drinking water and other household uses.

Acharya and Barbier (2002) combine stated preference valuation from the contingent behaviour (CB) method with a household production function model of observed behaviour in order to estimate the value placed on groundwater either purchased or collected from village wells by households in a floodplain region of Northern Nigeria. This combined approach overcomes two potential limitations to implementing CV in developing countries that are often mentioned in the literature (for example, see Whittington, 1998 and 2002). First, by focusing on a daily activity that is familiar to rural villagers – collecting and purchasing drinking water – there is little risk of misrepresenting the environmental commodity and behavioural scenario to the households surveyed. Second, supplementing the stated preference data on households' responses to changes in the price of water and collection times acquired through surveys with observed behaviour of the households' collection and purchasing decisions means that environmental valuation is not wholly dependent on hypothetical methods. The observed data provide a way of 'checking' the reliability and validity of the contingent behaviour surveys while ensuring that all the data available for the analysis – observed and stated – are being fully utilized in the valuation.

The results of the analysis suggest that the value of the recharge function is US$13 209 per day for the floodplain. The average welfare loss for a 1 metre drop in groundwater levels is approximately US$0.12 per household per day. This average figure suggests a daily loss of approximately 0.23 per cent of monthly income for purchase-only households, 0.4 per cent of monthly income for collect-only households, and 0.14 per cent of monthly income for collect and purchase households.

We have already noted the increasing importance of studies to assess the costs and benefits of different fuel choices on reducing indoor air pollution (for example, see An et al., 2002; Farsi et al., 2007; Heltberg, 2005; and Larson and Rosen, 2002). However, assessments of the health effects of air pollution, as well as valuing efforts to improve air quality, are also becoming more frequent.

For example, Alberini et al. (1997) have developed an averting behaviour model to determine a household's willingness to pay to avoid illness related to air pollution in three cities of Taiwan. The duration of the respiratory illness is assumed to depend on air pollution, the nature of the illness and an exogenous measure of its severity. However, the latter can be affected by mitigating behaviour, such as medication taken and medical attention received. Illness also affects the productive time available for work, and thus the income constraint of the household. The model indicates that the willingness to pay to reduce the duration of a single illness episode is therefore a function of income, prices, household characteristics, the nature of the illness, its severity (which in turn depends on mitigation) and illness duration before and after mitigation. The results of the analysis suggest a median willingness to pay by a household to avoid a one-day episode involving cold symptoms to be around US$20, and for non-cold symptoms $31. Based on previous dose-response estimates for Taiwan indicating the effects of air pollution controls on reducing symptoms of illness, the authors calculate that the morbidity value of this pollution abatement would be approximately US$262.58 million.

In follow-up studies, Alberini and Krupnik (1998 and 2000) show that the willingness to pay estimates to avoid minor respiratory illnesses from air pollution in Taiwan exceed cost of illness estimates by between 1.61 to 2.26 times, depending on the pollution levels. These ratios are similar to those for the United States, despite the differences between the two countries. This suggests that valuation methods to ascertain the health effects of air pollution in developing countries can produce results comparable to those attained for studies in developed countries.

Valuation studies are also being employed to analyse urban households' willingness to pay for policies to control urban air pollution in developing countries. For example, control of ozone pollution has become an increasingly important policy issue in many rapidly industrializing countries. Yoo and Chae (2001) used CVM to determine households' WTP for improved ozone pollution control in Seoul, Korea, which could involve a number of measures to limit car use and vehicle emissions. The average household's annual mean WTP ranged from $17.88 to $22.70 per household, which yielded a present value net benefits (over 8 years and at a 10 per cent discount rate) of between US$185 and US$283 million for the package of ozone control measures. Thus, as the authors conclude, 'the preliminary results apparently show that the ozone pollution control policy in Seoul is socially profitable, and rational households would support the policy if it were not costly to them' (Yoo and Chae, 2001, p. 58).

Instead of estimating the direct willingness to pay for pollution control, an alternative would be to adopt a choice model of households' responses to various control policy options. Takeuchi et al. (2007), for example, illustrate how a mode of transport and vehicular ownership choice model can be employed to examine the impact of various policies to reduce particulate emission (PM10) from buses, cars and two-wheelers in Mumbai, India. The choice model is relevant in this situation, as the three types of policies considered – conversion of city diesel buses to 'clean' natural gas (CNG), an increase in the price of gasoline, and a tax on vehicle ownership – will impact differently on how individuals choose to travel and their vehicle ownership. The behavioural responses to the various policies will determine in turn the effectiveness of each measure in reducing overall particulate emissions. The results of the Mumbai study suggest that the most effective policy to reduce total PM10 emissions from passenger vehicles is to convert diesel buses to CNG. The conversion of 3391 diesel buses to CNG would result in an emissions reduction of 663 tons of PM10 per year, 14 per cent of total emissions from transport, and would generate positive net benefits based on comparing the benefits to the estimated costs per life saved of the transport policy.

Another important source of pollution in rapidly expanding cities of the developing world is the growth in informal industries – low technology micro-enterprises that are generally unlicensed and unregulated by government authorities. Although responsible for significant employment of unskilled workers, especially migrants from rural areas, informal industries in urban areas, such as leather tanning, ceramics, brick kilning, metalworking, electroplating and mining, generate significant pollution. Blackman et al. (2006) employ three different models to estimate the benefits of policies to control particulate emissions from the informal brick kiln industry in Ciudad Juárez, Mexico. They find that the annual net benefits of controlling emissions from the informal brick kiln industry range from US$29 million for improved kiln technology to US$53 million for switching to natural gas. In comparison, the average net benefits from various pollution control measures on formal industries are US$12 million for a chemical plant and US$2 million for an iron foundry. The authors conclude that policy makers should include informal industry polluters as an important emission source to be targeted by major industrial pollution control initiatives.

As indicated in Table 8.2, unsafe sources of water and poor sanitation facilities are one of the leading environmental risk factors for mortality in the poorest economies. Increasingly, valuation and cost–benefit studies are being used to assess this critically important risk factor. Three approaches are commonly used. First, some studies value either the main health damages associated with unsafe water and sanitation or the willingness to pay for medicines and vaccines that treat these health effects. Second, some studies estimate the willingness to pay for improved water

supplies, and in some instances, compare the WTP to the coping or averting behaviour of households with access to unsafe supplies. Finally, some
studies conduct cost–benefit analysis of large-scale infrastructure investments that clean up water pollution or improve water supply.

Unsafe water, sanitation and hygiene are responsible for widespread
outbreaks of diarrhoea and typhoid, and are linked to the prevalence
of malaria and other fatal insect-borne diseases in developing countries.
Dasgupta (2004) develops a household 'health' production model to estimate the probability of diarrhoea illness incurred by an urban household
in India from unsafe drinking water. This probability measure is then
used, along with data on the incidence of illness, to determine both the
costs of medical treatment and wage losses accruing to each household.
This yields, in turn, an estimate of the total costs of diarrhoea outbreaks
arising from unsafe drinking water.

In some cases, it is also relevant to assess the willingness to pay by
households for medical treatments for the diseases arising from poor water
supplies and sanitation. For example, Canh et al. (2006) maintain that
improved sanitation and water supplies to eliminate typhoid fever in Hue,
Vietnam is a long-term prospect, but development of an effective vaccine
is a more feasible short to medium-term strategy to control the disease.
The authors find that the mean household *ex ante* WTP for typhoid
immunization through vaccinating all members of the household ranged
from US$21 to US$27, depending on the effectiveness and duration of the
vaccine. These estimates of private benefits suggest that a mass vaccina-
tion campaign against typhoid fever in Hue would be popular and would
be likely to pass a social cost–benefit analysis. Developing a vaccine for
malaria may also be an effective strategy for saving the maximum amount
of lives in poor developing regions. In an innovative study, Cropper et
al. (2004) compare the WTP of rural households in Ethiopia for malaria
immunization through vaccinating all household members with the total
cost of illness arising from contracting the disease. Their results indicate
that the value of preventing malaria with vaccines is about US$36 per
household per year, or about 15 per cent of imputed annual household
income. This private benefit is, on average, about twice the expected
household cost of illness, again suggesting that developing such a vaccine
would pass a cost–benefit test.

Various studies estimate households' willingness to pay for improved
water supplies. For example, Ready et al. (2002) calculate the WTP of
urban residents for an ambitious package of investments to upgrade
inadequate and deteriorated sewage treatment facilities over 800 small
and medium-sized towns in Latvia. While the WTP estimates alone yield
insufficient overall benefits needed to meet the costs of these investments,

the WTP is likely to increase rapidly as incomes in Latvia rise, suggesting that improved sanitation is an important public investment in the near term as incomes rise. Similarly, Casey et al. (2006) find that households in Manaus, Brazil are willing to pay more than US$6.12 per month for improved water treatment services.

Some studies take their analyses one step further and compare the WTP for improved water supply and sanitation to the implied costs of the coping or averting behaviour for households lacking such access. For example, Pattanayak et al. (2005) find that households in Kathmandu, Nepal cope with unsafe water by spending time on collecting water from public sources, storing water and treating it before consumption. Some households also spend money on bottled water, as well as water from public tankers and private vendors. In addition, households invest in storage tanks, water filters, tube wells and chemicals, plus the costs of maintaining these facilities. The authors find that these 'coping costs' average as much as US$3 per household per month, or about 1 per cent of current incomes. Not only are these coping costs almost twice as much as monthly water utility bills, but they are also significantly lower than the estimated WTP of the average household for improved water services.

Finally, large-scale improvements in water supplies, sanitation and hygiene require substantial investments in major projects and management programmes. The resulting increases in water quality often yield multiple benefits, which need to be assessed through a variety of environmental valuation methods to compare the costs and benefits of these investments. Box 8.3 summarizes such a CBA conducted by Markandya and Murty (2000 and 2004) performed for the major Ganga Action Plan to clean up the Ganges River in India. As the CBA indicates, the net present value of the project is significantly positive. In addition, because many important benefits occur to low-income groups, both the net present value and benefit–cost ratio of the plan rises when the distributional impacts of the clean-up are taken into account.

One of the important benefits, and indeed key motivations, of the Ganga Action Plan was to clean up the Ganges River to an acceptable bathing standard for recreational and religious use (see Box 8.3). As incomes rise in developing countries, such amenity benefits are likely to become increasingly important. For example, a study of Davao in the Philippines estimated the differences in the value households placed on recreation at a local beach, before and after a public health advisory on water pollution (Choe et al., 1996). Since two-thirds of the recreational users stopped visiting the site after the health advisory, a Tobit model was used to estimate the visitation rate equation. The results indicate that the average consumer surplus loss for each household due to the affects of

BOX 8.3   COST–BENEFIT ANALYSIS OF THE GANGA
          ACTION PLAN, INDIA

The Ganga Action Plan (GAP) was launched in February 1985 to raise
the water quality levels of the Ganges River in India to bathing standard
(Markandya and Murty, 2000 and 2004). The final investment cost of
implementing the GAP from 1985/86 to 1996/96 was US$318 million (in
1995/96 prices), with an operating cost over the same period of US$10
million. In addition, water-polluting industries were required to invest
in abatement, which amounted to an annual cost of effluent treatment
of US$10.5 million. Due to the plan, water quality in terms of dissolved
oxygen improved, biochemical oxygen demand and concentrates of
phosphates and nitrates were observed, although some places along
the Ganges were affected only marginally. The result, however, was that
the clean-up of the river produced multiple benefits to many different
stakeholders. Markandya and Murty (2000 and 2004) employed a variety
of environmental valuation methods to assess these multiple benefits,
and thus to conduct a complete cost–benefit analysis of the GAP investment.

The main user benefits were from increased amenity, especially
bathing, from the Ganges, which accrued to residents, tourists and
pilgrims (at bathing ghats) who visit the river. However, there were
also important non-user benefits from cleaning the Ganges, arising
from wanting to bequeath the biodiversity the river supports to future
generations, from reassurance that the Ganges River is kept clean
and its aquatic life protected, and from the desire to protect people
living along the river from water-borne diseases. Both these user and
non-user benefits of the GAP were estimated through CVM surveys
of households. In addition, improving water quality in the Ganges led
to various health benefits to nearby residents using the water, which
were estimated by the increased income due to the reduced number of
working days lost from illness by river water users. As sewage sludge
and waste water from towns and cities along the Ganges are used as
organic fertilizer and irrigation by small farmers, the increased number
of sewage treatment plants built by the GAP allowed farmers to irrigate more hectares and to substitute treated sewage for conventional
fertilizers. By estimating the fertilizer cost savings and the increased
yields from irrigation, the additional agricultural benefits arising from
the GAP could be calculated. Finally, there were substantial social
benefits from employing unskilled labour in the GAP projects, due to
increased income from employment and from redistribution of income
to the unskilled labourers who belong to the lowest income group in the
Indian economy.

The following table summarizes the present value estimates conducted by Markandya and Murty (2000 and 2004) of the various benefits
and costs of the GAP, along with the authors' sensitivity analysis of the
likely income distribution effects.

Cost–benefit analysis of GAP and income effects, US$ million (1995–96 prices)

	Present value[a]	Income distribution effects[b]	
		$\varepsilon = 1.75$	$\varepsilon = 1.75$
Benefits from:			
Recreation and amenities	0.83	0.08	0.06
Non-use	195.20	12.49	8.39
Health effects	23.49	72.42	81.64
Agricultural productivity	16.33	48.58	56.76
Employment of unskilled labour	54.53	162.17	189.49
Costs to:			
Industry	42.74	4.10	2.91
Government	129.81	129.81	129.81
Net present value	117.83	161.83	203.62
Benefit–cost ratio	1.68	2.21	2.53

Notes:
a   Estimated over 1985/86 to 1996/97 at 10 per cent discount rate.
b   The value of ε is the weight attached to the costs and benefits of each stakeholder group relative to the costs and benefits of a group with income equal to the national per capita income.

As the above CBA indicates, the net present value of the Ganga Action Plan is significantly positive. In addition, because many of the benefits accrue to poor income groups, such as farmers, river water users and unskilled labour, the income distribution effects of the GAP are substantial. When these are taken into account, the net present value and the benefit–cost ratio of cleaning up the Ganges River rise considerably.

pollution on recreation use amounted to between US$1.44 and US$2.04 per month.

Finally, rising incomes, especially in urban areas of developing countries, will also mean a higher demand for 'bundled' environmental benefits. These include both improvements in environmental quality associated with the choice of private goods, such as residential housing, and improvements in publicly provided environmental services. For example, Nokokure Humavindu and Stage (2003) utilize a hedonic pricing model of housing sales in Windhoek, Namibia to assess how environmental quality affects sales. They find that inhabitants in the township areas of Windhoek attach a high value to proximity to a conservation area, whereas proximity to a garbage dump reduces the value of a property significantly. Bluffstone and DeShazo (2003) estimate household willingness to pay for improved municipal landfill, sewage and recycling programmes in Ukmerge, Lithuania. Relative to estimated costs, households are willing to pay 80 to 90 per cent of costs for landfill improvement, but less than 10 per cent for an upgraded sewage service and virtually nothing for two recycling programmes. Thus, assessing private fees to recover the costs of landfill may be an option, but other sources of funding will be required for upgraded sewage and recycling.

8.6   CONCLUSION

The title of this chapter poses the question: what is different about cost–benefit analysis in developing countries? As we have shown in this chapter, neither the environmental valuation methods nor the application of cost–benefit analysis is substantially different. In fact, almost all of the valuation methods discussed in the various chapters of Part I are increasingly being applied to developing countries. But as we have stressed here, the context in which valuation and CBA is applied in developing countries is considerably different. The large numbers of rural poor dependent on fragile environments and critical environmental goods and services mean that valuation of ecosystem benefits and the quality and state of the surrounding environment on which poor people depend is extremely important. A growing concern is also the high mortality caused by certain environmental risk factors in developing economies, such as unsafe water, sanitation and hygiene, indoor pollution from solid fuels, urban air pollution and lead poisoning. Valuation methods are increasingly being employed to assess the willingness to pay for reducing these risk factors as well as for improving environmental quality in general. As more and more people in developing countries live in urban areas, and as incomes rise, the demand for controlling pollution and congestion problems in urban areas, as well as for improved environmental services generally, will be an increasingly important focus of CBA and valuation studies.

As the demand for environmental valuation for policy purposes in developing countries increases, it is important that researchers continue to apply the best market and non-market methods available for the task. In his review of contingent valuation studies in developing countries, Whittington (2002) points out that there is a significant risk that the current push for cheaper, simpler studies could discredit the CV methodology itself. Because such methods are increasingly being employed in a variety of policy decisions of tremendous importance to the welfare of many households in developing countries, such as improvements in water and sanitation services, control of urban pollution, vaccines for the poor and management of key natural ecosystems, Whittington (2002, p. 322) argues that it is even more critical that 'researchers push for excellence in this research enterprise and that funding agencies think more carefully about the value of policy-relevant information' resulting from these valuation methods. Whittington's advice pertains not just to CV methods but to the application of all environmental valuation methods and CBA in developing countries.

REFERENCES

Acharya, Gayatri and Edward B. Barbier (2002), 'Using domestic water analysis to value groundwater recharge in the Hadejia-Jama'are floodplain, Northern Nigeria', *American Journal of Agricultural Economics*, **84**(2), 415–26.

Adamowicz, Wiktor, Jordan Louviere and Michael Williams (1994), 'Combining revealed preference and stated preference methods for valuing environmental amenities', *Journal of Environmental Economics and Environmental Management*, **26**, 271–92.

Adamowicz, Wiktor, Peter Boxall, Michael Williams and Jordan Louviere (1998), *American Journal of Agricultural Economics*, **80**(1), 64–75.

Alberini, A. and A. Krupnick (1998), 'Air quality and episodes of acute respiratory illness in Taiwan cities: evidence from survey data', *Journal of Urban Economics*, **44**(1), 68–92.

Alberini, A. and A. Krupnick (2000), 'Cost-of-illness and willingness-to-pay estimates of the benefits of improved air quality: evidence from Taiwan', *Land Economics*, **76**(1), 37–53.

Alberini, A., M. Cropper, T.-T. Fu, A. Krupnick, J.-T. Liu, D. Shaw and W. Harrington (1997), 'Valuing health effects of air pollution in developing countries: the case of Taiwan,' *Journal of Environmental Economics and Environmental Management*, **34**, 107–26.

Alix-Garcia, Jennifer, Alain de Janvery, Elisabeth Sadoulet and Juan Manuel Torres (2005), 'An assessment of Mexico's payment for environmental services program', Report for the Comparative Studies Service, Agricultural and Development Economics Division, United Nations Food and Agriculture Organization (FAO), Rome.

Alpizar, Francisco and Fredrik Carlsson (2003), 'Policy implications and analysis of the determinants of travel mode choice: an application of choice experiments to metropolitan Costa Rica', *Environment and Development Economics*, **8**, 603–19.

Amacher, G., W. Hyde and B. Joshee (1993), 'Joint production and consumption in traditional households: fuelwood and crop residues in two districts in Nepal', *Journal of Development Studies*, **30**(1), 206–25.

An, Li, Frank Lupi, Jianguo Liu, Marc A. Linderman and Jinyan Huang (2002), 'Modeling the choice to switch from fuelwood to electricity: implications for giant panda habitat conservation', *Ecological Economics*, **42**, 445–57.

Ascher, William (1999), *Why Governments Waste Natural Resources: Policy Failures in Developing Countries*, Baltimore: Johns Hopkins University Press.

Aylward, Bruce and Jaime Echeverría (2001), 'Synergies between livestock production and hydrological function in Arenal, Costa Rica', *Environment and Development Economics*, **6**, 359–81.

Badola, Ruchi and S.A. Hussain (2005), 'Valuing ecosystems functions: an empirical study on the storm protection function of Bhitarkanika mangrove ecosystem, India', *Environmental Conservation*, **32**(1), 85–92.

Bandaranayake, W.M. (1998), 'Traditional and medicinal uses of mangroves', *Mangroves and Salt Marsh*, **2**, 133–48.

Barbier, Edward B. (1994), 'Valuing environmental functions: tropical wetlands', *Land Economics*, **70**(2), 155–73.

Barbier, Edward B. (2001), 'Environmental valuation in developing countries', Chapter 1 in Henk Folmer and Tom Tietenberg (eds), *The International Yearbook of Environmental and Resource Economics 2001/2002: A Survey of Current Issues*, Cheltenham, UK and Northampton, MA, USA: Edward Elgar, pp. 1–39.

Barbier, Edward B. (2003), 'Upstream dams and downstream water allocation: the case of the Hadejia-Jama'are Floodplain, Northern Nigeria', *Water Resources Research*, **39**(11), 1311–19.

Barbier, Edward B. (2005), *Natural Resources and Economic Development*, Cambridge: Cambridge University Press.

Barbier, Edward B. (2007a), 'Natural capital and labour allocation: mangrove-dependent households in Thailand', *The Journal of Environment and Development*, **16**(December), 398–431.

Barbier, Edward B. (2007b), 'Valuing ecosystem services as productive inputs', *Economic Policy*, **22**(49), 177–229.

Barbier, Edward B. (2008), 'In the wake of tsunami: lessons learned from the household decision to replant mangroves in Thailand', *Resource and Energy Economics*, **30**(2), May, 229–49.

Barbier, Edward B. and Mark Cox (2003), 'Does economic development lead to mangrove loss? A cross-country analysis', *Contemporary Economic Policy*, **21**(4), 418–32.

Barbier, Edward B. and S. Sathirathai (eds) (2004), *Shrimp Farming and Mangrove Loss in Thailand*, Cheltenham, UK and Northampton, MA, USA: Edward Elgar.

Barbier, Edward B. and Ivar Strand (1998), 'Valuing mangrove–fishery linkages: a case study of Campeche, Mexico', *Environmental and Resource Economics*, **12**, 151–66.

Barrett, Christopher B. (2004), 'Rural poverty dynamics: development policy implications', *Agricultural Economics*, **32**(1), 43–58.

Barrett, Christopher B., Thomas Reardon and P. Webb (2001), 'Nonfarm income diversification and household livelihood strategies in rural Africa: concepts, dynamics and policy implications', *Food Policy*, **26**, 315–31.

Berkes, Firkit (1999), *Sacred Ecology: Traditional Ecological Knowledge and Resource Management*, Philadelphia: Taylor & Francis.

Blackman, Allen, Jhih-Shyang Shih, David Evans, Michael Batz, Stephen Newbald and Joseph Cook (2006), 'The benefits and costs of informal sector pollution control: Mexican brick kilns', *Environment and Development Economics*, **11**, 603–27.

Bluffstone, Randall A. (1998), 'Reducing degradation of forests in poor countries when permanent solutions elude us: what instruments do we have?', *Environment and Development Economics*, **3**(3), 295–318.

Bluffstone, Randall and J.R. DeShazo (2003), 'Upgrading municipal environmental services to European Union levels: a case study of household willingness to pay in Lithuania', *Environment and Development Economics*, **8**(4), 637–54.

Bluffstone, Randall A., Marco Boscolo and Ramiro Molina (2008), 'Does better common property forest management promote behavioral change? On-farm tree planting in the Bolivian Andes', *Environment and Development Economics*, **13**(2), 137–70.

Brander, Luke M., Raymond J.G.M. Florax and Jan E. Vermaat (2006), 'The empirics of wetland valuation: a comprehensive summary and a meta-analysis of the literature', *Environmental and Resource Economics*, **33**, 223–50.

Cameron, Trudy A. (1992), 'Combining contingent valuation and travel cost data for the valuation of non-market goods', *Land Economics*, **68**(3), 302–17.

Canh, Do Gia, Dale Whittington, Le Thi Kim Thoa, Nugroho Utomo, Nguyen Thai Hoa, Christine Poulos, Dang Thi Dieu Thuy, Dohyeong Kim, Andrew Nyamete and Camilo Acosta (2006), 'Household demand for typhoid fever vaccines in Hue, Vietnam', *Health Policy and Planning*, **21**(3), 241–55.

Casey, James F., James R. Kahn and Alexandre Rivas (2006), 'Willingness to pay for improved water service in Manaus, Amazonas, Brazil', *Ecological Economics*, **58**, 365–72.

Caviglia-Harris, Jill L. (2004), 'Household production and forest clearing: the role of farming in the development of the Amazon', *Environment and Development Economics*, **9**,181–202.

Cesar, Herman S.J. (2000), 'Coral reefs: their functions, threats and economic value', in H.S.J. Cesar (ed.), *Collected Essays on the Economics of Coral Reefs*, Kalmar, Sweden: CORDIO.

Choe, KyeongAe, Dale Whittington and Donald T. Lauria. (1996), 'The economic benefits of surface water quality improvements in developing countries: a case study of Davao, Phillipines', *Land Economics*, **72**(4), 519–37.

Chomitz, Kenneth M. and Kanta Kumari (1998), 'The domestic benefits of tropical forests: a critical review', *The World Bank Research Observer*, **13**(1), 13–35.

Chomitz, Kenneth M. with P. Buys, G. De Luca, T.S. Thomas and S. Wertz-Kanounnikoff (2007), *At Loggerheads? Agricultural Expansion, Poverty Reduction, and Environment in the Tropical Forests*, Washington, DC: World Bank.

Chong, Jo (2005), *Protective Values of Mangrove and Coral Ecosystems: A Review of Methods and Evidence*, Gland, Switzerland: IUCN.

Cooke, Priscilla (1998), 'The effect of environmental good scarcity on own-farm labor allocation: the case of agricultural households in rural Nepal', *Environment and Development Economics*, **3**(4), 443–70.

Cooke, Priscilla, Gunnar Köhlin and William F. Hyde (2008), 'Fuelwood, forests, and community management – evidence from household studies', *Environment and Development Economics*, **13**(1),103–35.

Cropper, Maureen L., Mitiku Haile, Julian Lampietti, Christine Poulos and Dale Whittington (2004), 'The demand for a malaria vaccine: evidence from Ethiopia', *Journal of Development Economics*, **75**, 303–18.

Daily, Gretchen (ed.) (1997), *Nature's Services: Societal Dependence on Natural Ecosystems*, Washington, DC: Island Press.

Dasgupta, Partha (1993), *An Inquiry into Well-Being and Destitution*, New York: Oxford University Press.

Dasgupta, Purnamita (2004), 'Valuing health damages from water pollution in urban Delhi, India: a health production function approach', *Environment and Development Economics*, **9**, 83–106.

Dasgupta, Susmita, Uwe Deichmann, Craig Meisner and David Wheeler (2005), 'Where is the poverty–environment nexus? Evidence from Cambodia, Lao PDR, and Vietnam', *World Development*, **33**(4), 617–38.

Diwakara, H. and M.G. Chandrakanth (2007), 'Beating negative externality through groundwater recharge in India: a resource economic analysis', *Environment and Development Economics*, **12**, 271–96.

Englin, Jeff and Trudy A. Cameron (1996), 'Augmenting travel cost models with contingent behaviour data: Poisson regression analysis with individual panel data', *Environmental and Resource Economics*, **7**,133–47.

Farsi, Mehdi, Massimo Filippini and Shonali Pachauri (2007), 'Fuel choices in urban Indian households', *Environment and Development Economics*, **12**(6), 757–74.

Fisher, Monica (2004), 'Household welfare and forest dependence in Southern Malawi', *Environment and Development Economics*, **9**, 135–54.

Food and Agricultural Organization of the United Nations (FAO) (2001), 'Forest resources assessment 2000: main report', FAO Forestry Paper 140, Rome: FAO.

Food and Agricultural Organization of the United Nations (FAO) (2003), 'State of the world's forests 2003', Rome: FAO.

Gray, Leslie C. and William G. Mosley (2005), 'A geographical perspective on poverty–environment interactions', *The Geographical Journal*, **171**(1), 9–23.

Guo, Zhongwei, Xiangming Xiao, Yaling Gan and Yuejun Zheng (2001), 'Ecosystem functions, services and their values – a case study in Xingshan County of China', *Ecological Economics*, **38**, 141–54.

Hammitt, James K., Jin-Tan Liu and Jin-Long Liu (2001), 'Contingent valuation of a Taiwanese wetland', *Environment and Development Economics*, **6**, 259–68.

Hanley, Nick, Susana Mourato and Robert E. Wright (2001), 'Choice modeling approaches: a superior alternative to environmental valuation?', *Journal of Economic Surveys*, **15**(3), 435–62.

Heal, Geoffrey M., Edward B. Barbier, Kevin J. Boyle, Alan P. Covich, Stephen P. Gloss, Carl H. Hershner, John P. Hoehn, Catherine M. Pringle, Stephen Polasky, Kathleen Segerson and Kirstin Shrader-Frechette (2005), *Valuing Ecosystem Services: Toward Better Environmental Decision Making*, Washington, DC: The National Academies Press.

Hearne, Robert R. and Zenia M. Salinas (2002), 'The use of choice experiments in the analysis of tourist preferences for ecotourism development in Costa Rica', *Journal of Environmental Management*, **65**, 153–63.

Heltberg, Rasmus (2005), 'Factors determining household fuel choice in Guatemala', *Environment and Development Economics*, **10**(3), 337–62.

Houghton, R.A. (1995), 'Land use change and the carbon cycle', *Global Change Biology*, **1**, 257–87.

Islam, Mursaleena and John B. Braden (2006), 'Bio-economic development of floodplains: farming versus fishing in Bangladesh', *Environment and Development Economics*, **11**, 95–126.

Jackson, Jeremy B.C., Michael X. Kirby, Wolfgang H. Berger, Karen A. Bjørndal, Louis W. Botsford, Bruce J. Bourque, Roger H. Bradbury, Richard Cooke, Jon Erlandson, James A. Estes, Terence P. Hughes, Susan Kidwell, Carine B. Lange, Hunter S. Lenihan, John M. Pandolfi, Charles H. Peterson, Robert S. Steneck,

Mia J. Tegner and Robert R. Warner (2001), 'Historical overfishing and the recent collapse of coastal ecosystems', *Science*, **293**, 629–38.

Janssen, Ron and Jose E. Padilla (1999), 'Preservation or conservation? Valuation and evaluation of a mangrove forest in the Philippines', *Environmental and Resource Economics*, **14**(3), 297–331.

Kaiser, Brooks and James Roumasset (2002), 'Valuing indirect ecosystem services: the case of tropical watersheds', *Environment and Development Economics*, **7**, 701–14.

Kremen, C., J.O. Niles, M.G. Dalton, G.C. Daily, P.R. Ehrlich, J.P. Fay, D. Grewal and R.P. Guillery (2000), 'Economic incentives for rainforest conversion across scales', *Science*, **288**, 1828–32.

Landel-Mills, Natasha and Ina T. Porras (2002), 'Silver bullet or fool's gold? A global review of markets for forest environmental services and their impact on the poor', Instruments for Sustainable Private Sector Forestry Series, London: International Institute for Environment and Development.

Larson, Bruce A. and Sydney Rosen (2002), 'Understanding household demand for indoor pollution control in developing countries', *Social Science & Medicine*, **55**, 571–84.

Lemley, A. Dennis, Richard T. Kingsford and Julian R. Thompson (2000), 'Irrigated agriculture and wildlife conservation: conflict on a global scale', *Environmental Management*, **25**(5), 485–512.

Markandya, Anil and M.N. Murty (2000), *Cleaning Up the Ganges: The Cost–Benefit Analysis of Ganga Action Plan*, New Delhi: Oxford University Press.

Markandya, Anil and M.N. Murty (2004), 'Cost–benefit analysis of cleaning the Ganges: some emerging environment and development issues', *Environment and Development Economics*, **9**, 61–81.

Matthews, E., R. Payne, M. Rohweder and S. Murray (2000), *Pilot Analysis of Global Ecosystems: Forest Ecosystems*, Washington, DC: World Resources Institute.

Mekonnen, Alemu (2000), 'Valuation of community forestry in Ethiopia: a contingent valuation study of rural households', *Environment and Development Economics*, **5**, 298–308.

Millennium Ecosystem Assessment (2005), *Ecosystems and Human Well-being: A Framework for Assessment*, Washington, DC: Island Press.

Minot, Nicholas and Bob Baulch (2002), 'The spatial distribution of poverty in Vietnam and the potential for targeting', Policy Research Working Paper 2829, Washington, DC: World Bank.

Moberg, Frederik and Carl Folke (1999), 'Ecological goods and services of coral reef ecosystems', *Ecological Economics*, **29**, 215–33.

Moberg, Frederik and Patrick Rönnbäck (2003), 'Ecosystem services of the tropical seascape: interactions, substitutions, and restoration', *Ocean & Coastal Management*, **46**, 27–46.

Molden, David (ed.) (2007), *Water for Food, Water for Life: A Comprehensive Assessment of Water Management in Agriculture*, London: Earthscan, and Colombo, Sri Lanka: International Water Management Institute.

Narain, Urvashi, Klaas van't Veld and Shreekant Gupta (2008), 'Poverty and the environment: exploring the relationship between household incomes, private assets, and natural assets', *Land Economics*, **84**(1), 148–67.

Naylor, Rosalind and M. Drew (1998), 'Valuing mangrove resources in Kosrae, Micronesia', *Environment and Development Economics*, **3**, 471–90.

Nilsson, Christer, Catherine A. Reidy, Mats Dynesius and Carmen Revenga (2005), 'Fragmentation and flow regulation of the world's large river systems', *Science*, **308**, 405–8.

Nokokure Humavindu, Michael and Jesper Stage (2003), 'Hedonic pricing in Windhoek townships', *Environment and Development Economics*, **8**(2), 391–404.

Othman, Jamal, Jeff Bennett and Russell Blamey (2004), 'Environmental management and resource management options: a choice modelling experience in Malaysia', *Environment and Development Economics*, **9**, 803–24.

Pagiola, Stefano, Agustin Arcenas and Gunars Platais (2005), 'Can payments for environmental services help reduce poverty? An exploration of the issues and the evidence to date from Latin America', *World Development*, **33**(2), 237–53.

Pascual, U. and E.B. Barbier (2006), 'Deprived land-use intensification in shifting cultivation: the population pressure hypothesis revisited', *Agricultural Economics*, **34**, 155–65.

Pascual, U. and E.B. Barbier (2007), 'On price liberalization, poverty and shifting cultivation: an example from Mexico', *Land Economics*, **83**(2), 192–216.

Pattanayak, Subhrendu K. and Randall A. Kramer (2001), 'Worth of watersheds: a producer surplus approach for valuing drought mitigation in Eastern Indonesia', *Environment and Development Economics*, **6**, 123–46.

Pattanayak, Subhrendu K., Jui-Chen Yang, Dale Whittington and K.C. Bal Kumar (2005), 'Coping with unreliable public water supplies: averting expenditures by households in Kathmandu, Nepal', *Water Resources Research*, **41**, W02012–W02023.

Population Division of the United Nations Secretariat (2008), *World Urbanization Prospects: The 2007 Revision: Executive Summary*, New York: United Nations.

Postel, Sandra L. and Barton H. Thompson, Jr. (2005), 'Watershed protection: capturing the benefits of nature's water supply services', *Natural Resources Forum*, **29**, 98–108.

Ready, Richard C., Jânis Malzubris and Silva Senkane (2002), 'The relationship between environmental values and income in a transition economy: surface water quality in Latvia', *Environment and Development Economics*, **7**(1), 147–56.

Reardon, Thomas and Stephen A. Vosti (1995), 'Links between rural poverty and the environment in developing countries – asset categories and investment poverty', *World Development*, **23**, 1495–506.

Richards, Michael (1997), 'The potential for economic valuation of watershed protection in mountainous areas: a case study from Bolivia', *Mountain Research and Development*, **17**(1), 19–30.

Rodwell, Lynda D., Edward B. Barbier, Callum M. Roberts and Timothy R. McClanahan (2003), 'The importance of habitat quality for marine reserve–fishery linkages', *Canadian Journal of Fisheries and Aquatic Sciences*, **60**, 171–81.

Rolfe, John, Jeff Bennett and Jordan Louviere (2000), 'Choice modelling and its potential application to rainforest preservation', *Ecological Economics*, **35**, 289–302.

Rönnbäck, Patrik (1999), 'The ecological basis for economic value of seafood production supported by mangrove ecosystems', *Ecological Economics*, **29**(2), 235–52.

Rönnbäck, Patrick, Beatrice Crona and Lisa Ingwall (2007), 'The return of ecosystem goods and services in replanted mangrove forests: perspectives from local communities in Kenya', *Environmental Conservation*, **34**(4), 313–24.

Rosado, Marcia A., Maria A. Cunha-E-Sá, Maria M. Ducla-Soares and Luis C.

Nunes (2006), 'Combining averting behavior and contingent valuation data: an application to drinking water in Brazil', *Environment and Development Economics*, **11**, 729–46.

Rosegrant, Mark W., Ximing Cai and Sarah A. Cline (2002), *World Water and Food to 2025: Dealing with Scarcity*, Washington, DC: International Food Policy Research Institute.

Ruitenbeek, H.J. (1994), 'Modeling economy–ecology linkages in mangroves: economic evidence for promoting conservation in Bintuni Bay, Indonesia', *Ecological Economics*, **10**(3), 233–47.

Sarntisart, Isra and Suthawan Sathirathai (2004), 'Mangrove dependency, income distribution and conservation', Chapter 6 in E.B. Barbier and S. Sathirathai (eds), *Shrimp Farming and Mangrove Loss in Thailand*, Cheltenham, UK and Northampton, MA, USA: Edward Elgar.

Scherr, Sara J. (1999), 'Poverty–environment interactions in agriculture: key factors and policy implications', Paper 3, United Nations Development Program and European Community, Poverty and Environment Initiative, New York: UNDP.

Scherr, Sara J. (2000), 'A downward spiral? Research evidence on the relationship between poverty and natural resource degradation', *Food Policy*, **25**, 479–98.

Shutz, Steven, Jorge Pinazzo and Miguel Cifuentes (1998), 'Opportunities and limitations of contingent valuation surveys to determine national park entrance fees: evidence from Costa Rica', *Environment and Development Economics*, **3**, 131–49.

Shyamsundar, P. and R.A. Kramer (1996), 'Tropical forest protection: an empirical analysis of the costs borne by local people', *Journal of Environmental Economics and Management*, **31**, 129–44.

Silvano, Renato A.M., Shana Udvardy, Marta Ceroni and Joshua Farley (2005), 'An ecological integrity assessment of a Brazilian Atlantic forest watershed based on surveys of stream health and local farmers' perceptions: implications for management', *Ecological Economics*, **53**, 369–85.

Takeuchi, Akie, Maureen Cropper and Antonio Bento (2007), 'The impact of policies to control motor vehicle emissions in Mumbai, India', *Journal of Regional Science*, **47**(1), 27–46.

Tockner, Klement and Jack A. Stanford (2002), 'Riverine flood plains: present state and future trends', *Environmental Conservation*, **29**(3), 308–30.

Turner, R. Kerry, Jouni Paavola, Philip Cooper, Stephen Farber, Valma Jessamy and Stavros Georgiou (2003), 'Valuing nature: lessons learned and future research directions', *Ecological Economics*, **46**, 493–510.

United Nations Environment Programme (UNEP) (2006), 'Marine and coastal ecosystems and human wellbeing: a synthesis report based on the findings of the Millennium Ecosystem Assessment', Nairobi: UNEP.

Valiela, I.J.L. Bowen and J.K. York (2001), 'Mangrove forests: one of the world's threatened major tropical environments', *BioScience*, **51**(10), 807–15.

Vedeld, Paul, Arild Angelsen, Espen Sjaastad and Gertrude K. Berg (2004), 'Counting on the environment: forest incomes and the rural poor', Environment Department Paper 98, Washington, DC: World Bank.

Walton, Mark E.M., Giselle P.B. Samonte-Tan, Jurgenne H. Primavera, Gareth Edwards-Jones and Lewis Le Vay (2006), 'Are mangroves worth replanting? the direct economic benefits of a community-based reforestation project', *Environmental Conservation*, **33**(4), 335–43.

Wassenaar, T., P. Gerbera, P.H. Verburgb, M. Rosalesa, M. Ibrahimc and H. Steinfelda (2007), 'Projecting land use change in the neotropics: the geography of pasture expansion into forest', *Global Environmental Change*, **17**, 86–104.

Whittington, Dale (1998), 'Administering contingent valuation surveys in developing countries', *World Development*, **26**(1), 21–30.

Whittington, Dale (2002), 'Improving the performance of contingent valuation studies in developing countries', *Environmental and Resource Economics*, **22**, 323–67.

Whittington, Dale, X. Mu and R. Roche (1990), 'Calculating the value of time spent collecting water: some estimates for Ukundu, Kenya', *World Development*, **18**(2), 269–80.

World Bank (2003), *World Development Report 2003*, Washington, DC: World Bank.

World Bank (2006), *World Development Indicators*, Washington, DC: World Bank.

World Bank (2008), *Poverty and the Environment: Understanding Linkages at the Household Level*, Washington, DC: World Bank.

World Health Organization (WHO) (2002), *World Health Report: Reducing Risks, Promoting Healthy Life*, Geneva: WHO.

World Resources Institute (WRI) (2001), *World Resources 2000–2001. People and Ecosystems: The Fraying Web of Life*, Washington, DC: World Resources Institute.

Worm, Boris, Edward B. Barbier, Nicola Beaumont, J. Emmett Duffy, Carl Folke, Benjamin S. Halpern, Jeremy B.C. Jackson, Heike K. Lotzke, Fiorenza Micehli, Stephen R. Palumbi, Enric Sala, Kimberly A. Selkoe, John J. Stachowicz and Reg Watson (2006), 'Impacts of biodiversity loss on ocean ecosystem services', *Science*, **314**, 787–90.

Yoo, Seung-Hoon and Kyung-Suk Chae (2001), 'Measuring the benefits of the ozone pollution control policy in Seoul, Korea: results of a contingent valuation survey', *Urban Studies*, **38**(1), 49–60.

Young, Carlos E.F. (1998), 'Public policies and deforestation in the Brazilian Amazon', *Planejamento e Políticas Públicas*, **18**, 201–22.

PART II

Case studies

9.   Valuing ecosystem services

9.1   INTRODUCTION

Global concern over the disappearance of many ecosystems and habitats
has prompted policy makers to consider the implications of this loss for
human welfare and environmental decision-making. The result has been
a number of inter-disciplinary assessments by economists, ecologists and
other scientists highlighting the need to 'value' the goods and services provided by key global ecosystems (Daily, 1997; Heal et al., 2005; Millennium
Ecosystem Assessment, 2005; Pagiola et al., 2004; World Resources
Institute, 2001). This interest in 'valuing' ecosystem services raises two
important questions. What are ecosystem services, and what are the particular measurement issues that must be addressed when valuing these
environmental flows?

This chapter discusses the implications of valuing ecosystem services for
the application of cost–benefit analysis to environmental decision making.
We begin by explaining the concept of ecosystem services and why this term
provides a useful insight for classifying and quantifying a variety of important benefits that arise from the 'functioning' of ecosystems. The chapter
then discusses what challenges ecosystem services pose for conventional
environmental valuation methods, such as those described in Chapters
3–6. Despite these challenges, we explain why valuing ecosystem services
is increasingly important for a variety of economic decisions concerning
the decision of whether to 'develop' or 'conserve' ecosystems. The chapter
illustrates some of these issues by focusing on examples from coastal and
marine systems, as well as other valuation studies of ecosystem services.

9.2   WHAT ARE ECOSYSTEM SERVICES?

Broadly defined, 'ecosystem services are the benefits people obtain from
ecosystems' (Millennium Ecosystem Assessment, 2005, p. 53). Such benefits are typically described by ecologists in the following manner:

> Ecosystem services are the conditions and processes through which natural
> ecosystems, and the species that make them up, sustain and fulfill human

life. . . . In addition to the production of goods, ecosystem system services are the actual life-support functions, such as cleansing, recycling, and renewal, and they confer many intangible aesthetic and cultural benefits as well. (Daily, 1997, p. 3)

Thus in the current literature the term 'ecosystem services' lumps together a variety of 'benefits', which in economics would normally be classified under three different categories: (i) 'goods' (for example products obtained from ecosystems, such as resource harvests, water and genetic material), (ii) 'services' (for example recreational and tourism benefits or certain ecological regulatory functions, such as water purification, climate regulation, erosion control, and so on), and (iii) cultural benefits (for example, spiritual and religious, heritage, and so on).

Regardless of how one defines and classifies 'ecosystem services', as a report from the US National Academy of Science has emphasized, 'the fundamental challenge of valuing ecosystem services lies in providing an explicit description and adequate assessment of the links between the structure and functions of natural systems, the benefits (i.e., goods and services) derived by humanity, and their subsequent values' (Heal et al., 2005, p. 2). Moreover, it has been increasingly recognized by economists and ecologists that the greatest 'challenge' they face is in valuing the ecosystem services provided by a certain class of key ecosystem functions – regulatory and habitat functions. Table 9.1 provides some examples of the links between regulatory and habitat functions and the ecosystem services that ultimately benefit humankind.

9.3   THE VALUATION CHALLENGE

The literature on ecological services implies that ecosystems are assets that produce a flow of beneficial goods and services over time. In this regard, they are no different from any other asset in an economy, and in principle, ecosystem services should be valued in a similar manner. That is, regardless of whether or not there exists a market for the goods and services produced by ecosystems, their social value must equal the discounted net present value (NPV) of these flows.

For example, let's suppose that the flow of ecosystem services in any time period, t, can be quantified and that we can measure what each individual is 'willing to pay' for having these services provided to him or her. If we sum up, or aggregate, the willingness to pay by all the individuals benefiting from the ecosystem services in each period, we will have a monetary amount – call it B_t – which indicates the social benefits in the given time

Table 9.1 *Some services provided by ecosystem regulatory and habitat functions*

Ecosystem functions	Ecosystem processes and components	Ecosystem services (benefits)
Regulatory Functions		
Gas regulation	Role of ecosystems in biogeochemical processes	Ultraviolet-B protection Maintenance of air quality Influence of climate
Climate regulation	Influence of land cover and biologically mediated processes	Maintenance of temperature, precipitation
Disturbance prevention	Influence of system structure on dampening environmental disturbance	Storm protection Flood mitigation
Water regulation	Role of land cover in regulating runoff, river discharge and infiltration	Drainage and natural irrigation Flood mitigation Groundwater recharge
Soil retention	Role of vegetation root matrix and soil biota in soil structure	Maintenance of arable land Prevention of damage from erosion and siltation
Soil formation	Weathering of rock and organic matter accumulation	Maintenance of productivity on arable land
Nutrient regulation	Role of biota in storage and recycling of nutrients	Maintenance of productive ecosystems
Waste treatment	Removal or breakdown of nutrients and compounds	Pollution control and detoxification
Habitat Functions		
Niche and refuge	Suitable living space for wild plants and animals	Maintenance of biodiversity Maintenance of beneficial species
Nursery and breeding	Suitable reproductive habitat and nursery grounds	Maintenance of biodiversity Maintenance of beneficial species

Source: Adapted from Heal et al. (2005, Table 3-3) and De Groot et al. (2002).

period t of those services. Hopefully, there will be a stream of such benefits generated by ecosystem services, from the present time and into the future. Because society is making a decision today about whether or not to preserve ecosystems, we want to consider the flow of benefits of these services, net of the costs of maintaining the natural ecosystems intact, in terms of their *present value*. To do this, any future net benefit flows are discounted into present value equivalents. In essence, we are treating natural ecosystems as a special type of capital asset – a kind of 'natural wealth' – which just like any other asset or investment in an economy is capable of generating a current and future flow of 'income' or 'benefits'.

However, what makes environmental assets special is that they give rise to particular measurement problems that are different from those for conventional economic or financial assets. This is especially the case for the beneficial services that are derived from the regulatory and habitat functions of ecosystems.

For one, these assets and services are a special type of 'natural capital' (Just et al., 2004, p. 603). Ecosystems comprise the abiotic (non-living) environment and the biotic (living) groupings of plant and animal species called communities. As with all forms of capital, when these two components of ecosystems interact, they provide a flow of services (Barbier and Heal, 2006). If the ecosystem is left intact, then the flow services from the ecosystem's regulatory and habitat functions are available in quantities that are not affected by the rate at which they are used. Although like other assets in the economy an ecosystem can be increased by investment, such as through restoration activities, ecosystems can also be depleted or degraded, for example through habitat destruction, land conversion, pollution impacts and so forth.

However, whereas the services from most assets in an economy are marketed, the benefits arising from the regulatory and habitat functions of ecosystems generally are not. If the aggregate willingness to pay for these benefits, B_t, is not revealed through market outcomes, then efficient management of such ecosystem services requires explicit methods to measure this social value. In fact, the failure to consider the 'values' provided by key ecosystem services in current policy and management decisions is a major reason for the widespread disappearance of many ecosystems and habitats across the globe (Millennium Ecosystem Assessment, 2005). The global expansion of human populations and economic activity are important causes of this disappearance, due to, among other things, increased demand for land, pollution or over-exploitation of resources (Kareiva et al., 2007; Millennium Ecosystem Assessment, 2005; UNEP, 2006; Valiela et al., 2001; Worm et al., 2006). The failure to measure explicitly the aggregate willingness to pay for otherwise non-marketed ecological

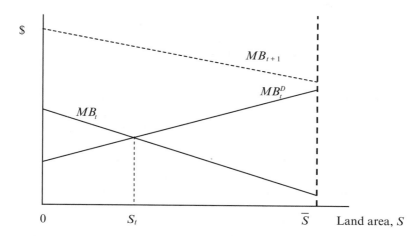

Figure 9.1   Optimal ecosystem conversion to coastal zone development

services exacerbates these problems, as the benefits of these services are underpriced and may lead to excessive land conversion, habitat fragmentation, harvesting and pollution caused by commercial economic activity undertaken by humans.

Figure 9.1 illustrates the difficulty that these environmental measurement problems pose – and why valuation is important especially to land management decisions. In this figure, the example of the conversion of an area of coastal zone to commercial development is used.

In Figure 9.1, the marginal social benefits of ecological services at any time t are represented by the line MB_t for a coastal ecosystem of given area $\overline{S}$. For the purposes of illustration, this line is assumed to be downward-sloping, which implies that for every additional square kilometre of coastal habitat land area, S, preserved in its original state, more ecosystem service benefits will be generated at a decreasing amount. Note that it is straightforward to determine the aggregate willingness to pay for the benefits of these services, B_t, from this line; it is simply the area under the MB_t line. If there is no other use for the land occupied by the ecosystem, then the opportunity costs of maintaining it are zero, and B_t is at its maximum size when the entire coastal ecosystem is left intact at its original land area size $\overline{S}$. The ecosystem management decision is therefore simple; the coastal ecosystem should be completely preserved and allowed to provide its full flow of services in perpetuity.

However, population and economic development pressures in many areas of the world usually mean that the opportunity cost of maintaining the land for coastal ecosystems is not zero, due to increased demand for land accompanying economic development in coastal zones. The eco-system management decision needs to consider these alternative uses of coastal areas, and we therefore need to add into Figure 9.1 these oppor-tunity costs. For example, suppose that the marginal social benefits of converting natural ecosystem land for these development options is now represented by a new line MB_t^D in the figure. Thus efficient use of land would require that an amount $\bar{S} - S_t$ of coastal ecosystem area should be converted for development, leaving S_t of the original ecosystem intact.

Both of these outcomes assume that the willingness to pay for the mar-ginal benefits arising from coastal and surrounding marine ecosystem services, MB_t, is explicitly measured, or 'valued'. But if this is not the case, then these non-marketed flows are likely to be ignored in the land use deci-sion. Only the marginal benefits, MB_t^D, of the 'marketed' outputs arising from coastal economic development activities will be taken into account, and as indicated in the figure, this implies that the entire ecosystem area $\bar{S}$ will be converted for development.

A further problem in valuing environmental assets is the uncertainty over their future values. It is possible, for example, that the benefits of ecosys-tem services are larger in the future as more scientific information becomes available over time. This is illustrated in Figure 9.1. Recall that, if the benefits of ecosystem services in the current period are correctly valued and incorporated in the development decision, then only $\bar{S} - S_t$ of ecosystem area should be converted for coastal zone development at time t. However, as we shall now see, even this may be too much development *today* if we are uncertain about *future* ecosystem service benefits. For example, suppose that in some future period $t+1$ it is discovered that the value of coastal and marine ecosystem services is actually much larger, so that the marginal ben-efits of these services, MB_{t+1}, in present value terms (that is, 'discounted', or measured in terms of today's dollars) is now represented by the dotted line in the figure. If the present value marginal benefits from coastal zone devel-opment in the future are largely unchanged, that is $MB_{t+1}^D \approx MB_t^D$, then as Figure 9.1 indicates, the future benefits of ecosystem services exceed these costs, and the coastal ecosystem area should be 'restored' to its original area $\bar{S}$. Unfortunately, in making development decisions today we often do not know today that the future value of ecosystem services will turn out to exceed future development benefits. Our simple example shows that, if we have already made the decision today to convert the $\bar{S} - S_t$ area of the coastal zone, then we will have to reverse this decision in the future period and 'restore' the original coastal ecosystem.

It should be immediately apparent from this simple example that taking into account future ecosystem service values is further complicated by the problem of *irreversibility*. If development today leads to irreversible loss

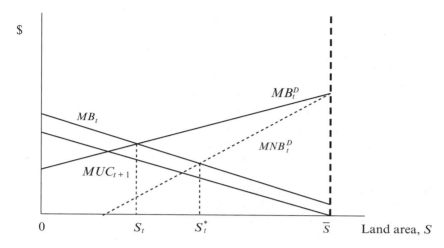

Figure 9.2 Irreversible conversion of ecosystems and uncertainty

(or reversible only at high cost) of coastal and marine ecosystems, and the values of the services provided by these environments are uncertain, then this gives an additional reason for conserving ecosystems (Arrow and Fisher, 1974; Dixit and Pindyck, 1994; Henry, 1974). As pointed out by Krutilla and Fisher (1985), if environmental assets are irreversibly depleted, their value will rise relative to the value of other reproducible and accumulating economic assets. This is a likely scenario for any coastal and marine ecosystem that is irreversibly converted or degraded as a result of expansion of coastal zone development or the cumulative generation of pollution by this activity. Because natural ecosystems are in fixed supply and are difficult to substitute for or restore, the beneficial services provided by their regulatory and habitat functions will decline as these assets are converted or degraded. The increasing relative scarcity of these services means that their value will rise relative to other goods and services in the economy. This also implies that any decision today that leads to irreversible conversion imposes a 'user cost' on individuals who face a rising scarcity value of future coastal and marine ecosystem benefits as a consequence. This user cost should be part of a cost–benefit analysis of a development proposal.

Figure 9.2 illustrates the additional measurement problem arising from irreversible conversion of fixed ecosystem assets.

As in the original example of Figure 9.1, if only the current benefits, MB_t, and opportunity costs, MB_t^D, of maintaining the original ecosystem are considered, then an amount $\overline{S} - S_t$ of ecosystem area would be converted today. But suppose that the loss of coastal and marine eco-system services arising from converting $\overline{S} - S_t$ causes the value of these services to rise. As a result, individuals benefiting from these services in a future time period $t + 1$ would optimally choose to have less land con-verted to coastal zone development. However, if ecosystem conversion is irreversible, then land development remains at $\overline{S} - S_t$ in time period $t + 1$. But this additional development means that individuals in the future will be deprived of valuable coastal and marine services. This loss in welfare for individuals in the future is the 'user cost' of irreversible loss of coastal and marine ecosystem services due to conversion today. In Figure 9.2, the marginal user cost of development, measured in present value terms, is represented as the straight line MUC_{t+1}, which rises as more coastal land is converted. The correct land use decision should take into account this additional cost of irreversible ecosystem conversion due to expansion of coastal zone development today. Deducting the marginal user cost from MB_t^D yields the net marginal benefits of the development option, MNB_t^D. The latter is the appropriate measure of the opportunity costs of maintain-ing coastal and marine ecosystems intact, and equating it with the mar-ginal social benefits of ecosystem services determines the intertemporally optimal land allocation. Only $\overline{S} - S_t^*$ of coastal ecosystem area should be converted for development, leaving S_t^* of the original ecosystem intact.

Valuation of environmental assets under conditions of uncertainty and irreversibility clearly poses additional measurement problems. There is now a considerable amount of literature advocating various methods for estimating environmental values by measuring the additional amount, or 'premium', that individuals are willing to pay to avoid the uncertainty surrounding such values (see Ready, 1995 for a review). Similar methods are also advocated for estimating the user costs associated with irrevers-ible development, as this also amounts to valuing the 'option' of avoiding reduced future choices for individuals (Just et al., 2004). However, the problem with such welfare measures is that they cannot be estimated from the observed behaviour of individuals and are therefore difficult to imple-ment empirically, particularly when there is uncertainty not only about the future state of the environmental asset but also over the future preferences and income of individuals. The general conclusion from the few empirical attempts to implement environmental valuation under uncertainty is that 'more empirical research is needed to determine under what conditions we can ignore uncertainty in benefit estimation. . . . where uncertainty is over economic parameters such as prices or preferences, the issues surrounding uncertainty may be empirically unimportant' (Ready, 1995, p. 590).

However, ignoring uncertainty and irreversibility may not be wise for many ecosystems in the case of assessing their resilience, that is their capacity to avoid breaching thresholds that cause the systems to 'flip' from one functioning state to another (Elmqvist et al., 2003; Folke et al., 2004; Perrings, 1998). In principle, the methods outlined here of incorporating the 'user costs' of irreversible development are the same for taking into account the value of preserving the 'resilience' of a natural ecosystem. For example, returning to Figure 9.2, suppose that we know that if coastal development is limited to S_{t+1}, then the thresholds of the original coastal and marine ecosystem are unlikely to be breached. However, as additional coastal area is converted, the resilience of the system is likely to decline – that is there is an increasing risk that the ecosystem will 'breach' its thresholds and 'flip' to a different type of system that yields poorer quality and less beneficial ecological services. If we are able to estimate the probability of the system breaching its thresholds as land conversion proceeds beyond S_{t+1}, and if we can measure and value the changes to ecosystem services that result from the 'altered' ecosystem state, then we might be able to construct a similar 'marginal user cost' curve as MUC_{t+1} in Figure 9.2. Once again, the correct land use decision should take into account this additional 'resilience' cost of irreversible ecosystem conversion today.

In principle, therefore, taking into account the 'resilience' cost of irreversible conversion of any ecosystems can be handled through economic valuation. Actually measuring this cost, however, does impose a formidable challenge. As this simple example of coastal habitats makes clear, the two key components of valuing the marginal user cost associated with reducing the resilience of ecosystems is determining: a) the probability of 'breaching' thresholds as natural habitat area is converted or damaged; and b) the loss in valuable ecological services that result from any 'flip' in ecosystems to an altered state. We return to the problem of including resilience with a CBA in Chapter 13.

9.4 VALUATION METHODS

Uncertainty, irreversible loss and resilience costs are important issues to consider in valuing ecosystem service tradeoffs affected by economic development and population growth. However, even before we tackle these 'second-order' valuation issues, we are faced with a more basic problem of how to go about valuing the various services of ecosystems. As emphasized by Heal et al. (2005), the 'fundamental challenge' in valuing these flows is that ecosystem services are largely not marketed. In other words, returning to Figure 9.1, unless some attempt is made to value the aggregate willingness to pay for these services, B_t, then it will be difficult to succeed at effective land use management to balance development and conservation tradeoffs.

In recent years substantial progress has been made by economists working with ecologists and other natural scientists on this 'fundamental challenge' to improve environmental valuation methodologies. Table 9.2 indicates there are now various methods that can be used for valuing the services derived from ecological regulatory and habitat functions.

As shown in the table, the various valuation methods employed for ecosystem services are essentially the standard techniques that are available to economists. It is therefore not necessary to discuss the valuation methods listed in Table 9.2, since these have already been described in detail earlier in this book. Instead, however, this section will make a few observations concerning how these standard valuation methods are best applied to ecosystem services, emphasizing in particular both the advantages and shortcomings of the different methods and their application. More discussion of such issues can be found in Barbier (2007), Freeman (2003), Heal et al. (2005) and Pagiola et al. (2004).

First, the application of some valuation methods is often limited to specific types of ecological services. For example, the travel cost method is used principally for those environmental values that enhance individuals' enjoyment of recreation and tourism (see Chapter 4); averting behaviour models are best applied to the health effects arising from environmental pollution (see Chapter 8). Similarly, hedonic wage and property models are used primarily for assessing work-related environmental hazards and environmental impacts on property values, respectively (see Chapter 5).

In contrast, stated preference methods, which include contingent valuation methods, conjoint analysis and choice experiments, have the potential to be used widely in valuing ecosystem goods and services (see Chapter 3). These valuation methods share the common approach of surveying individuals who benefit from an ecological service or range of services, in the hope that analysis of these responses will provide an accurate measure of the individuals' willingness to pay for the service or services. In addition, stated preference methods can go beyond estimating the value to individuals of single and even multiple benefits of ecosystems and in some cases elicit 'non-use values', that is the additional 'existence' and 'bequest' values that individuals attach to ensuring that a preserved and well-functioning system will be around for future generations to enjoy. For example, a study of mangrove-dependent coastal communities in Micronesia demonstrated through the use of contingent valuation techniques that the communities 'place some value on the existence and ecosystem functions of mangroves over and above the value of mangroves' marketable products' (Naylor and Drew, 1998, p. 488). Similarly, choice experiments have the potential to

Table 9.2   Various valuation methods applied to ecosystem services

Valuation method[a]	Types of value estimated[b]	Common types of applications	Ecosystem services valued
Travel cost	Direct use	Recreation	Maintenance of beneficial species, productive ecosystems and biodiversity
Averting behaviour	Direct use	Environmental impacts on human health	Pollution control and detoxification
Hedonic price	Direct and indirect use	Environmental impacts on residential property and human morbidity and mortality	Storm protection; flood mitigation; maintenance of air quality
Production function	Indirect use	Commercial and recreational fishing; agricultural systems; control of invasive species; watershed protection; damage costs avoided	Maintenance of beneficial species; maintenance of arable land and agricultural productivity; prevention of damage from erosion and siltation; groundwater recharge; drainage and natural irrigation; storm protection; flood mitigation
Replacement cost	Indirect use	Damage costs avoided; freshwater supply	Drainage and natural irrigation; storm protection; flood mitigation
Stated preference	Use and non-use	Recreation; environmental impacts on human health and residential property; damage costs avoided; existence and bequest values of preserving ecosystems	All of the above

Table 9.2   (continued)

Notes:
a   See Freeman (2003), Heal et al. (2005) and Pagiola et al. (2004) for more discussion of
     these various valuation methods and their application to valuing ecosystem goods and
     services.
b   Typically, use values involve some human 'interaction' with the environment whereas
     non-use values do not, as they represent an individual valuing the pure 'existence' of a
     natural habitat or ecosystem or wanting to 'bequest' it to future generations. Direct use
     values refer to both consumptive and non-consumptive uses that involve some form of
     direct physical interaction with environmental goods and services, such as recreational
     activities, resource harvesting, drinking clean water, breathing unpolluted air and so
     forth. Indirect use values refer to those ecosystem services whose values can only be
     measured indirectly, since they are derived from supporting and protecting activities
     that have directly measurable values.

Source: Adapted from Heal et al. (2005, Table 4-2).

elicit the relative values that individuals place on different ecosystem services. A study of wetland restoration in southern Sweden revealed through choice experiments that individuals' willingness to pay for the restoration increased if the result enhanced overall biodiversity, but decreased if the restored wetlands were used mainly for the introduction of Swedish crayfish for recreational fishing (Carlsson et al., 2003).

However, as emphasized by Heal et al. (2005), to implement a stated-preference study two key conditions are necessary:

1. The information must be available to describe the change in a natural ecosystem in terms of service that people care about, in order to place a value on those services.
2. The change in the natural ecosystem must be explained in the survey instrument in such a manner that people will understand and not reject the valuation scenario.

For many of the specific services arising from the type of ecological regulatory and habitat functions listed in Table 9.1, one or both of these conditions may not hold. For instance, it has proven very difficult to describe accurately through the hypothetical scenarios required by stated-preference surveys how changes in ecosystem processes and components affect ecosystem regulatory and habitat functions and thus the specific benefits arising from these functions that individuals value. If there is considerable scientific uncertainty surrounding these linkages, then not only is it difficult to construct such hypothetical scenarios but also any responses elicited from individuals from stated-preference surveys are likely to yield inaccurate measures of their willingness to pay for ecological services.

Valuation workshop methods may, however, help in terms of conveying information about complex ecological goods, and investigating the effects on people's values of scientific uncertainty about linkages within the system (see, for example, Christie et al., 2006).

In contrast to stated preference methods, the advantage of production function (PF) approaches is that they depend on only the first condition, and not both conditions, holding (see Chapter 6). That is, for those regulatory and habitat functions where there is sufficient scientific knowledge of how these functions link to specific ecological services that support or protect economic activities, then it may be possible to employ the PF approach to value these services. As we discussed in Chapter 6, the basic modelling approach underlying PF methods, also called 'valuing the environment as input', is similar to determining the additional value of a change in the supply of any factor input. If changes in the regulatory and habitat functions of ecosystems affect the marketed production activities of an economy, then the effects of these changes will be transmitted to individuals through the price system via changes in the costs and prices of final goods and services. This means that any resulting 'improvements in the resource base or environmental quality' as a result of enhanced ecosystem services, 'lower costs and prices and increase the quantities of marketed goods, leading to increases in consumers' and perhaps producers' surpluses' (Freeman, 2003, p. 259).

An adaptation of the PF methodology is required in the case where ecological regulatory and habitat functions have a protective value, through various ecological services such as storm protection, flood mitigation, prevention of erosion and siltation, pollution control and maintenance of beneficial species (see Chapter 6). In such cases, the environment may be thought of as producing a non-marketed service, such as 'protection' of economic activity, property and even human lives, which benefits individuals through limiting damages. Applying PF approaches requires modelling the 'production' of this protection service and estimating its value as an environmental input in terms of the expected damages avoided by individuals.

However, PF methods have their own measurement issues and limitations. Some of these issues were discussed in Chapter 6. Here, we review the measurement problems and limitations that pertain especially to the valuation of ecosystem services.

For instance, applying the PF method raises questions about how changes in the ecological service should be measured, whether market distortions in the final goods market are significant, and whether current changes in ecological services may affect future productivity through biological 'stock effects'. A common approach in the literature is to assume that an estimate of ecosystem area may be included in the 'production function' of marketed output as a proxy for the ecological service input. For example, this is the standard approach adopted in coastal habitat–fishery PF models, as allowing the wetland area to be a determinant of fish catch is thought by economists and ecologists to proxy some element of the productivity contribution of this important habitat function (Barbier, 2000 and 2007; Freeman, 2003, ch. 9). In addition, as pointed out by Freeman (1991), market conditions and regulatory policies for the marketed output will influence the values imputed to the environmental input. For instance, in the previous example of coastal wetlands supporting an offshore fishery, the fishery may be subject to open access conditions. Under these conditions, profits in the fishery would be dissipated, and price would be equated to average and not marginal costs. As a consequence, producer values are zero and only consumer values determine the value of increased wetland area. Finally, a further measurement issue arises in the case where the ecological service supports a natural resource system, such as a fishery, forestry or a wildlife population, which is then harvested or exploited through economic activity. In such cases, the key issue is whether or not the effects on the natural resource stock or biological population of changes in the ecological service are sufficiently large that these stock effects need to be modelled explicitly. In the production function valuation literature, approaches that ignore stock effects are referred to as 'static models' of environmental change on a natural resource production system, whereas approaches that take into account the intertemporal stock effects of the environmental change are referred to as 'dynamic models' (Barbier, 2000 and 2007; Freeman, 2003, ch. 9).

Finally, measurement issues, data availability and other limitations can prevent the application of standard valuation methods to many ecosystem services. In circumstances where an ecological service is unique to a specific ecosystem and is difficult to value, then economists have sometimes resorted to using the cost of replacing the service or treating the damages arising from the loss of the service as a valuation approach. However, economists consider that the replacement cost approach should be used with caution (Barbier, 1994 and 2007; Ellis and Fisher, 1987; Freeman, 2003; Shabman and Batie, 1978). For example, a number of studies that have attempted to value the storm prevention and flood mitigation services of the 'natural' storm barrier function of mangrove and other coastal wetland systems have employed the replacement cost method by simply estimating the costs of replacing mangroves by constructing physical barriers to perform the same services (Chong, 2005). Shabman and Batie (1978) suggested that this method can provide a reliable valuation estimation for an ecological service, but only if the following conditions are met:

(1) the alternative considered provides the same services; (2) the alternative compared for cost comparison should be the least-cost alternative; and (3) there should be substantial evidence that the service would be demanded by society if it were provided by that least-cost alternative. Unfortunately, very few replacement cost studies meet all three conditions.

However, one study that did meet these criteria for valuing an ecosystem service was the well-known analysis of the policy choice of providing clean drinking water by the Catskills Mountains for New York City (Chichilnisky and Heal, 1998; Heal et al., 2005). The case study is summarized in Box 9.1.

The rest of this chapter provides examples of other economic methods applied to valuing ecosystem services, and the use of this information in

---

BOX 9.1   VALUING WATER SUPPLY TO NEW YORK CITY
            BY THE CATSKILLS WATERSHED

The policy decision of whether or not to protect the Catskills watershed in upstate New York in order to provide clean drinking water to New York City is a good example of valuing a single ecosystem service through the replacement cost method (Chichilinsky and Heal, 1998; Heal et al., 2005).

Historically, the Catskills watersheds have supplied New York City 'freely' with high-quality water with little contamination as part of the 'natural filtration' process of the rich and diverse ecosystems on the banks of streams, rivers, lakes and reservoirs comprising these watersheds. However, increasing housing developments and pollution from vehicles and agriculture have threatened water quality in the region. By 1996, New York City faced a choice: either it could build water filtration systems to clean its water supply or the city could protect the Catskill watersheds to ensure high-quality drinking water. In retrospect, the decision was an easy one for New York City. It was not necessary to value all the services of the Catskills watershed ecosystems; instead, it was sufficient simply to demonstrate that protecting and restoring the ecological integrity of the Catskills was less costly than replacing this ecosystem service with a human-constructed water filtration system. It was estimated that the total costs of building and operating the filtration system were in the range of $6 billion to $8 billion. In comparison, to protect the water provision service of the Catskills, New York is obligated to spend $250 million during a ten-year period to purchase and set aside over 140 000 hectares in the watershed. In addition, a series of land regulations were implemented, controlling development and land use in other parts of the watershed. Overall, New York City estimated that it would cost $1 billion to $1.5 billion to protect and restore the natural ecosystem processes in the watershed, thus preserving the clean drinking water service provided by the Catskills.

policy decisions, by exploring two separate case studies. The first case study is valuing the various ecosystem services provided by The Great Lakes bordering the United States and Canada. The second case study is how valuing the ecosystem services of mangroves in Southern Thailand can inform the type of development versus conversion land use decision depicted in Figure 9.1.

9.5   CASE STUDIES

9.5.1   Case Study 1: Great Lakes, United States

As indicated in Box 9.2, the Great Lakes ecosystem bordering Canada and the United States is the largest single freshwater system in the world. However, since the 1800s, population growth, industrial development and the introduction of exotic species have altered this system dramatically, with important consequences in terms of water pollution, biological invasion and lakeshore erosion. The box summarizes some studies that have been conducted on these impacts from loss of ecosystem services in the Great Lakes.

The Great Lakes studies show how various valuation methods discussed in this book can be usefully applied to a wide range of ecosystem

---

BOX 9.2   VALUING THE ECOSYSTEM SERVICES OF THE
           GREAT LAKES

The Great Lakes system, comprising Lakes Michigan, Superior, Huron, Erie and Ontario, borders Canada and the United States. Covering an area of 94 000 square miles, the Great Lakes are the largest freshwater ecosystem in the world, and drain an even larger territory of 201 000 square miles. The ecosystem is currently inhabited by 33 million people, and is visited by numerous tourists and visitors all year round.

Since the 1800s, steady growth in economic activities, such as agriculture, industry, mining and timber harvesting, and in human populations have led to significant ecological change, including biological invasions, water pollution and lake erosion. In recent years, several economic studies have attempted to value the ecosystem services affected by these impacts, including the overall economic consequences of multiple ecosystem changes over time. The following table lists some of the valuation studies, the methods employed and the main findings for a wide range of disturbances to ecological services of the Great Lakes, including a biological invasion affecting native fish, toxic pollution reducing water quality and lake shore erosion.

Ecosystem service affected	Economic activity affected	Valuation method and purpose	Key policy findings
Sea lamprey invasion affecting habitat and populations of lake trout	Recreational trout fishing	Travel cost (Hoehn et al., 1996), used to calculate the benefits to anglers of different control strategies	Net benefits were greatest for annual lampricide and a one-time release of sterile males
Deteriorating water quality due to polychlorinated biphenyls (PCBs)	Recreational fishing	Travel cost (Breffle et al., 1999), used to estimate the benefits from reducing PCB levels so that fish consumption advisories are no longer necessary	Restoration efforts that reduced recovery time to 20 years reduced damages to $106 million, resulting in clean-up benefits of $42 million
Deteriorating water quality due to polychlorinated biphenyls (PCBs)	Welfare of households in Great Lakes region	Stated preference survey (Bishop et al., 2000), used to assess different levels of PCB removal, wetland restoration, enhanced recreation and reducing non-point source pollution	Restoration to reduce PCBs to safe levels in 20 years resulted in benefits of $254 million by reducing damages to $356 million over the 20-year clean-up period.
Lake shoreline erosion	Impact of increased erosion on property values	Hedonic price (Kriesel et al., 1993 and Heinz, 2000), used to estimate the impact of erosion risk on residential shoreline property values	For a $500 000 residence, the annual cost of erosion is $18 400 at 5 years before actual loss; $10 400 at 10 years before loss; and $2 500 for 50 years.

Source: Based on valuation studies reviewed in Heal et al. (2005).

services. However, a comparison of the studies also indicates how the application of some valuation methods is often limited to specific types of ecological services. For example, the travel cost method to value the economic damages caused by lamprey eel invasion is limited to assessing these damages solely in terms of the recreational benefits to anglers who fish trout. Although recreational trout fishing benefits were sufficiently substantial to allow identification of an appropriate lamprey control programme, it is likely that other ecological and species effects in the Great Lakes occur as a result of the biological invasion. Similarly, using hedonic methods to estimate the effect of shoreline erosion of property prices is, by definition, limited to assessing how improved shoreline stabilization influences residential property values.

An interesting comparison is between the travel cost study of the impact of polychlorinated biphenyls (PCBs) water pollution on recreational fishing and the stated preference valuation of PCB pollution impact on households in the Great Lakes region. As indicated in Box 9.2, both studies provide an assessment of the benefits of a lake restoration programme that aims to reduce PCBs to safe levels in 20 years. However, because it is limited to assessing the impacts of PCB pollution on recreational fishing only, the travel cost study estimates that the benefits of the 20-year restoration programme are reduced present-value damages to anglers of $106 million and that the resulting clean-up benefits are $42 million. In contrast, the stated preference studies of households suggest that the 20-year restoration programme would result in present value reduced damages of $356 million for the households, and clean-up benefits of $254 million. The reason for these larger damages avoided and benefits for households is that clearly the stated preference survey is capturing the willingness to pay by Great Lakes households for not just a single ecosystem service, such as recreational fishing, but a wide variety of services that would be improved by PCB clean-up in the Great Lakes. Such an outcome illustrates both the advantage and disadvantage of using stated preference methods for valuing ecosystem services. On the one hand, such methods are not tied to estimating the value to individuals of single and even multiple benefits of ecosystems but instead can elicit a 'total value' comprising various use as well as non-use values associated with an improvement in a wide array of ecosystem services. On the other hand, the 'total value' of the change in ecosystem services cannot be easily disaggregated by type of value or even service. For example, in the Great Lakes stated preference survey of households, it is unclear whether the estimated benefits can be attributed to the value households place on improved quality for recreational water activities, drinking and household water use, improved lake biodiversity, or the 'non-use' value of handing on to future generations an unpolluted lake environment.

9.5.2 Case Study 2: Mangrove Land Use, Thailand

In Thailand, aquaculture expansion has been associated with mangrove wetlands destruction. Since 1961 Thailand has lost from 1500 to 2000 km^2

of coastal mangroves, or about 50–60 per cent of the original area (FAO, 2003). Over 1975–96, 50–65 per cent of Thailand's mangroves was lost to shrimp farm conversion alone (Aksornkoae and Tokrisna, 2004).

Mangrove deforestation in Thailand has focused attention on the two principal services provided by mangrove ecosystems, their role as nursery and breeding habitats for offshore fisheries, and their role as natural 'storm barriers' to periodic coastal storm events, such as wind storms, tsunamis, storm surges and typhoons. In addition, many coastal communities exploit mangroves directly for a variety of products, such as fuelwood, timber, raw materials, honey and resins, and crabs and shellfish. Various studies have suggested that these three benefits of mangroves are significant in Thailand (Barbier, 2003 and 2007; Sathirathai and Barbier, 2001).

Valuation of the ecosystem services provided by mangroves is therefore important for two land use policy decisions in Thailand. First, although declining in recent years, conversion of remaining mangroves to shrimp farm ponds and other commercial coastal developments continues to be a major threat to Thailand's remaining mangrove areas. Second, since the December 2004 tsunami disaster, there is now considerable interest in rehabilitating and restoring mangrove ecosystems as 'natural barriers' to future coastal storm events. Thus valuing the goods and services of mangrove ecosystems can help to address two important policy questions: do the net economic returns to shrimp farming justify further mangrove conversion to this economic activity, and is it worth investing in mangrove replanting and ecosystem rehabilitation in abandoned shrimp farm areas?

To illustrate how improved and more accurate valuation of ecosystems can help inform these two policy decisions, Table 9.3 compares the per hectare net returns to shrimp farming, the costs of mangrove rehabilitation and the value of mangrove services. All land uses are assumed to be instigated over 1996–2004 and are valued in 1996 US$ per hectare (ha).

Several analyses have demonstrated that the overall commercial profitability of shrimp aquaculture in Thailand provides a substantial incentive for private landowners to invest in such operations (Barbier, 2003; Sathirathai and Barbier, 2001; Tokrisna, 1998). However, many of the conventional inputs used in shrimp pond operations are subsidized, below border-equivalent prices, thus increasing artificially the private returns to shrimp farming. In Table 9.3 the net economic returns to shrimp farming, which are calculated once the estimated subsidies are removed, are based on non-declining yields over a five-year period of investment (Sathirathai and Barbier, 2001). After this period, there tend to be problems of drastic yield decline and disease; shrimp farmers then usually abandon their ponds and find a new location. In Table 9.3 the annual economic returns to shrimp aquaculture are estimated to be $322 per hectare (ha), and when

Table 9.3 Comparison of land use values per hectare, Thailand, 1996–2004 (US$)

Land use	Net present value per ha (10–15% discount rate)
Shrimp farming	
Net economic returns[a]	1078 – 1220
Mangrove ecosystem rehabilitation	
Total cost[b]	8812 – 9318
Ecosystem goods & services	
Net income from collected forest products[c]	484 – 584
Habitat–fishery linkage[d]	708 – 987
Storm protection service[e]	8966 – 10 821
Total	10 158 – 12 392

Notes and sources:

a Based on annual net average economic returns US$322 per ha for five years from Sathirathai and Barbier (2001), updated to 1996$.
b Based on costs of rehabilitating abandoned shrimp farm site, replanting mangrove forests and maintaining and protecting mangrove seedlings. From Sathirathai and Barbier (2001), updated to 1996 US$.
c Based on annual average value of $101 per ha over 1996–2004 from Sathirathai and Barbier (2001), updated to 1996 US$.
d Based on a dynamic analysis of mangrove–fishery linkages over 1996–2004 and assuming the estimated Thailand deforestation rate of 3.44 sq km per year (see Barbier, 2007).
e Based on marginal value per ha of expected damage function approach of Barbier (2007).

discounted over the five-year period at a 10–15 per cent rate yield a net present value of $1078 to $1220 per ha.

There is also the problem of the highly degraded state of abandoned shrimp ponds after the five-year period of their productive life. Across Thailand those areas with abandoned shrimp ponds degenerate rapidly into wasteland, since the soil becomes very acidic, compacted and too poor in quality to be used for any other productive use, such as agriculture. To rehabilitate the abandoned shrimp farm site requires treating and detoxifying the soil, replanting mangrove forests and maintaining and protecting mangrove seedlings for several years. As shown in Table 9.3, these restoration costs are considerable, $8812 to $9318 per ha in net present value terms. This reflects the fact that converting mangroves to establish shrimp farms is almost an 'irreversible' land use, and without considerable additional investment in restoration, these areas do not regenerate into mangrove forests. What should happen is that, before the decision to allow shrimp farming to take place, the restoration costs could be treated as one measure of the 'user cost' of converting mangroves irreversibly, and this cost should be deducted from the estimation of the net returns to shrimp aquaculture. As the restoration costs exceed the net economic returns per ha, the decision should be to prevent the shrimp aquaculture operation from occurring.

Unfortunately, past land use policy in Thailand has ignored the user costs of shrimp farming, and as a result many coastal areas have been deforested of mangroves. Many short-lived shrimp farms in these areas have also long since become unproductive and are now abandoned. Thus, an important issue today is whether it is worth restoring mangroves in these abandoned areas. If the forgone benefits of the ecological services of mangroves are not large, then mangrove restoration may not be a reasonable option. Table 9.3 therefore indicates the value of three of these benefits: the net income from local mangrove forest products, habitat–fishery linkages and storm protection.

Sathirathai and Barbier (2001) estimate the value to local communities of using mangrove resources in terms of the net income generated from the forests in terms of various wood and non-wood products. If the extracted products were sold, market prices were used to calculate the net income generated (gross income is minus the cost of extraction). If the products were used only for subsistence, the gross income was estimated based on surrogate prices, that is the market prices of the closest substitute. Based on surveys of local villagers in Surat Thani Province, the major products collected by the households were various fishery products, honey, and wood for fishing gear and fuelwood. As shown in Table 9.3, the net annual income from these products is $101 per ha, or a net present value of $484 to $584 per ha.

The coastal habitat–fishery of mangroves in Thailand may also be modelled through incorporating the change in wetland area within a multi-period harvesting model of the fishery, following the methodology outlined in Chapter 6. The key to this approach is to model a coastal wetland that serves as a breeding and nursery habitat for fisheries as affecting the growth function of the fish stock. As a result, the value of a change in this habitat-support function is determined in terms of the impact of any change in mangrove area on the dynamic path of the returns earned from the fishery. As Table 9.3 indicates, the net present value of this service ranges from $708 to $987 per ha.

The value of the coastal protection service of mangroves in Table 9.3 is derived by employing the expected damage function (EDF) valuation methodology for estimating the expected damage costs avoided through increased provision of the storm protection service of coastal wetlands (see Chapter 6). By applying this EDF approach, Table 9.3 estimates the

benefits from the storm protection service of mangroves in Thailand to be
$1879 per ha, or $8966 to $10 821 per ha in net present value terms.

Table 9.3 indicates that the net present value of all three mangrove ecosystem benefits ranges from $10 158 to $12 392 per ha. These ecosystem
service values clearly exceed the net economic returns to shrimp farming.
In fact, the net income to local coastal communities from collected forest
products and the value of habitat–fishery linkages total $1192 to $1571
per ha, which is greater than the net economic returns to shrimp farming.
However, the value of the storm protection is critical to the decision as to
whether or not to replant and rehabilitate mangrove ecosystems in abandoned pond areas. As shown in Table 9.3, storm protection benefit makes
mangrove rehabilitation an economically feasible land use option.

To summarize, this case study has shown the importance of valuing the
ecological services in land use decisions, as outlined in Figure 9.1. The
irreversible conversion of mangroves for aquaculture results in the loss of
ecological services that generate significantly large economic benefits. This
loss of benefits should be taken into account in land use decisions that
lead to the widespread conversion of mangroves, but typically are ignored
in private sector calculations. Finally, the largest economic benefits of
mangroves appear to arise from regulatory and habitat functions, such as
coastal storm protection and habitat–fishery linkages. This reinforces the
importance of measuring the value of such ecological services.

9.6   MODELLING MULTIPLE ECOSYSTEM
SERVICES

Most natural ecosystems provide more than one beneficial service, and
it may be important to model any tradeoffs among these services as an
ecosystem is altered or disturbed. Integrated economic–ecological modelling could capture more fully the ecosystem functioning and dynamics
underlying the provision of key services, and can be used to value multiple
services arising from natural ecosystems. In Chapter 6 we noted that such
modelling is essentially an extension of the production function approach,
but from a single environment–economic production relationship to
encompassing multiple, possibly interrelated, relationships. Examples
of such multi-service ecosystem modelling include analysis of salmon
habitat restoration (Wu et al., 2003); eutrophication of small shallow lakes
(Carpenter et al., 1999); changes in species diversity in a marine ecosystem
(Finnoff and Tschirhart, 2003); introduction of exotic trout species (Settle
and Shogren, 2002); rangeland management with dynamic interactions
between livestock, grass, shrubs and fire (Janssen et al., 2004); and cattle

stocking on rangeland threatened by invasive plants and nitrogen deposition (Finnoff et al., 2008).

Such integrated ecological–economic modelling allows the ecosystem functioning and dynamics underlying the provision of ecological services to be modelled and can be used to value multiple rather than single services. For example, returning to the Thailand case study, integrated modelling of an entire wetland–coral reef–sea grass system could measure simultaneously the benefits of both the habitat–fishery linkage and the storm protection service provide by the system. In addition, it is well known that both coral reefs and sea grasses complement the role of mangroves in providing both the habitat–fishery and storm protection services (Cochard et al., 2008; Halpern, 2004; Mumby et al., 2004). Thus full modelling of the integrated mangrove–coral reef–sea grass system could improve measurement of the benefits of both services. The result could be that the 'integrated' benefits exceed the valuation of each single ecosystem service estimated on its own (see Table 9.3). As we learn more about the important ecological and economic role played by such services, it may be relevant to develop multi-service ecosystem modelling to understand more fully what values are lost when such integrated coastal and marine systems are disturbed or destroyed.

Integrated modelling of ecosystem services also has the advantage of showing explicitly the relationship between different environmental 'threats'. A good example is shown in Box 9.3, which discusses the integrated model developed by Finnoff et al. (2008) to analyse the problem of invasive plants, nitrogen deposition and stocking rates affecting rangelands in western Canada and the United States.

9.7 NON-LINEAR ECOLOGICAL FUNCTIONS

As noted previously, a principal aim of valuing ecosystem services is often to determine appropriate land use policies, such as how much of an area of ecosystem to conserve and how much to convert to another use (see Figure 9.1). We have noted that, because natural ecosystems are subject to stresses, rapid change and irreversible losses, they tend to display threshold effects and other 'non-linearities' that are difficult to incorporate into any valuation yet may be very important to the land use outcome (see Figure 9.2). However, non-linearities may also have a bearing on the valuation and land use policy outcome, separate to the concerns of 'resilience' and irreversible ecosystem change. The reason is that the connection between ecosystem structure, function and economic value may change due to these non-linearities.

BOX 9.3   INTEGRATED ECOLOGICAL–ECONOMIC
MODELLING OF CATTLE RANGELAND
THREATENED BY INVASIVE PLANTS AND
NITROGEN DEPOSITION

The productivity of cattle rangelands in western Canada and the United States is affected by two important environmental changes: invasive plants, such as cheat grass and leafy spurge, and nitrogen deposition, nitrogen oxides and ammonia which precipitate on terrestrial ecosystems. Both these environmental threats interact, and vary with how much cattle graze on rangeland. For example, stocking rates can determine whether rangeland gravitates toward a socially desirable or undesirable plant community, in terms of the balance of invasive species and native perennials (Huffaker and Cooper, 1995). Nitrogen deposition increases the fertilization of the rangelands, which is good for the native grasses. However, fertilization also benefits cheat grass, and allows this less nutritious invasive to dominate rangeland (McLendon and Redente, 1991).

Finnoff et al. (2008) develop an integrated ecological–economic model of cattle stocking on rangeland threatened by invasive plants and nitrogen deposition to see how maintaining the quality of rangelands and determining optimal stocking rates are complicated by the threat of invasive species and increased levels of nitrogen deposition. They show that improved rangeland policies that take into account these interconnections would require lower optimum stocking in order to avoid low-production rangelands dominated by cheat grass, or zero-production rangelands dominated by leafy spurge. This outcome contrasts with standard 'grazing optimization theory', which maintains that grazers can promote plant primary production either by increasing nitrogen cycling or reducing plant competition, and has been used by land managers to justify heavy stocking on western rangelands (Painter and Belsky, 1993). Instead, by modelling the relationship between nitrogen deposition, along with stocking rates, to plant competition, Finnoff et al. show that current policies may encourage rangeland degradation.

For instance, a common assumption is often made that the 'value' of an ecosystem service changes 'linearly' with critical habitat variables, such as size (for example, area). One reason for invoking such an assumption is that little data exists for examining the marginal losses associated with changes in non-linear ecological functions, making it difficult to value accurately the changes in ecosystem services in response to incremental changes in habitat characteristics (for example, area). Thus, a 'point estimate' for the value of an ecosystem service, in terms of benefits per hectare, is simply multiplied by the total land area of an ecosystem to obtain the value of the service provided by the entire system. If, however, relationships between ecosystem structure and function are non-linear, then assuming that the value of an ecosystem service varies linearly with respect to changes in habitat or ecosystem area will mislead management decisions.

In Box 9.4 we illustrate the potential problem by revisiting the case study of Thailand mangrove use discussed earlier. As shown in the box, if we assume that all ecosystem services are 'uniform' across a mangrove ecosystem covering a 10 km² land area, then their benefits increase linearly as we choose to preserve each additional km² of the coastal landscape. Since these linearly increasing ecosystem benefits exceed the returns from converting the ecosystem to shrimp aquaculture, then the land use decision should be to preserve the entire mangrove ecosystem. But, as the box shows, if the largest ecosystem benefit of the mangroves, which is coastal storm protection, varies across the coastal landscape, then a different land use outcome emerges. Because small losses in mangroves will not cause the economic benefits of storm buffering by mangroves to fall precipitously, the correct land use decision now is to allow up to 2 km² of mangroves to be converted to shrimp aquaculture and to preserve the remainder of the ecosystem.

BOX 9.4 NON-LINEAR WAVE ATTENUATION AND THE
ECONOMIC VALUE OF MANGROVE LAND USE
CHOICES

Table 9.3 depicts a comparison of land use values between various mangrove ecosystem benefits and conversion of the mangrove to a shrimp pond in Thailand. As indicated in the table, the highest value of the mangrove is its storm protection service, which yields an annual benefit of $1879 per hectare (ha) annually, or $8966 to $10 821 per ha in net present value terms over the 1996 to 2004 period of analysis.

But what if the per hectare values in Table 9.3 were used as the basis for a land use decision to convert a mangrove ecosystem, such as a forest extending 1000 m seaward along a 10 km coastline? As pointed out by Barbier et al. (2008), the decision as to how much of this forest to convert to shrimp aquaculture may depend critically on whether or not all the mangroves in the 10 km² ecosystem are equally beneficial in terms of coastal storm protection.

For example, suppose it is assumed that the annual per hectare values for the various ecosystem benefits in Table 9.3 are 'uniform' across the entire 10 km² land area. Consequently, these benefits are essentially 'linear' with respect to the area of mangroves; that is, to derive the total benefits of an area of mangrove we simply multiply the 'point estimate', or per unit value, of each benefit times the total number of hectares of a mangrove ecosystem. For example, according to this assumption, a mangrove area of 10 km² would have an annual storm protection value of 1000 times the $1879 per ha 'point estimate', which yields an annual total benefit estimate of nearly $1.9 million. Barbier et al. (2008) show how this assumption translates into a comparison of the net present value (10 per cent discount rate and 20-year horizon) of shrimp farming to three mangrove services – coastal protection, wood product collection and habitat support for offshore fisheries – as a function of mangrove area (km²) for the example of a 10 km² coastal landscape. The following figure shows the comparison of benefits:

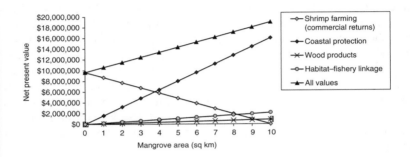

The figure also aggregates all four values to test whether an 'integrated' land use option involving some conversion and some preservation yields the highest total value. When all values are linear, as shown in the figure, the outcome is a typical 'all or none' scenario; either the aggregate values will favour complete conversion or they will favour preserving the entire habitat. Because the ecosystem service values are large and increase linearly with mangrove area the preservation option is preferred. The aggregate value of the mangrove system is at its highest ($18.98 million) when it is completely preserved, and any conversion to shrimp farming would lead to less aggregate value compared to full preservation; thus any land use strategy that considers all the values of the ecosystem would favour mangrove preservation and not shrimp farm conversion.

However, it is also clear from the above figure that the most valuable ecosystem service is storm protection, and the assumption that this service increases linearly with mangrove area is critical to the land use decision to preserve all the mangroves. But not all mangroves along a coastline are equally effective in storm protection. It follows that the storm protection value is unlikely to be uniform across all mangroves either. The reason is that the storm protection 'service' provided by mangroves depends on their critical ecological function in terms of 'attenuation' of storm waves. That is, the ecological damages arising from tropical storms come mostly from the large wave surges associated with these storms. Ecological and hydrological field studies suggest that mangroves are unlikely to stop storm waves that are greater than 6 m (Alongi, 2008; Cochard et al., 2008; Forbes and Broadhead, 2007; Wolanski, 2007). In fact, large and prolonged wave surges from extreme storm events, such as tsunamis and violent cyclones, can uproot mangroves, thus increasing damages and fatalities (Forbes and Broadhead, 2007). Fortunately, such large storm events are rare; even with respect to extremely large events, such as the 2004 Indian Ocean tsunami, mangroves may have acted as natural barriers to some degree: 'in several locations (particularly farther away from the tsunami source), mangroves and other vegetation probably provided some protection against the 2004 tsunami' (Cochard et al., 2008). On the other hand, where mangroves are effective as 'natural barriers' against storms that generate waves less than 6 m in height, field studies show that the wave height of a storm decreases quadratically for each 100 m that a mangrove forest extends out to sea (Mazda et al., 1997; Barbier et al., 2008). In other words, wave attenuation is greatest for the first 100 m of mangroves but declines as more mangroves are added to the seaward edge.

Barbier et al. (2008) employ the non-linear wave attenuation function for mangroves based on the field study by Mazda et al. (1997) to revise the estimate of storm protection service value for the Thailand case study. The result is depicted in the figure below.

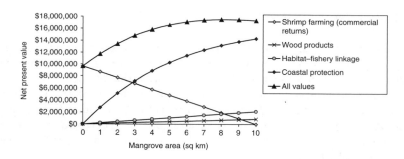

The storm protection service of mangroves still dominates all values, but small losses in mangroves will not cause the economic benefits of storm buffering by mangroves to fall precipitously. The consequence is that the aggregate value across all uses of the mangroves, shrimp farming and ecosystem values, is at its highest ($17.5 million) when up to 2 km² of mangroves are allowed to be converted to shrimp aquaculture and the remainder of the ecosystem is preserved.

Thus, taking into account the 'non-linear' relationship between an ecological function and the value of the ecosystem service it provides can have a significant impact on a land use decision at the landscape scale.

The non-linearity of the ecological functions underlying many ecosystem services can therefore have an important bearing on the valuation of these services and land use decisions. A number of ecological functions appear to have this property (Gaston and Blackborn, 2000). For instance, the example of wave attenuation highlighted in Box 9.4 appears to be non-linear not just for mangroves but for a wide variety of interface coastal habitat, including salt marshes, seagrass beds, nearshore coral reefs and sand dunes. For example, Barbier et al. (2008) show that for salt marshes, there are exponential decreases in wave height with increasing habitat distance inland from the shoreline. In the case of seagrasses and near-shore coral reefs, wave attenuation is a function of the water depth above the grass bed or reef, and these relationships are also non-linear. Additionally, there is an exponential relationship between the percentage cover of dune grasses and the size of oceanic waves blocked by sand dunes produced by the grass. These data suggest that the assumption of linearity is likely to be inaccurate for many ecosystem services that depend on habitat size, a result that could have important implications for both the valuation of these services across landscapes and the land use decisions based on such valuations.

9.8   CONCLUSIONS

Valuing the non-market benefits of ecological services is becoming increasingly important in assisting policy makers to manage critical environmental assets. As we have seen in this chapter, estimating the benefits of these services can be accomplished through applying many of the valuation methods and techniques discussed earlier in the book, although valuing ecosystem services has its own measurement issues. However, further progress to applying valuation methods to value ecological services faces two broad challenges.

First, for these methods to be applied effectively to valuing ecosystem services, it is important that the key ecological and economic relationships are well understood. Unfortunately, our knowledge of the ecological functions, let alone the ecosystem processes and components underlying many of the services listed in Table 9.1, is still incomplete.

Second, natural ecosystems are subject to stresses, rapid change and irreversible losses; they tend to display threshold effects and other non-linearities that are difficult to predict, let alone model in terms of their economic impacts. These uncertainties can affect the estimation of values from an *ex ante* ('beforehand') perspective. The economic valuation literature recognizes that such uncertainties create the conditions for option values, which arise from the difference between valuation under conditions of certainty and uncertainty (for example, see Freeman, 2003 and Just et al., 2004). The standard approach recommended in the literature is to estimate this additional value separately, through various techniques to measure an option price, that is the amount of money that an individual will pay or must be compensated to be indifferent from the status quo condition of the ecosystem and the new, proposed condition. However, in practice, estimating separate option prices for unknown ecological effects is very difficult. Determining the appropriate risk premium for vulnerable populations exposed to the irreversible ecological losses is also proving elusive. As one review of these studies concludes: 'Given the imperfect knowledge of the way people value natural ecosystems and their goods and services, and our limited understanding of the underlying ecology and bio-geochemistry . . . calculations of the value of the changes resulting from a policy intervention will always be approximate' (Heal et al., 2005, p. 218).

Nonetheless, in a world in which many ecosystems are increasingly disappearing or degraded as a result of economic activity and human population expansion, we must continue to make progress in applying valuation methods to assess the myriad benefits provided by these important systems.

REFERENCES

Aksornkoae, S. and R. Tokrisna (2004), 'Overview of shrimp farming and mangrove loss in Thailand', in E.B. Barbier and S. Sathirathai (eds), *Shrimp Farming and Mangrove Loss in Thailand*, Cheltenham, UK and Northampton, MA, USA: Edward Elgar.

Alongi, D.M. (2008), 'Mangrove forests: resilience, protection from tsunamis, and responses to global climate change', *Estuarine, Coastal and Shelf Science*, **76**, 1–13.

Arrow, K. and A. Fisher (1974), 'Environmental preservation, uncertainty, and irreversibility', *Quarterly Journal of Economics*, **88**, 312–19.

Barbier, E.B. (1994), 'Valuing environmental functions: tropical wetlands', *Land Economics*, **70**, 155–73.

Barbier, E.B. (2000), 'Valuing the environment as input: applications to mangrove–fishery linkages', *Ecological Economics*, **35**, 47–61.

Barbier, E.B. (2003), 'Habitat–fishery linkages and mangrove loss in Thailand', *Contemporary Economic Policy*, **21**, 59–77.

Barbier, E.B. (2007), 'Valuing ecosystem services as productive inputs', *Economic Policy*, **22**(49), 177–229.

Barbier, E.B. and G.R. Heal (2006), 'Valuing ecosystem services', *The Economists' Voice*, **3**(3), Article 2, www.bepress.com/ev/vol3/iss3/art2.

Barbier, E.B. and S. Sathirathai (eds) (2004), *Shrimp Farming and Mangrove Loss in Thailand*, Cheltenham, UK and Northampton, MA, USA: Edward Elgar.

Barbier, E.B., E.W. Koch, B.R. Silliman, S.D. Hacker, E. Wolanski, J.H. Primavera, E. Granek, S. Polasky, S. Aswani, L.A. Cramer, D.M. Stoms, C.J. Kennedy, D. Bael, C.V. Kappel, G.M. Perillo and D.J. Reed (2008), 'Coastal ecosystem-based management with nonlinear ecological functions and values', *Science*, **319**, 321–3.

Bishop, R.C., W.S. Breffle, J.K. Lazo, R.D. Rowe and S.M. Wytinck (2000), *Restoration Scaling Based on Total Value Equivalency: Green Bay Natural Resource Damage Assessment*, Boulder, CO: Stratus Consulting Inc.

Breffle, W.S., E.R. Morey, R.D. Rowe, D.M. Waldman and S.M. Wytinck (1999), *Recreational Fishing Damages from Fish Consumption Advisories in the Waters of Green Bay*, Boulder, CO: Stratus Consulting Inc.

Carlsson, F., P. Frykblom and C. Lijenstolpe (2003), 'Valuing wetland attributes: an application of choice experiments', *Ecological Economics*, **47**, 95–103.

Carpenter, S.R., D. Ludwig and W.A. Brock (1999), 'Management of eutrophication for lakes subject to potentially irreversible change', *Ecological Applications*, **9**(3), 751–71.

Chichilnisky, G. and G.M. Heal (1998), 'Economic returns from the biosphere', *Nature*, **391**, 629–30.

Chong, J. (2005), 'Protective values of mangrove and coral ecosystems: a review of methods and evidence', Gland, Switzerland: IUCN.

Christie, M., N. Hanley, J. Warren, K. Murphy, R. Wright and T. Hyde (2006), 'Valuing the diversity of biodiversity', *Ecological Economics*, **58**(2), 304–17.

Clark, C.W. (1996), 'Marine reserves and precautionary management of fisheries', *Ecological Applications*, **6**, 369–70.

Cochard, R., S.L. Ranamukhaarachchi, G.P. Shivakoti, O.V. Shipin, P.J. Edwards and K.T. Seeland (2008), 'The 2004 tsunami in Aceh and Southern Thailand: a review on coastal ecosystems, wave hazards and vulnerability', *Perspectives in Plant Ecology, Evolution and Systematics*, **10**, 3–40.

Daily, G. (ed.) (1997), *Nature's Services: Societal Dependence on Natural Ecosystems*, Washington, DC: Island Press.

De Groot, R.S., M.A. Wilson and R.M.J. Boumans (2002), 'A typology for the classification, description and valuation of ecosystem functions, goods and services', *Ecological Economics*, **41**, 393–408.

Dixit, A. and R. Pindyck (1994), *Investment under Uncertainty*, Princeton, NJ: Princeton University Press.

Ellis, G.M. and A.C. Fisher (1987), 'Valuing the environment as input', *Journal of Environmental Management*, **25**, 149–56.

Elmqvist, T., C. Folke, M. Nyström, G. Peterson, J. Bengtsson, B. Walker and J. Norberg (2003), 'Response diversity, ecosystem change, and resilience', *Frontiers in Ecology & Environment*, **1**(9), 488–94.

FAO (2003), 'Status and trends in mangrove area extent worldwide', by M.L. Wilkie and S. Fortuna, Forest Resources Assessment Working Paper, No. 63, Forest Resources Division, Food and Agricultural Organization of the United Nations, Rome.

FAO (2005), *The State of World Fisheries and Aquaculture 2004*, Rome: Food and Agricultural Organization of the United Nations.

Finnoff, D. and J. Tschirhart (2003), 'Harvesting in an eight-species ecosystem', *Journal of Environmental Economics and Management*, **45**, 589–611.

Finnoff, D., A. Strong and J. Tschirhart (2008), 'A bioeconomic model of cattle stocking on rangeland threatened by invasive plants and nitrogen deposition', *American Journal of Agricultural Economics*, **90**(4), 1074–90.

Folke, C., S. Carpenter, B. Walker, M. Scheffer, T. Elmqvist, L. Gunderson and C.S. Holling (2004), 'Regime shifts, resilience, and biodiversity in ecosystem management', *Annual Review of Ecology, Evolution and Systematics*, **35**(1), 557–81.

Forbes, K. and J. Broadhead (2007), 'The role of coastal forests in the mitigation of tsunami impacts', RAP Publication 2007/1, Food and Agricultural Organization of the United Nations, Regional Office for Asia and the Pacific, Bangkok.

Freeman, A.M. III (1991), 'Valuing environmental resources under alternative management regimes', *Ecological Economics*, **3**, 247–56.

Freeman, A.M. III (2003), *The Measurement of Environmental and Resource Values: Theory and Methods*, 2nd edn, Washington, DC: Resources for the Future.

Gaston, K. and T. Blackborn (2000), *Pattern and Process in Macroecology*, 2nd edn, Oxford: Blackwell Science.

Goldburg, R. and R. Naylor (2005), 'Future seascapes, fishing and fish farming', *Frontiers in Ecology & Environment*, **3**(1), 21–8.

Grafton, R.Q. and T. Kompas (2005), 'Uncertainty and the active adaptive management of marine reserves', *Marine Policy*, **29**, 471–79.

Halpern, B.S. (2004), 'Are mangroves a limiting resource for two coral reef fisheries?', *Marine Ecology Progress Series*, **272**, 93–8.

Heal, G., E. Barbier, K. Boyle, A. Covich, S. Gloss, C. Hershner, J. Hoehn, S. Polasky, C. Pringle, K. Segerson and K. Shrader-Frechette (2005), *Valuing Ecosystem Services: Toward Better Environmental Decision Making*, Washington, DC: The National Academies Press.

Heinz (H. John Heinz III Center for Science, Economics and the Environment) (2000), 'Evaluation of erosion hazards', EMC-97-CO-0375, Federal Emergency Management Agency, Washington, DC.

Henry, C. (1974), 'Investment decisions under uncertainty: the "irreversibility effect"', *American Economic Review*, **64**(6), 1006–12.

Hoehn, J.P., T. Tomasi, F. Lupi and H.Z. Chen (1996), 'An economic model for valuing recreational angling resources in Michigan', Report to the Michigan Department of Natural Resources and the Michigan Department of Environmental Quality, Michigan State University, East Lansing.

Huffaker, R. and K. Cooper (1995), 'Plant succession as a natural range restoration factor in private livestock enterprises', *American Journal of Agricultural Economics*, **77**, 901–13.

Janssen, M.A., J.M. Anderies and B.H. Walker (2004), 'Robust strategies for managing rangelands with multiple stable attractors', *Journal of Environmental Economics and Management*, **47**, 140–62.

Just, R.E., D.L. Hueth and A. Schmitz (2004), *The Welfare Economics of Public Policy: A Practical Approach to Project and Policy Evaluation*, Cheltenham, UK and Northampton, MA, USA: Edward Elgar.

Kareiva, P., S. Watts, R. McDonald and T. Boucher (2007), 'Domesticated nature: shaping landscapes and ecosystems for human welfare', *Science*, **316**, 1866–9.

Kriesel, W., A. Randall and F. Lichtkoppler (1993), 'Estimating the benefits of shore erosion protection in Ohio's Lake Erie housing market', *Water Resources Research*, **29**(4), 795–801.

Krutilla, J.V. and A.C. Fisher (1985), *The Economics of Natural Environments: Studies in the Valuation of Commodity and Amenity Resources*, Washington, DC: Resources for the Future.

Mardle, S., C. James, C. Pipitone and M. Kienzle (2004), 'Bioeconomic interactions in an established fishing exclusion zone: the Gulf of Castellammare, NW Sicily', *Natural Resource Modeling*, **17**(4), 393–447.

Mazda, Y., M. Magi, M. Kogo and P.N. Hong (1997), 'Mangroves as a coastal protection from waves in the Tong King Delta, Vietnam', *Mangroves and Salt Marshes*, **1**, 127–35.
McLendon, T. and E. Redente (1991), 'Nitrogen and phosphorus effects on secondary succession dynamics on a semi-arid sagebrush site', *Ecology*, **72**(6), 2016–24.
McLeod, K.L., J. Lubchenco, S.R. Palumbi and A.A. Rosenberg (2005), 'Scientific consensus statement on marine ecosystem-based management', signed by 221 academic scientists and policy experts with relevant expertise and published by the Communication Partnership of Science and the Sea at http://compassonline. org/marinescience/solutions_ecosystem.asp.
Millennium Ecosystem Assessment (2005), *Ecosystems and Human Well-being: A Framework for Assessment*, Washington, DC: Island Press.
Mumby, P.J., A.J. Edwards, J.E. Arias-Gonzalez, K.C. Lindeman, P.G. Blackwell, A. Gall, M.I. Gorczynska, A.R. Harborne, C.L. Pescod, H. Renken, C.C. Wabnitz and G. Llewellyn (2004), 'Mangroves enhance the biomass of coral reef fish communities in the Caribbean', *Nature*, **427**, 533–6.
Naylor, R. and M. Drew (1998), 'Valuing mangrove resources in Kosrae, Micronesia', *Environment and Development Economics*, **3**, 471–90.
Naylor, R., R. Goldburg, J. Primavera, N. Kautsky, M. Beveridge, J. Clay, C. Folke, J. Lubchenco, H. Mooney and M. Troll (2000), 'Effect of aquaculture on world fish supplies', *Nature*, **405**, 1017–24.
Pagiola, S., K. von Ritter and J. Bishop (2004), *How Much is an Ecosystem Worth? Assessing the Economic Value of Conservation*, Washington, DC: World Bank.
Painter, E.L. and A.J. Belsky (1993), 'Application of herbivore optimization theory to rangelands in the western United States', *Ecological Applications*, **3**(1), 2–9.
Perrings, C. (1998), 'Resilience in the dynamics of economic–environmental systems', *Environmental and Resource Economics*, **11**(3–4), 503–20.
Ready, R.C. (1995), 'Environmental valuation under uncertainty', in Daniel W. Bromley (ed.), *The Handbook of Environmental Economics*, Cambridge, MA: Blackwell Publishers, pp. 568–93.
Rodwell, L.D., E.B. Barbier, C.M. Roberts and T.R. McClanahan (2002), 'A model of tropical marine reserve–fishery linkages', *Natural Resource Modeling*, **15**(4), 453–86.
Rodwell, L.D., E.B. Barbier, C.M. Roberts and T.R. McClanahan (2003), 'The importance of habitat quality for marine reserve–fishery linkages', *Canadian Journal of Fisheries and Aquatic Sciences*, **60**, 171–81.
Sanchirico, J.N. (2005), 'Additivity properties in metapopulation models: implications for the assessment of marine reserves', *Journal of Environmental Economics and Management*, **49**, 1–25.
Sanchirico, J.N. and J.E. Wilen (2002), 'The impacts of marine reserves on limited-entry fisheries', *Natural Resource Modeling*, **15**(3), 291–310.
Sathirathai, S. and E. Barbier (2001), 'Valuing mangrove conservation, Southern Thailand', *Contemporary Economic Policy*, **19**, 109–22.
Settle, C. and J.F. Shogren (2002), 'Modeling native-exotic species within Yellowstone Lake', *American Journal of Agricultural Economics*, **84**(5), 1323–8.
Shabman, L.A. and S.S. Batie (1978), 'Economic value of natural coastal wetlands: a critique', *Coastal Zone Management Journal*, **4**(3), 231–47.

Sumaila, U.R. (2002), 'Marine protected area performance in a model of a fishery', *Natural Resource Modeling*, **15**(4), 439–51.

Tokrisna, R. (1998), 'The use of economic analysis in support of development and investment decision in Thai aquaculture: with particular reference to marine shrimp culture', a paper submitted to the Food and Agriculture Organization of the United Nations.

UNEP (2006), 'Marine and coastal ecosystems and human well-being: a synthesis report based on the findings of the Millennium Ecosystem Assessment', Nairobi: United Nations Environment Programme.

US Army Corps of Engineers (2006), *2006: Louisiana Coastal Protection and Restoration*, Washington, DC: US Army Corps of Engineers.

Valiela, I., J. Bowen and J. York (2001), 'Mangrove forests: one of the world's threatened major tropical environments', *BioScience*, **51**, 807–15.

Wolanski, E. (2007), *Estuarine Ecohydrology*, Amsterdam: Elsevier.

World Resources Institute (2001), *World Resources 2000–2001. People and Ecosystems: The Fraying Web of Life*, Washington, DC: World Resources Institute.

Worm, B., E.B. Barbier, N. Beaumont, J.E. Duffy, C. Folke, B.S. Halpern, J.B.C. Jackson, H.K. Lotzke, F. Micehli, S.R. Palumbi, E. Sala, K.A. Selkoe, J.J. Stachowicz and R. Watson (2006), 'Impacts of biodiversity loss on ocean ecosystem services', *Science*, **314**, 787–90.

Wu, J., K. Skelton-Groth, W.G. Boggess and R.M. Adams (2003), 'Pacific salmon restoration: trade-offs between economic efficiency and political acceptance', *Contemporary Economic Policy*, **21**(1), 78–89.

10. Costs and benefits of water quality improvements

In this chapter, we consider ways in which CBA methods have been used to assess policies aimed at improving water quality, focusing mainly on freshwater issues in Europe. In fact, the policy environment in Europe has recently become one in which CBA is extensively involved in implementing a key piece of legislation – the Water Framework Directive. The chapter covers the following issues:

- The main aspects of CBA used in designing and implementing water quality policies.
- Issues involved with measuring *costs*, including the distribution of costs, the importance of non-point source pollution, and the identification of cost-effective approaches to achieving targets.
- Issues involved in estimating *benefits*, including the development and use of Benefits Transfer systems.

10.1 MAIN ASPECTS TO THE USE OF CBA IN DESIGNING AND IMPLEMENTING WATER QUALITY POLICY

Policy makers and environmental regulators have become increasingly interested in the costs and benefits of meeting water quality targets. Costs will include the costs to those responsible for polluting emissions to rivers, lakes and coastal waters of taking remedial action: for example, the costs to municipalities of improving sewage treatment, to industry of reducing emissions, and to consumers in terms of higher water bills. Land use is also an important source of water quality problems, due to non-point pollution from sediments, nutrients and pathogens originating from farmland and forests. Farmers, then, might also bear some of the costs of improving water quality.

The costs of meeting a particular target, such as an improvement to 'Good ecological status' under the European Union's Water Framework Directive (WFD), or of reducing ambient Biological Oxygen Demand below some maximum, will depend on how this target is met, particularly in terms of the flexibility in achieving reductions in emissions across sources. Under the WFD, regulators are supposed to identify cost-effective means of achieving targets, and to put plans in place to achieve these cost-effective reductions, rather than aiming for some more expensive way of achieving the same water quality target. Regulators will often also be interested in how the burden of costs is shared, both between producers and consumers, and across industry (for example between the electricity industry and the food and drinks industry).

Estimating benefits is also important. Whilst some of the benefits of improved water quality may be valued by the market – such as impacts on commercial fisheries, or aquaculture operations – most will not, requiring the application of the non-market valuation methods set out in Chapters 3–6. The non-market benefits of water quality improvements might include:

- increases in consumers' surplus to anglers, swimmers and kayakers;
- benefits to informal users of a river, such as people who walk beside it;
- improvements to in-stream ecology, bird populations and riverbank vegetation;
- amenity benefits from cleaner rivers which impact on house prices.

A range of valuation methods will be appropriate for measuring these benefits. For instance, site choice travel cost models might be used to estimate changes in consumers' surplus for anglers; choice experiments could be used to value benefits to informal users and to in-stream ecology; hedonic pricing could be used to value those aspects of amenity improvements which impact on house prices. Many benefits will be a mixture of use and non-use values. For certain pollutants (for example pathogens from livestock wastes running off into coastal bathing waters), health benefits could also be important. In situations where water is used for drinking, health-related benefits will also be key (see Boxes 10.4 and 10.6 below).

Due to the costs and time necessary to undertake original valuation studies, a growing interest has arisen in using benefits transfer to value the benefits of water quality improvements. As we saw in Chapter 3, benefits transfer means taking WTP estimates from one or several studies, adjusting them in some way, and then applying them to a new context. For example, if there is a need to measure angling benefits at the River X from a reduction in pollution, then WTP values taken from studies of other rivers could be used to estimate this value. Adjustments can be made for: (i) differences in the environmental characteristics of the site to which values are transferred, relative to the site or sites where the original surveys were undertaken; and (ii) differences in the socio-economic characteristics of beneficiaries between the original site(s) and the site to which benefits are being transferred. Errors will arise in this transfer process, and economists have been working on how to minimize such errors. We return to the issue of benefits transfer in section 10.3.

BOX 10.1   COST–BENEFIT ANALYSIS AND
            TARGET SETTING FOR UK WATER
            COMPANIES

Water supply and sewerage services in England are undertaken by private sector companies. This means that water companies are both sources of water pollution (through their ownership and operation of sewage treatment works), and the beneficiaries of improvements in water quality. The Environment Agency is the regulator responsible for achieving improvements in water quality in rivers, lakes, estuaries and coastal waters, and does this through a system of 'consents' which specify the allowable pollution inputs to water bodies. By tightening consents, the Environment Agency can achieve reductions in pollution. As part of the process of reviewing consents issued to water companies, the Agency is required to consider the benefits and costs of proposed tightening of pollution regulation across the water bodies it is responsible for. This process, known as 'Periodic Review', is overseen by Ofwat, the Office of Water Regulation.

The first programme-wide assessment of proposed improvements occurred under the 'PR99' plan in 1999. The Agency carried out 700 individual multi-criteria assessments to prioritize and rank proposed improvements in water quality (for example by upgrading sewage works on a particular river). However, this process was criticized by Ofwat, on the grounds that multi-criteria analysis did not show which schemes would generate benefits in excess of costs (Fisher, 2008). The Agency then developed a *Benefits Assessment Guidance* manual to allow it to measure benefits under the next Periodic Review, due to be undertaken in 2004. This Guidance recommended extensive use of simple benefits transfer techniques. The PR04 assessment then used these guidelines to generate benefit–cost ratios for 437 individual water quality improvement schemes. This took 19 person-years of work at the Agency. Costs were provided by the water companies (that is by the polluters): this led to an apparent overestimate of around 40 per cent in costs, once these figures had been scrutinized by Ofwat and the Agency (Fisher, 2008).

Based on the benefits estimates generated by the Agency, and the (moderated) cost figures provided by industry, schemes were then classified according to benefit/cost ratio (Environment Agency, 2003). Some results are shown below:

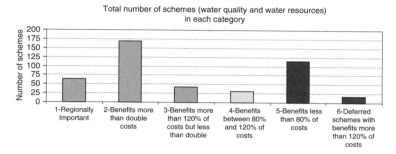

Number of non-statutory schemes in various benefit/cost categories

Total number of schemes (water quality and water resources)
in each category

Summary findings of costs and benefits of schemes

	Categories 1 to 3 Proposed schemes (% of total)	Categories 4 to 6 Deferred schemes (% of total)	All categories
Total number of schemes	274 (63%)	163 (37%)	437
Total costs	£649m (37%)	£1,035m (63%)	£1,684m
Total benefits	£1,160m (80%)	£286m (20%)	£1,446m

Source: Fisher (2008).

Based on these findings, the Agency recommended that the water quality projects in categories 1–3 above went ahead. Budgetary constraints meant that in the end many of these recommended projects were not implemented. However, the Agency still felt that the exercise had been worthwhile in terms of demonstrating their ability to assess a large number of possible projects on CBA criteria.

10.2 MEASURING COSTS

Consider a policy target to improve the quality of a river from a currently degraded status to what is defined in the WFD as 'Good Ecological Status'. How would costs be estimated? The first step is to identify the sources of the water quality problem. This might include direct pollution inputs from factories or sewage works, non-point run-off from farm fields, abstraction of water by various users leading to lower dilution of pollutants, and 'morphological' changes – that is, changes to the physical shape and operation of the water body, such as the building of weirs, which limit

Table 10.1   Sources of failure to meet GES for water bodies in the UK

Country	Water body	Abstraction	Alien species	Diffuse pollution	Flow regulation	Morph. alteration	Point source pollution	Unknown
		Proportion of water bodies affected by pressures 1=<20% of water bodies at risk from pressure, 5=>80%.						
England	Coastal	1	3	2	1	4	1	–
England	Groundwater	2	1	4	2	1	1	–
England	Lakes	1	1	3	1	3	2	–
England	Rivers	1	2	5	1	3	2	–
England	Transitional	1	2	2	1	5	3	–
Scotland	Coastal	1	1	1	1	1	4	1
Scotland	Groundwater	1	1	3	1	1	2	1
Scotland	Lakes	1	1	1	2	2	1	1
Scotland	Rivers	1	1	2	1	2	1	1
Scotland	Transitional	1	1	2	1	2	3	1
Wales	Coastal	1	3	2	1	4	1	–
Wales	Groundwater	2	1	4	2	1	1	–
Wales	Lakes	1	1	3	1	3	2	–
Wales	Rivers	1	2	5	1	3	2	–
Wales	Transitional	1	2	2	1	5	3	–

Source: Jacobs (2006).

fish migration. Table 10.1 shows the distribution of problem sources for water bodies in the UK in terms of the need to achieve Good Ecological Status (GES).

As may be seen, diffuse pollution (that is non-point source pollution) is the main problem for groundwater in England, whilst point source pollution is the main source of problems with 'transitional waters' – estuaries – in Scotland.

Next, the possible measures which could be taken to achieve water quality targets need to be identified. Even for a particular water body, these could include a very wide range of measures, according to which pressures are targeted. For example, a programme to achieve GES for Loch Leven in Scotland, which currently suffers from algal bloom problems due to high nutrient inputs, could include:

- changes in farming practices to reduce phosphate run-off;
- capital investments at sewage works to install nutrient-stripping capacity;
- reduced abstraction of water during the summer;
- improved effluent treatment at a number of factory sites around the loch;
- changing the management of fish farms situated in the loch.

The costs of a particular package of measures depend on how cost-effective these measures are. Cost-efficiency implies that the regulator implements policies which enable the marginal cost of pollution reduction to be equalized both across source categories (for example between farmers and factories) but also within categories (for example across all farmers). The least-cost outcome will be one where the marginal costs of damage reduction are equal across all sources of pollution (Baumol and Oates, 1985). Market mechanisms such as pollution taxes and tradeable pollution permits could, ideally, produce such an outcome. The expectation is that in most cases CBA analysis will be undertaken on sub-optimal policies, since governments rarely depend solely on market mechanisms to achieve pollution reduction targets. However, the key message is that the cost of achieving a water quality target will depend very much on the mix of policy instruments or practical measures taken to achieve it. For example, Hanley et al. (1998) found that achieving a 20 per cent improvement in dissolved oxygen levels in the Forth Estuary using process regulation was nine times more expensive compared to the outcome using a tradeable permits system.

BOX 10.2 THE ROLE OF CBA WITHIN THE EU'S WATER FRAMEWORK DIRECTIVE

The Water Framework Directive is a unifying measure passed by the European Union to harmonize water resource management, and to achieve a default target of 'Good Ecological Status' (GES) for all surface waters in the EU. Good Ecological Status is defined with respect to biological, chemical and morphological criteria. River basins are the focus for management actions. The timetable for implementing the Directive is as follows:

Year	Issue
2000	Directive entered into force
2003	Transposition in national legislation
	Identification of River Basin Districts and Authorities
2004	Characterization of river basin: pressures, impacts and economic analysis
2006	Establishment of monitoring network
	Start public consultation (at the latest)
2008	Present draft river basin management plan
2009	Finalize river basin management plan including programme of measures
2010	Introduce pricing policies
2012	Make operational programmes of measures
2015	Meet environmental objectives
	First management cycle ends
	Second river basin management plan & first flood risk management plan
2021	Second management cycle ends
2027	Third management cycle ends, final deadline for meeting objectives

It is in the drafting of 'River Basin Management Plans' that CBA comes into play. National agencies must, for each water body, identify cost-effective programmes of measures which achieve the target of GES by 2015. However, they must also consider whether the costs of achieving GES on a particular water body are 'disproportionately costly'. This means a comparison is necessary between the likely benefits and costs of improvements to GES – potentially for every water body in each country! Because of this burden of work, countries have been seeking proformas for identifying which rivers and other water bodies are likely candidates for designation as 'disproportionate cost' cases (see RPA, 2004). If the Environment Agency finds that benefits are considerably lower than costs for a particular water body, then the government can ask that either (i) a longer time scale be allowed for that water body to achieve GES; or (ii) that a lower target for improvement be set. However, even if benefits exceed costs, a derogation for improvements to GES can still be sought if 'disproportionate costs are imposed on one particular sector or operator'. In other words, distributional criteria are seen as very important.

One particularly difficult aspect of costing water quality improvements relates to non-point source (NPS) pollution. As Table 10.1 shows, this is the major source of water quality problems for rivers in England, and this would also be true for many other countries in Europe and for the US. As noted above, NPS pollution consists of sediments, nutrients and pathogens running off from farmland and forests into surface waters, and leaching into groundwater: run-off of pollutants from roads and other paved areas can also contribute to NPS loads. As for point source pollution, the costs of achieving a water quality target by reducing NPS emissions will depend on how this is undertaken, particularly the flexibility with which different sources can respond. However, because it is very expensive to measure actual emissions of, say, nitrates from individual farm fields, we must use estimates of emissions instead, and relate these to how land is managed. For example, the run-off of nitrates from farmland can depend on how many livestock are grazed on land adjoining a river, how much fertilizer is applied, and what kind of crops are grown. In general, the expectation is that economic instruments will yield lower-cost outcomes than regulatory approaches (Shortle and Horan, 2001), but applying these is more difficult for NPS problems, since a pollution tax, for instance, must be levied on inputs, or expected emissions, or ambient pollution, rather than actual emissions from a given farm (since these are too expensive to monitor). Moreover, it will often be desirable to allow for tradeoffs in pollution control efforts between non-point sources of a particular pollutant (say phosphate) and point sources such as sewage works. All this makes for a complicated task in identifying the cost-efficient way of reducing NPS pollution, yet we know that costs will be sensitive to how the NPS pollution reduction target is achieved. As an illustration of this, Larson et al. (1996) find that taxing nitrogen fertilizer as a way of reducing nitrate pollution from vegetable growing in California would involve a cost which was three times higher per hectare than increasing the price of irrigation water.

Having said this, the CBA analyst will typically be faced with a predetermined plan of action which must then be costed. This plan might consist of a set of required actions from farmers, such as reducing livestock numbers or fertilizer inputs, or creating buffer strips on land near to water courses. The costs of these activities can be estimated by comparing farm profits in the 'no-restrictions' case with profits under the water quality management programme, although it is important that transfer payments such as any government subsidies for crops are excluded from this cost calculation. A recent example is provided in Aftab et al. (2007) for nitrate pollution from farmland in Scotland; see also the survey in Shortle and Horan (2001). Box 10.6 below discusses an example of costs and benefits for a NPS pollution problem.

Finally with respect to costs, it will often be helpful to consider the distribution of costs of a particular programme of measures in terms of who loses as a result of the policy measure. Indeed, this kind of detail is required under the WFD and the EU Impact Assessment guidelines

Table 10.2   Incidence of costs of a water quality improvement plan

Measure	Sector paying for this measure	Present Value of Costs assuming 3.5% discount rate: one-off costs plus annual costs, £m.			Ratio of annual equivalent of best estimate of costs to typical operating profit
		Low estimate	Best Estimate	High Estimate	%
Nutrient surplus charge on farmers	Agriculture	0.32	0.40	0.65	65%
Invest in tertiary level treatment at sewage works	Central government	40.4	62.4	84.4	–
Improve effluent treatment at paper works	Industry	11.3	14.75	16.55	11%

Source: Adapted from supporting documents to Jacobs (2006).

(Chapter 13). In the Loch Leven example above, we saw that a plan to reduce phosphate levels in the loch could include actions by a number of different 'sources' of the problem – farmers, firms, local water companies. An analysis of who bears the costs of an action plan might look something like Table 10.2. Going ahead with the water quality improvement plan in this case would impose the highest costs on taxpayers, but significant costs would also fall on industry. Costs to farming seem small in relative terms compared with other sectors, but as the last column shows, these might be high relative to current profits in agriculture.

10.3   ESTIMATING BENEFITS

The potential benefits from water quality improvements are many and various, spanning the continuum of market-valued and non-market impacts. Market-valued benefits can include benefits to commercial fisheries and aquaculture operations. Non-market effects include benefits to water-based recreational users (fishermen, sailors, kayakers, swimmers);

people using waterways for informal recreation such as walking along a canal; ecosystem benefits to fish, birds and aquatic plants; and aesthetic improvements in the appearance of river banks.

Use of Stated Preference Methods

Stated preference methods have frequently been used to value water quality improvements. For example, Morrison and Bennett (2006) used choice modelling to value the benefits of improvements to five rivers in New South Wales. The policy context was a desire by government to improve the efficiency of allocation of scarce water resources, to which end Water Management Committees were established to advise on the consequences of alternative water sharing arrangements between agriculture, recreation and conservation. Conservation impacts were measured in terms of the health of vegetation and wetlands, native fish species and waterfowl.

In the choice experiment, respondents were households located mainly within the catchments of each river. Information was provided to these respondents on current water uses and environmental conditions. For example, for the Bega River, respondents were told that:

- there had been declines in native fish and water birds;
- there had been a loss of areas suitable for swimming or fishing;
- various factors including the extraction of water for irrigating crops, erosion of river banks, and sewage inputs, had contributed to these problems;
- remedial projects could be undertaken, but that this would require funding through a once-off levy on water rates payable by households in the area.

The choice experiment was designed using recreational potential, healthy riverside vegetation and wetlands, native fish and waterbirds, and a once-off increase in water rates as the attributes. A no-additional-cost status quo was included in each choice set. For the Bega River, the status quo consisted of:

- no fishing or swimming possible in parts of the river;
- 30 per cent healthy vegetation;
- 15 native species of fish;
- 48 species of waterbirds.

Table 10.3 shows some results obtained from the choice experiment for mean WTP for improvements in each attribute above this baseline. It is

Table 10.3　Willingness to pay (implicit prices) for improvements in two rivers in New South Wales, Australia (in AUS $)

	Vegetation	Fish species	Swim	Fish	Fauna
Bega River – locals	2.33	7.23	100.98	51.33	0.88
Gwydir River – locals	1.46	2.12	104.07	48.94	1.76
Gwydir River – non-locals	1.98	3.51	59.98	29.93	0.55

Notes:　Vegetation: % of riverbank vegetation in healthy condition; *Fish species:* per species; *Swim:* being able to swim in whole river; *Fish:* being able to fish in whole river; *Fauna:* per species conserved.

Source:　Morrison and Bennett (2006, p. 85).

interesting to see that non-use values for healthy vegetation are present in the out-of-catchment sample (non-locals), and indeed this non-local value for healthy vegetation is higher than the locals are WTP in the case of the Gwydir River. Use values for swimming and fishing are higher for locals than for non-locals. Comparing the implicit prices (willingness-to-pay measures) between the two rivers, it is apparent that the ranking of benefits is virtually identical: improving swimming quality is valued most highly. The implicit prices are also very similar between the Gwydir (locals) and Bega (locals), although we cannot test whether they are statistically different since the authors did not report confidence intervals for these implicit prices. However, one can imagine that water resource managers in these catchments would gain useful information from this choice experiment in formulating future plans for management.

Use of Revealed Preference Methods

Revealed preference measures of water quality improvements rely on water quality being an input to recreational demand, in the sense that water quality partly determines the consumers' surplus from a day's fishing, or a day's hunting in a wetland. Two examples worth considering are the studies by Train (1998) and Larson and Shaikh (2003). Train uses the site choice travel cost model explained in Chapter 4 to study the effects of variations in fishing site quality and access for fishermen in Montana, USA. His paper is particularly interesting since it introduced the 'random parameters logit' model to environmental valuation. This model, as noted in Chapter 3, is a way of measuring the variability in preferences across

BOX 10.3   DISTANCE DECAY FUNCTIONS FOR
              AGGREGATING BENEFITS

One big problem in applying CBA to environmental quality improvements
is determining how many people will benefit from this change. This is an
important piece of information, since along with mean WTP it determines
the size of aggregate benefits. For instance, if water quality on the River
Garonne in France is improved, how many recreational users of the river
will benefit? How many people will experience an increase in non-use
values?

A recent suggestion for trying to quantify the number of beneficiaries from an environmental improvement is to rely on a *distance decay
function* (Bateman et al, 2006). This is a function which shows how
WTP for an environmental improvement – such as an increase in river
water quality – depends on how far away an individual lives from that
river:

$$WTP_i = f(D_i, S_i)$$

where for individual i, D_i is the distance they live from the river and
S_i is a vector of socio-economic and other characteristics of the
individual which also determine their WTP for an improvement. By
sampling people at varying distances from the river, the researcher
could identify the relationship between WTP and distance, and then
use this to calculate how far away from the river one must go for WTP
to become zero, or some arbitrarily low value (say, £0.05). Once this
'zone of beneficiaries' has been identified, Geographic Information
Systems (GIS) could be used to work out how many people live in this
zone – this is then the number of people over whom benefits should
be aggregated.

Two obvious problems with distance decay functions are, first, that
they might not exist for some kinds of benefit (for example for non-use
values: why should these depend on how far one lives from a resource?);
and that they may be unique to particular improvements, and so cannot
be 'transferred' to other settings. Moreover, the researcher might mistake
a distance effect for the effect of some missing variable. For example, if
average incomes fall as we move away from a river, but if income is not
included in the distance decay function, then what looks like a relationship between WTP and distance could actually be a relationship between
WTP and income.

Nevertheless, researchers have succeeded in estimating distance
decay functions for water quality improvements. For instance, Hanley
et al. (2003) measured WTP for improvements in the condition of the
River Mimram in South-East England, using contingent valuation.
Households were sampled at varying distances from the river, as
shown below:

Distance category (km)	Number of respondents interviewed
0–0.5	71
0.6–5	96
6–15	100
16–30	80
31–50	82
51–70	104
71–100	75
101–150	42
Total	**650**

Next, mean WTP was calculated for each respondent for an improvement in flow rates on the river (low flows being the major water quality problem at issue here): this seemed to vary by distance band, with a stronger relationship apparently existing for people who actually used the river for recreation:

Willingness-to-pay estimates by distance band

Users

Distance category (kms)	Sample size	Mean	S. Dev	95% confidence limit-lower	95% confidence limit-upper	Median
0–0.5	43	17.27	26.90	8.04	25.31	13.59
0.5–3	50	13.20	16.26	4.51	17.71	11.03
3–12	16	4.12	6.92	3.39	7.51	3.10
12–130	5	–	–	–	–	–
Sum	114					

Non-users

Distance category (kms)	Sample size	Mean	S. Dev	95% confidence limit-lower	95% confidence limit-upper	Median
0–0.5	1	–	–	–	–	–
0.5–3	21	12.78	20.19	8.64	21.42	10.18
3–12	45	3.73	8.95	2.61	6.34	1.87
12–130	233	1.71	3.57	0.46	2.17	1.16
Sum	300					

Then, a regression analysis was undertaken which related distance to WTP. Other variables included were household income (INC), highest level of education achievement of the respondent (EDUC), age of respondent (AGE), the log of distance from their house to the river (LOGDIST), and a dummy variable for whether their property had a boundary with the river (RIVBOUND). We can see that, for use values, there is a strong negative relationship between distance from the river and WTP. Interestingly, there is also a statistically-significant effect of distance on WTP for non-use values: perhaps this reflects the degree of 'ownership' or affection with which people view their local river. However, the distance decay effect is stronger for use values.

	Use values			Non-use values		
	Coefficient	Stnd error	P-value	Coefficient	Stnd Error	P-value
Constant	5.7353	13.2079	0.6641	5.2009	2.5657	0.0427
INCOME	0.2070	0.1145	0.0706	0.0808	0.0210	0.0001
EDUC	−2.1072	2.5646	0.4113	0.3041	0.4974	0.5410
AGE	1.3944	1.7999	0.4385	0.0357	0.2827	0.8994
LOGDIST	−2.7997	1.3979	0.0452	−2.0248	0.4016	0.0000
RIVBOUN	5.9328	7.3063	0.4168	−3.6546	1.9514	0.0611

The authors then used this relationship to calculate the number of households for which WTP was greater than a small positive number, in order to calculate aggregate benefits for the water quality improvement.

recreationalists. The method has become widely used in choice modelling and well as in revealed preference work. Train's sample includes 962 fishing trips taken by 258 anglers to 59 possible fishing sites in Montana. The site characteristics on which data existed for each site were:

- fish stock;
- landscape quality rating;
- size of site;
- number of camp grounds;
- listing of the site in a popular guidebook;
- number of fishing restrictions (e.g. catch limits);
- the travel cost for each angler to each site.

Train then estimates a standard conditional logit model of site choice, and compares it to a random parameters logit (RPL) version. In the RPL model, two coefficients (parameters) are estimated for each attribute: a mean value, showing the average importance of the attribute to site choice,

Table 10.4   Travel cost results for fishing sites in Montana

	Conditional Logit		Random Parameters Logit (RPL)	
	Coefficient	Standard error	Coefficient	Standard error
Fish stock	0.1061	0.02	−2.876	0.66
			(1.01)	(0.24)
Aesthetics	0.5654	0.06	−0.7942	0.22
			(0.8493)	(0.13)
Travel cost	−0.0756	0.002	−2.402	0.06
			(0.8012)	(0.07)
Listed in guide	0.3718	0.13	1.018	0.28
			(2.195)	(0.35)
Camp sites	−0.1380	0.22	0.1158	0.32
			(1.655)	(0.43)
Access	0.4592	0.16	−0.949	0.36
			(1.88)	(0.35)
Restrictions	−0.3084	0.05	−0.4989	0.13
			(0.8989)	(0.16)
Log (size)	0.5847	0.07	0.9835	0.11
Likelihood ratio index	0.4324		0.5018	

Note: In the RPL results, the numbers in parentheses refer to the standard deviation terms for each attribute.

Source: Adapted from Train (1998).

and a standard deviation term, showing how variable preferences are within the sample for this attribute. The analyst must make an assumption about how each of the random parameters is distributed across the population. For example, is it likely that some people will prefer more camp grounds to fewer camp grounds? Will everyone prefer a lower travel or a higher landscape quality? Table 10.4 shows Train's results.

As can be seen from Table 10.4, in the standard conditional logit model, higher fish stocks increase the likelihood of people choosing a site – and thus increase the utility of each fishing trip. Since the value of this coefficient (0.1061) is more than twice the standard error (0.02), then this effect is statistically significant at the 95 per cent level of confidence. Similarly, higher travel costs mean fewer trips, whilst a higher aesthetics score for landscape quality increases utility. Greater access also increases trips to a site, as does a larger size (implying more choice within a site of where to fish). People, though, seem to prefer sites with fewer camp grounds

– perhaps they see this as an indicator of potential crowding. Turning to the RPL model, we can see that there is substantial evidence of variations in preferences, since all the standard deviation coefficients – which are shown in parentheses – are statistically significant. Moreover, the RPL model fits the data better than the conditional logit, since the likelihood ratio index is higher. Based on the RPL results shown in the table, Train computes some welfare measures for changes in fishing site quality and availability. These show that doubling fish stocks would increase consumers' surplus by around $4.25 per trip (based on the RPL model), whilst closing sites along the Madison River would impose a welfare loss of about $30 per trip.

A rather different approach is taken by Larson and Shaikh (2003). In Chapter 4, we saw how *visitation models* are an extension of the traditional form of travel cost analysis which try to predict how many trips will be taken to a particular site. Larson and Shaikh propose a variant of this approach which allows them to consider demand (visits to) a number of substitute sites when visitors are constrained both by trip costs and by their limited leisure time available. Changes in site quality can, to a limited extent, be included in the model. They refer to this approach as a 'double log demand system', and apply it to recreational whale-watching off the coast of Northern California. Site quality here is measured by the number of whale sightings. Based on data from 432 visitor surveys, they find that the 'access value' of the sites for whale watching (that is, people's maximum WTP to maintain access to whale watching at each site – how much of a loss would be sustained if access was removed) was $779 for the Point Reyes site (where whales could be seen from the shore) and $128 for the Monterey site (where a boat trip was necessary). Interestingly, they found that whilst the own-price elasticity of demand for each site was negative as expected – as the travel cost goes up, people make fewer trips – the income elasticity of demand was positive for two of the sites, but negative for Monterey. This means that rising income levels would lead, other things being equal, to more trips being demanded at Point Reyes, but fewer trips being demanded at Monterey. They are also able to calculate how many more trips would be taken at each site as the number of expected sightings rose, for instance if whale migration patterns were to change due to changes in pollution affecting food supplies.

The Distribution of Benefits

Water quality improvements do not benefit everyone, and do not benefit in equal measure all those who gain. From a policy viewpoint, it is often as important to identify who will gain from a policy compared to how

---

BOX 10.4   THE HEALTH BENEFITS OF WATER QUALITY
            IMPROVEMENTS (1)

Drinking water supplies in many developing countries are polluted,
posing a health risk to those who depend on them. In West Bengal
(India), contamination of surface waters by pollution led for a search for
alternative sources of drinking water. One such source is groundwater
from relatively shallow aquifers. However, groundwaters have become
polluted with arsenic over time, as abstraction from the aquifer for agriculture has led to a falling water table coming into contact with arsenic-
bearing rocks. High arsenic levels in drinking water are associated with a
range of health problems such as damage to the nervous system, cancer
and birth defects. Technologies exist for removing arsenic but these are
costly. An important question is thus: what are the economic benefits of
removing arsenic contamination?

   This question is addressed by Roy (2008). She surveys 473 households to uncover data on the 'cost of illness': this includes wage losses
due to sickness, medical expenditures, and averting behaviour such
as time spent in obtaining water from less-polluted sources. Villages
were selected across a range of arsenic concentrations from 3370μg/l
to 330μg/l (500μg/l is considered a safe level of exposure). For each
village, there was a variation in recorded arsenic levels over time, and in
the percentage of households consuming contaminated water. Around 5
per cent of households reported symptoms of arsenic-related disease,
although this was higher amongst the sub-sample of households reporting any sickness over a year. A three-equation model is estimated relating arsenic levels, days of illness, medical expenditures and averting
expenditure. Results from this three-equation system are then used
to calculate the benefits of reducing arsenic to safe levels by treating
drinking water. For the average household, this is equal to 297 rupees/
month. Poor households experience lower benefits (335 rupees) than
mid-income households (446 rupees) since the value of their lost earnings due to sickness is lower.

   Comparing the costs of arsenic removal technologies with the aggregate benefits shows that benefits are roughly double the costs: on CBA
grounds, then, we would recommend this investment in water treatment
to go ahead.

---

big the total benefits are, just as it is informative to know how costs are
distributed across the population of stakeholders.[1] Improvements in water
quality which confer mainly recreational benefits would have a rather different profile of beneficiaries to a policy which is mainly targeted at health
benefits from water quality investments. An example of an analysis which
distinguishes between different types of beneficiary is provided by Birol et
al. (2008). The Upper Silesia region in Poland has a long history of mining

which has resulted in an increase in flood risks to people living in the area. However, the combination of mining earthworks and flood episodes has created unique habitats which are rich in biodiversity. Policy makers thus face a tradeoff between reducing flood risks and protecting biodiversity. Actions might also be expected to have very different impacts on people, depending on whether they live in flood-prone areas, and, if WTP for biodiversity is related positively to income, on whether they are rich or poor.

A choice experiment was conducted with people living in the region. The attributes were flood risks (low, high), biodiversity (low, high), recreational access to the river (easy, difficult) and increases in local taxes. A summary of results for the implicit prices (willingness to pay) is given in Table 10.5. For the 'average' household, reductions in flood risks are the most highly valued aspect of policy. However, we see that the benefits of risk reduction to households who have been flooded before are much higher. For biodiversity conservation, wealthy households are willing to pay the most, but poor households place almost no value on conservation. Their biggest benefits come from flood risk reductions. This suggests that a policy that prioritized biodiversity conservation over flood risk reduction would produce benefits that would disproportionately accrue to the better-off: is this what the local government would want? Those who have been flooded before are also unlikely to benefit from protecting biodiversity or improving recreation – all they are willing to pay for is reductions in flood risk.

Table 10.5   Willingness to pay for river management in Poland, zloty/ household

	'Average' household	Previously flooded household	Visitors	Wealthy households	Poor households
Reduce flood risk from high to low	14.5	45.5	21.5	27.8	11.2
Increase biodiversity from low to high	4.6	4.6*	12.5	20.2	−0.6*
Improve recreational access to river from difficult to easy	6.6	−2.1*	12.7	21.7	1.3*

Notes:

For confidence intervals on implicit prices, see the original article.
* = not significantly different from zero.

Source: Birol et al. (2008, p. 287).

BOX 10.5   BENEFITS OF REDUCING WATER POLLUTION FROM CONTROLLING SOIL EROSION

Soil erosion has both on-site and off-site costs. On-site costs are the discounted value of lost future production to farmers due to declines in soil resources. However, the off-farm (external) effects of soil erosion are likely to be significant too. These off-farm effects include the siltation of reservoirs, sediment impacts on fisheries, the loss of wildlife habitat, the enhancement of flooding risks, landscape degradation, land abandonment and desertification. Actions to reduce soil erosion can be costly: for example, in terms of changes in cultivation practice, or the creation of buffer strips. The social efficiency of decision-making could thus be enhanced if estimates of the social benefits of reducing soil erosion were available to policy makers.

Colombo et al. (2005) use the choice experiment (CE) method to estimate the benefits of reducing off-site impacts from soil erosion in the Genil and Guadajoz watersheds, situated in the Andalusian region of South-East Spain. The area is characterized by steep slopes and is mainly cultivated with olive orchards. It is a typical Mediterranean landscape of fragile natural ecosystems, insufficient rainfall for fast vegetation recovery and a long history of human exploitation. The climate is dry, with precipitation averaging 400–600 mm/year. Natural factors in the watersheds, together with current management practices by farmers have led to an erosion rate from olive orchards on sloping lands of up to 80 tonnes per hectare per year. This has had harmful effects on local surface water quality. The attributes used in the CE were as follows:

Attributes	Levels
Landscape desertification	● Degradation due to desertification: (the current situation) ● Small improvement: reducing desertification risks in high erosion areas ● Moderate improvement: reducing risks in all areas
Surface and groundwater quality	● Low: water not potable, reservoirs and rivers polluted due to high turbidity, and unsuitable for swimming (current situation), high concentrations of toxic materials. ● Medium: water now potable, turbidity problems remain but now suitable for swimming, acceptable levels of toxic materials ● High: potable waters, turbidity problems now absent, suitable for swimming, toxic materials absent

Attributes	Levels
Flora and fauna quality	• Poor: reduction of ecological quality index over next 50 years by 20%, so that number of birds per km² decrease by about 350 individuals • Medium: increase in ecological quality index by 50%, so that numbers of birds per km² rise by about 700 individuals • Good: increase in ecological quality index by 90%, number of birds rises by 1650 per km²
Rural jobs created in watershed (number)	0 100 200
Area covered by the project (km² of catchment area treated against erosion)	330 660 990
Extra taxes (Euros per individual/yr, over next 5 years)	6.01 12.02 18.03 24.04 30.05 36.06

Based on a survey of 505 local households, a multinomial logit model was estimated describing choices between alternative policy options for the future, described in terms of their impacts on the attributes shown above. Using results from this model, the authors calculated the benefits of three alternative policies:

• *Scenario 1*: Landscape desertification is characterized by a small improvement; surface and groundwater quality is improved to the medium level; flora and fauna quality is improved to the medium level; 100 extra jobs are created; and the watershed's degraded area treated is 330 km².
• *Scenario 2*: Landscape desertification is characterized by a small improvement; surface and groundwater quality is improved to a high level; flora and fauna quality is improved to a medium level; 200 extra jobs are created; and the watershed's degraded area treated is 660 km².
• *Scenario 3*: Landscape desertification is characterized by a small improvement; surface and groundwater quality is improved to a high level; flora and fauna quality is improved to a high level; 200 extra jobs are created; and the watershed's degraded area treated is 990 km².

Results were as follows:

Scenarios	Compensating surplus compared to status quo (euros/yr)
Scenario 1	26.23
Scenario 2	49.60
Scenario 3	63.61

This study shows how the CE method can be used to obtain benefit estimates for catchment-wide management schemes. The authors also report estimates of implicit prices for each attribute: these show, for example, that improvements in water quality were more highly valued by local residents than equivalent improvements in biodiversity.

Benefits Transfer for Water Quality Improvements

As noted in section 10.1, benefits transfer is a topic of increasing relevance in policy applications of CBA, and there is now a considerable amount of literature which tests out benefit transfer techniques in the context of water quality improvements. One example is the study carried out by Hanley et al. (2006) for two rivers in Eastern Scotland, the Brothock and the Motray. Both rivers run through predominately agricultural land, and both are characterized by the same water quality problems – periods of low flow, which are attributable to variations in rainfall and water abstraction for irrigation; and high nutrient levels, which depress ecological quality. Nutrients originate in non-point run-off from farmland and emissions from sewage works. A choice experiment was undertaken with local residents in both catchments, using three attributes to describe the effects of alternative future catchment management options:

- impacts on ecology, in terms of mammals such as otters, fish life and water plants;
- the number of months in an average year when flows would fall below some critical level;
- the impacts on agricultural employment in the area.

The price attribute used was increases in local taxation. Table 10.6 shows the information given to respondents on the ecological quality attribute, whilst Table 10.7 shows an example choice card.

The results from a random parameters logit model were then used to calculate the compensating surplus (WTP) for three different policy

Table 10.6   Ecological information for the Motray/Brothock study

	What will happen if we do nothing	What will happen if we do something	
Ecol. Condition Impact on	Worsening	Slight Improvement	Big Improvement
Large mammals	Large mammals unlikely to be present	Medium sized mammals such as water vole **possible**	Small populations of large mammals such as otter **possible**
Plants	Algae – pond scum main vegetation type	Algae – pond scum main plant type but a few aquatic plants present	A mixture of aquatic plants and algae
Fish	Few fish species with small populations	Few fish species with large populations	Many fish species large populations
Other factors	Smell of rotting vegetation noticeable	Occasional smell of rotting vegetation	No smell noticeable

options, relative to the status quo, using the formula shown as equation (3.12) in Chapter 3. These policy options were:

- Status quo: two local jobs lost, low flow occurs 5 months of the year, ecological condition is 'worsening'.
- Plan A: no jobs lost, low flows occur in 3 months of the year, ecological change is 'a slight improvement'.
- Plan B: gain of 2 local jobs, low flow falls to 2 months/year, ecological change is a 'slight improvement'.
- Plan C: gain of 5 local jobs, low flow falls to 1 month/year, ecological change is 'a big improvement'.

We can see from Table 10.8 that WTP rises as more 'ambitious' plans are put in place (the gain from plan C relative to the status quo is much bigger than the gain from plan A). We can also see that the WTP estimates seem quite similar between the two rivers for a given plan. In fact, a formal benefits

Table 10.7   Example choice card from the Motray/Brothock study

Policy option / Impact	Do nothing	A	B
Number of agricultural jobs lost or gained in the local area	No loss no creation	Loss of 5 jobs	Creation of 2 jobs
Visual impact: number of months of low flow condition	5 months	2 months	3 months
Ecological condition	Worsening	Slight improvement	Big improvement
Increase in water rates per year	£0	£2	£2
Please tick the option you prefer			

Table 10.8   Compensating surplus (WTP) for three different future management plans for two Scottish rivers (all values are £/ household/year)

	Motray River		Brothock River	
	Mean WTP	95% confidence interval	Mean WTP	95% confidence interval
Plan A	56.80	45.80–67.90	62.00	44.00–84.00
Plan B	67.70	55.30–80.50	72.00	53.60–93.30
Plan C	97.20	79.70–115.50	103.30	80.90–133.30

Source: Adapted from Hanley et al. (2006).

transfer test of whether the mean values are equal fails to reject this hypothesis at the 95 per cent level. In this instance, then, we could use WTP values from one river as a reasonable guess for WTP values at the other river.

10.4   CONCLUSIONS

As noted above, the role of CBA has been greatly increasing in recent years for the appraisal of water quality improvements. In Europe, the main driver of this process has been the Water Framework Directive,

BOX 10.6   THE HEALTH BENEFITS OF WATER QUALITY
IMPROVEMENTS (2)

As noted in the main text, non-point source pollution is a major source of water quality problems in the UK and US. One aspect of such pollution is run-off of pathogens contained in livestock wastes (for example from dairy farms), which leads to concentrations in coastal bathing waters which can have adverse health effects on people swimming. Undertaking a CBA of measures to reduce such problems is complicated: a dose-response relationship between agricultural land use (for example stocking rates) and pathogen concentrations in coastal waters must be discovered, along with the relationship between concentrations of pathogens and cases of illness.

Johnson et al. (2008) present results from a model which tries to represent most of this picture for bathing water quality in Irvine, Scotland. Water quality here has a history of high levels of intestinal enterocci (IE), which are linked to gastro-enteritis in bathers. Dairy farming higher up the catchment has been identified as a major source of these pathogens. Johnson et al.'s model relates concentrations of IE in the catchment to levels of IE in bathing waters, and then calculates the change in exposure for people swimming from an increase in predicted IE concentrations. This increase in risk is then valued in monetary terms using a benefits transfer of a WTP value for reduced risks of a stomach upset from bathing in polluted water. This model is then used to calculate the present value of aggregate benefits from a 25 per cent, 50 per cent and 75 per cent reduction in IE concentrations. A 50 per cent reduction in IE concentration gives a PV of benefits of £1.8 million, at a 6 per cent discount rate. The authors comment that measures to reduce the run-off of IE from dairy farms by installing 'best management practices' are unlikely to pass a cost–benefit test, and that it was unlikely that these management practices could actually achieve the higher-end reductions in concentration, especially during periods of heavy rainfall.

For a comparable exercise undertaken within a US context, see Dwight et al. (2005).

whilst in the UK the 'Periodic Review' process has also been important (Box 10.1). How can we summarize what emerges as important for the application of CBA within this policy framework?

In terms of measuring *costs*, the main issues which emerge as important would seem to be:

- quantifying how costs are distributed across those having to take actions to improve water quality;
- that the costs of achieving a given water quality target will depend on what measures are put in place to achieve it.

Moreover, we should recognize that costs will depend on the ambition levels set within targets: more ambitious targets, other things being equal, mean higher costs.

In terms of measuring *benefits*, the most important areas are:

- the need to develop systems of benefits transfer with 'acceptably low' errors, and errors that are also predictable;
- uncertainty over the ecological effects of reductions in pollution, and thus problems in knowing what changes in environmental quality need to be valued;
- being able to quantify how many people will gain from a particular water quality improvement.

We should also recognize that policy makers and water quality managers may be uneasy over the lack of precision of non-market benefit estimates, and their dependence on how benefits are measured. But equal or greater uncertainty may also exist over programme costs.

NOTE

1. Indeed, the most recent OFWAT guidance on the use of CBA in regulatory review of future water quality improvements requires this to be done (OFWAT, 2007).

REFERENCES

Aftab, A., N. Hanley and A. Kampas (2007), 'Co-ordinated environmental regulation: controlling non-point nitrate pollution while maintaining river flows', *Environmental and Resource Economics*, **38**(4) 573–93.

Bateman, I., B. Day, S. Georgiou and I. Lake (2006), 'The aggregation of environmental benefit values: welfare measures, distance decay and total WTP', *Ecological Economics*, **60**, 450–60.

Baumol, W. and W. Oates (1985), *The Theory of Environmental Policy*, Cambridge: Cambridge University Press.

Birol, E., P. Koundouri and Y. Kountouris (2008), 'Using the choice experiment method to inform river management in Poland: flood risk reduction versus habitat conservation in the Upper Silesia region', in E. Birol and P. Koundouri (eds), *Choice Experiments Informing Environmental Policy*, Cheltenham, UK and Northampton, MA, USA: Edward Elgar.

Brouwer, R. (2000), 'Environmental value transfer: state of the art and future prospects', *Ecological Economics*, **32**(1), 137–52.

Colombo, S. and N. Hanley (2008), 'How can we reduce the errors from benefits transfer? An investigation using the Choice Experiment method', *Land Economics*, **84**(1), 128–47.

Colombo, S., Nick Hanley and Javier Calatrava-Requena (2005), 'Designing policy for reducing the off-farm effects of soil erosion using Choice Experiments', *Journal of Agricultural Economics*, **56**(1), 81–96.

Downing, M. and T. Ozuna (1996), 'Testing the reliability of the benefit function transfer approach', *Journal of Environmental Economics and Management*, **30**, 316–22.

Dwight, R.H., L. Fernandez, D. Baker, J. Semenza and B. Olson (2005), 'Estimating the economic burden from illnesses associated with recreational coastal water pollution – a case study in Orange County, California', *Journal of Environmental Management*, **76**, 95–103.

Environment Agency (2003), *Economic Appraisal for the Environment Programme in PR04*, London: Environment Agency.

Fisher, J. (2008), 'Challenges for applying Cost Benefit Analysis and valuation of environmental benefits to aid decision making in practice', Paper presented to the European Association of Environmental and Resource Economists' conference, Goteborg, Sweden, June.

Hanley, N., F. Schlapfer and J. Spurgeon (2003), 'Aggregating the benefits of environmental improvements: distance-decay functions for use and non-use values', *Journal of Environmental Management*, **68**, 297–304.

Hanley, N., R. Faichney, A. Munro and J. Shortle (1998), 'Economic and environmental modelling for pollution control in an estuary', *Journal of Environmental Management*, **52**, 211–25.

Hanley, N., S. Colombo, D. Tinch, A. Black and A. Aftab (2006), 'Estimating the benefits of water quality improvements under the Water Framework Directive: are benefits transferable?', *European Review of Agricultural Economics*, **33**, 391–413.

Jacobs UK Ltd (2006), 'Guidance on the evidence required to justify disproportionate cost decisions under the Water Framework Directive', report to DEFRA under the Collaborative Research programme, Project 3, available from DEFRA website on the Water Framework Directive CRP.

Jiang, Y., S.K. Swallow and M.P. McGonagle (2005), 'Context-sensitive benefit transfer using stated choice models: specification and convergent validity for policy analysis', *Environmental and Resource Economics*, **31**, 477–99.

Johnson, E.K., D. Moran and A. Vinten (2008), 'A framework for valuing the health benefits of improved bathing water quality in the River Irvine catchment', *Journal of Environmental Management*, **87**, 633–8.

Larson, D.M. and S. Shaikh (2003), 'Whalewatching demand and value: estimates from a new empirical demand system', in N. Hanley, W.D. Shaw and R.E. Wright (eds), *The New Economics of Outdoor Recreation*, Cheltenham, UK and Northampton, MA, USA: Edward Elgar.

Larson, D.M., G.E. Helfand and B.W. House (1996), 'Second-best tax policies to reduce nonpoint source pollution', *American Journal of Agricultural Economics*, **78**(4), 1108–17.

Morrison, M. and J. Bennett (2006), 'Valuing New South Wales rivers for use in benefit transfer', in J. Rolfe and J. Bennett (eds), *Choice Modelling and the Transfer of Environmental Values*, Cheltenham, UK and Northampton, MA, USA: Edward Elgar.

Morrison, M., J. Bennett, R. Blamey and J. Louviere (2002), 'Choice modelling and tests of benefit transfer', *American Journal of Agricultural Economics*, **84**, 161–70.

Muthke, T. and K. Holm-Muller (2004), 'National and international benefit transfer testing with a rigorous test procedure', *Environmental and Resource Economics*, **29**, 323–36.

OFWAT (2007), 'Further guidance on the use of cost benefit analysis for PR09', London: Office of Water Regulation.

Roy, J. (2008), 'Economic benefits of arsenic removal from ground water – a case study of West Bengal, India', *Science of the Total Environment*, **397**, 1–12.

Rozan, A. (2004), 'Benefit transfer: a comparison of WTP for air quality between France and Germany', *Environmental and Resource Economics*, **29**, 295–306.

RPA (2004), 'CEA and developing a methodology for assessing disproportionate costs', report to DEFRA and others by Risk and Policy Analysis, available at www.defra.gov.uk/environment/water/wfd/economics/research.htm.

Shortle, J.S. and R. Horan (2001), 'The economics of non-point pollution control', *Journal of Economic Surveys*, **15**(3), 255–89.

Train, K.E. (1998), 'Recreation demand models with taste differences over people', *Land Economics*, **74**(2), 230–39.

WATECO (2004), 'Economics and the environment – the implementation challenge of the water framework directive', Luxembourg: European Commission, available at http://ec.europa.eu/environment/water/water-framework/index_en.html.

11.   Valuing habitat protection

11.1   INTRODUCTION

In Chapter 9 we saw that loss of natural habitats worldwide is one of
the main causes of the decline in 'ecosystem services' – the benefits that
people derive from natural environments and systems. In that chapter,
we addressed methods of valuing these benefits and their incorporation
in cost–benefit analysis (CBA). In this chapter we explore the related
theme of valuing natural habitats – the unique natural environments that
generate many important ecosystem services. As we explored in Chapter
9, these two values are clearly interconnected; if a natural habitat generates ecological services, then the latter can be considered to be simply the
flow of 'values' generated by a unique economic asset, which is the natural
habitat responsible for these services. It follows that, by valuing correctly
the range of ecosystem services of a natural habitat, we can determine how
much of the natural area should be converted to another economic use or
protected in its original state.

Although valuing the decision whether or not to create a protected area
is extremely important, especially given the decline in important natural
ecosystems globally, there are other important issues concerned with managing natural habitat that also require input from cost–benefit analysis. In
particular, there are three additional themes that need to be considered.

First, the tradeoff between conservation and development means that
the opportunity cost of habitat protection must also be considered carefully. In Chapter 9, we focused almost exclusively on the benefits associated with ecosystem preservation in terms of maintaining ecological
services and the methods required to value these services. But we noted
that both the decision whether or not to preserve a natural environment,
as well as determining how much area of the environment should be conserved, will depend crucially on the forgone opportunities of the next-best
economic use of the resources and land that comprise the protected area.
In this chapter we will focus more closely on the opportunity costs of protection and how these costs can be assessed. We will also discuss briefly
the other costs associated with protecting habitats, such as the direct costs
of acquiring, setting up and managing the protected area and any external
damages inflicted through preserving wildlife and their habitat.

Second, conservation areas are not simply 'preserved' natural environments. Many protected areas serve as important parks and sites that are visited frequently for recreation and tourism. Nature-based tourism and recreation are therefore often important additional benefits generated by protected areas once they are created. Assessing the benefits from tourism, and in particular the willingness to pay by individuals to visit one or more sites with different and unique environmental attributes, is an important part of determining the overall benefits of a protected area. In this chapter we will also examine how many of the valuation methods discussed in this book can be applied to the problem of determining this willingness to pay.

Finally, determining the appropriate fees to charge for visits to protected areas and parks is an increasingly important issue in the management of natural habitat, although charging for entrance is not always possible for legal or cultural reasons. For example, in some European countries, such as in the UK or throughout Scandinavia, national parks are not permitted to charge visitors' fees. On the one hand, where entrance fees and other use permits are levied, they should not be set too low so that congestion reduces the enjoyment of visitors or that overuse of the environment leads to a deterioration in the natural habitat; on the other hand, fees and permits cannot be prohibitively expensive so that individuals are discouraged from visiting the park. As we shall discuss in this chapter, CBA is increasingly being used to assess both the optimal management strategy and the fee structure necessary to balance competing stakeholder interest in protected areas.

All three of these themes have emerged as important issues for CBA in recent years, because of global trends in habitat protection (see Table 11.1). As the table indicates, since 1970 an increasing amount of territory has been designated as marine and terrestrial protected areas. By 2006, all other regions have caught up with or even exceeded the percentage of total area protected in Europe and North America. Currently, almost 13 per cent of the world's territory is protected, and there are nearly 900 World Heritage sites set aside because of their outstanding natural or natural/cultural value.

11.2   THE COSTS OF PROTECTION

As pointed out by Naidoo et al. (2006), most environmental conservation plans focus on the benefits of establishing protected areas and conserving habitats, often expressed in terms of specific biological targets, such as the number of endangered species saved, preservation of biodiversity 'hot

Table 11.1   Global trends in protected areas, 1970 to 2007

Region	Terrestrial and marine protected areas as percent of total territorial area[a]					Number of World Heritage sites (2007)[b]
	1970	1980	1990	2000	2006	
Africa	5.07	7.83	9.23	9.65	9.90	112
Asia and Pacific	2.41	4.46	7.40	9.90	10.55	174
West Asia	0.25	0.26	4.22	21.76	21.80	25
Latin America and Caribbean	6.39	8.92	13.07	16.32	17.71	117
Europe	5.06	6.12	7.45	9.05	9.17	395
North America	6.47	10.65	11.43	14.09	14.20	33
World	4.56	7.40	9.78	12.21	12.74	856

Notes:

a   Based on data from the World Conservation Union (IUCN), downloaded from http:// wcpa.iucn.org/. Total territorial area includes terrestrial area plus territorial sea area (up to 12 nautical mile limit). A protected area is defined by IUCN as an area of land and/or sea especially dedicated to the protection and maintenance of biological diversity, and of natural and associated cultural resources, and managed through legal or other effective means.

b   Based on data from the World Heritage Committee, United Nations Educational, Scientific, and Cultural Organization (UNESCO), downloaded from http://whc.unesco. org/en/list. World heritage sites represent areas of 'outstanding universal value' for their natural features, their cultural value, or for both natural and cultural values. This table only lists natural or natural/cultural sites.

spots' or the area of critical species habitat conserved. But, as the authors argue, 'By ignoring the cost side of conservation planning, ecologists and conservation biologists are missing great opportunities to achieve more efficiently conservation objectives in a world of limited conservation resources.' Instead, more efficient conservation planning 'attempts to solve a cost-effectiveness problem: how to achieve a given conservation target (e.g. represent at least 10% of every species range) at least cost; that is, how to achieve the most conservation given limited resources' (Naidoo et al., 2006, p. 681). Thus, an increasingly important role for cost–benefit analysis (CBA) is to determine the cost effectiveness of alternative conservation plans for achieving desired targets (Busch and Cullen, 2009).

As we discuss in Box 11.1, such a cost effectiveness analysis is often used as a fallback position when a full CBA of the benefits and costs of establishing a protected area cannot be achieved. Usually, this happens when we cannot measure benefits in monetary terms or when there is a legally binding target to be met. However, even if one is limited to conducting a

BOX 11.1   COST–BENEFIT ANALYSIS RULES AND HABITAT
           PROTECTION

There are three types of economic costs associated with the establishment and maintenance of protected areas (Barbier et al., 1997; Naidoo et
al., 2006). There are the *direct costs* of acquiring, setting up and managing the protected area, C^P. There are the *opportunity costs* of any land or
other natural resources that are allocated to the protected area and could
possibly have other alternative economic uses, C^O. Finally, there are the
external costs that might be imposed on others, such as wildlife damage
inflicted on surrounding communities, by the creation of protected areas
and wildlife habitats, C^E. The following table, adapted from Naidoo et al.
(2006, Box 1), summarizes and gives examples of these three categories
of costs.

Type of Cost	Definition	Example
Direct Costs (C^D)		
Acquisition cost	The costs of acquiring property rights to an area of land.	Sale of land and title; short-term land rental, conservation easements, and contracts between conservation agents and landowners.
Transaction cost	Any additional costs associated with negotiating the transfer of property rights to an area of land.	The costs of searching for properties, negotiating with individual landholders and obtaining approval for title transfer.
Maintenance cost	Ongoing costs of managing and maintaining an established protected area.	Costs of monitoring conservation, guarding against illegal activities, maintaining upkeep of protected area and facilities.
Opportunity Costs (C^O)	The costs of forgone opportunities; i.e., the net present value of the next-best economic use of the resources and land that comprise the protected area.	In protected forested areas, the next best use of the land and resources might be for agriculture or forestry; in wetlands, for aquaculture or water diversion; in marine protected areas, fishing.
External Costs (C^E)	Damages and costs imposed on others that arise through the creation maintenance of the protected areas.	Wildlife damages to property and economic activities; predation of livestock; biological invasion.

A full cost–benefit analysis (CBA) of establishing a protected area must take into account not only the benefits of creating and maintaining the conserved natural environment but also these costs (Barbier et al., 1997). For example, as we discussed in Chapter 9, conserving a natural habitat or ecosystem is likely to yield a range of 'services', or benefits, and the aggregate willingness to pay for these benefits can be denoted as B_t. Of course, these benefits occur not just in one time period but are a flow of benefits over time; thus, by discounting this flow, we will have an estimate of the net present value of benefits, which we can denote as $PV(B_t)$. The decision to conserve a natural ecosystem must therefore compare the net present value of the benefits from conservation against the opportunity cost of next best use of the land and resources tied up in creating the protected area (Table 10.6). As noted in the above table, this opportunity cost, C^O, is also a net present value of the forgone 'development' benefits, such as from commercial agriculture, forestry, fishing or water diversion, or $PV(B_t^D)$. It follows that the protected area should be established if the net present value of its benefits exceeds the opportunity costs, or $PV(B_t) > C^O = PV(B_t^D)$. But there are also the direct and external costs associated with setting up and running the protected area. These costs must also be considered in the decision of whether or not to create a protected area. So, the full CBA rule is that the protected area should be established, if $PV(B_t) > C^O + C^D + C^E = PV(B_t^D) + C^D + C^E$.

However, given the difficulties in quantifying the economic benefits, B_t, of protected areas in advance, efficient conservation planning can still take place provided that the principles of cost-effective analysis are used. For example, Naidoo et al. (2006, p. 682) suggest:

Such analyses express the costs of conservation in monetary terms, but the benefits remain in the original units (e.g. numbers of species or area of forest). The most efficient plan is the one that delivers a given conservation target for the least cost or, alternatively, maximizes the conservation target level for a given cost.

Consequently, such a cost effectiveness rule would mean selecting the conservation or protected area plan that seeks to minimize the overall costs of achieving the plan's goal or targets, that is, min $C = C^O + C^D + C^E = PV(B_t^D) + C^D + C^E$.

cost effectiveness analysis of alternative protected area or conservation plans, one needs to account carefully for the costs associated with setting up and running the protected area. As noted in Box 11.1, three types of costs are crucial: the *direct costs* of acquiring, setting up and managing the protected area; the *opportunity costs* of any land or other natural resources that are allocated to the protected area and could possibly have other alternative economic uses; and finally any *external costs* that might be imposed on others from establishing a protected area. All these costs are critical to assess, but it is the opportunity cost of land that is often most important for determining whether creating a protected area is economically worthwhile (that is, whether the benefits of protection are bigger than the costs).

One important reason for considering carefully the opportunity costs of establishing protected areas and parks is that these costs tend to vary spatially, especially in the case of terrestrial conservation decisions (Ando et al., 1998; Balmford et al., 2003; Carwardine et al., 2008b; Naidoo et al., 2006). Allowing for the spatial variability of costs across heterogeneous landscapes will have an important bearing on the decision as to how much land area to protect, which landscapes to include cost effectively for achieving overall conservation targets, and the selection of alternative possible sites for protected areas. Accounting for spatial heterogeneity in measuring the overall opportunity costs of habitat protection can improve markedly the cost effectiveness of conservation plans, thus reducing their costs within a CBA.

For example, Polasky et al. (2001) consider the cost effectiveness of alternative biodiversity reserve plans for preserving various endangered terrestrial vertebrates in Oregon. They show that reserve plans that took into account the spatial heterogeneity of landscapes in estimating the opportunity costs exhibited just 10 per cent of the costs of plans that ignored the spatial variability of the opportunity costs. Similarly, Ando et al. (1998) examine the effect of heterogeneous land prices on the efficient selection of endangered species reserve sites across the United States. The authors show that accounting for spatial variability in land prices can lead to a more cost effective reserve selection strategy by avoiding costly sites and selecting nearby sites that have fewer species but are less costly. Thus, by including twice as many sites at 30 per cent of the cost, the cost per site under the cost-minimizing solution is less than one-sixth of that under the solution that minimizes the number of sites selected to conserve a given target of species.

Of course including the opportunity cost of establishing protected areas has its most dramatic impacts when conservation plans are at the global scale. For example, Ceballos et al. (2005) construct a method of selecting priority areas for global terrestrial mammal conservation, which concludes that 11 per cent of Earth's land surface could be managed for conservation to achieve the goal of preserving at least 10 per cent of terrestrial mammal geographic ranges. However, the authors failed to take into account the site-specific opportunity costs involved in such an immense global habitat conservation strategy. Carwardine et al. (2008b) revisit the problem of establishing global priority areas for mammal conservation and derive a new set of priority areas for investment in mammal conservation based on:

(i) agricultural opportunity cost and biodiversity importance; (ii) current levels of international funding; and (iii) degree of threat. The authors find that their cost effective analysis of global mammals achieves the same biodiversity outcomes and desired targets as Ceballos et al. (2005) and reduces the opportunity costs and conflicts with agriculture by up to 50 per cent.

But accounting for the heterogeneous opportunity costs of biodiversity conservation and habitat protection is also important at the local and regional level. This may particularly be the case in developing regions, where fragmented but biologically diverse 'hotspots' are under threat from conversion to agriculture and other economic activities. Chomitz et al. (2005) consider this potential conflict in their analysis of the opportunity costs of protecting biodiversity 'hotspots' in southern coastal Bahia, Brazil. The authors use a hedonic price model to analyse and impute site-specific agricultural land values as a measure of the opportunity cost of biodiversity hotspot conservation. They identified the least expensive 10 000 hectares of 'high forest cover' land in each of eight biologically distinct ecological zones within the study region, and found that the mean agricultural land value of these lands was only $146 per hectare. The results suggest that the opportunity cost of conserving these biologically unique areas in south Bahia is very low relative to the benefits of hotspot conservation.

However, not all biodiversity benefits may be large enough to cover the opportunity costs of conservation. Box 11.2 discusses the case of 'capturing' the pharmaceutical value of biodiversity conservation to justify the costs of establishing protected areas in developing countries. As the box indicates, studies show that the returns from the potential pharmaceutical value of biodiversity may be sufficient to cover the costs of bioprospecting activities, such as collecting biotic samples and screening them for useful pharmaceutical properties, but the returns are unlikely to cover the full opportunity costs (such as forgone timber and agricultural revenues) of establishing biodiversity reserves in developing countries. Other benefits from conservation, such as ecotourism or watershed values, would have to make up the difference.

Determining the direct costs of conservation may also be critical to the successful creation of protected habitat and ecosystems. In particular, assessing acquisition costs can be important when establishing protected areas is for landscape-specific ecosystem benefits other than species or biodiversity conservation. For example, the use of riparian land buffers to protect water quality for human consumption has become a key conservation goal in many countries and regions. Azzaino et al. (2002) and Ferraro (2003 and 2004) examine the case of managing a riparian buffer zone to

BOX 11.2   THE PHARMACEUTICAL VALUE OF FORESTS
AND THE OPPORTUNITY COSTS OF
PROTECTION

The widely publicized agreement in 1991 by Merck pharmaceutical company to enter into a bioprospecting agreement with the National Institute for Biodiversity (INBio) in Costa Rica led to much speculation in the environmental community and the media about the possibility that developing countries could 'capture' the pharmaceutical value of biodiversity as a mechanism for paying for biodiversity conservation. Several studies, including economic analyses, pointed out that 25 per cent of the drugs sold in the developing world and 75 per cent in developing countries were based on chemicals made originally by biological organisms, yet only a small fraction of the world's biodiversity has been fully accessed for its potential 'pharmaceutical value'. With annual global drug sales exceeding $200 billion, these studies have argued that developing countries could justify preserving tropical forests and other biological biodiversity habitats through marketing their potential value as a source of future pharmaceuticals (see Firn, 2003 for a review).

However, Barbier and Aylward (1996) maintain that, in order to capture a share of the pharmaceutical value from their biological diversity, developing countries have to invest in the protection of biodiversity as well as the collection and identification of biotic samples that may have potentially useful pharmaceutical properties. By using data from the international pharmaceutical industry and from INBio and its bioprospecting activities in Guanacaste National Park in Costa Rica, the authors determine the net returns to a developing country from investing in biodiversity protection as opposed to 'bioprospecting', which involves collecting biotic samples and assessing their useful taxonomic properties as pharmaceuticals. Barbier and Aylward find that the expected royalty returns and fees from screening 2000 samples every year for 40 years amounts to US$5.79 million, or US$9.65 per hectare (ha) conserved as a biodiversity reserve. The costs of the bioprospecting – procuring biotic samples and testing their pharmaceutical properties – amount to US$1.96 million or US$3.27 per ha. Thus, the authors suggest that the pharmaceutical value of prospecting can cover the costs of bioprospecting for a developing country. But they also find that the opportunity costs of preserving 600 000 ha forests in Costa Rica for biodiversity conservation amount to US$244.48 million, or $407.47 per ha. Consequently, Barbier and Aylward (1996, p. 176) conclude that 'the full social costs of biodiversity protection are simply too high to be compensated through prospecting on its own. Other economic benefits of establishing protected natural areas – from ecotourism to watershed protection – must make up the difference if the full costs of biodiversity protection are to be justified.'

Other studies concur with these findings. For example, Simpson et al. (1996) calculate that the maximum possible pharmaceutical value for bioprospecting in 18 critical biodiversity hotspots identified as potential protected areas in developing countries is US$20 per ha, and in areas with less genetic diversity this value falls to a dollar per hectare or less. Thus, the authors also conclude that 'considerable caution and skepticism should be employed when considering the potential for genetic prospecting as a conservation tool'. The conclusion by Firn (2003, p. 207) is even more stark; given the scientific and economic difficulties in protecting, generating and capturing the pharmaceutical value of biodiversity, 'there should be no reliance on large-income streams being available from bioprospecting agreements to help fund the preservation of biodiversity.'

provide water for urban residents in New York state. The city of Syracuse in central New York has a population of just under 200 000 and draws its water from the nearby Skaneateles Lake. The high quality of the lake's water is due to a relatively small watershed-to-lake ratio, and the city of Syracuse has sought to maintain this high quality by establishing a 'riparian buffer' consisting of strips of land purchased from private landowners that intercepts and sequesters pollutant run-off from the watershed into the lake. When the economic studies of the riparian buffers include both the benefits (reduction in pollutants and sediments in the watershed) and the costs (acquisition costs of land parcels for the buffer zone), the conservation plans resulted in expenditures that were 16–67 per cent of the total costs of plans that considered benefits only. Taking account of acquisition costs not only allowed for more efficient selection of land parcels for the buffer zone but also allowed targeting of parcels to fit heterogeneous landscapes. Similarly, Carwardine et al. (2008a) show for Australia that a typical conservation planning objective is to identify protected areas that can achieve specific biodiversity targets with the minimum possible area of land or sea set aside for this purpose. However, because the acquisition and 'stewardship' (that is management) costs differ throughout a landscape, the authors demonstrate that taking account of such spatially variable costs can halve the overall costs of achieving conservation targets.

One of the most important external costs of conservation projects and the establishment of protected habitats is wildlife damage, especially to agriculture. In the United States, 55 per cent of agricultural producers report some damage to crops from wildlife, and total estimated damage costs can be as high as $1.26 billion (Yoder, 2002). Currently, 25 state and provincial agencies in the United States and Canada run programmes that compensate for wildlife crop damages. For the state of Wisconsin, Yoder (2002) analyses county-level compensation programme claims data, and find that the aggregate crop damages from deer range from $45 million to $57 million. In Scotland, rising wild geese numbers due to greater conservation of wetland habitat have increased losses of crops and grassland from goose grazing. Although damages vary between seasons and locations, the average cost of damage is around £21.5 and £72 per ha, or £6000 to £11 000 per affected farm (MacMillan et al., 2004). In addition, the economic costs per farm tended to change with goose density; for example, for farms surveyed in the Strathberg catchment, damages per farm ranged from £1932 for low density to £3671 for medium densities, and finally to £10 241 for high densities.

The costs of wildlife damage can be extensive in developing countries as well. Sutton et al. (2008) employ a contingent value survey of smallholder farmers in the Caprivi Region of Namibia, which also contains protected habitat for elephant, lion, hippo, buffalo and other wildlife that are considered important to international and local tourism. The survey reveals that the mean household willingness to pay (WTP) to deter one predator from attacking a farmer's livestock one time is $25.97 in cash or 343.89 kg in maize; the mean WTP to deter one elephant from trampling crops is $0.16 or 2.09 kg of maize; and the mean WTP to prevent wild herbivore crop damage is $3.03. In addition, however, Johannesen (2005) finds that there may be another indirect cost of wildlife damage in Africa. In her survey of rural households in the western Serengeti of Tanzania, she finds that wildlife-induced damage to crops and domestic animals increases the probability that the households will engage in illegal hunting activity in nearby protected areas.

11.3 NATURE-BASED TOURISM AND RECREATION

Many protected areas serve as important parks and sites that are visited frequently for recreation and tourism. Nature-based tourism and recreation are therefore often important additional benefits generated by protected areas once they are created. Assessing these benefits from tourism, and in particular the willingness to pay by individuals to visit one or more sites with different and unique environmental attributes, is therefore important in determining the overall benefits of a protected area.

Most studies that estimate the benefits from nature-based tourism and recreation usually involve application of the stated preference and travel cost methods discussed in this book (see Chapters 3 and 4). As we saw in Chapter 4, variants of the travel cost approach have been developed into site choice models, which are applied to the case where individuals may have the choice of one or more sites to visit and the choice is likely to be affected by the various attributes of each site. Extensions of this approach estimate the site choice model first and then connect it to an estimation of the number of visits made to the preferred site (see Freeman, 2003, ch. 13; Haab and Hicks, 2000; Haab and McConnell, 2002, ch. 7 and 8; Phaneuf and Smith, 2005 for reviews). Choice Experiment models are also being employed more frequently to assess tourist preferences for the establishment of protected areas and supporting infrastructure (Hanley et al., 2003; Hearne and Salinas, 2002; Huybers and Bennett, 2003; Mansfield et al., 2008; Naidoo and Adamowicz, 2005; Rolfe et al., 2000).

Choice models are also frequently important in assessing tradeoffs between competing uses for a preserved habitat. For example, in the United States a major controversy has emerged in recent years over the use of snowmobiles for winter recreation in national parks. Opponents of increased snowmobile access complain about the crowding, noise and fumes generated by the activity and assert that snowmobiles disrupt the wilderness and wildlife as well as other winter activities such as snow-shoeing and cross-country skiing. The focus point of this debate has been Yellowstone National Park in Wyoming, where the National Park Service has tried to implement policies to curtail snowmobile use in the park. Mansfield et al. (2008) assess the effect of various policy options by employing a stated preference choice experiment to quantify welfare changes for snowmobilers and other visitors under different restrictions of snowmobile use in the park. The authors find that the welfare losses to snowmobilers of various restrictions on their use of the park could be offset by the welfare gains to other recreationists. However, the outcome depends on the current visitors of each type and how the mix of visitor types would change in response to a new policy.

Traditionally, studies that value recreation and nature-based tourism focus on the single choice of deciding whether or not to visit a protected area, or choosing between different alternative areas to visit, or between different activities at the same protected area. However, such recreation choices can often be related to other important considerations, which suggests that the choice may be 'bundled' benefits. For example, in more affluent countries households may choose to purchase houses because of the proximity to a protected area that not only affords them easy access for recreation but also a host of other ecosystem services, such as improved water quality and amenity values. Phaneuf et al. (2008) show that it is possible to employ a combination of hedonic property value and random utility models for local recreation to consider the welfare impacts on households of these multiple benefits. Similarly, Landry and McConnell (2007) include a hedonic price schedule in a recreation demand model to account for the on-site expenditures on associated services, such as accommodation, dining, excursions and tours, equipment rental and sightseeing, as the cost of these activities may also affect the number of visits to a protected area as well as the time spent on-site. Cutter et al. (2007) also analyse individuals' choice between on-site attributes and site activities. Their purpose was to test whether a change in the level of a site attribute may simultaneously increase the welfare of some individuals, while reducing the welfare of others, depending upon the activities in which individuals are engaged. Cutter et al. explored this hypothesis with a survey of domestic visitors to seven national parks in Costa Rica, which consisted primarily of forested beaches offering similar on-site activities. The results indicate that incorporating on-site activities was critical to understanding individuals' derived demand for site attributes, and the welfare changes associated both with site attributes and regulations affecting on-site activities.

Given the long history of stated preference and travel cost studies of recreation in certain locales, economists are finding novel ways of utilizing this track record of studies for improving estimates of nature-based tourism. For example, as indicated in Box 11.3, in European countries there have been more valuation studies of woodland recreation than any other nature-based tourism activity. Two studies from the UK and Denmark show that information from these past studies, combined

---

BOX 11.3   EMPLOYING PAST RECREATIONAL DEMAND
            STUDIES TO INFORM CURRENT WTP
            ESTIMATES

Because of the long history of estimating the willingness to pay (WTP) for recreation, some economic studies have tried to find ways to utilize this information. For example, in Europe there have been more applications of stated preference and travel cost methods to value woodland recreation than any other form of nature-based tourism. This is not surprising; as the table below shows, recreation is the highest value of forests in Great Britain.

Environmental benefit	Annual value (£ million, 2002 prices)	Capitalized value (£ million, 2002 prices)
Recreation	392.65	11,218
Biodiversity	386.00	11,029
Landscape	150.22	4,292
Carbon sequestration	93.66	2,676
Air pollution absorption	0.39	11
Total	**1,022.92**	**29,226**

Source: Willis et al. (2003).

Previous valuation studies of recreation therefore are potentially useful sources of information for new studies. One approach, taken by Bateman et al. (2005, ch. 2–4), was to review all stated preference studies of recreation in the United Kingdom and conduct a meta-analysis on a selected number. They concluded that the results of such studies are subject to design effects, but could be usefully employed to quantify the limits of such effects. In addition, the authors concluded that previous studies suggest that there is scope for combining Geographical Information Systems (GIS) techniques within a travel cost model of recreational demand. An important advantage of using GIS techniques in travel cost studies is that it allows standardization and improvement in the accuracy of measuring travel distance and duration variables, which are key determinants in estimating travel time and expenditure by individuals. Bateman et al. apply this methodology to a follow-up study of visitors to Lynford Stag, a major woodland recreation site near Thetford, East Anglia. They found that the use of GIS-based measures of travel offered substantial improvement in the robustness of benefit estimates compared either to conventional straight-line or road-fitted measures, and were more reliable compared to the highly variable recreational values produced by previous stated preference studies of recreation at Thetford. In particular, the use of GIS allowed better measurement of journey outset location, modelling journey routing and conducting sensitivity analysis on journey outset locations. In addition, the GIS information could be used effectively to model the predicted number of visitors to a particular woodland site and to test the efficiency of the resultant arrivals function in estimating visits to other sites. Again, Bateman et al. employ their Thetford study to use GIS information to predict future visits, both to Thetford and to similar recreational forests found in Wales.

There are other ways that past recreation information can be used to improve current valuation estimates. For example, Zandersen et al. (2007), which we also reviewed in Box 4.4 of Chapter 4, evaluate two separate random utility model estimations based on 1977 and 1997 national visitor surveys of recreation in 52 forests in Denmark for possible changes in preferences towards forest characteristics and travel over the 20-year period. GIS techniques were also employed to account for site heterogeneity and the spatial pattern of population density and other demographic characteristics. The authors then combine the 1997 random utility model with a count data model to determine total demand for visits at each forest site, and controlling for changes in trip demand, they conduct a value transfer from 1977 to 1997. Finally, Zanderson et al. use sensitivity analysis to determine whether the 20-year benefits transfer improves the estimation of the present total demand for recreation. They find that the error margins improve by 282 per cent, although the average errors of the best transfer model remain at 25 per cent.

with new techniques such as Geographical Information Systems (GIS) and benefit transfers, can be used to improve current WTP estimates for nature-based tourism.

Estimating the benefits of recreation and nature-based tourism may be especially critical to the establishment of new marine protected areas in developing countries. For example, as we discussed above and show in Table 11.1, the growth of terrestrial and marine protected areas around the world has accelerated in recent years. Some of the fastest growth has been for marine protected areas in developing regions. For example, in 1970 Latin America and the Caribbean had nearly 18 million hectares (ha) of marine protected areas, Asia and the Pacific 10.5 million ha, Africa 7.3 million ha and West Asia less than 16 000 ha. By 2006, Latin America and the Caribbean had nearly 48 million ha of marine protected areas, Asia and the Pacific over 101 million ha, Africa nearly 30 million ha and West Asia almost 4 million ha (these data are from the World Conservation Union (IUCN), downloaded from http://wcpa.iucn.org/). Much of the recent growth in marine protected areas has occurred through the establishment of marine reserves, which have the primary purpose of aiding the recovery of overfished stocks and marine habitats. However, given the high 'opportunity costs' to local fishing communities of closing commercial and subsistence fisheries, marine reserves and other protected areas are often keen to promote additional recreational benefits, such as snorkelling, scuba diving, coral reef tours and other forms of nature-based tourism.

To assess such marine tourism benefits, Mathieu et al. (2003) conducted a stated preference study to determine the willingness to pay (WTP) of tourists to visit marine national parks in the Seychelles. They find that the average consumer surplus per tourist is US$2.20, giving a total consumer surplus estimate of US88 000 for the 40 000 tourists visiting the Seychelles in 1997. The authors found that country of origin, expectations, and reasons for visiting the parks were more important in determining WTP responses than socio-demographic factors, such as age, sex, education and income. In addition, respondents indicated much higher WTP for certain parks (for example Curieuse and Ile de Coco) compared to others (Baie Terney).

11.4   VISITORS' FEES

Once protected areas and parks are established, it becomes vitally important to determine the appropriate fees to charge for visitors, in instances where this is institutionally and culturally possible. The entrance fees and other use permits cannot be set too low so that congestion reduces the enjoyment of visitors or that overuse of the environment leads to a deterioration in the natural habitat. But permits cannot also be prohibitively expensive so that individuals are discouraged from visiting the park. The determination of the correct visitors' fee has been a particularly important issue in developing countries, where the number and size of protected areas have grown rapidly in recent years (see Table 11.1) and governments count increasingly on the revenues from park fees to pay for the management and other costs of conservation.

For instance, from their study of marine parks in the Seychelles, Mathieu et al. (2003) conclude that entrance fees to parks could be increased from the current institutional rate of $10 per visitor to $12 without affecting visitors' rates significantly. Fee revenues from the marine parks would increase from $445 560 to $525 560, which would reduce their operating deficit from $365 500 to $285 500. In fact, the authors calculate from their sensitivity analysis of WTP estimates that the fee charged per visitor could be safely raised to $24, in which case the marine parks in the Seychelles would be making a profit of $249 172.

Similarly, Naidoo and Adamowicz (2005) used choice experiments to determine the contribution of biodiversity and other attributes of national parks in Uganda to the willingness to visit by tourists and foreign residents. The authors employ their results to devise a revenue-maximizing park management strategy for Ugandan parks. One important finding is that, as the number of bird species seen by visitors increased, tourists demonstrated increased willingness to visit a protected area. As a result, Naidoo and Adamowicz calculate that revenue accruing to the park ecotourism centre was maximized at an average entrance fee of $47.53, yielding average revenue flows of $29 919 per year. But if a visitor expected to see 20 bird species, revenue flows at the maximum entrance fee were $18 032; and if a tourist expected to see 80 birds, maximum revenue flows were $40 423. Currently, nature-based tourism at one Ugandan park, Mabira Forest Reserve, generates approximately US$7000 in revenue per year. Thus, Naidoo and Adamowicz recommend raising entrance fees for tourists and foreign residents to at least $47 per visit.

One country that has experimented with raising entrance fees to protected areas to generate more revenue and capture the benefits from nature-based tourism has been Costa Rica. Chase et al. (1998) was one of the first studies to evaluate the effects of this new entrance fee policy. They found that actual entrance fees and tourists' maximum WTP for visits were similar, suggesting that the overall policy was a success. However, there were problems too; many political factors, including the distributional implications of higher park fees, were making universal application of the new policy across all Costa Rican parks and for domestic as well as foreign visitors problematic. Alpizar (2006) tries to address in particular the distributional aspects of the policy by focusing on price discrimination in entrance fees. Since May 2002, the Costa Rican park agency has set the prices for entering a national park at US$7 per foreign visitor and approximately US$2 per national visitor. Alpizar's analysis indicates that better price discrimination can successfully raise revenues while simultaneously achieving a more optimal pricing policy. Although the fee charged to nationals is approximately optimal, the prices to foreign visitors could be raised to $10–15.

11.5   CONCLUSION

As the demand for increased conservation of natural habitats grows, and more protected areas are established (see Table 11.1), cost–benefit analysis is capable of providing increasingly vital information to assist in both the efficient creation and management of protected areas, reserves and parks. In Chapter 9, we addressed some of the important issues concerning the application of CBA to the decision of whether or not to convert or conserve natural habitat. In this chapter, we have focused more on the other important issues concerned with managing natural habitat that also require input from cost–benefit analysis.

There is a growing amount of economics literature that is trying to improve the efficiency of conservation plans. A key and growing role for CBA is to determine the opportunity costs of protection and how these costs can be assessed. Economists are also helping to improve conservation plans by examining the other costs associated with protecting habitats, such as the direct costs of acquiring, setting up and managing the protected area and any external damages inflicted through preserving wildlife and their habitat.

Once they are established, many protected areas are visited frequently for recreation and nature-based tourism. Determining the willingness to pay by visitors for such benefits has also become a growing focus of many valuation studies. As we have shown in this chapter, the techniques used in such studies draw on many of the methods discussed throughout Part I of this book – stated preference methods, random utility models, travel cost methods and choice experiments. One of the more exciting innovations in recent years is that economists are increasingly combining one or more of these methods to tackle more complex 'bundles' of benefits from recreation and nature-based tourism, such as the location of residential housing to take advantage of nearby recreation in protected habitats as well as their other ecosystem benefits, the value of visits combined with the costs and benefits of on-site recreational activities and the use of meta-analysis and benefit transfers from past recreation studies to improve current ones. Given that distance and location matter in assessing recreation and nature-based tourism demand, the use of valuation methods in combination with GIS techniques is an encouraging development.

Finally, in many developing countries especially, the need for governments to earn sufficient revenues from national parks and protected areas has meant that the price of entrance fees charged to visitors is an important consideration. Most studies point to the problem that current fees charged are often too low, and revenue could be increased by raising fees without significantly discouraging visits. Where countries have experimented with increasing visitor fees, the use of price discrimination, especially between foreign and domestic visitors, might also improve revenues without affecting visits unduly.

REFERENCES

Alpizar, Francisco (2006), 'The pricing of protected areas in nature-based tourism: a local perspective', *Ecological Economics*, **56**, 294–307.

Ando, Amy, Jeffrey Camm, Stephen Polasky and Andrew Solow (1998), 'Species distributions, land values, and efficient conservation', *Science*, **279**, 2126–28.

Azzaino, Zevi, Jon M. Conrad and Paul Ferraro (2002), 'Optimizing the riparian buffer: Harold Brook in Skaneatles Lake Watershed, New York', *Land Economics*, **78**(4), 501–14.

Balmford, Andrew, Kevin J. Gaston, Simon Blyth, Alex James and Val Kapos (2003), 'Global variation in terrestrial conservation costs, conservation benefits, and unmet conservation needs', *Proceedings of the National Academy of Sciences*, **100**(3), 1046–50.

Barbier, Edward B. and Bruce A. Aylward (1996), 'Capturing the pharmaceutical value of biodiversity in a developing country', *Environmental and Resource Economics*, **8**, 157–81.

Barbier, Edward B., Mike Acreman and Duncan Knowler (1997), *Economic Valuation of Wetlands: A Guide for Policy Makers and Planners*, Gland, Switzerland: Ramsar Convention Bureau.

Bateman, Ian J., Andrew A. Lovett and Julii S. Brainard (2005), *Applied Environmental Economics: A GIS Approach to Cost–Benefit Analysis*, Cambridge: Cambridge University Press.

Busch, Jonah and Ross Cullen (2009), 'Effectiveness and cost-effectiveness of yellow-eyed penguin recovery', *Ecological Economics*, **68**(3), 762–76.

Carwardine, Josie, Kerrie A. Wilson, Matt Watts, Andres Etter, Carissa J. Klein and Hugh P. Possingham (2008a), 'Avoiding costly conservation mistakes: the importance of defining actions and costs in spatial priority setting', *PLoS ONE*, **3**(7), 1–6.

Carwardine, Josie, Kerrie A. Wilson, Gerardo Ceballos, Paul R. Ehrlich, Robin Naidoo, Takuya Iwamura, Stefan A. Hajkowicz and Hugh P. Possingham (2008b), 'Cost-effective priorities for global mammal conservation', *Proceedings of the National Academy of Sciences*, **105**(32), 11446–50.

Ceballos, Gerardo, Paul R. Ehrlich, Jorge Soberón, Irma Salazar and John P. Fay (2005), 'Global mammal conservation: what must we manage?', *Science*, **309**, 603–7.

Chase, L.C., D.R. Lee, W.D. Schulze and D.J. Anderson (1998), 'Ecotourism demand and differential pricing of national park access in Costa Rica', *Land Economics*, **74**(4), 466–82.

Chomitz, Kenneth M., Keith Alger, Timothy S. Thomas, Heloisa Orlando and Paulo Vila Nova (2005), 'Opportunity costs of conservation in a biodiversity hotspot: the case of southern Bahia', *Environment and Development Economics*, **10**, 293–312.

Christie, Mike, Nick Hanley, John Warren, Kevin Murphy, Robert Wright and Tony Hyde (2006), 'Valuing the diversity of biodiversity', *Ecological Economics*, **58**, 304–17.

Cutter, W. Bowman, Linwood Pendleton and J.R. DeShazo (2007), 'Activities in models of recreational demand', *Land Economics*, **83**(3), 370–81.

Ferraro, Paul J. (2003), 'Assigning priority to environmental policy interventions in a heterogeneous world', *Journal of Policy Analysis and Management*, **22**(1), 27–43.

Ferraro, Paul J. (2004), 'Targeting conservation investments in heterogeneous landscapes: a distance-function approach and application to watershed management', *American Journal of Agricultural Economics*, **86**(4), 905–18.

Firn, Richard D. (2003), 'Bioprospecting – why is it so unrewarding?', *Biodiversity and Conservation*, **12**, 207–16.

Freeman, A. Myrick III (2003), *The Measurement of Environmental and Resource Values*, 2nd edn, Washington, DC: Resources for the Future.

Haab, Timothy C. and Robert L. Hicks (2000), 'Choice set considerations in models of recreation demand: history and current state of the art', *Marine Resource Economics*, **14**, 271–81.

Haab, Timothy C. and Kenneth E. McConnell (2002), *Valuing Environmental and Natural Resources: The Econometrics of Non-Market Valuation*, Cheltenham, UK and Northampton, MA, USA: Edward Elgar.

Hanley, N., D. MacMillan, I. Patterson and R. Wright (2003), 'Economics and the design of nature conservation policy: a case study of wild goose conservation in Scotland using choice experiments', *Animal Conservation*, **6**, 123–9.

Hearne, Robert R. (2002), 'The use of choice experiments in the analysis of tourist preferences for ecotourism development in Costa Rica', *Journal of Environmental Management*, **65**, 153–63.

Hearne, Robert R. and Zenia M. Salinas (2002), 'The use of choice experiments in the analysis of tourist preferences for ecotourism development in Costa Rica', *Journal of Environmental Management*, **65**(2), 153–63.

Huybers, Twan and Jeff Bennett (2003), 'Environmental management and the competitivenes of nature-based tourism', *Environmental and Resource Economics*, **24**, 213–33.

Johannesen, Anne Borge (2005), 'Wildlife conservation policies and incentives to hunt: an empirical analysis of illegal hunting in Western Serengeti, Tanzania', *Environment and Development Economics*, **10**(3), 271–92.

Landry, Craig E. and Kenneth E. McConnell (2007), 'Hedonic onsight cost model of recreation demand', *Land Economics*, **83**(2), 253–67.

MacMillan, Douglas, Nick Hanley and Mike Daw (2004), 'Costs and benefits of wild goose conservation in Scotland', *Biological Conservation*, **119**, 475–85.

Mansfield, Carol, Daniel J. Phaneuf, F. Reed Johnson, Jui-Chen Yang and Robert Beach (2008), 'Preferences for public lands management under competing uses: the case of Yellowstone National Park', *Land Economics*, **84**(2), 282–305.

Mathieu, Lawrence F., Ian H. Langford and Wendy Kenyon (2003), 'Valuing marine parks in a developing country: a case study of the Seychelles', *Environment and Development Economics*, **8**, 373–90.

Naidoo, Robin and Wiktor L. Adamowicz (2005), 'Biodiversity and nature-based tourism at forest reserves in Uganda', *Environment and Development Economics*, **10**, 159–78.

Naidoo, Robin, Andrew Balmford, Paul J. Ferraro, Stephen Polasky, Taylor H. Ricketts and Matheiu Roget (2006), 'Integrating economic costs into conservation planning', *TRENDS in Ecology and Evolution*, **21**(12), 681–7.

Phaneuf, Daniel J. and V. Kerry Smith (2005), 'Recreation demand models', Chapter 15 in Karl-Göran Mäler and Jeffrey R. Vincent (eds), *Handbook of Environmental Economics, Vol. 2 Valuing Environmental Changes*, Amsterdam: Elsevier, pp. 671–761.

Phaneuf, Daniel J., V. Kerry Smith, Raymond B. Palmquist and Jaren C. Pope (2008), 'Models to value ecosystem services in urban watersheds', *Land Economics*, **84**(3), 361–81.

Polasky, Stephen, Jeffrey D. Camm and Brian Garber-Yonts (2001), 'Selecting biological reserves cost-effectively: an application to terrestrial vertebrate conservation in Oregon', *Land Economics*, **77**(1), 68–78.

Rolfe, John, Jeff Bennett and Jordan Louviere (2000), 'Choice modelling and its potential application to tropical rainforest preservation', *Ecological Economics*, **35**, 289–302.

Simpson, R. David, Roger A. Sedjo and J.W. Reid (1996), 'Valuing biodiversity for use in pharmaceutical research', *Journal of Political Economy*, **104**, 163–85.

Sutton, William R., Douglas M. Larson and Lovell S. Jarvis (2008), 'Assessing the costs of living with wildlife in developing countries using willingness to pay', *Environment and Development Economics*, **13**(4), 475–96.

Willis, Kenneth G., Guy Garrod, Riccardo Scarpa, Neil Powe, Andrew Lovett, Ian J. Bateman, Nick Hanley and Douglas C. Macmillan (2003), *The Social and Environmental Benefits of Forests in Great Britain*, report to Forestry Commission , UK Forestry Commission, Edinburgh, Scotland.

Yoder, Jonathon (2002), 'Estimation of wildlife-inflicted property damage and abatement based on compensation program claims data', *Land Economics*, **78**(1), 45–59.

Zanderson, Marianne, Mette Termansen and Frank Søndergaard Jensen (2007), 'Testing benefits transfer of forest recreation values over a twenty-year time horizon', *Land Economics*, **83**(3), 412–40.

12. Cost–benefit analysis and renewable energy

This chapter aims to:

- provide a general overview of the costs and benefits of renewable energy;
- give more detail on how both costs and benefits can be measured;
- provide a range of case studies which try to value both the market and non-market impacts of renewable energy schemes.

The focus here is on renewable energy as a source of electricity, rather than issues such as the use of biomass in cars.

12.1 INTRODUCTION

This chapter reviews applications of CBA methods to policy over renewable energy. Many governments worldwide now have policies in place to encourage the development of renewable sources of energy, partly as a component of climate change strategy, and partly as a way of reducing strategic dependence on fossil fuels for, in particular, electricity production. An example is provided by Scotland, where the government has a target for renewable electricity production that 31 per cent should be met by renewable sources by 2011 and 50 per cent by 2020. Targets for reductions in greenhouse gases by 2020 for all EU member states include sub-targets for the proportion of energy demand (not just electricity demand) which must be met by renewable energy by 2020. For Germany, this means that 18 per cent of final energy demand should be met by renewables as part of a 14 per cent cut in 2005 emissions by 2020. For France, 23 per cent of final energy demand must come from renewables as part of a 14 per cent cut in emissions (Ernst and Young, 2007).

Such targets are typically met by private sector investments, incentivized by a variety of methods such as higher 'green' tariffs, green credit schemes where electricity suppliers are compelled to meet a certain percentage of supply from renewables (these obligations can be traded for

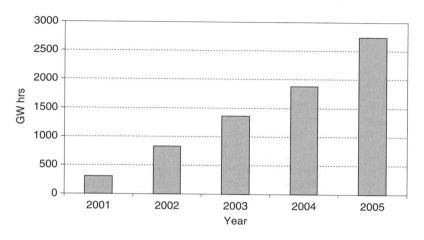

Source: Compiled from Scottish Environmental Statistics (various years).

Figure 12.1 Renewable energy expansion in Scotland, 2001–2006

example in the UK), and investment grants for capital projects, such as subsidies for solar energy plants in Spain. Since renewable energy is exempt from carbon taxes or participation in tradeable carbon schemes (such as the EU Emissions Trading Scheme), this can also be a form of subsidy to the renewables industry. In many countries, renewables capacity is rising fast in response to these incentives, and to changes in oil and gas prices. For instance, Figure 12.1 shows renewables capacity growth for Scotland.

Renewable energy includes wind power (onshore and offshore), tidal power, wave energy plants, biomass plants (producing heat and electricity), hydroelectric plants on rivers, geothermal and solar energy. A unifying characteristic of renewables is that their operation produces little or no net carbon dioxide emissions – although their construction may well involve net carbon releases, for example if a wind farm is built on peat moorland which leads to erosion of Total Organic Carbon in sediments in drainage waters. Building access roads and fabricating wind turbines will also emit CO_2, whilst the policy of replacing fossil fuel with biofuels can also lead to net increases in emissions (see Box 12.1). Typically, though, CBA of energy options has not considered these 'indirect' effects.

The application of CBA to renewable energy projects and policies is relevant since (i) it is the government that sets targets for renewable generation, and incentivizes this growth; (ii) in doing so, governments may make

BOX 12.1   COSTS AND BENEFITS OF BIOFUELS IN
            THE US

Much attention has recently been given to policies that encourage the growing of biofuels as a substitute for fossil fuel-derived energy in the transport sector. The US government has encouraged farmers to grow corn and soybeans for conversion into ethanol and biodiesel respectively, as a way of reducing dependence on imports and as part of agricultural policy; in 2006, subsidy rates were $0.29 per energy equivalent litre for ethanol, and $0.20 per litre for biodiesel. The growing of biofuels is also presented as a part of climate policy, in that replacing gasoline and diesel derived from oil by ethanol and biodiesel can, in principle, reduce net greenhouse gas emissions.

Hill et al. (2006) consider this issue from the viewpoint of net environmental impact. They note that in the context of rising world food demands and rising energy demand for transport there is a need to promote biofuels that (i) do not compete with food production; and (ii) offer a genuine net reduction in greenhouse gases, once a lifecycle perspective is taken. Hill et al. find that biodiesel from soybeans seems preferable to ethanol production from corn on the second of these criteria, although neither do well in terms of the first criterion. Biodiesel from soybeans provides 93 per cent more usable energy than the fossil-fuel energy needed to produce each unit of energy, and reduces greenhouse gas emissions by 41 per cent compared with oil-derived diesel. However, ethanol from corn production yields only a 25 per cent net energy gain and a 12 per cent reduction in greenhouse gases, at the expense of a large increase in nitrate and phosphate pollution of waterways, and an increase in pesticide use. All of these impacts should be included in a social CBA of the policy of encouraging biofuel production on US farmland. Neither technology seems capable of making significant contributions to total US energy consumption for transport, saving at most 3 per cent of total energy demand.

Fargione et al. (2008) look at the issue of how the net carbon savings of biofuel production vary according to where they are grown. They consider the conversion of rainforests, peatlands, savannas and grasslands to biofuel production in Brazil, Southeast Asia and the US. Results show that land conversion implies a big net *increase* in carbon emissions: this 'carbon debt' is highest for the conversion of tropical forest and peatland rainforest to either biodiesel produced from palm oil plantations or from soybean crops. This is because land conversion releases the carbon stored in soils and vegetation. However, using abandoned or 'marginal' cropland in the US to produce biofuels from native perennial grasses could have a positive carbon offsetting effect, and thus create a benefit in terms of net greenhouse gas reduction. However, we are not aware at present of any CBA analysis which has taken this scientific work forward in a policy context.

explicit or implicit judgements about the 'best' renewable technology to invest in; whilst (iii) as noted below, renewable energy schemes result in externalities, in terms of impacts on wildlife and landscape quality.

What are the *benefits* of renewable energy investments? Consider a proposal to construct a new tidal hydroelectric station in Sweden. The output from this project will be so many megawatt hours of electricity: actual output will be some fraction of the installed capacity. If the project is sufficiently 'small' in relation to total Swedish electricity supply (including imports of electricity from Norway and Finland), then it will have no impact on the wholesale price of electricity. Thus, if the price is 550 Krona per MWh, and the station is expected to generate 750MWh of power, then the annual benefits of the station are (550 * 750) or 412 500 Krona/year. If a policy or project is expected to increase or decrease the price of electricity paid by industry consumers, then the analyst would instead calculate the likely change in consumers' and producers' surplus. If electricity is taxed, then there will be a difference between the consumer price and the producer price. The consumer price shows the marginal WTP of consumers for electricity, and thus the value to them of an increase in output; this will now be different from the marginal cost to producers of supplying greater output.

A somewhat different approach to valuing the outputs of renewable energy projects was advanced by Krutilla and Fisher (1985), who consider the case of irreversible wilderness developments for hydroelectric power. They focused on a number of case studies, including the Hells Canyon site on the Snake River, lying on the Oregon/Idaho border. Krutilla and Fisher argued that (i) the benefits of development – hydroelectricity – were best viewed as an intermediate good, indistinguishable to the consumer from electricity supplied from another source; (ii) the costs of these alternatives would be likely to decline over time due to technological progress, whilst the cost of hydroelectric output from the project would be 'frozen in concrete', like its technology. However, the costs of development – wilderness benefits forgone – were not reproducible, were of increasing value over time as incomes increased, and were to an extent unique. This, they saw, meant that a fundamental asymmetry existed between the benefits and costs of development. In this context, they calculate the benefits of hydropower as 'the savings in costs over its least-cost alternative' (p. 98). In other words, we assume that so much electricity must be generated by the nation, and that in building a new hydropower station, we avoid the need to generate that power by the (next) cheapest source – in the case of Krutilla and Fisher, this is nuclear power. As the costs of generating from the 'next cheapest source' fall as time passes, this causes the benefits of the hydropower station to decline over time in real terms.

Besides the value of electricity output, which is valued by the market, there are other, non-market benefits from renewable energy:

- Renewable energy can displace CO_2 emissions from fossil-fuel power stations. Precisely how much depends on how the electricity grid is operated, and on the load factor of the renewable source.[1]
- Similarly, it displaces emissions of local and regional pollutants such as SO_2 and NOx from fossil fuel generation.
- It can help diversify a country's energy supply situation, for example in terms of lowering dependence on imports of oil or gas for power generation.
- Hydroelectric dams can create new recreational opportunities for water-based recreation in artificial lakes.
- Hydroelectric schemes could be managed in a manner which reduces flood risks lower down the catchment.

In addition, several studies have noted that consumers are WTP a higher price for electricity from renewable energy, in other words that they are WTP a 'green premium' for power (see section 12.2, and the overview in Longo et al., 2008). This willingness to pay may be motivated by any of the benefits listed above, including pollution reduction and security of supply. Electricity companies do indeed partly differentiate their produce on the basis of a separate demand existing for renewable energy, and the choice available to consumers has increased in many countries due to deregulation of the electricity sector (for example in Sweden in 1996).

The *costs* of renewable power investments and policies can also be broken down into market- and non-market-valued impacts. Market-valued aspects include construction, land take (including the opportunity costs of land use in some instances), and operating and maintenance expenses. Other than forecasting completion dates, there is little that is complicated in principle for inclusion of such items in a CBA. However, renewable power investments can also have external costs which vary by technology. For wind power, people may be concerned about impacts on landscape, of soil erosion on some sites, and effects on birds (see Box 12.2). For hydro schemes, there are well-known conflicts with fisheries, in particular with salmon migration (Boxes 12.3 and 12.4). Biomass planting will have a mixture of external costs and benefits, depending on the type of crop grown (for example short rotation willow) and location (Hanley and Nevin, 1999). Tidal power schemes can have very significant impacts on bird habitats (Box 12.5). Policies to encourage renewables investments may require upgrading and relocation of transmission lines, which can also impact on landscape quality.

Finally, if a renewable power source cannot be relied upon to generate electricity on demand, then a move to expand the renewables capacity of the economy might need to be accompanied by an investment in fossil fuel generated electricity which can be started up at short notice (for example on cold winter mornings with a high pressure system keeping both the temperature and the wind speed low!). To the extent to which this back-up power source is at a higher cost than would have been constructed in the absence of a renewable expansion, then the incremental costs of building and running this back-up source also need to be added to the costs of the renewables programme.

BOX 12.2   VALUING EXTERNALITIES FOR OFFSHORE
            WIND FARMS IN DENMARK

Denmark has long been one of the leading European countries in the development of wind energy, and sees expanding wind power still further as an important part of its climate change strategy. Due to the large number of onshore wind farms in operation, further expansions are likely to be offshore. This reduces the visual impact of wind farms (impact might be linearly-decreasing with distance from the shore), at the cost of higher cost per kWh of electricity generated. There is thus a tradeoff to be evaluated with regard to how far offshore one plans to locate new wind farms.

Ladenburg et al. (2005) use the choice experiment method to investigate this tradeoff. The attributes used were the price of electricity, size of wind farms, distance from coast and number of wind farms. Three samples of people were used: two living close to existing offshore wind farms at Horns Rev and Nysted, and the third being drawn from the general public across Denmark. Respondents were less concerned about future offshore developments than with future onshore expansion.

Results showed that there was a significant WTP to move wind farms further away from the shore, from 8 km (the closest) to 18 km. However, WTP was lower to move the wind farms still further away, to 50 km offshore, with marginal WTP declining sharply. Looking at the effects of existing 'experience' with offshore wind farms produced interesting results. People living in the Horns Rev area were WTP less than the national sample to move a new development further away, whilst people living in Nysted were WTP considerably more.

Finally, the authors note that due to the lack of cost data, they were not able to use CBA to calculate the optimal distance of new wind farms from the shore – although as is clear in the previous paragraph, this optimal distance might vary across different communities since their preferences differ.

BOX 12.3 TRADEOFFS BETWEEN SALMON AND HYDROELECTRICITY

In the main text, we saw how hydropower operations can adversely impact salmon populations by restricting their movement up-river to spawn. Options to alleviate this impact are: (i) to abandon hydroelectric production on a river, dismantling all associated structures; (ii) building fish passes to allow salmon to swim up-river; (iii) catching salmon below the dam and then releasing them above the dam; and (iv) reducing the amount of river flow through turbines, and increasing compensation flows to the river.

Cecilia Håkansson (2007) has quantified these tradeoffs for the Ume and Videln rivers in Northern Sweden. Operation of the Stornorrfors hydropower station has been linked with declines in salmon numbers in the upper river system. Using a fisheries model, five scenarios for salmon restoration were devised, varying in terms of how many extra salmon would be present in the upper river, and how long this increase would take to occur. A mail survey of 1192 Swedes was undertaken, using contingent valuation to measure WTP for each of these scenarios. The author also analyses differences in WTP according to whether people live in Southern Sweden or in the North, reasoning that people living further away may have lower WTP than those living closer, whether they are fishermen or not. Based on a scenario where there is an increase in the salmon population from 3000 to 4000, aggregate WTP was estimated at between 96–234 million SEK (Swedish Krona), with a point estimate of 140 million SEK.

Costs of achieving this increase were based on the necessary reduction in water flows through the power plant, the amount of electricity that this would have produced, and the price of electricity: this gave a figure for the present value of costs which depended critically on assumptions about the future price of electricity, and how long the recovery programme would take (choice of discount rate did not seem to matter too much in this instance, within the range 1–5 per cent). Hakansson concludes that the net present value of the proposal will only be positive if electricity prices are towards the lower end of the range investigated, and benefits towards the higher end, since the range of NPVs in the sensitivity analysis runs from −2005 million SEK to +403 million SEK.

12.2 MEASURING BENEFITS

As noted above, measuring the benefits of renewable energy is, in a sense, straightforward, since electricity is traded in markets. However, the benefits of displaced pollution will not be valued by markets: calculating such benefits is complex since we need to know what power source the new renewable energy capacity will be replacing. This requires an

BOX 12.4 ENVIRONMENTAL COSTS OF HYDROPOWER
DEVELOPMENT IN ICELAND

Iceland uses several sources of renewable energy, notably geothermal and hydro power. A proposal to construct a new hydropower scheme in Karahnjukar to provide energy for a planned aluminium smelter provoked controversy, partly due to the fact that the proposed development is very large-scale (a system of dams and tunnels), and partly because the location is currently an undeveloped wilderness area, which provides a habitat for reindeer and birds, whilst the proposal would also affect canyons and waterfalls in the area, reducing their flow rates greatly. To measure the negative externalities of this project to Icelanders, Bothe (2003) undertook a contingent valuation study. The scenario developed was one whereby respondents could choose between two alternatives: the current hydroelectric plan for Karahnjukar; and an alternative, which would still provide enough power for the smelter to be built, but through expansions in the capacity of existing hydro and geothermal stations, and the provision of undersea transmission lines. This alternative was described as being more expensive than the Karahnjukar hydro plan.

A mail survey of 1000 Icelanders was undertaken, and a response rate of 34 per cent obtained. Maps and photos were provided to respondents showing them the area with and without the hydro project in place. Some 69 per cent of respondents preferred the alternative proposal for energy supply, even though it would impose higher taxes on them. Mean WTP to have the alternative energy supply option rather than the Karahnjukar project was 4962 ISK (Icelandic Krona) (standard deviation 6493). Important factors determining individual WTP amounts included their attitude towards whether economic growth could only come at the expense of environmental deterioration; knowledge of the area did not seem to influence WTP. Motivations for WTP were also dominated by moral considerations and by people's desire to protect the area for future generations, rather than current use of the area for hiking. Finally, aggregating the sample mean WTP up to the level of the population of Iceland showed an aggregate WTP to protect this wilderness area of around 2 billion ISK.

understanding of the process by which power stations are switched into the national supply grid. It makes a difference since the saving in carbon dioxide outputs, for example, will depend on whether renewable power displaces oil, gas or coal-fired electricity generation at the margin. If we can calculate how many fewer tonnes of emissions of CO_2, SO_2 and NOx are emitted from supplying a given level of demand, then these benefits can be valued using avoided damage costs per tonne of pollutant. For example, the EU has produced estimates of the marginal damage costs of a range of air pollutants for use in policy analysis (see AEA, 2005).

BOX 12.5   COSTS AND BENEFITS OF TIDAL POWER
          SCHEMES

Tidal power schemes offer the promise of predictable, reliable renewable
energy. However, rather few actual schemes exist worldwide (three at
present), perhaps due to the cost of barrage construction, the difficulty
of finding suitable sites, problems over technology for in-stream tidal
devices, and worries over the ecological impacts of barrages on estuaries. The site at La Rance in Brittany (France) was the world's first tidal
power station, opening in 1967. It provides an annual output of around
68 megawatts, which is a rather small fraction of total French electricity
consumption (<1 per cent). Wave energy seems to offer a more attractive option at present, with new wave energy plants starting up in the UK,
US, Portugal and India in 2008.

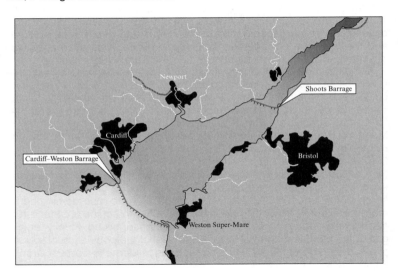

Source: SDC (2007).

Site of Severn estuary proposals for a tidal barrage

For many years, plans have been put forward for a tidal barrage in
South-West England on the Severn Estuary (Frontier Economics, 2008).
The Severn Estuary has the second largest tidal range in the world, but
also provides an important habitat for birds and fish. The UK Sustainable
Development Commission undertook a review of plans for construction of such a barrage in 2007 (SDC, 2007). Two alternative sites were
considered (see figure above) at Weston–Cardiff and at Shoots. The
former would have a capacity of 8.6 GW, generating around 17 TWh of

electricity per year (about 4 per cent of UK electricity output); the latter would be smaller, with a capacity of 1 GW and an output of 2.75 TWh. Construction costs for the former scheme were put at £15 billion, and at £1.5 billion for the latter. Benefits aside from power output would include displaced CO_2 and other emissions from fossil fuel power stations in England, and a reduction in expected flood damages: these were calculated as follows:

	Cardiff–Weston scheme	Shoots scheme
Annual carbon savings (million tonnes CO_2), assuming displaces new power station (combined cycle gas turbine)	5.6	0.91
Annual carbon savings if displaces current average mix of power generation	8.15	1.32

Note that the benefits of carbon savings are higher if one assumes that the current mix of power generation is the relevant comparison, rather then a new CCGT plant. Costs would include the legal requirement to construct compensatory habitats for those damaged by the barrage. The SDC found that the economic case for either scheme rested on the choice of discount rate, with a rate as low as 2 per cent being required to justify the larger scheme. At a discount rate of 2 per cent, the unit cost of electricity from the Cardiff-Weston scheme would be around 2.5 pence/kWh. This compares with a figure of around 12 pence/kWh for a 10 per cent discount rate. These figures can be compared with the equivalent current costs of alternative technologies. At 10 per cent, tidal power is more expensive than any technology except advanced biomass. At 2 per cent, it is cheaper than all the alternatives considered.

These relate mainly to health costs of air pollution. For CO_2, a number of estimates for the PV of avoided damages per tonne of emission now exist in the literature (see Stern, 2007). The European Union has tended to favour avoided abatement costs rather than damage costs as the basis for valuing reductions in CO_2 emissions, recommending a figure of 19 €/tonne CO_2 in 2005 (Longo et al., 2008). Using avoided abatement costs makes sense if a target has been set for total emissions, so that avoiding emissions from one source means less must be spent to reduce emissions from another. Reductions in CO_2 could also be valued using the market price of tradeable carbon permits, as in the European Union's Emissions Trading Scheme.

Partly because of this pollution displacement effect, some individuals are willing to pay a price premium for electricity supplied from renewable sources. This is an additional benefit of renewables compared to the market average (wholesale) price of electricity, although care should be taken not to double-count this price premium with the value of avoided damages if this is all it represents. The size and determinants of this premium have been investigated by a number of authors. In the US, the Energy Policy Act of 1992 allowed the deregulation of the supply sector, and increased competition and consumer choice. Roe et al. (2001) compare choice modelling results from surveys of electricity consumers as to their WTP a higher price for green energy with hedonic price estimates of the actual premium paid in parts of the US. In the choice modelling exercise, respondents were offered hypothetical supply options differentiated in terms of price (monthly bill), contract terms, fuel mix and pollution emissions relative to the regional average. The results showed that the premiums people said they were WTP were small (around $0.50 increase in annual bill at most for the biggest reduction in pollution considered), and varied by socio-economic grouping and by region.

The authors also analyse market data from 21 green supply deals available in 2000 to US consumers. These showed price premiums ranging from −$102 to +$263 per year, with a median of $59; these numbers relate to a great variation in the percentage of 'new' renewables included in the supply package.[2] The authors then undertake a linear regression to explain the variation of these price premia in terms of percentage generation from all renewables, percentage generation from new renewables, whether the scheme is certified under the 'Green-e' scheme, and the geographic region in which the scheme operates. If one interprets the choice modelling results as showing WTP for *new* renewables supply, then the real market data marginal effect of a $6 per annum price premium for a 1 per cent increase in new renewables lies within the range of estimates for an equivalent change for the stated preference data.

Other applications of stated preference methods to WTP for green electricity in the US are Champ and Bishop (2001) and Poe et al. (2002). Champ and Bishop compared hypothetical and actual WTP for a wind energy option offered by the Madison Gas and Electric Company, and estimated the premium as being in the range of $59–101 per year. Vossler et al. (2003) carried out a similar exercise for a renewable energy option offered by the Niagara Mohawk company in New York State. They found that about 20 per cent of respondents were willing to pay a positive premium for green electricity.

A more recent example is provided by Whitehead and Cherry (2007), who employ contingent valuation to study preferences for consumers in North Carolina. A hypothetical green power scheme funded by a monthly levy on electricity bills was offered to consumers, with the likely effects of this on acid rain, visibility and health effects should 10 per cent of all North Carolina utility consumers sign up being described. The questionnaire asked people:

> In a voluntary Green Energy scheme, households that chose to participate would pay an extra $A per month . . . this would cover the higher production costs of green energy.

The amount $A was varied between $5, $15, $30 and $50 across respondents. People answered yes, no, or don't know to this question. Those who said yes were later asked how certain they were about this, on a scale of 1–10. Two versions of the questionnaire were used: half of these included a cheap talk script (see Chapter 3), and half did not. Some 431 responses were collected by phone survey, with a 61 per cent response rate. Depending on the predicted reduction in environmental and health impacts, mean WTP for green electricity varied from $4 to $12 per household per month,[3] with the highest amount referring to a 20-mile increase in visibility (due to lower particulates), a 20 per cent fall in the number of lakes and streams affected by acidification, and a 20 per cent fall in the number of illnesses due to breathing problems. This value of $12 was roughly one-third of that obtained from respondents who were not given a cheap talk script.

Finally, Longo et al. (2008) use the choice experiment to investigate the determinants of people's WTP a green premium. Their choice experiment design includes the following attributes, all presented as aspects of alternative energy policy:

- reductions in greenhouse gas emissions (with levels: no additional cuts, 1 per cent, 2 per cent, and 3 per cent annual reductions due to renewable energy programmes);
- possible future shortages of energy supply (with levels: current level, 30 minutes, 60 minutes and 120 minutes/year);
- numbers of people employed in the energy sector (with levels: no change, +1000 jobs in electricity sector, −1000 jobs);
- increases in electricity bills (no price increase, +6.5 per cent, +16 per cent, +25 per cent, +38 per cent).

The sample was drawn from people living in the city of Bath, England.

Results showed that most people ranked 'reductions in greenhouse gases' as the most important aspect of energy policy. In the choice model, all of the attributes were statistically significant. Implicit prices (marginal WTP) were calculated as shown in Table 12.1.

Table 12.1   Implicit prices from Longo et al. (2008)

	Implicit price	Standard error
Reduction in greenhouse gases: decrease by 1 per cent/yr.	£29.65	£5.50
Decrease in blackouts by 1 minute/yr.	£0.36	£0.08
Increase in jobs in sector, per job	£0.02	£0.00

Source: Adapted from Longo et al. (2008).

WTP for greenhouse gas emission reductions via renewable energy investments is thus seen as being a considerable motivation, but increasing supply security and jobs also matter. Whilst one could comment that a large increase in renewable capacity might actually lead to a rise in blackouts (depending on technology choice), the results are still of interest.

12.3   MEASURING COSTS

One of the more interesting aspects of applying CBA to renewable energy is how one costs the negative externalities that can arise. The main negative externalities involved are:

- For wind power, people may be concerned about impacts on landscape, of soil erosion on some sites, and effects on birds.
- For hydropower schemes, there are well-known conflicts with fisheries, in particular with salmon migration. Creation of new dams and reservoirs will also affect landscape quality and lead to the loss of wildlife habitats. In developing countries, the displacement of people by the creation of new dams is a major issue.
- Biomass planting will have a mixture of external costs and benefits, depending on the type of crop grown (for example short rotation willow) and location.
- Biofuel programmes may have a variety of impacts on water and air quality and on greenhouse gas emissions – see Box 12.1.
- Tidal power schemes can have very significant impacts on bird habitats.
- Renewables investments may require upgrading and relocation of transmission lines, which can also impact on landscape quality.

One study which considers many of these potential impacts together is Bergmann et al. (2008). Their choice experiment was conducted in

Table 12.2   Example of a choice card from Bergmann et al. (2008)

	PLAN A	PLAN B	Neither plan
LANDSCAPE: visual impact caused by location/size	HIGH	NONE	No increase in renewable energy
WILDLIFE: health of habitat	SLIGHT HARM	NO IMPACT	Alternative climate change programmes used instead
AIR POLLUTION	NONE	NONE	
EMPLOYMENT: new jobs in the local community	8–12 JOBS	1–3 JOBS	
PRICE OF ELECTRICITY: additional cost per year to you	£16 PER YEAR	£7 PER YEAR	North Sea gas-fired power stations built instead
YOUR CHOICE:			

Scotland, a country which has set ambitious targets for growing its renewable energy capacity. Respondents were told that promoting renewable energy could have a variety of effects on wildlife and landscape according to which technology mix was involved; changes in local air pollution could also result from investments in biomass-burning power stations. Policies might have an effect on long-term local employment, whilst electricity prices to households would be likely to increase. An example choice card is shown as Table 12.2. As may be seen, respondents could choose between two alternative 'plans' for renewable energy increases, or for neither plan, in which case no increase in renewables would result.

A random parameters logit model (see Chapter 3) was estimated on the data, first for all respondents together, and then having divided people up into those living in urban versus rural areas. The rationale for this division was that most of the negative externalities from renewables are likely to be experienced in rural areas, where such schemes are located, although all electricity consumers would face higher prices. It is thus reasonable to suspect that rural households might place different values on these impacts than urban households. In short, this is what the researchers find, although the differences are not great. Implicit prices were derived (Table 12.3) and showed that, for example, reductions in air pollution and the avoidance of high landscape impacts increased people's utility, whilst low or moderate landscape impacts had no significant

Table 12.3   Implicit prices from Bergmann et al. (2008): whole sample

Attributes	WTP per household/year (£)
Landscape change: high versus moderate	2.77 (–2.52; 9.06)
Landscape change: high versus low	3.36 (–4.71; 10.16)
Landscape change: high versus none	7.00* (2.73; 11.79)
Wildlife: no impact rather than slight decrease	4.94* (0.96; 10.16)
Wildlife: slight improvement rather than slight decrease	10.95* (6.74; 14.61)
Air pollution: none rather than an increase	13.84* (10.78; 18.45)

Note: * Statistically different from 0 at 95 per cent confidence level.

effect. People were also willing to pay higher electricity prices to avoid impacts on wildlife.

Finally, the researchers used the choice model results to compare the welfare effects of alternative policies to increase renewable energy. The policy options were:

- Reference case: Fossil fuel power station – 200 MW expansion of a natural gas power plant resulting in an increase in the facility's size, emissions and employment; no change in exhaust stack visibility.
- A: Large offshore windmill farm – 200 MW, 100 turbines each at 80 metres nacelle hub height, 6–10 kilometres from shore.
- B: Large onshore windmill farm – 160 MW, 80 turbines each at 80 metres nacelle hub height.
- C: Moderate windmill farm – 50 MW, 30 turbines each at 60 metres nacelle hub height.
- D: Biomass power plant – 25MW, emissions stack height up to 40 metres, portions of building up to 30 metres, fuelled by energy crops.

These policy options can be translated into their implications for the attribute levels in the choice experiment, and then welfare measures calculated, based on the results of the random parameters model estimates (see Table 12.4).

This shows three things of interest: first, that relative to base case of fossil expansion, the net effect of almost all schemes on welfare is positive (so not a cost, but a benefit). Second, that the size of the effect varies between technologies (compare the consumers' surplus gain, in terms of

Table 12.4 Welfare effects of alternative renewable energy projects

Scenario:	Base Case	A	B	C	D
	Fossil fuel power station expansion	Large offshore wind farm	Large onshore wind farm	Small onshore wind farm	Biomass power plant
Attribute levels:					
Landscape	Low	None	High	Moderate	Moderate
Wildlife	None	None	None	None	Improve
Air pollution	Increase	None	None	None	Increase
Employment	+2	+5	+4	+1	+70
Welfare change (£/hsld/yr.): **Total sample**		31.88 (19.02, 48.29)	11.57 (−2.67, 29.63)	26.91 (12.98, 44.52)	18.14 (−12.97, 52.80)
Welfare change (£/hsld/yr.): **Urban sample**		17.87 (5.74, 37.57)	0.08 (−15.40, 21.65)	11.17 (−0.59, 30.57)	−12.99 (−47.72, 20.73)
Welfare change (£/hsld/yr.): **Rural sample**		53.71 (29.90, 91.82)	33.04 (5.70, 70.80)	50.16 (24.30, 96.54)	97.95 (38.83, 176.63)

external effects, from a large offshore wind farm with a large onshore wind farm). Third, there are noticeable differences between the impacts on rural and urban households.

Hydroelectricity and Salmon

Most other studies of the external costs of renewable energy focus on a particular technology type, such as wind or hydro. For *hydroelectricity*, the major debate has been on the effects of dam construction and operation on salmon migration (Scruton et al., 2008). Salmon spawn in up-river parts of catchments, where gravel beds provide sites for egg-laying. The salmon then spend their early lives in these parts of the river, before swimming downstream and into the ocean. For example, in northern Sweden, salmon swim down to the Baltic Sea. They then spend a variable number of years at sea, feeding and growing, until attempting to return to the river where they were hatched in order to reproduce. It is this stage of their life cycle that concerns many researchers. The construction of hydro dams and weirs acts as a barrier to migration. For example, about 70 per cent of adult salmon entering the mouth of the Ume River in Northern Sweden are estimated to fail to reach the upper parts of the catchment for breeding, due to the operation of the Stornorrfors power station (Lundqvist et al., 2005). The numbers who succeed in passing up the river are thought to be a function of the amount of water flowing through the power station: there is thus a direct tradeoff between producing more electricity and having more salmon in the upper part of the river. Since this is where salmon breed, the long-term viability of a river's salmon stock can be put at risk by hydro operations (Rivinoja et al., 2001).

The economic value of the impacts of hydro operations on salmon populations have been studied by several authors. An early study by Loomis et al. (1986) used the travel cost approach to calculate the value of recreational fishing to people living in Idaho, relating this to specific fishing sites. A hydropower development at the Henry's Fork site was then costed by calculating the predicted loss in aggregate consumers' surplus per annum from the loss of all fishing at the site, and for 50 per cent and 75 per cent reductions in expected catch. For a 50 per cent decline in expected catch, the loss of consumers' surplus was just under $1 million/year (in 1983 US$). For a total loss of the fishery, the net present value of lost consumers' surplus over the life time of the dam was $38 million. Note that these figures would understate the values of losses if there are non-use values associated with the condition of fish populations: for example, people other than fishermen might feel worse off if salmon disappeared from Scottish rivers. Bell et al. (2003) find that local residents in coastal communities in Oregon and Washington states were willing to pay for salmon conservation programmes, irrespective of whether they went fishing or not.

Another example of this type of calculation is provided by Morey et al. (1993). They use a random utility site choice model based on revealed preference (travel cost) data to estimate the value of salmon fishing in Maine, in the context of threats from hydro operations on salmon rivers, and in terms of the benefits of fish re-stocking activities. Data from a 1988 survey of Maine anglers was used, distinguishing trips between eight different fishing sites in Maine and Eastern Canada. The model predicts both participation (total trips to all sites) and site choice as a function of expected catch and travel costs. The model is then used to predict the change in annual consumers' surplus, on average, for (i) a total loss of fishing on the principal salmon fishing site in Maine, the Penobscot River; and (ii) a 50 per cent decline in catch rates. However, these fishery scenarios are not directly linked to changes in hydro operations. In Box 12.3, calculations from the Ume River example are presented which do directly link changes in the benefits of fish stocks to changes in hydro operations and the value of lost electricity output.

Another example of directly linking changes in salmon numbers to the value of hydro operations is given in Hanley and Black (2006). This uses a much simpler way of calculating the losses to salmon fisheries, by considering the market value of salmon fishing permits on Scottish rivers. One can think of the value of such permits (without which it is illegal to fish for salmon on certain rivers) as reflecting the WTP of anglers for the right to fish salmon at a particular location. The authors assessed the ecological condition of water bodies in the catchment of the River Tummel in Scotland as largely failing to meet Good Ecological Status under the EU Water Framework Directive (see Chapter 10). The authors considered that assessing the effects of removing all hydro operations was rather unrealistic in terms of implementation of the Directive, and thus they considered two measures which would allow hydro operations to continue with lower impacts on salmon stocks. These were (i) increasing compensation flows to waterbodies downstream of dams; and (ii) improving fish ladders and passes. The capital costs of these measures, plus the value of reduced electricity output associated with each, were then estimated. The likely increase in salmon numbers was then calculated for each option, and this was valued using the current market value of salmon permits per salmon caught on the nearest comparable river. The conclusion reached was that, for all options, costs exceeded benefits, partly due to the low numbers of salmon which were predicted to become available for anglers. The analysis was then repeated for similar modifications to hydro operations on another Scottish river catchment, the Dee in Galloway. Here, benefits were greater than costs for some options, partly because some low-cost options were identified, and partly because there was a higher predicted increase in salmon numbers from these options (even though the value per additional salmon caught was lower).

Wind Power Schemes

Wind power is, in many ways, a renewable source with few environmental impacts which has commanded a high degree of public support (Krohn and Damborg, 1999). However, some wind farm developments, particularly large, onshore wind farms, have landscape impacts that people have objected to, especially in the context of rapid expansions in wind power in many countries. These landscape effects are a negative externality. Other negative externalities include disruption to bird breeding sites, noise and soil erosion from wind farm construction. Several studies have tried to quantify these impacts, focusing on landscape effects.

Kristina Ek uses the choice experiment method to quantify landscape externalities for wind power in Sweden (Ek, 2006). Respondents, chosen from the general public, were asked to choose between alternative schemes described in terms of noise levels, location (mountain location, onshore but not mountain, offshore), height (higher than 60 metres or not), grouping (small clusters, large clusters, or individual turbines) and the effects on electricity price (five levels of increase, with the highest being equal to about a 25 per cent increase on average bills). Attribute descriptions were developed using extensive focus group work. The survey was mailed to 1000 Swedish households, and 547 responses were obtained. Analysis showed that noise levels, location, grouping and price were all significant determinants of choice. Siting wind farms in mountainous areas caused the biggest loss in utility relative to non-mountain and offshore locations, with the latter being preferred. Large wind farms caused a bigger disutility than small wind farms, although only for onshore locations. Comparing implicit prices showed that the biggest disutility was from mountain locations compared to large rather than small groupings. Ek concludes that electricity companies competing for market share might want to sell wind energy on the basis of where it is produced, since consumers, on this evidence, would be willing to pay more for wind energy generated offshore. However, producing offshore power has higher costs than onshore power at present.

Alvarez-Farizo and Hanley (2002) also conducted a choice experiment on the impacts of wind energy, but this time focusing on planned developments at one particular site in Spain (La Plana, near Zaragoza). The attributes used were impacts on landscape quality and birds, along with the price of electricity. A mixture of manipulated photographs and text were used to inform respondents about the likely effects of the project. Wind energy expanded rapidly in Spain in the 1990s. Results showed that respondents were willing to pay higher electricity prices to mitigate impacts on both landscape and wildlife, with the highest value attributed to potential impacts on birds. As in the Ek study referred to above, the authors claim that such results can help governments plan wind energy developments in a way that minimizes their social costs.

Effects of New Transmission Lines

Expansion of renewable energy capacity is often focused on those parts of a country that have a natural advantage in terms of potential power output, and where land prices are relatively low. This is true for hydro and wind schemes, although less so for biomass projects (which could be located nearer to centres of population if their fuel is municipal solid waste, for example). In Scotland, wind farm expansion has been focused geographically on upland sites in the north, west and south of the country.

However, this means that power generation is moved away from centres of electricity demand. National electricity grids have evolved in a way that mirrors generation capacity location in a system dominated by fossil fuel in most countries, taking power out from the 'centre' to the 'periphery'. Such transmission networks can be unsuitable for the new geographical spread of renewable energy.

If this is so, then part of a strategy to expand renewable energy capacity may involve plans to create new high-voltage transmissions lines from the 'periphery' to the 'centre'. Such lines also impose negative externalities in terms of their landscape impact. Public opposition may lead to calls for such new lines to be placed underground, although this then gives rise to concern regarding the higher construction costs of underground transmission lines. The policy question is thus: do the incremental benefits (avoided landscape damages) justify the incremental costs?

One attempt to answer such a question is Navrud et al. (2008). The authors focus on a proposal to expand overhead transmission lines around Oslo in Norway. Contingent Valuation was used to assess whether the benefits of avoiding this landscape impact by laying the cables underground would be big enough to justify the costs of doing so. Results showed that benefits were indeed bigger than costs, by a factor of around three. The authors note there might be external costs from burying transmission lines – such as short-term effects on water quality – which should also be taken into account. One might also look at the housing market, using the hedonic price method to uncover the relationship between house prices and proximity to power lines (Sims and Dent, 2005).

12.4 CONCLUSIONS

Renewable energy seems destined for a large expansion worldwide, due to concerns over the climatic effects of rising CO_2 levels. Renewable energy schemes involve a range of benefits and costs which depend both on the technology and on location. External costs (for example landscape effects) and benefits (displaced pollution) figure strongly in the analysis of renewable energy, making it a challenging topic for CBA.

NOTES

1. The load factor shows what fraction of maximum possible power output per year is actually achieved.
2. For details on which technologies this included, see Swezey and Bird (2000). A more up-to-date review is given in Bird et al. (2007).

3. These figures come from column 10, Table 3 in Whitehead and Cherry (2007). The
    authors provide other figures dependent on how the data is analysed.

REFERENCES

AEA Technology (2005), 'Damages per tonne emission of PM2.5, NH3, NOx, SO2
    and VOCS from each EU25 member state', report to European Commission,
    available at http://ec.europa.eu/environment/archives/air/cafe/activities/esti-
    mates.htm.
Alvarez-Farizo, B. and N. Hanley (2002), 'Using conjoint analysis to quantify
    public preferences over the environmental impacts of wind farms', *Energy
    Policy*, **30**(2), 107–16.
Bell, K., D. Huppert and R. Johnson (2003), 'Willingness to pay for local coho
    salmon enhancement in coastal communities', *Marine Resource Economics*,
    18(1), 15–31.
Bergmann, A., C. Colombo and N. Hanley (2008), 'Rural versus urban preferences
    for renewable energy developments', *Ecological Economics*, **65**, 616–25.
Bird, L., L. Dagher and B. Swezey (2007), 'Green power marketing in the United
    States: a status report (tenth edition)', NREL/TP-670-42502, Golden, CO:
    National Renewable Energy Laboratory, December.
Bothe, D. (2003), 'Environmental costs due to the Karahnjukar hydro power
    project on Iceland', discussion paper 2003-01, Department of Economic and
    Social Geography, University of Cologne.
Champ, P. and R. Bishop (2001), 'Donation payment mechanisms and contingent
    valuation: an empirical study of hypothetical bias', *Environmental and Resource
    Economics*, **19**, 383–402.
Ek, K. (2006), 'Quantifying the environmental impacts of renewable energy: the
    case of Swedish wind power', in D.W. Pearce (ed.), *Environmental Valuation in
    Developing Countries*, Cheltenham, UK and Northampton, MA, USA: Edward
    Elgar.
Ernst and Young (2007), 'Renewable Energy Country Attractive Indices', www.
    ey.com/renewables.
Fargione J., J. Hill, D. Tilman, S. Polasky and P. Hawthorne (2008), 'Land clear-
    ing and the biofuel carbon debt', *Science*, **319**, 1235–8.
Frontier Economics (2008), *Analysis of a Severn Barrage*, Report to the NGO
    Steering Group, London: Frontier Economics.
Håkansson, C. (2007), 'Cost–benefit analysis and valuation uncertainty: empirical
    contributions and methodological developments for trade-offs between hydro-
    power and wild salmon', doctoral thesis 2007:41, Faculty of Forest Sciences,
    Swedish University of Agricultural Sciences.
Hanley, N. and A. Black (2006), 'Cost–benefit analysis and the Water Framework
    Directive in Scotland', *Integrated Environmental Assessment and Management*,
    2(2), 156–65.
Hanley, N. and C. Nevin (1999), 'Appraising renewable energy developments in
    remote communities: the case of the North Assynt Estate, Scotland', *Energy
    Policy*, **27**, 527–47.
Hill, J., E. Nelson, D. Tilman, S. Polasky and D. Tiffany (2006), 'Environmental,

economic and energetic costs and benefits of biodiesel and ethanol biofuels', *PNAS*, **103**(30), 11206–10.

Krohn, S. and S. Damborg (1999), 'On public attitudes towards wind power', *Renewable Energy*, **16**, 945–60.

Krutilla, J.V. and A.C. Fisher (1985), *The Economics of Natural Environments*, Baltimore: Johns Hopkins University Press.

Ladenburg, J., A. Dubgaard, L. Martinsen and J. Tranberg (2005), 'Economic valuation of the visual externalities of off-shore wind farms', report 179/2005, Institute of Food and Resource Economics, University of Copenhagen.

Longo, A., A. Markandya and M. Petrucci (2008), 'The internalization of externalities in the production of electricity: willingness to pay for the attributes of a policy for renewable energy', *Ecological Economics*, **67**, 140–52.

Loomis, J., C.F. Sorg and D. Donnelly (1986), 'Economic losses to recreational fisheries due to small-head hydro power development: a case study of Henry's Fork in Idaho', *Journal of Environmental Management*, **22**, 85–94.

Lundqvist, H., P. Rivinoja, K. Leonnardsson and S. McKinnell (2005), 'Upstream passage problems for wild Atlantic salmon in a flow controlled river', Department of Wildlife, Fish and Environmental Studies, SLU, Sweden.

Morey, E., R. Rowe and M. Watson (1993), 'A repeated nested logit model of Atlantic salmon fishing', *American Journal of Agricultural Economics*, **75**, 578–92.

Navrud, S., R. Ready, K. Magnussen and O. Bergland (2008), 'Valuing the social benefits of avoiding landscape degradation from overhead power transmission lines: do underground cables pass the benefit–cost test?', *Landscape Research*, **33**(3), 281–96.

Poe, G., J. Clark, D. Rondeau and W. Schulze (2002), 'Provision point mechanisms and field validity tests of contingent valuation', *Environmental and Resource Economics*, **23**, 105–31.

Rivinoja, P., S. McKinnell and H. Lundquist (2001), 'Hindrances to upstream migration of Atlantic salmon in a northern Swedish river', *Regulated Rivers: Research and Management*, **17**, 101–15.

Roe, B., M. Teisl, A. Levy and M. Russell (2001), 'US consumers' willingness to pay for green electricity', *Energy Policy*, **29**, 917–25.

Scruton, D.A., C. Pennell, L.M.N. Ollerhead, K. Alfredsen, M. Stickler, A. Harby, M. Robertson, K.D. Clarke and L.J. LeDrew (2008), 'A synopsis of "hydropeaking" studies on the response of juvenile Atlantic salmon to experimental flow alteration', *Hydrobiologia*, **609**(1), 263–75.

Sims, S. and P. Dent (2005), 'High voltage power lines and property values: a residential study for the UK', *Urban Studies*, **42**(4), 665–94.

Stern, N. (2007), *The Economics of Climate Change: The Stern Review*, Cambridge: Cambridge University Press.

Sustainable Development Commission (SDC) (2007), 'Turning the tide: tidal power in the UK', London, SDC, available at www.sd-commission.org.uk/publications.

Swezey, B. and L. Bird (2000), 'Green power marketing in the United States: a status report', NREL/TP-620-28738, Golden: CO: National Renewable Energy Laboratory, August.

Vossler, C., R. Ethier, G. Poe and M. Welsh (2003), 'Payment certainty in discrete choice contingent valuation: results from a field validity test', *Southern Economic Journal*, **69**(4), 886–902.

Whitehead, J. and T. Cherry (2007), 'Willingness to pay for a green energy program', *Resource and Energy Economics*, **29**, 247–61.

WWF (2008), 'Analysis of a Severn barrage', Report from Frontier Economics for WWF, Godalming, Surrey, available at www.wwf.org.uk/filelibrary/pdf/frontier_economics_barrage_repo.pdf.

13. The strengths and weaknesses of environmental CBA

This final chapter is in some ways the most important in this book. Here, we take the opportunity to stand back from the details of how to undertake CBA to ask: 'what are the advantages and disadvantages of CBA, as applied to the environment?'. In other words, we want to undertake a cost–benefit analysis of the technique, highlighting its strengths and weaknesses and thinking about the opportunities for future developments. To do this, discussion is organized into four sections:

- What is the role of CBA within current decision-making processes in government?
- What are the main challenges to the individual component parts of a CBA?
- What are the main challenges to the overall approach and basis of CBA?
- What are the principal future challenges and opportunities?

13.1 THE ROLE OF CBA WITHIN GOVERNMENT

How, in principle, can CBA improve the process of policy analysis? How can it contribute to a firm 'evidence base' for decision making in the public sector?

- CBA can make clear the tradeoffs that decision makers face, for example in terms of increasing the extent to which we generate power from renewable energy sources and how much we pay for electricity; or between investing in new roads or hospitals.
- By consistently applying the Kaldor–Hicks criteria, CBA ensures that government policies can contribute to increasing the average level of well-being over time amongst voters.
- If one believes that government actions should be based on voters' preferences, then CBA provides a way of measuring and representing these as part of decision making.

- The application of CBA to government decision making can improve its effectiveness: for example, the UK Government Economic Service's strategic plan states that 'rigorous cost–benefit analysis informs choices on spending to *ensure value for money and effective delivery*' (Fisher, 2008; emphasis added).
- If standard values are adopted for the key parameters of CBAs (such as the value of a statistical life, or the value of reducing CO_2 emissions, or the social rate of discount), CBA can ensure greater consistency in decision making. Arrow et al. (1997) point out that the implicit value per life saved for recent US health and safety legislation varied from $200 000 to $6.3 trillion. This suggests (i) rather inconsistent decision making and (ii) the scope for achieving a large increase in the number of lives saved for no increase in costs, by reallocating resources across policies.
- CBA can identify 'switching values' for particular choices. For example, how highly would we have to value each tonne of CO_2 saved for investing in offshore wind energy to yield positive net benefits? By how much would oil prices have to rise before investing in new forms of re-using economically-exhausted oil deposits becomes cost effective?
- CBA is a way of encouraging people to think about, describe and then measure the multiple impacts of different policies and projects in a consistent manner. In principle, this can be done in a very transparent way which encourages debate over the important parameters of a decision: how many people will visit a new marine national park? What will be the short-run costs of lost fishing revenues? What resources will be needed to monitor compliance with park regulations? What external factors are important in determining the status of marine ecosystems in the 'without protection' and 'with protection' cases? CBA can be a very useful framework for presenting information on the advantages and disadvantages of different options for government policy and environmental management.
- The CBA process can reveal what important information on the likely impacts of a new policy is currently missing, and how sensitive the recommendation to proceed or not might be to the content of this missing information.

We certainly do not expect that CBA will be the *only* piece of information that policy makers take into account in making decisions: CBA is an important source of information about one aspect of a policy choice or environmental management decision, summarizing this impact in terms of efficiency over time. But other criteria are of course important, such as distributional impacts and political expediency. CBA thus provides insights, not decisive answers.

CBA in the Policy World

Both the UK and US governments have produced detailed guidance on how to conduct CBA (US EPA, 2000; HM Treasury, 2003). In the case of the UK guidance, the objective is clear: 'The Government is committed to continuing improvement in the delivery of public services. A major part of this is ensuring that public funds are spent on activities that provide the greatest benefits to society, and that they are spent in the most efficient way' (HM Treasury, 2003, p. v).

Applying a uniform mode of analysis (which is described as 'not rocket science') at both the pre-project/pre-policy stage of decision making, and at the *ex post*, evaluative stage, is intended to help achieve this goal of efficiency in public spending. Note the emphasis on efficiency. Cost–Benefit Analysis is seen as the main way of undertaking such an appraisal, with other methods being used to weight impacts which cannot be valued in monetary terms. The guidance notes that: 'As decisions will often have far reaching consequences, the presentation of the conclusions and recommendations to decision makers and key stakeholders can be as important as the analysis itself. In all cases, transparency is vital' (HM Treasury, 2003, p. vi). Detailed guidance is then provided on valuing benefits and costs (including non-market valuation), on the treatment of uncertainty, and on discounting.

As Chapter 10 showed, CBA is used extensively in the UK for the management of water quality. Other uses of environmental CBA within the UK include flood risk management, coastal zone protection actions, major land drainage projects and the assessment of major transport projects; although in many cases the assessment procedures also allow for the consideration on non-monetized impacts (Hanley, 2001; Turner, 2007).

In the case of the US Environmental Protection Agency guidelines for policy appraisal, the objective is 'improved guidance on the preparation and use of sound science in support of the decision making process' (US EPA, 2000, p. i). However, the EPA guidelines are also firmly based in terms of the statutory requirements for undertaking such analyses, which date from requirements for Regulatory Impact Analyses (RIAs) introduced by Executive Order 12291. This measure, brought in by President Reagan, required the review of all proposed new federal laws and regulations in terms of their benefits, costs and economic impacts.

The process was overseen by the Office of Management and the Budget under guidelines issued by them in 1996; six other legal requirements (Acts and Executive Orders) for economic analysis of new policies and projects are also noted in the EPA guidelines. The Guidelines recommend three approaches for policy assessment: benefit–cost analysis (CBA), economic impact analysis, and identifying impacts on particular groups. CBA deals with the efficiency criterion, whilst the other two methods address distributional concerns. The Guidelines are clear on the limitations of CBA. For example, they state:

> Benefit-cost analysis is not a precise tool that yields firm numerical results, rather, it is a general framework for more carefully accounting for the potential and varied effects of government programs. Some of these effects can be quantified, whereas others can only be assessed qualitatively. Some may be relatively certain, whereas others may be quite speculative. (US EPA, 2000, p. 33)

Detailed guidance is then provided on issues such as choice of the discount rate and sensitivity analysis, the selection of a baseline for describing the 'policy off' or counterfactual against which options can be compared, and methods for dealing with uncertainty. An outline of non-market valuation methods is provided, along with a review of estimates of the value of a statistical life. The guidance reviews tools for calculating the social costs of regulations, and concludes with advice on how to present the results of policy analyses. Box 13.1 contains more information on the US EPA guidelines, whilst Box 13.2 asks 'how well does the US government undertake CBA?'.

The European Commission has recently introduced a system of Impact Assessment guidelines (European Commission, 2005). These contain elements of CBA, but are a rather broader set of principles on how regulatory proposals can be assessed in a consistent, transparent manner. Like CBA, the guidelines offer a way of bringing together the economic, environmental and social impacts of a policy, including how these impacts are spread across different groups within society. Box 13.1 gives more detail. Introduction of such a formal appraisal system for new policy proposals was seen by many as overdue, since evidence existed that a significant number of EU directives would have failed a CBA test had it been applied (Pearce, 2004). Interestingly, the procedure also involves the use of an independent quality-checking body, the 'Impact Assessment Board', created in 2006 to vet the results of individual assessments. Box 13.3 gives brief information on the Board's main conclusions after its first year of operation.

BOX 13.1   POLICY APPRAISAL GUIDELINES IN THE US
AND EUROPEAN UNION

The US EPA guidelines were issued in 2000, following an extensive period of consultation and review. They are an update of the *Guidelines for Performing Regulatory Impact Analysis (RIAs)* issued by the EPA in 1983. The Office of Management and the Budget had issued its own guidelines on conducting RIAs in 1996. According to the *Guidelines*, the main audiences are: 'those performing or using economic analysis, including policy makers, the Agency's Program and Regional Offices, and contractors providing economic reports to the EPA.'

As noted in the main text, the guidelines provide very detailed advice on how to conduct a cost–benefit analysis, but also contain much valuable information which would enable public servants to judge CBAs undertaken by other parties (for example by consultants or industry groups). Care is taken to explain the various tools available for estimating costs and benefits, and for quantifying distributional impacts.

The EU Impact Assessment Guidelines were issued in 2005. As a general rule, all major EU policy initiatives and legislative proposals are required to undergo an impact assessment. The main aims of the Impact Assessment system, as summarized by a review undertaken of the system in 2007 (TEP, 2007), were to:

1.   Improve the quality of Commission proposals, in particular by
     ● facilitating a more systematic, coherent, analytical, open, and evidence-based approach to policy design;
     ● providing a thorough, balanced and comprehensive analysis of likely social, economic and environmental impacts.
2.   Provide an effective aid to decision making, in particular by
     ● providing policy makers with relevant and comprehensive information on the rationale behind proposed interventions, and their likely impacts;
     ● enabling policy makers to assess tradeoffs and compare different scenarios when deciding on a specific course of action.
3.   Serve as a valuable communication tool, in particular by
     ● fostering internal communication and ensuring early and effective coordination within the Commission;
     ● enhancing external communication by making the policy development process more open and transparent to external stakeholders.

The Impact Assessment procedure replaces the previous single-sector type assessments and assesses the potential impacts of new legislation or policy proposals in economic (including competitiveness), social, and environmental fields. These are known as the 'three pillars' of assessment. Impact assessment is seen as an aid to political decision making, not a substitute for it. The impact assessment informs the political decision makers of the likely impacts of proposed measures to tackle an identified problem, but leaves it to them to decide if and how to proceed.

The EU guidelines do not correspond to a guide on how to undertake CBA, since the recommended assessment procedure is much broader than CBA alone. For instance the Guide states the main steps as follows:

- Identify (direct and indirect) environmental, economic and social impacts and how they occur.
- Identify who is affected (including those outside the EU) and in what way.
- Assess the impacts in qualitative, quantitative and monetary terms where possible and appropriate.
- Consider the risks and uncertainties in the policy choices, including obstacles to compliance.

Moreover, the types of impact included are broader than would be the case in a standard CBA: for example, including the effects on EU competitiveness and internal markets (although this could be represented in a CBA using predicted changes in consumers' and producers' surplus), and impacts on EU foreign policy and livelihoods in developing countries. Finally, the overall assessment of policy options is not undertaken simply as a Net Present Value: different impacts may be evaluated in different ways (qualitative, quantitative, monetary), and the final outcome can be a ranking of preferred options in terms of impacts on criteria chosen specifically for the case in hand. Tradeoffs between different groups of people and sectors affected by each option are an important aspect of the impact assessment process.

BOX 13.2   HOW WELL DOES THE US GOVERNMENT DO CBA?

In the main text, we noted the comment by Arrow et al. (1997) that there was evidence of inconsistency in regulatory behaviour in the US, which could be moderated by the wider and more consistent use of CBA. We also saw that the US EPA has produced guidelines for the conduct of CBA, and that such analysis is now required in the case of new federal legislation. Since the Reagan administration, federal agencies have been required to assess the benefits and costs of proposed legislation, and consider how benefits and costs would vary if alternative regulation was put in place. But how well is this done? Robert Hahn and Patrick Dudley (2007) provide a view.

Hahn and Dudley review 74 CBAs undertaken by the US EPA over the period 1982–99. Their method is to score each of the analyses on the extent to which they met the requirements for 'proper' CBA set out in Presidential Orders 12291 and 12866 and the OMB (Office of Management and the Budget, which oversees the process) guidelines of 1996.

One of their key findings is that the quality of analysis is highly variable, and does not seem to be improving over time. In detail, their findings were:

- On *costs*, 15 per cent of early studies provided no figure for total costs. More recent studies present either point or range estimates of total costs, but these costs often excluded costs incurred by government itself (for example in monitoring compliance).
- On *benefits*, only 50 per cent of studies presented at least some benefits in monetary terms, although most studies quantified benefits to a degree.
- More studies reported on the cost effectiveness of measures (physical benefits relative to monetary costs) than reported on the *net benefits*, although the proportion of studies reporting net benefits rose over time to 40 per cent in the Clinton presidency.

Hahn and Dudley concluded that although part of the explanation for 'missing reports' in these CBAs was likely be the difficulty of obtaining information on the costs and benefits of regulatory reform, 'there is evidence of . . . non-compliance with the executive orders and OMB guidelines . . . Limited knowledge and resource constraints do not offer a complete explanation'. The reasons they put forward for this include:

- Regulatory analyses are expensive to perform (well).
- Agency staff have little incentive to conduct analyses effectively.
- Agencies may not wish evidence that benefits are less than costs for policies which they wish to pursue on other grounds.
- There is no political pressure for good analysis, but rather for a box-ticking exercise.
- Agencies may not see a comparison of benefits and costs as particularly helpful for them, even though it is necessary to ensure efficiency in public policy choice.

CBA thus emerges as a 'necessary evil' for federal agencies – not the role that most economists would see for it! However, the authors end by saying that they are more optimistic about the conduct of CBA in regulatory appraisal in the future, as experience builds and people learn how to undertake analyses correctly.

BOX 13.3   REVIEWING THE QUALITY OF CBAS: THE EU
            IMPACT ASSESSMENT BOARD

In a speech to the Commission, senior civil servant Catherine Day stated
that 'Existing quality control mechanisms in the Commission could in the
past not fully ensure that all impact assessments were of a consistently
high quality'. In response to such worries, an Impact Assessment Board
was created. Since starting work in February 2007, it has scrutinized
102 impact assessments, corresponding to virtually all initiatives in the
Commission's 2007 work programme. Examples of impact assessments
looked at include:

- proposals for a regulation to reduce CO_2 emissions from passenger cars;
- simplifications to the EURO VI regulations for heavy duty vehicles;
- proposals for a Directive concerning carbon capture and storage;
- protection of vulnerable deep sea ecosystems.

In all cases, it has given detailed recommendations for improvements
in these assessments. The Board's initial report recommended that EC
departments undertaking Impact Assessment should:

- reinforce their analytical capacity;
- start impact assessment work earlier, especially to facilitate adequate data collection;
- enhance inter-departmental cooperation from the earliest stages of the impact assessment.

13.2   WHAT ARE THE MAIN CHALLENGES TO THE INDIVIDUAL COMPONENT PARTS OF A CBA?

Here we consider problems that have arisen with some of the tools which
economists use as part of undertaking a CBA.

The Problems of Environmental Valuation

One of the most controversial and difficult aspects of environmental applications of CBA is that we would ideally like to be able to measure all non-market environmental impacts in monetary terms. Chapters 3–6 explained the main methods through which this can be done, and also discussed some of the challenges in using these methods. Summing up, we can say that revealed preference methods are limited in terms of their applicability (for example, they cannot be used to measure non-use values), whilst stated preference methods are still challenged since the values produced are for hypothetical changes in environmental quality. Whether people would actually pay the amounts they say they would pay, either directly in a contingent valuation exercise, or indirectly in a choice experiment, is still doubted by some, and seems to depend crucially on context (this issue of hypothetical market bias was discussed in Chapter 3).

The issue of 'part–whole bias' is also important. For instance, if the goal is to estimate the benefits of a new policy of protecting habitats across the UK, then the researcher might proceed by asking people to value changes in specific habitats individually. The question is then whether summing up the individual habitat values produces a reliable estimate of the overall value of protecting all habitats. There are actually good reasons why this would not be so in theory: if individual habitats are partial substitutes in terms of the utility they provide people, then adding up individual habitat values (obtained in isolation) will produce a bigger number than asking people to value all habitats together.

Another problem in stated preference surveys relates to information. We assume that people 'know enough' for their expressed WTP to be meaningful as a way of measuring social benefits and costs. But this is difficult when a contingent valuation study is being undertaken on a good that people are unfamiliar with. The effects of providing information on stated WTP have been studied for many years in contingent valuation (see the review in Munro and Hanley, 1999); we know that as people learn more about the 'good' characteristics of an environmental resource, their WTP tends to increase. This is, of course, what is also observed in markets for traded goods and services. But it does leave the awkward issue of how much information is enough, and how best to provide it (MacMillan et al., 2006).

Production function valuation methods, as discussed in Chapter 6, are promising, but problems exist in terms of the availability of appropriate statistical or simulation models linking human actions and well-being with future changes in environmental goods and services. The complexity and non-linearities in ecosystems add to the difficulties of predicting how systems will respond to varying pressures from human behaviour (see Chapters 9 and 11; also see Maler, 2008).

For instance, a common assumption is often made that the 'value' of an ecosystem service changes 'linearly' with critical habitat variables, such as size (for example, area). One reason for invoking such an assumption is that little data exists for examining the marginal losses associated with changes in non-linear ecological functions, making it difficult to value accurately the changes in ecosystem services in response to incremental changes in habitat characteristics (for example, area). Thus, a 'point estimate' for the value of an ecosystem service, in terms of benefits per hectare (ha), is simply multiplied by the total land area of an ecosystem to obtain the value of the service provided by the entire system. If, however, relationships between ecosystem structure and function are non-linear, then assuming that the value of an ecosystem service varies linearly with respect to changes in habitat or ecosystem area will mislead management decisions. Box 9.4 illustrates with an example from Thailand how taking into account such non-linear values affects the CBA decision of how much of a mangrove landscape to convert to shrimp ponds.

Using any of the economic valuation methods contained in Chapters 3–6 means that we are basing our measurement of the value of environmental gains and losses on an underlying theory of rational behaviour. This is because all of the methods set out in these chapters assume that people, on average, behave according to the assumptions of the 'rational' economic model: in other words, people make the best choices they can, in terms of maximizing their individual utility, based on their resources and on the information they have about the problem. However, over many years, a body of evidence has accumulated suggesting that people's behaviour can diverge from the predictions of the rational economic model: this is sometimes referred to as *preference anomalies*. Hanley and Shogren (2005) summarize the principal anomalies as:

i.   the observed differences between willingness to pay (WTP) and willingness to accept compensation (WTAC) measures of value;
ii.   preference uncertainty and preference construction;
iii. hypothetical market bias;
iv.   perceptions toward risk;
v.   preference reversals.

We have already discussed points (i) and (iii) in Chapter 3: the fact that WTP can differ from WTAC by an amount greater than predicted by theory creates awkward problems in that the analyst now has to use subjective criteria to choose which measure to use in valuing an environmental gain or loss. Use of WTAC designs may also lead to higher levels of protest bidding, whilst the willingness in principle of people to be compensated for an environmental loss might depend on how compensation was offered, and to whom. Point (ii) relates to the assumption that people have pre-formed preferences for environmental goods about which they are certain; the researcher's task is then to 'uncover' these preferences. However, people may construct their preferences for environmental goods in a way that is context-specific, implying that the measured benefits from an environmental improvement would depend on the wider context for this improvement (for example, whether the burden of the improvement was shared equally, or whether the decision to proceed was taken democratically). For more discussion of this, see Payne and Bettman (1999) or Slovic (2000). Points (iv) and (v) are taken up in the next section.

Attitudes to Risk

Risk perceptions are interesting because of the phenomenon whereby subjective risk assessments can differ systematically from objective (scientific) risk assessments (this point was raised in Chapter 5). This perception gap occurs, in part, because many environmental risks are ambiguous low-probability events of high severity. In contrast to the benchmark rational model of expected utility, evidence suggests that people have a bimodal response to low probability risks – they either ignore the risk completely, or overreact to it. When the outcome is potentially very bad, experience tells them little about how to think about such very low-probability risks (see Camerer and Kunreuther, 1989). As Hanley and Shogren (2005) say, 'People confronting risk have a tendency to be conservative and alarmist. They both plan for the worst, and hope for the best, and then over-invest in the worst-case prevention policy rather than balancing the costs and benefits of alternative options'. One explanation of anomalous behaviour toward risk is therefore that people do not think about odds and consequences simultaneously, as expected utility requires. Rather people seem to separate the two elements and make their decision based on the most attractive element – either certain odds or a big prize (Machina, 1987). People use this heuristic to simplify their choices.

One problem that subjective perceptions of risk cause for CBA applied to environmental policy is that actual legislation, monitoring and enforcement of environmental quality is typically based on scientific measures of risk, for example in setting upper limits on faecal coliforms in bathing water, based on a dose-response relationship between coliform counts and the risk of getting sick after swimming. But when the analyst seeks to estimate the benefits of raising such standards, what they measure is benefits based on different levels of subjective risk in people's minds, which may be quite different. A lack of a common risk currency thus exists between people and regulators, managers and scientists.

In the preceding section, 'preference reversals' were listed as one of the anomalies which seem to exist in the context of risky choices. A preference reversal occurs when rankings of two bundles differ according to whether people rank on the basis of their preferences or on the basis of value – their willingness to pay (Lichtenstein and Slovic, 1971; Sugden, 1999). Normally, we assume that a project (such as investing in different rail safety improvements) which would be ranked first out of a set of competing projects would also be the project for which WTP would be highest. But the experimental economics evidence suggests that preference and value rankings can differ. If researchers ask people what they are willing to pay for a risk reduction option, and people state values that are inconsistent with their underlying preferences, then basing decisions on NPV grounds may produce choices that people would prefer not to have go ahead. Stated values should match up with underlying preferences to judge the relative net benefits of alternative policies. Moreover, if risk-reduction values are context specific such that they change with the policy being proposed, we cannot compare two risk-reduction policies using CBA because it would be like comparing apples and oranges (Hanley and Shogren, 2005).

Back to the Discount Rate

In Chapter 7, we saw that the choice of discount rate and the discounting method (constant rate or declining rate) could be very influential for CBAs of policies with long-term benefits and/or costs. A striking illustration of this is the application of CBA to decisions over climate change, but many other examples exist: decisions over nuclear power programmes, and policy choices concerning toxic chemicals, biodiversity conservation and forest planting. For example, Turner et al. (2007) show how moving from a constant discount rate of 3.5 per cent to a declining discount rate starting out at 3.5 per cent changes the NPV of alternative coastal management policies for managed realignment strategies in the Humber Estuary, England. Choosing a higher discount rate (constant *or* declining) will swing decisions away from policies where benefits occur far into the future but costs occur now, and toward policies which postpone costs in favour of present-day benefits. Moreover, if benefits and costs stretch across generations, then there are profound ethical implications of choosing a particular discount rate.

Whilst there is now some agreement in the literature over the way in which discounting should be carried out – that declining discount rates should be used – the choice of what the discount rate should be is still very open to debate. We know the broad principles which should guide our choice: the productivity of capital, the rate of pure time preference, the future growth of per capita consumption, and the elasticity of the marginal utility of income; but we can disagree on precisely what weight should be given to each of these components and on the values they take. This means that a search for *the* correct social rate of discount is pointless. Instead, the value of the social discount rate emerges as a political choice. This might appear a little unsettling. However, the good economist will always undertake a sensitivity analysis of their baseline CBA, paying particular attention to the value of the discount rate. This means we can ask sensible questions such as: do we believe the social discount rate to be somewhere in the range of 2–8 per cent for a go-ahead decision for a new biomass technology to be desirable?

13.3   CHALLENGES TO THE OVERALL APPROACH OF CBA

The issues raised in the preceding section relate to the 'tools' of CBA – how the analysis is undertaken in practice. Here, we consider some objections to the underlying principles of CBA as a way of informing public decisions. These principles could be summarized as follows:

- the Kaldor–Hicks potential compensation test is a reasonable way of thinking about the net welfare effects of a decision, in terms of adding up and comparing benefits and costs;
- individuals' preferences, and the aggregation of these, are a reasonable basis for making decisions on what society should do.

We can then bring together the many 'objections in principle' to CBA under the following four headings:

A. objections to the Kaldor–Hicks test;
B. objections to adding up benefits and costs as a way of determining overall impacts;
C. ethical objections to the 'realm' within which CBA is applied (that is, to what kind of decisions);
D. objections to CBA as a decision-making mechanism in terms of long-term well-being.

A.   Objection to the Kaldor–Hicks Test

In Chapter 2, we saw that the ideas proposed separately by John Hicks and Nicholas Kaldor, which are now merged together as the 'Kaldor–Hicks Test', or KHT, form the underlying basis for CBA. This is because the KHT provides an apparently simple answer to the question: how can we tell whether a project will improve social well-being, when some people will be better off as a result, and some worse off? The KHT answers this question by adding up the total benefits of a project, adding up the total costs and then asking a different question: could the gainers compensate the losers and still be better off? Within CBA, this is interpreted as being the same as asking whether aggregate, discounted benefits are greater than aggregate, discounted costs (that is, whether the Net Present Value is positive or not). Recall that no requirement is set in place that compensation for losses is actually paid.

What objections can be made against use of the KHT as a way of judging net gains in social well-being? One obvious objection is that it may not be possible to compensate for some losses. For instance, if a project will destroy an ancient woodland and some people state that they would refuse *any* compensation to restore their utility if the project went ahead, then these people are not potentially compensatable. The question then is whether the KHT should only be used when losers indicate that they *could* be compensated for losses. But this offers the prospect of the tyranny of the few – one person with an infinite WTA could stymie a project even if everyone else in the community would benefit from it. Another issue relates to *how* compensation is paid: for example, if those who would suffer a loss in utility from the felling of the forest are told that money will be set aside to construct a new wetland, they may be less likely to veto the project than if net benefits stayed with the beneficiary, or if compensation was offered to them as cash payments (Frey and Jegen, 2001; Mansfield et al., 2002). A further problem relates to how gains and losses are measured. If losses are measured using WTP – for instance, mean WTP to prevent the forest being felled – then this will understate losses to the extent that WTAC is greater than WTP (Knetsch, 2005).

B.   Objections to Adding up Gains and Losses as a Way of Determining Overall Impacts

One Achilles heel for CBA is that it implicitly assumes we can compare changes in utility across people and over time, since in arriving at a predicted change in social welfare, this is what is required. A Social Welfare Function considers changes in utility across all parties deemed as relevant to the decision. This implies that utility is something that can be compared across people, and that it is possible to measure how much utility changes in moving from one outcome to another. Yet for many years economics has struggled with the concept of a cardinal measure of utility, building its demand analysis and welfare economics frameworks instead on ordinal utility.[1] Despite advances in 'neuro-economics', we still cannot measure utility! The implementation of the KHT criteria gets around this problem by expressing gains and losses in terms of WTP and WTA. It also assumes that the marginal social utility is equal for each person, as Chapter 2 made clear – that is, that additions to or losses in utility for any person count equally in the adding up of social gains and losses.[2] We can then assess the contribution of a project to social welfare by comparing the summation of the monetary equivalents of gains and losses in utility. However, some critics would argue that, especially in CBA analyses of long-term policy impacts, we are making strong implicit value judgements in using the KHT to compare gains and losses across generations.

A related issue has been raised by Aldred (2006), who discusses whether environmental gains and losses are really *commensurable* with other impacts of a policy. Commensurability is a key aspect of environmental valuation: the assumption is that, for any change in environmental quality say from $Q1$ to $Q2$, there is some change in income which will keep people at either their initial or subsequent utility level. In other words, we assume the existence of a unique value m for any particular environmental change, where m is defined as:

$$v(Q1, y - m) = v(Q2, y) \qquad (13.1)$$

where y is income, v is indirect utility, and $Q1$ and $Q2$ are two levels of the desirable environmental good Q. Changes in environmental quality are thus capable of being measured using the same tape measure as changes in income or changes in any market-valued good. This tape measure is money. Aldred reviews both empirical evidence and conceptual arguments against this proposition. He notes the existence of protest bids and 'incommensurability statements' in stated preference surveys, the idea that preferences for environmental goods may be lexicographic, and evidence that people have vague preferences for environmental goods, which means that the amount m in equation (13.1) might be defined more by the idea of 'rough equivalence', than by strict indifference. He wonders whether our choices can be relied upon to reveal our preferences for non-market goods, given the unobserved impacts of choice context and information. He also argues that variations in the marginal utility of income across people, and experimental evidence on what people see as adequate compensation for environmental losses, both imply that money is not a neutral measuring rod. His conclusion is that there are no strong arguments for environmental losses to be considered as commensurable with other project impacts, although this does not mean that environmental outcomes cannot be compared with other outcomes. We return to Aldred's ideas in the next section on possible future developments of CBA.

C.   Ethical Objections to the 'Realm' Within Which CBA is Applied

CBA can in principle be used to look at the net effects of any act of government policy. However, this might make us feel uneasy in some cases.
For instance, do you think that it would be appropriate to have used CBA
to help the UK Parliament decide whether to ban slavery in 1807? This
would have meant, in the limit, putting a monetary value on the suffering of slaves and their families, and comparing this with the benefits of
lower-cost agricultural outputs or returns to UK capitalists. Most people
would feel that this would be morally wrong. Yet using CBA to appraise
competing projects for road safety improvements also involves putting a
monetary price on human lives. As another example, would it have been
acceptable to use CBA in making decisions over limiting the use of child
labour in manufacturing and retail in the US in the 1930s?

Some authors have argued that, when societies make decisions over
issues of human rights, environmental protection and health and safety,
a consensus of 'reasonable opinion' would be that such decisions should
be made with reference to criteria other than benefits and costs (Sagoff,
1988). Economic efficiency is thus the wrong framing for decisions that
impinge on ethical concerns, so the argument goes. Instead, we should
use the democratic process to ensure that morals are brought to bear on
such decisions. In part, this is a philosophical debate: should we use a
utilitarian criterion, or a rights-based one, as the means of thinking about
desirable actions? In part, it is a pragmatic argument: we would not expect
the average person to approach issues of ethical importance simply from a
comparison of selfish costs and benefits. Sagoff (1988) has also argued that
in thinking about environmental or health and safety issues, people are
more likely to think and behave as citizens rather than as consumers. Since
CBA can be interpreted as simulating the outcome of an efficient market,
and is thus based on values which people would reveal as consumers
through their Willingness to Pay, CBA is the wrong way to frame public
policy questions touching on environment or health and safety.

And yet: people can state their WTP for tougher environmental regulation with their citizen's hat on, as much as with their consumer's hat on
(Alvarez-Farizo and Hanley, 2006). The citizen–consumer split is thus
perhaps not the most fruitful way of thinking about the moral limits of
CBA. Alan Randall (2002) has suggested what might be a more useful
approach to these ethical issues. He suggests that we set moral limits
within which CBA is used. For example, these limits could be determined
with regard to environmental policy by saying that, on ethical grounds, we
think that no new nuclear power stations should be constructed in the UK
because of the implications for future generations of waste storage. CBA

could then be used to analyse low-carbon options for energy supply, given this 'no nuclear' constraint. Similarly, the Indian state could decide to ban child labour on ethical grounds, and then use CBA to evaluate different training and education programmes which could, over time, replace children's earnings for low-income households. This has links with the Safe Minimum Standards approach discussed in the next section. An alternative perspective on Randall's method is to say that any policy that is likely to produce an impact that transcends commonly-accepted standards of morality would not be permitted to go ahead. But so long as no such standards are likely to be violated, the CBA can usefully weigh up benefits and costs in a way that makes clear the tradeoffs which are involved in decision making over the use of scarce resources.

D. Objections to CBA as a Decision-making Mechanism in Terms of Long-term Well-being

As we noted in Chapter 7, there is a potentially poor fit between the use of CBA in policy analysis and the goal of sustainable development. CBA concerns itself with economic efficiency over time – maximizing the present value of net benefits. Sustainable development, on the other hand, is defined in terms of fairness in the allocation of wealth or well-being over time. One might argue that these are not necessarily inconsistent *if* one recasts the Kaldor–Hicks criterion as being concerned with testing for projects that increase net wealth – the discounted value of benefits minus costs over time. If sustainability is defined as total wealth being non-declining over time, then, provided one assumes 'weak sustainability' – perfect substitutability of all forms of wealth/capital – a policy that passes the CBA test also enhances sustainability. However, not all would agree with this interpretation of the CBA rule or with this interpretation of sustainability.

However, there is another concern relating to the use of CBA and long-term well-being. This is the extent to which the application of CBA can be relied on to guarantee the ecosystem functioning and global life support services on which humanity depends. There is no reason to suppose that application of CBA will provide these guarantees. This is for two reasons. First, if avoiding 'disastrous' climate change requires us to ensure that atmospheric CO_2 concentrations never rise above a particular limit, then applying CBA to climate policy cannot guarantee this. Instead, governments would have to limit the set of acceptable policies to those that would lead to this ceiling not being breached. CBA would then be used to decide amongst alternatives that all meet this constraint. In general, having an overarching environmental target is just like the kind of moral or ethical 'trump cards' considered by Randall. The environmental target is used to act as a top-level filter (selection criterion) for policies, and CBA is then only used to inform choices from amongst policies that pass this selection test.

This idea of CBA operating within environmental limits can be related to the economics of the Safe Minimum Standard (Farmer and Randall, 1998). This idea was first suggested in the context of decisions over the protection of biodiversity in the face of uncertainty about future benefits and costs from irreversible developments which would harm biodiversity. Scientists would indentify the minimum viable population for a particular species. Society would then decide to safeguard this minimum, for example by protecting habitat, so long as the opportunity costs of so doing were not 'unacceptably large'. These opportunity costs would be identified from a search for the most cost-effective way of defending the safe minimum standard. Whether a cost of, say, £2 million for protecting the minimum viable population of Yellow Eyed Penguin in New Zealand was 'unacceptable' or not would then be decided by the political process, *not* through the application of CBA. CBA could, however, be used in identifying the best way of meeting this target, although this could also be identified using cost criteria alone (Busch and Cullen, 2009). Farmer and Randall (1998) have extended the concept to natural resources which are essential at some level for maintaining an adequate standard of living, and showed an alternative way of defining the 'tolerable limit of sacrifice' to defend the SMS even when there is no uncertainty about the future dynamics of the resource. However, they point out that it only makes sense to sacrifice consumption now to defend the SMS into the future (for the benefit of far-in-the-future generations) if the intervening generations can also be 'signed up' to the contract.

An alternative way of thinking about maintaining the sustainability of natural systems is through the concept of resilience. Resilience is a concept taken from systems ecology which has recently been promoted as a useful way of thinking about the economics of sustainable development (Levin et al., 1998; Maler, 2008). Resilience refers to the ability of the processes within an ecosystem to remain functional in the presence of exogenous shocks such as drought or fire. Ecosystem variables may well undergo large changes as a result of such shocks, but the overall functioning of the system is maintained within bounds. Resilience is determined by flexibility and the ability to change adaptively (Peterson et al., 2003). As economic growth increases our demands on ecosystems via resource depletion and rising emissions, so society becomes more sensitive to external shocks as the environmental system itself becomes more sensitive. This is important, since the nature of the dynamics of the economy–environment system (non-linear, adaptive and far-from-equilibrium) means that the system can suddenly lurch from one state to another, radically different state. Whilst such changes do not have to be undesirable, in an environmental context they have often been so in the recent past (for example the collapse of certain ocean fisheries).

Levin et al. (1998) argue that, in general, resilience is a desirable property. For the environment–economy system, maintaining resilience might be viewed as a sustainable development strategy since it maintains system functioning over time. The 'stock' of resilience in a system might be seen as a valuable asset, much like other forms of capital, changes in which need to be recognized and reacted to. Moreover, projects or policies might deplete the 'stock' of resilience in an ecosystem. If so, then according to Walker et al. (2008), this is a cost which should in principle be recognized in sustainability accounting as part of a CBA. Walker et al. focus on the risks of exceeding critical thresholds in an underlying control variable for an ecosystem. Resilience is measured by the distance from the current state of the system to this threshold. It is the costs of increasing this risk that could be included in a CBA, measured as changes in 'distance to the threshold', valued through the expected change in future wealth from a marginal change in resilience. This approach in fact restores the use of marginal analysis in systems where non-marginal changes might occur because of a policy or project decision, since the extra marginal cost of a change in probability of crossing the threshold can now, in principle, be factored into the CBA.

Walker et al. show how this idea can be applied to the management of irrigated agriculture in South-East Australia, using thresholds for the level of the groundwater table, which is linked to increasing salinity in soils, and native vegetation cover. Changes in resilience are linked to the value of agricultural output. The authors show how the value of a project to address the problem of rising salinity can be augmented by an estimate of the change in the value of the stock of resilience. Options for achieving further integration of CBA methods with ecological sustainability are an important avenue for future research.

13.4   THE FUTURE OF CBA?

As we have seen above, CBA has many advantages as a decision-aiding process. However, CBA also faces a number of practical and conceptual challenges when applied to environmental policy analysis. The standard economist's defence for CBA is that it is transparent way of recognizing the choices which resource scarcity faces decision makers with, and that it allows for people's preferences – what they want – to play a key role in public policy choice. The standard critique is that CBA is a technocratic, black box which is based on subjective views on what constitutes social well-being. In one sense, the strength of CBA – its focus on efficiency – is also its weakness.

Three important tensions seem to exist. The first concerns environmental values. If environmental impacts are expressed in monetary terms, then the advantage is that this elevates environmental concerns to the same level as more electricity output, or faster commuting times. On the downside, this also implies that the environment is no longer special, requiring a separate and perhaps more favourable treatment, for example through the setting of absolute limits on pollution, rather than judging air quality standards on the grounds of costs and benefits. The second tension concerns the focus of CBA on economic efficiency alone. The positive aspect of this is a greater consistency in policy decisions, the avoidance of expensive mistakes (a check against bad government decisions), and over time, an increase in average well-being. The downside is too narrow a focus, which does not prioritize distributional concerns, either in the present day or over time. The third tension sees an open, consistent, transparent and democratic mechanism on one hand, and a technocratic, non-participatory device on the other.

This last concern is being addressed by current attempts to combine aspects of CBA with more participatory methods of decision making, such as citizen juries. This is being done both by using methods such as valuation workshops to undertake environmental valuation in a group setting

---

BOX 13.4   A COST–BENEFIT ANALYSIS OF PROPOSED AIR QUALITY STANDARDS FOR THE EU

The European Union has long been concerned with regulating air pollution, initially with regard to problems such as acid rain and eutrophication, and latterly through a concern with human health effects. The Air Quality Framework Directive of 1996 led to the setting up of a 'Clean Air for Europe' programme in 2001 – shortened to CAFÉ – which would inform a new Thematic Strategy on Air Pollution. Much of the work of the CAFÉ programme was to examine the costs and benefits across the EU of setting alternative new targets, known as levels of ambition, for a range of pollutants including SO_2, NOx, VOCs, NH_3 and $PM_{2.5}$. Three increasingly strict targets for improvements in ambient quality were compared to a business-as-usual baseline running to 2020, and a 'Maximum Technically Feasible Reduction' or MTFR scenario which disregarded costs entirely.

This was a large programme of work. Details can be found at the air pollution section of the EU Environment website (http://ec.europa.eu/environment/archives/air/cafe/index.htm), both in terms of the main report (CEC, 2005a) and the summary report (CEC, 2005b). Watkiss et al. (2008) also give an overview of the analysis.

The main impacts considered from air pollution were those on health, agriculture, buildings and ecosystems. These formed the benefit categories for the CBA. Health effects turned out to dominate total benefits; ecological impacts were not monetized, but were presented in qualitative terms. Health benefits were calculated both in terms of the value of a statistical life saved (mean = €2 million) and the value of a life year saved (mean value €120 000). Costs were calculated using the 'RAINS' model of cost-effective emission reductions across the EU, and were presented both in terms of impacts on specific sectors, and aggregate costs. Uncertainty was modelled using Monte Carlo analysis.

The two tables below, which are taken from CEC (2005a) show the scenarios considered, and the partial benefits and costs of each. As may be seen, for all scenarios, benefits seem to greatly exceed costs. By comparing marginal benefits and marginal costs, the report's authors found that the biggest net benefits – and therefore the optimal target, given what was included in the CBA – was somewhere between targets B and C. Monte Carlo analysis was used to show the probability that benefits would be greater than costs for a given target: this revealed that there was a 90 per cent chance that benefits would exceed costs for target B; although this probability fell for option C, it was still 'very likely' that benefits would exceed costs.

In the end, the Commission set targets for air quality somewhere in between scenarios A and B.

(1) Scenarios

	2000	Baseline 2020	Scenario A	Scenario B	Scenario C	MTFR
EU-wide cumulative life years lost, million	203	137	110	104	101	96
Acidification: index of hectares exceeding critical loads	120	30	15	11	10	2
Eutrophication: index of hectares exceeding critical loads	422	266	173	138	120	87
Ozone exposure index	4081	2435	2111	2003	1949	1895

(2) Benefits and costs

Alternative environmental interim objectives up to 2020

Ambition level	Cost of reduction (€bn)	Human health		Natural environment					
		Life Years Lost due to $PM_{2.5}$ (million)	Premature deaths due to $PM_{2.5}$ and ozone (thousands)	Range in monetized health benefits[10] (€bn)	Ecosystem area exceeded acidification (000 km^2)			Ecosystem area exceeded eutrophication (000 km^2)	Forest area exceeded ozone (000 km^2)
					Forests	Semi-natural	Fresh-water		
2000		3.62	370	–	243	24	31	733	827
Baseline 2020		2.47	293	–	119	8	22	590	764
Scenario A	5.9	1.97	237	37–120	67	4	19	426	699
Scenario B	10.7	1.87	225	45–146	59	3	18	375	671
Scenario C	14.9	1.81	219	49–160	55	3	17	347	652
MTFR	39.7	1.72	208	56–181	36	1	11	193	381
Strategy	**7.1**	**1.91**	**230**	**42–135**	**63**	**3**	**19**	**416**	**699**

Notes:
Ecosystem benefits and the damage to materials and buildings have not been monetized but still need to be considered.
MTFR is the Maximum Feasible Technical Reduction and includes the application of all possible technical abatement measures irrespective of cost.
Only costs and benefits of moving beyond the baseline are presented.
Lower value is based on the median of the value of a life year lost (VOLY) and higher value is based on mean value of a statistical life (VSL).
Costs and benefits are annual amounts. In addition to the benefits, the damage to agricultural crops is around €0.3–0.5 billion lower in 2020 under scenarios A–C.

Source: CEC (2005b, p. 14).

In reviewing the process, Watkiss et al. (2008) comment that the following factors were important in achieving a high level of recognition and buy-in from top-level policy makers to the results of the CBA. These were:

- A process of external peer review.
- Presenting results in as simple a manner as possible, for example as benefit/cost ratios.
- Presenting impacts in physical terms as well as just monetary terms – this reassured some stakeholders. However, non-monetized benefits (such as ecosystem effects here) were then often forgotten in the discussion.

- Uncertainty analysis using Monte Carlo techniques provided confidence in the recommendations, when presented in terms of the probability that benefits would exceed costs.
- Having a senior official in charge of the impact analysis who was sympathetic to CBA helped a lot in terms of how best to convey the results to other stakeholders (in fact, he was an economist).

However, the authors note that the CBA was very expensive and time consuming, and proved 'challenging' within the externally-set policy timetable.

which encourages discussion and reflection (MacMillan et al., 2006; Alvarez-Farizo and Hanley, 2006); but also by seeing CBA and citizens' juries as being complementary methods. By this, we mean that appraisal methods can be used alongside each other to provide a fuller picture of the effects of policy options, and of public views on desirable choices. Indeed, CBA can also be used alongside methods such a multi-criteria analysis to address issues such as trust, accountability and social justice (Turner et al., 2007). In this general regard, the use of CBA as a way of setting out the impacts of policies in a clear, consistent manner (including impacts differentiated by income group, or by stakeholder type or industry group) holds many attractions.

From the practical viewpoint of civil servants and agency staff faced with actually using CBA day-to-day, a key issue is that of making sure that *how* and *when* CBA is applied is proportional to the size or cost of a policy initiative. Moreover, time pressures for government decision making also constrain the extent to which full-blown CBAs can be used. This means that academics need to come up with better ways of performing 'quick and dirty' CBAs, and of producing frameworks for transferring values across studies (see Box 13.5). Of particular relevance to environmental issues is the development of acceptable methods for *benefits transfer*. As

---

BOX 13.5   A 'RAPID APPRAISAL' COST–BENEFIT ANALYSIS OF CHEMICAL REGULATIONS IN THE EU

David Pearce and Phoebe Koundouri (2004) present a 'rapid' CBA of a new regulatory procedure proposed by the EU in 2003, known as REACH. REACH is an acronym for Registration, Evaluation and Assessment of Chemicals, and applies to almost all chemicals produced in the EU. Firms must register, and in some cases evaluate the benefits, costs and risks of chemicals in order to be allowed to sell them. This clearly imposes costs on the chemical industry – estimated by the EU at around 5.2 billion euros – but might also impose costs on consumers in terms of higher product prices. Benefits are in terms of avoided risks from the use of chemicals associated with increased illness or death.

However, undertaking a full CBA of the REACH proposal was not possible, according to Pearce and Koundouri, since (i) information on dose-response or exposure–response relationships in terms of health effects did not exist for all the thousands of products likely to be covered by the legislation and (ii) since the likely effects on ecosystems was uncertain. Costs are also uncertain, since we do not know how the industry will respond to the legislation in terms of which products continue to be offered for sale, and at what price.

Pearce and Koundouri therefore undertake a 'rough' CBA analysis, based on some simplifying assumptions. Environmental impacts are ignored. Health impacts are summarized in terms of changes in Disability-Adjusted Life Years, or DALYs. This concept has been used by the World Bank to jointly consider changes in morbidity and mortality. The authors then assume that the decline in health effects due to REACH will be proportional to the likely percentage of chemicals withdrawn from sale, weighted by the percentage of DALYS lost in industrialized countries due to 'agro-industrial pollution'. Two approaches are taken to valuing this predicted change in DALYS due to the REACH legislation. First, a value per DALY is calculated from avoided health-care costs. However, we know that people's WTP to avoid illness is typically greater than the cost of treating illness. Thus, a second scenario is constructed which values DALYs using a link to the Value of a Statistical Life (see Chapter 3): the VOSL used is €1.67 million: this gives a value per DALY saved of between €90 000 and €50 000.

The results are shown in the table below:

Summary of present value of costs and benefits of REACH at the EU level in billion euros

	Costs	Benefits	Benefit–cost ratio
Avoided cost approach	5.2	−0.4 – 14.9	0.92 – 3.87
WTP-based approaches:			
With DALY = €90 000	5.2	17.2 – 88.1	4.3 – 17.94
With DALY = €50 000	5.2	7.1 – 46.1	2.17 – 9.87

As can be seen, benefits are bigger than costs in almost all cases. This is at the level of the EU as a whole – the picture may vary, though, by individual country, depending on their populations, health levels, incomes and chemical industries. Pearce and Koundouri are able to convince us that even this 'rapid' or 'quick and dirty' CBA gives valuable information. This is important since rapid appraisal may well describe the way in which CBA gets used in many situations.

we saw in Chapter 3, benefits transfer means applying the results of valuation studies carried out in one context to another setting. Economists are gradually learning how to make such transfers more accurate, by controlling for more of the social and environmental factors that can be expected to impact on WTP. But much more remains to be done.

Finally, as Kerry Turner says, 'despite its limitations, CBA still has an important role to play in environmental policy assessment, but given the increasingly contested nature of public policies, its prescriptive importance will decline. Future CBA will be a component in a wider policy analysis and decision support system' (Turner, 2007, p. 254). This is a sensible way to conclude our exploration: CBA does not provide all the answers. But the insights it does provide are extremely valuable, provided that the analysis itself is well done and open to external scrutiny.

NOTES

1. For a detailed discussion concerning the merits of cardinal and ordinal utility, see Ng (1983).
2. In Chapter 2, we also saw how weighting systems can be used to address this issue.

REFERENCES

Aldred, J. (2006), 'Incommensurability and monetary valuation', *Land Economics*, **82**(2), 141–61.

Alvarez-Farizo, B. and N. Hanley (2006), 'Improving the process of valuing non-market benefits: combining citizens' juries with choice modelling', *Land Economics*, **82**(3), 465–78.

Arrow, K., M. Cropper, G. Eads, R. Hahn, L. Lave, R. Noll, P. Portney, M. Russell, R. Schmalensee, V.K. Smith and R. Stavins (1997), 'Is there a role for benefit–cost analysis in environmental, health and safety regulation?', *Environment and Development Economics*, **2**, 196–201.

Busch, J. and R. Cullen (2009), 'Effectiveness and cost-effectiveness of yellow-eyed penguin recovery', *Ecological Economics*, **68**(3), 762–76.

Camerer, C. and H. Kunreuther (1989), 'Decision processes for low probability events: policy implications', *Journal of Policy Analysis and Management*, **8**, 565–92.

CEC (2005a), 'Impact assessment for the thematic strategy on air pollution', SEC (2005) 1133, COM (2005) 446 and 447, Brussels: Commission of the European Communities.

CEC (2005b), 'Impact assessment for the thematic strategy on air pollution: summary', SEC (2005) 1133, Brussels: Commission of the European Communities.

Colombo, S. and N. Hanley (2008), 'How can we reduce the errors from benefits transfer?', *Land Economics*, **84**(1), 128–47.

European Commission (2005), *Impact Assessment Guidelines*, Brussels: European Commission.

Farmer, M. and A. Randall (1998), 'The rationality of a safe minimum standard', *Land Economics*, **74**(3), 287–302.

Fisher, J. (2008), 'Challenges for applying cost–benefit analysis and valuation of environmental benefits to aid environmental decision-making in practice', paper prepared for the 2008 annual conference, European Association of Environmental and Resource Economists.

Frey, B. and R. Jegen (2001), 'Motivation crowding theory', *Journal of Economic Surveys*, **15**, 589–611.

Hahn, R.W. and P.M. Dudley (2007), 'How well does the US government do benefit–cost analysis?', *Review of Environmental Economics and Policy*, **1**(2), 192–211.

Hanley, N. (2001), 'Cost–benefit analysis and environmental policy making', *Environment and Planning C*, **19**, 103–18.

Hanley, N. and J. Shogren (2005), 'Is cost–benefit analysis anomaly-proof?', *Environmental and Resource Economics*, **32**(1), 13–34.

HM Treasury (2003), *The Green Book: Appraisal and Evaluation in Central Government*, London: The Stationery Office.

Knetsch, K. (2005), 'Gains, losses and the US–EPA economic analysis guidelines: a hazardous product?', *Environmental and Resource Economics*, **32**, 91–112.

Levin, S., S. Barrett, S. Anikyar, W. Baumol, C. Bliss, B. Bolin, P. Dasgupta, P. Ehrlich, C. Folke, I.-M. Gren, C. Holling, A. Jansson, B.-O. Jansson, K. Maler, D. Martin, C. Perrings and E. Sheshinski (1998), 'Resilience in natural and socioeconomic systems', *Environment and Development Economics*, **3**, 222–35.

Lichtenstein, S. and P. Slovic (1971), 'Reversals of preferences between bids and choices in gambling decisions', *Journal of Experimental Psychology*, **101**, 16–20.

Machina, M. (1987), 'Choice under uncertainty: problems solved and unsolved', *Journal of Economic Perspectives*, **1**, 121–54.

MacMillan, D., N. Hanley and N. Lienhoop (2006), 'Contingent valuation: environmental polling or preference engine?', *Ecological Economics*, **60**(1), 299–307.

Maler, K.-G. (2008), 'Sustainable development and resilience in ecosystems', *Environmental and Resource Economics*, **39**(1), 17–24.

Mansfield, C., G. Van Houtven and J. Huber (2002), 'Compensating for public harms: why public goods are preferred to money', *Land Economics*, **78**, 368–89.

Munro, A. and N. Hanley (1999), 'Information, uncertainty and contingent valuation', in I.J. Bateman and K.G. Willis (eds), *Contingent Valuation of Environmental Preferences: Assessing Theory and Practice in the USA, Europe, and Developing Countries*, Oxford: Oxford University Press, pp. 258–79.

Ng, Y.-K. (1983), *Welfare Economics: Introduction and Development of Basic Concepts*, Basingstoke: Macmillan.

Payne, J.W. and J.R. Bettman (1999), 'Measuring constructed preferences: towards a building code', *Journal of Risk and Uncertainty*, **19**, 243–70.

Pearce, D.W. (2004), 'Does European Union environmental policy pass a cost–benefit test?', *World Economics*, **5**(3), 115–37.

Pearce, D.W. and P. Koundouri (2004), 'Regulatory assessment for chemicals: a rapid appraisal cost–benefit approach', *Environmental Science and Policy*, **7**, 435–49.

Peterson, G., S. Carpenter and W. Brock (2003), 'Uncertainty and the management of multistate ecosystems: an apparently rational route to collapse', *Ecology*, **84**(6), 1403–11.

Randall, A. (2002), 'B–C considerations should be decisive when there is nothing more important at stake', in D. Bromley and J. Paavola (eds), *Economies, Ethics and Environmental Policy*, Oxford: Blackwell.

Sagoff, M. (1988), *The Economy of the Earth*, Cambridge: Cambridge University Press.

Slovic, P. (2000), 'The construction of preferences', in D. Kahneman and A. Tversky (eds), *Choices, Values and Frames*, Cambridge: Cambridge University Press.

Sugden, R. (1999), 'Alternatives to the neo-classical theory of choice', in I. Bateman and K. Willis (eds), *Valuing Environmental Preferences: Theory and Practice of the Contingent Valuation Method*, Oxford: Oxford University Press.

TEP (2007), 'Evaluation of the Commission's Impact Assessment System', report to the European Commission, Secretariat General, by The Evaluation Partnership.

Turner, R.K. (2007), 'Limits to CBA in UK and European environmental policy: retrospect and future prospects', *Environmental and Resource Economics*, **37**, 253–69.

Turner, R.K., D. Burgess, D. Hadley, E. Coombes and N. Jackson (2007), 'A cost–benefit appraisal of coastal managed realignment policy', *Global Environmental Change*, **17**, 397–407.

US EPA (2000), 'Guidelines for preparing economic analyses', Washington, DC: US Environmental Protection Agency.

Walker, B., L. Pearson, M. Harris, K.-G. Maler, C.-Z. Li, R. Biggs and T. Baynes (2008), 'Incorporating resilience in the assessment of inclusive wealth: an example from South East Australia', discussion paper 209, Beijer Institute, available at www.beijer.kva.se.

Watkiss, P., M. Holland, F. Hurley, A. Hunt and S. Pye (2008), 'Assessing the costs and benefits of the European air pollution policy (CAFÉ): results and lessons from experience', in J. Le Roux, T. Sherpa and E. Williams (eds), *Economic Appraisal of Environmental Regulation*, Stirling: Scottish Environmental Protection Agency.

Index